encyclopedia
of
HOME BUILDING
and
DECORATING

encyclopedia
of
HOME
BUILDING
and
DECORATING

Stanley Schuler

RESTON PUBLISHING COMPANY, INC.
Reston, Virginia 22090
A Prentice-Hall Company

Library of Congress Cataloging in Publication Data

Schuler, Stanley.
    Encyclopedia of home building and decorating.

    1. House construction—Dictionaries. 2. Interior
decoration—Dictionaries. I. Title.
Th4812.S36   690'.03   74-34323
ISBN 0-87909-243-2

©1975 by
Reston Publishing Company, Inc.
A Prentice-Hall Company
Reston, Virginia 22090

10 9 8 7 6 5 4 3 2 1

Printed in the United States of America.

Preface

Trying to understand what an architect, builder, interior designer, real estate agent, carpenter, or anyone involved with building and decorating homes means when he uses an unfamiliar word or term is a problem that confronts just about every family in the United States at some time or other. Like doctors and lawyers, these people speak a language of their own; and even though I have been closely connected with housing for close to 40 years, I sometimes have as much difficulty interpreting them as anyone. This book stemmed from my desire to clarify the situation.

I realized, however, that a simple dictionary would be of relatively limited value. When you're buying property, building, remodeling, repairing, decorating, appealing for a zoning change, etc., in many cases you need more than the definition of a term. You also want to know how the thing described affects you, whether you can put it to use and how or whether the professional you hire is using it as he should, and so forth. So my dictionary became an encyclopedia.

Then to make the encyclopedia more useful, I added the lists of words and terms at the end of the book so that if you can't think of the right word for whatever you want to know about, you can run down the appropriate list and find it. The result is a unique book which both laymen and professionals can use in many ways—

- To figure out what somebody is talking about.
- To run down the materials, equipment, and furnishings you might use to improve your home or to solve a problem you have in the home.

v

- To plan and/or decorate your home.
- To design your house, room, closet, etc., so it is both utilitarian and aesthetically pleasing.
- To determine the desirable or proper dimensions for a part of the house.
- To ascertain the advantages and disadvantages of specific products—both the oldest and the newest.
- To make sure that the workman you hire is making an installation properly and also to help you make your own repairs, improvements, etc., properly (but be warned that this is not a step-by-step instruction book).
- To employ and deal more effectively with professionals.
- To give you at least a clue as to what may be causing difficulties in your home.
- In short, to make your home the convenient, safe, comfortable, attractive place you want it to be.

STANLEY SCHULER

A ANCHOR
    A plastic device shaped like a sleeve which expands to an A shape when a screw is driven into it. It is used to fasten objects on hollow walls with very shallow hollows (for example, a plywood surface applied over furring strips).

ABS
    Acrylonitrile-butadiene-styrene. A plastic used to make drainage pipe. *See* Pipe.

ABSTRACT OF TITLE
    A summary of the instruments effecting title to a property.

ACCELERATOR
    A chemical, such as calcium chloride, which is added to concrete to make it set more rapidly. It must be used sparingly.

ACCESSORIES
    The innumerable small objects completing the decoration of a room. They include such things as art objects, vases, bookends, candlesticks, pillows, scatter rugs, plaques, and wind chimes.

ACETATE
    A plastic made from cellulose which is used in taffeta. satin, faille, crepe, brocade, and tricot. Produced in filament and spun

1

yarns, it is often combined with other fibers. It has luster, body, good draping qualities, a crisp hand, good color fastness, and resistance to moths and mildew.

Some solid objects such as lampshades and playing cards are also made of acetate.

ACOUSTICAL BOARD

A paneling material of cellulose fibers used to deaden sound in rooms. It is made for application to walls, although it can be applied to ceilings. The panels are 2 or 4 ft. wide; 6, 7, 8, 9, 10, 11, or 12 ft. long; and 1 in. thick.

ACOUSTICAL PLASTER

Special plaster which absorbs sound and thus reduces the noise level in rooms. Applied like ordinary plaster in a continuous sheet, it is usually given a stipled or perforated finish.

ACOUSTICAL TILE

Large tiles made of compressed cellulose fibers which absorb sound. They are used on ceilings and sometimes walls.

Standard tiles are generally ½ in. thick and are made in 12 x 12-in. or 16 x 16-in. squares with a surface that is slightly rough or perforated with small holes. Larger square and rectangular tiles and tiles with sculptured surfaces are also available. Selection should be based primarily on the noise reduction coefficient (NRC) of the tiles. For kitchens, family rooms, bathrooms, and other very noisy rooms, the NRC should be in the 0.60 to 0.70 range; for other rooms, 0.40 to 0.50.

The tiles can be installed with adhesive to any level, clean surface; or they can be stapled to either furring strips applied over open joists or an imperfect solid surface. They are also frequently used in suspended ceilings (*see* Ceiling, Suspended).

New tiles do not require finishing, but they can be painted repeatedly with alkyd or latex paint without impairing their sound absorption characteristic.

ACRE

A quantity of land containing 43,560 sq. ft. A parcel 200 x 200 ft. is roughly an acre.

ACRYLIC (1)

A multi-purpose, widely used plastic. As a solid material, it goes into light diffusers, skylights, and windows because of its strength and its resistance to impact and to yellowing when exposed to the sun or bright light. It is easily scratched, however.

Acrylic fabrics, resembling wool, are strong, resilient, slow to soil, easy to clean, and resistant to abrasion, mildew, and moths. They are used in carpets and other furnishings.

Acrylic is also a principal ingredient of some superior latex paints.

ACRYLIC (2)

A painting done with acrylic paints. The effect is similar to that of an oil painting, and the painting is cared for in the same way.

ADAM

A style of architecture and design inspired by books of Robert Adam (1728-1792), a Scottish architect and decorator. A return to the classic principles and motifs of the Greeks and Romans, it is characterized by exceptional lightness and three-dimensionality. Sheraton and Hepplewhite furniture and Federal houses are outstanding examples of the style.

ADAPTATION

Furniture, furnishings, and architecture with the general feeling of a definite style but not designed according to Hoyle. Many of the things we live with are adaptations.

ADAPTER

Any device which allows two unmatched things to be fitted together. The most common adapter used in building is a pipe fitting which connects a threaded pipe to a copper tube.

ADDITION

An alteration which increases a building's size. The change need not, of course, increase the ground area covered by the building, since it is often feasible to add floor space by building up rather than out.

ADDITIVE

Something added to another material, as a mildewcide may be mixed into paint. The word can be used interchangeably with *admixture*.

ADHESIVE

Since no one adhesive will glue every material used by man, it is hardly surprising that manufacturers have flooded the market with a vast and confusing array of compounds—some with unusual capabilities, others exactly like their competitors. The following is a short list of basic types which builders, decorators, and homeowners frequently need:

Cellulose Cement • A transparent, quick-drying, ready-to-use adhesive which glues a variety of materials but is outstanding for glass and ceramics, provided they are not exposed to heat or very much moisture.

Epoxy Glue • Extremely strong and moisture resistant, but fairly expensive and therefore best saved for jobs which other adhesives cannot do. It is especially good for bonding dense materials such as metal, stone, and glass. It is usually packaged in two parts, which are mixed together as needed.

Plastic-Mending Adhesive • A clear, waterproof adhesive needed to fix vinyl, phenolic, acrylic, and styrene plastics, among others. It is not suitable for gluing polyethylene, polypropylene, or nylon.

Polyvinyl-Acetate Glue • Also called *PVA glue* or *white glue*, this is a white liquid which dries colorless. It is excellent for most wood-to-wood and fabric-to-wood fastening jobs, provided it is used indoors. It is not waterproof.

Resorcinol Glue • The best glue for fastening wood to wood outdoors or in damp locations. It consists of a powder and a liquid which are mixed together as needed. The adhesive dries slowly and leaves a red stain.

Silicone Rubber Adhesive • A very thick, rubbery adhesive sold everywhere as bathtub caulking, but useful for many other caulking and gluing projects. It is available in clear, white, gray, or black colors. The glue is unique in that it will fasten things which do not fit together tightly; in fact, it can span a gap almost 1 in. wide.

Wallpaper Paste • The most common wallpaper paste is a dry wheat paste which is mixed with water. Cellulose paste is also a powder to which water is added. Both are used for hanging paper and sometimes light vinyl wallcoverings. But vinyls are generally hung with heavy viscous materials recommended by the wallcovering manufacturers.

Contact Cement • A waterproof rubber-base adhesive most often used to bond laminated plastic sheets to a rigid base. It is tricky to use because once the surfaces that have been coated with glue touch each other, they cannot be pulled apart.

Asphalt Roofing Cement • A black mastic used to install asphalt roofing but useful for sticking down many other types of roofing and for waterproofing basement walls. It retains some elasticity even in cold weather. Cement containing fibers is very viscous and can be used in considerable thicknesses. Nonfibered cement is thin enough to be applied with a brush.

In addition to the above, a miscellaneous assortment of mastics is used to glue down resilient flooring, hardboard paneling, gypsum board, ceramic tile, etc. The type recommended by the manufacturer of the material should always be used.

ADHESIVE ANCHOR

A gadget for fastening things to masonry walls. Shaped like a common nail, it has a very large, flat, perforated head with a projecting nail or bolt. The head is stuck to the wall with mastic, and the object being hung is then slipped over the shank.

ADMIXTURE

An substance added to another material. A coloring powder added to a concrete mix is an *admixture.*

ADOBE

A clay soil which is mixed with water and straw, shaped into bricks, and baked in the sun for about two weeks. The bricks are then laid up with a clay mortar to form the exterior and interior walls of houses in desert regions. In such regions, walls protected by wide roof overhangs last for many years.

AFRICAN MAHOGANY

See Mahogany.

AFRICAN SATINWOOD
See Avodire.

AFRICAN TEAK
See Iroko.

AFRORMOSIA
A West African wood used in furniture veneer, flooring, and paneling. It is strong, heavy, hard, and reddish brown with bands of golden brown.

AGBA
A light, fairly soft West African furniture wood with straight grain and a warm, medium-brown color.

AGGREGATE
The sand, pebbles, or crushed rock used in cement mortar. The sand is *fine aggregate*, though it is not usually called anything except sand. The pebbles or crushed rock is always referred to as *coarse aggregate* in order to make it unnecessary to specify what the actual material is.

AGREEMENT OF SALE
A written document by which the owner agrees to sell his property to the buyer at an agreed price. It constitutes a contract. But in real estate title to the property does not pass until delivery of the deed.

AIR CHAMBER
A plumbing device which is installed in the wall behind a lavatory, sink, or tub to prevent water hammer—pounding in the pipes—when a faucet is opened. The usual air chamber is a capped length of pipe installed vertically—as an extension of the supply riser—above the T fitting into which the faucet is connected. Each faucet serving a fixture has an air chamber.

AIR CLEANER
A device for removing dirt, dust, pollen, and other particles from the air in a house.

Of the several types made, the best is a two-stage electronic, or electrostatic, unit which filters out large particles with a screen and traps small particles on charged plates. Its efficiency ranges from 70% to 96%. This type of cleaner is usually built into the return duct of a warm-air heating system or central air conditioning system, and is capable of cleaning the air in an entire house. Portable cleaners are used in houses without ducts. The largest can clean the air in a room with floor space of up to 600 sq. ft.

Less efficient air cleaners for installation in ducted heating or air conditioning systems include charged-media filters, self-charging electrostatic filters, and ordinary fiber filters coated on one side with a viscous liquid.

AIR CONDITIONING

Man has found ways of cooling his home for hundreds of years; but it wasn't until the electrically powered air conditioner was developed that he was able to lower house temperature far below the outside temperature and simultaneously dehumidify and filter the air. Today, he air conditions his home in four ways. All are different, but all operate on the same principle. As the indoor air is pulled into the air conditioner, it gives up its heat to the refrigerant circulating through an evaporator. The cooled, dehumidified air is then returned to the house through the supply ducts. Meanwhile, the refrigerant, which is now hot, passes into a compressor and then into a condenser exposed to the outdoor air. Here it loses its heat and returns once more to the evaporator, where the cycle starts all over again.

Central Air Conditioners • A central air conditioner is a large unit for cooling the entire house. Along with a heat pump, it is the most efficient method of air conditioning because sooner or later all the air in the house passes through it. Thus, balanced comfort is maintained throughout the house. In addition, the system can be equipped with a high-efficiency electronic air cleaner which removes most of the contaminants in the house air.

Two types of central air conditioner are used: the *single-package system* and the *split system*. Since one is as efficient as the other, the choice depends on the technical and economic requirements of the particular installation.

In a single-package air conditioner, all parts are enclosed in one cabinet which can be installed in the house or outside. In the split system, the evaporator and the blower which circulates the air are installed indoors while the condenser and compresser are outdoors.

In the majority of new homes, a central air conditioner is coupled with a forced warm-air heating system, and both use the same blower and the same system of ducts to circulate air. The supply ducts carry the cooled (or heated) air to the rooms where it is discharged through registers mounted in the exterior walls. In cold climates, where heating is more important than cooling, the registers are located just above the floors and are equipped with adjustable deflectors which direct cool air upward and warm air downward. In warm climates, where cooling is more important than heating, the registers are installed high in the walls or even in the ceilings.

Air from the rooms is returned to the air conditioner (or furnace) through return ducts. The registers for these are installed in interior partitions near the floor.

The same system is used in old houses with forced warm-air heating. In this case, however, the existing ducts are usually too small to carry a proper volume of cold air, so a larger blower must be installed.

If a house is heated by hot water, steam, or electricity, a central air conditioner is installed separately from the heating plant, and a special system of ducts must be put in. The exact kind of installation depends on the design of the house. In a one-story house with an attic, for instance, the air conditioner is located in the attic, and cooled air is ducted into the rooms through ceiling registers. In a house without an attic, the air conditioner is installed in the basement or crawl space. In a two-story house, two small air conditioners are used—one in the attic to serve the second floor, the other in the basement for the first floor.

All central air conditioners require their own 240-volt wiring circuits.

Heat Pumps • A heat pump is a central unit which cools the house in summer and heats it in winter. It is installed in a new house like a central air conditioner and uses the same type of ductwork and registers. *See* Heat pump.

Small Room Air Conditioners • A room air conditioner is a self-contained cooling unit which is mounted on a windowsill or installed in a hole cut through an outside wall below a window, over a door, or in any other suitable location. No ductwork is required. The unit simply pulls in stale air from the room, cools and dehumidifies it, and blows it right back into the room.

Most room conditioners are large enough to cool only the room in which they are installed; they can be used to cool an entire house only if a separate unit is installed in each principal room. This is less desirable than putting in a central air conditioner because the noise level is much higher and uniform cooling of all parts of the house is impossible. On the other hand, the total cost is somewhat lower, and it is possible to cool each room to a different comfort level. It is also possible to reduce operating cost by shutting off the conditioners in unoccupied rooms.

Room conditioners which are designed to operate on 120 volts and 7½ amps or less can be plugged directly into any 120-volt, 15-amp wiring circuit, provided the circuit is not also used to serve lamps and appliances with a total wattage exceeding 860. Room conditioners rated above 7½ amps, however, require their own circuits.

Large-Capacity Room Air Conditioners • These are identical to small room conditioners except that they operate on 240-volt circuits to which nothing else is connected. In addition, because of their size, installation should almost always be made through an outside wall—not in a window.

Large room conditioners can often be used to cool an entire house of average size (about 1500 sq. ft.). But they do an efficient job only in houses with forced warm-air heating systems. In this case, the heating system is set for continuous air circulation (*see below*), and the conditioner is installed in a room that has a return duct leading to the furnace. This register is kept open, but the supply registers in the room are closed. All other return ducts in the house are also closed.

Chilled Water Air Conditioners • Very rarely used in houses, chilled water air conditioners operate by cooling water in an electric chiller and circulating it through the pipes of a forced hot-water heating system. Air in the house is cooled as it circulates through convectors connected to the pipes.

Sizing an Air Conditioner • Regardless of the system used to cool a house, the air conditioner must be sized carefully because if it is too small, it will not cool the house adequately, and if it is too large, it will be inefficient and expensive to operate.

The size of an air conditioner is stated in terms of its cooling capacity, which is measured in British thermal units (Btu's) or tons per hour. (One ton equals 12,000 Btu's.) The capacity required for a given installation should be determined by a qualified air conditioning contractor after making a survey of the house. The points he must consider are the total area of the house; the width, depth, and height of each window; the number and types of windows; the construction of the exterior walls and roof; the direction the house faces; the extent to which the house is shaded by trees, hills, and other buildings; the mean temperature of the community; the number of people in the family; and the extent to which guests and visitors are entertained.

As a rule of thumb, 12,000 Btu's of air conditioning are needed for every 500 sq. ft. of floor space.

AIR-DRIED LUMBER

Lumber seasoned at normal temperatures by air circulating naturally around it. If the seasoning is properly done, there is no difference between air-dried and kiln-dried lumber. In either case, the moisture content of rough construction boards and timbers under 8 in. in width should not exceed 19%; that of wider material should not exceed 15%. Finish lumber should contain even less moisture. (Air-dried may be abbreviated *AD*.)

ALABASTER

A fine-grained, smooth, white stone which is carved into decorative objects.

ALCOHOL

Denatured alcohol is the vehicle in shellac, stainkillers, and alcohol-base wood stains. It is also used as a thinner for these finishes.

ALCOVE

A small recessed area in a room. If a fireplace projects out from the middle of a wall, there are alcoves on both sides.

ALKALI

A soluble mineral salt in concrete and plaster. Concentrations of alkalis can damage some paints and wallcoverings.

ALKYD

A manufactured resin used to make alkyd paint and some types of varnish. *See* Paint.

ALLIGATORING
A paint problem similar to checking but worse. The paint surface is badly roughened by interlaced cracks. Removal is necessary before new paint is applied.

ALLOWANCE
See Builder's Allowance.

ALPACA
Soft, silky, wool-like hair from a llama-like South American animal called the alpaca. It is woven into a fabric and sometimes used in rugs.

ALTERATION
An alteration involves a change in a building, but exactly what type of change depends on the local building authority. In some communities, an alteration is an alteration only if it involves changes in the structural members of a building. Elsewhere it may be more broadly defined.

ALTERNATING CURRENT
The type of power used in all home wiring systems. A current of constantly changing voltage and constantly reversing polarity. It is abbreviated *AC*.

ALUMINUM
Although uses for aluminum in the home are increasing steadily, the strong, lightweight material presents problems.

Even though it does not rust, it does corrode—often very badly in cities and near the seacoast. This can be avoided only by specifying top-grade alloys. Additional protection is afforded by having aluminum covered with a baked-on enamel finish at the factory. The alternative is to paint the metal after purchase with a zinc chromate primer followed by any suitable finish paint. The natural color of aluminum can be retained in a corrosive atmosphere only by applying a clear, nonyellowing acrylic or cellulose-butyrate lacquer.

Also, to prevent corrosion—even of the best aluminum—the metal should not be placed in direct contact with concrete.

Another problem with aluminum is that because it has excellent thermal conductivity, moisture condenses rapidly on inside surfaces of aluminum window frames in cold climates. The condensation in turn drips off and damages adjacent surfaces of wood, paint, and clear finish. This problem is not preventable.

ALUMINUM PAINT

A paint made with tiny aluminum flakes in a varnish or asphalt base. The varnish type can be used as a final finish or as a primer-sealer to prevent knots from bleeding through a finish paint and to protect the back of wood and plywood paneling against moisture.

Asphalt-base aluminum paint is a roof coating used to prolong the life of old asphalt roofing.

ALUMINUM ROOFING

The most common type of aluminum roofing—used primarily on farm and utility buildings—consists of long strips which are laid up and down a roof. The strips are corrugated, ribbed, or flat, and are usually left unpainted. They are put down over a solid deck, spaced boards, or purlins. The roof must be pitched at least 3 in. per foot.

Aluminum shingles are striated to resemble cedar shingles or shakes and painted at the factory. They are installed on a solid deck with a minimum slope of 4 in. per foot.

One of aluminum's advantages as a roofing material is that if left natural or painted a light color, it reflects sun rays and helps to keep the house cool. It is also fire and wind resistant, and durable in all areas except those with very corrosive atmospheres.

ALUMINUM SIDING

A relatively new prefinished siding which is being heavily promoted to owners of old homes as a re-siding material that will reduce maintenance. It is also installed on new houses.

The siding is produced in the form of vertical boards or horizontal clapboards. The latter are made in conventional narrow widths like wooden clapboards and also in double widths molded to look like two or more narrow boards. Called *double-lap siding*, these cut installation time.

All the boards have interlocking edges that keep out water. They should be installed over mineral-fiber backer boards, which help to insulate the house against cold and noise. Grounding of the siding is required to prevent electrical shock.

Aluminum siding is made with a tough, semi-permanent acrylic or baked-enamel finish in a variety of colors. This is generally guaranteed against blistering, cracking, and chipping for 10 to 25 years, depending on the brand and quality. But it is generally not guaranteed against fading, which may occur after a period of years.

AMERICANA

Anything related to America's past. Weathervanes, cigar-store Indians, scrimshaw, warming pans, fireplace cranes, and captain's walks are all part of Americana.

AMORTIZE

To pay off a debt by periodic installments.

AMPERE

The unit of electric current intensity (abbreviated *amps*). It is commonly used to express an amount of electric current—the electrical rate of flow, like gallons per minute in a water system.

The amount of amperage varies with the electrical devices in use. Lights in the house, for example, operate on 15 amps; small appliances such as toasters and irons and some large appliances such as refrigerators and dishwashers operate on 20 amps. Other appliances such as dryers and ranges require 30 to 50 amps.

Because of the American family's dependence on electrical appliances, no house should be built today without a service of 100 amps or more. Houses heated by electricity require a 200-amp service.

ANCHOR

An anchor is most commonly thought of as a piece of metal used to attach wood to masonry, but it can be anything which holds something securely in place.

Anchor is also the name of an anchor-like ornament carved into moldings or other pieces of wood.

ANGLE IRON

A stiff strip of steel or brass bent at a right angle and used to reinforce a joint in wood or sometimes other materials. It is attached to the joined pieces with screws or with nuts and bolts.

One kind of angle iron is called a *flat corner brace* because the arms lie in the same plane and are screwed flat to the wood. Another angle iron called simply a *corner brace* is set inside the corner between the pieces of wood. It may also be used to support cantilevered shelves, etc.

ANGLO-JAPANESE STYLE

A decorating and furniture style of the second half of the 19th century. It combines Japanese and Gothic elements.

ANGORA

See Mohair.

ANIDEX

A synthetic elastic fiber with exceptional resistance to sunlight and heat, good hand, and easy-to-care-for properties. Blended with other fabrics and used to upholster furniture, it allows unusual freedom of design because it stretches to conform to the contours of the furniture.

ANTIFREEZE

A chemical which lowers the freezing point of concrete poured in very cold weather. Calcium chloride is one of the commonest. None, however, should be used for this purpose since it has a deleterious effect on concrete. *See* Accelerator.

ANTIQUE FINISH

A multi-toned finish for wooden furniture and paneling. It consists of a base coat of white or colored paint covered with a semi-transparent glaze which is brushed or wiped while wet to produce shading effects. A second color may be applied before the glaze coat.

APPLIED ORNAMENT

A decorative piece applied—usually with adhesive or mortar—to a wall, ceiling, piece of furniture, etc.

APPLIQUÉ

An ornament sewed, glued, or otherwise fastened to another material.

APPORTIONMENT

The dividing between the seller and buyer of the expenses and income connected with a property. The seller is responsible until the deed to the property is conveyed; then the buyer takes over. For example, at the closing, the buyer pays for any oil left in the tank at the time of the closing. Similarly, the seller is entitled to any rent due for that part of the month prior to the closing.

APPRAISAL

An estimate of the value of a piece of property, furniture, etc. Although any appraisal should be made by a qualified appraiser, it is to some extent a subjective evaluation which may be colored by the circumstances under which it is made. The amount actually offered by a prospective buyer who is not trying to horse-trade is the most accurate measure of a property's worth at the time the offer is made.

APRON

A horizontal board set on edge used to conceal whatever is behind it. The board under a windowsill is an apron. The name is also given to the vertical board under the edge of a table top or chair seat or below the bottom drawer of a chest.

ARCADE

A covered passageway—originally with an arched roof.

ARCH

An upwardly curved structure spanning an opening. It may be made of brick, stone, other masonry, wood, or metal.

When an opening is made in a wall, an arch is one of the two methods used to support the wall above it. The other is a *lintel*. The latter is a horizontal beam of sufficient strength that when laid across the opening, it resists the downward pressure of the weight it supports. By contrast, an arch is formed in such a way that it resists the load by balancing thrusts and counterthrusts. It is supported at the sides by buttresses or walls.

Arches are also used to span the space between parallel walls.

ARCH BACK

A Windsor chair back in which the arms and rail seem to be formed of one piece suggestive of a wishbone. The entire member is supported on slender spindles.

ARCHITECT

The person best qualified to develop the plan and design of a new or remodeled house. He combines design skill with understanding of construction, and is competent to undertake the planning of any project involving erection of a building.

In order to be licensed to practice architecture in a state, an architect must usually be a graduate of an accredited professional institution and have had a certain number of years of practice in an architectural office. No person can call himself an architect unless licensed (registered by one or more of the 50 states). Most, but not all, architects are members of the American Institute of Architects (AIA).

The work that an architect does for a client is agreed to at the time he is employed. He may do nothing more than draw up the preliminary and then the detailed plans and specifications for the house to be built or remodeled. Or he may go on to help the homeowner find and hire a contractor, and then to supervise the construction of the house. For these services his only compensation is a fee paid by the homeowner. This is usually a percentage of the total cost of construction. The percentage depends on the fame of the architect and the area in which he practices, as well as on the size and type of project. Since construction of a house stretches out over a period of several months, partial payments of the fee are made to the architect at times stipulated in his contract with the homeowner.

ARCHITECTURAL DETAIL

The small details incorporated in the structure of a house to make it more beautiful or authentic. Good architectural detail derives from the skill with which the architect selects and/or uses such things as moldings, door styles, balusters, mantels, wall textures, hardware, etc. Frequently, a successful house is distinguished from a so-so house only by its architectural detail.

ARCHITECTURAL REVIEW BOARD

A community-type board set up to approve or disapprove the construction of buildings on aesthetic grounds. Such boards are rare but are found in a number of U.S. communities such as Santa Fe, N.M.; Alexandria, Va.; and Rye, N.Y. Their purpose is simply to prevent the construction of eyesores in the community. They have no authority to dictate design or rule out a design because it is unusual.

ARCHITRAVE

In classic architecture, an architrave is the lowest division of an entablature. It is also a molded frame around a door or window.

AREAWAY

A walled opening in the ground outside a basement window or door. Its purpose is to let light and air into the basement through the window and to permit access through the door.

The areaway for a basement door usually has walls of concrete block or poured concrete and a floor of poured concrete. Because of the size of the opening, a floor drain should be provided.

Window areaways formerly had masonry walls but now almost always have walls of heavy galvanized steel shaped to form a shallow U. They can be bolted to the foundation walls or simply laid against them and held in place by the pressure of the soil. The top edge of the walls can be level with the grade if the ground slopes away from the house; but if the ground slopes toward the house even slightly, the walls should be an inch or two above grade to prevent entrance of water.

To stop flooding of a window areaway, the dirt bottom should be several inches below the bottom of the window opening. If the soil is dense, the areaway should be deepened and lined on the bottom with several inches of crushed rock. In extremely dense soil, a drain should be provided to carry water into the footing drain.

ARMOIRE

A piece of furniture for hanging clothes. It is a tall, rather deep cabinet, usually of refined design and choice wood. It stems from earlier days when closets were rare but is now being manufactured again.

ARMORED CABLE

See BX Cable.

ARM STUMP

In some chairs an arm is supported at the front by an extension of the leg. In others the support is separate from the leg. The latter is an arm stump.

ARRIS

The sharp edge formed when two flat surfaces meet at an outside corner. For example, there is an arris where the side piece of a picture frame meets the top piece, or where the two sides of a gable roof meet at the ridge.

ARROW BACK

A chair back shaped like a flower pot in outline and curving slightly backward. The top rail is supported by three to five splats shaped like the feather end of an arrow.

ART NOUVEAU

A style or design popular in the late 19th and early 20th centuries. It is characterized by curvilinear lines taken mainly from life. Tiffany glassware is an example.

ASBESTOS-CEMENT BOARD

A smooth, gray panel made of asbestos-cement fibers and portland cement. It is fireproof, moisture-proof, and rodentproof; very hard and resistant to damage; stable; and inert. It serves as a wall surface inside or outside a house. It can also be used to fireproof walls, ceilings, and flush doors.

The panels are 4 ft. wide; 4, 8, 10, or 12 ft. long; and 1/8, 3/16, or ¼ in. thick. The thinnest panels are easily bent to a rounded contour. If the panels are painted, chlorinated rubber paint should be used.

ASBESTOS-CEMENT SHINGLE

A roofing and siding shingle made out of asbestos fibers and portland cement to resemble deeply striated wood shingles in a variety of colors. Both individual and strip shingles up to 30 in. long are available.

Asbestos-cement shingles are heavy, fire resistant, and very durable. They are applied to a solid roof deck covered with building paper. Minimum roof pitch is 5 in. per foot. Normal shingle exposure is 6 to 8 in.

Shingles used for exterior siding are similar. In addition, there are strips simulating wooden clapboards. Many styles come from the factory with a colorful acrylic coating.

Asbestos-cement shingles and siding are also called *mineral-fiber shingles* and *siding*.

ASH

An extremely tough hardwood used in furniture and tool handles. It is a very pale brown—almost white. It is cut from several American tree species as well as from European and Japanese species.

ASHLAR

A stone with sides and edges that are roughly or carefully squared so it can be laid up in a wall like a brick or concrete block. The word is also applied to artificial rectangular stones and burned clay units larger than bricks. Used as an adjective, ashlar describes a wall made of squared stones, etc.

To carpenters, an ashlar is a short stud between an attic floor and roof. The studs forming knee walls are ashlars.

ASH PIT

A hollow space in the foundation of a fireplace. Ashes from the fireplace are dropped into it through a small metal door, called an *ash dump*, installed in the hearth. Ashes are removed through a clean-out door near the base of the foundation.

Ash pits are an optional part of fireplaces, not necessities. In houses without basements, the pits are simply metal buckets under the hearth. They are removed for emptying through the ash dump.

ASPHALT ROLL ROOFING

An economical, utilitarian roofing material made of asphalt-saturated felt covered with mineral particles. It is normally sold in long, 36-in.-wide rolls which are laid parallel with the eaves, but 18-in.-wide rolls in several colors are also available.

The drab material produces a wind- and semi-fire-resistant roof with a life expectancy of about 20 years. It can be laid on decks with a pitch of only 2 in. per foot. In normal installations, the strips are overlapped 2 in. But for greater durability and better protection against rain, so-called *double-coverage roofing* is made. With this, the top strip overlaps the upper half of the bottom strip, with the result that the roof is covered with two layers of roofing at all points. Colored 18-in. roll roofing is also laid in this way.

Roll roofing can be applied over a smooth deck or any old nailable roofing material.

ASPHALT SHINGLE

A roofing and siding material made of thick felt saturated and coated with asphalt, and surfaced with colored mineral particles. The shingles are most commonly produced in 3-ft. strips with three 1-ft.-wide tabs with square butts. The surface is smooth or slightly textured.

Asphalt shingles have become the most popular residential roofing material because they are economical, have a life expectancy of approximately 20 years, are available in a wide range of colors, and have good resistance to fire.

In new construction, the shingles are applied directly over a solid plywood deck or over a deck covered with building paper. In reroofing, application can be made over any surface that is reasonably smooth, sound, and nailable. In all cases, the minimum roof pitch is 4 in. per foot. (However, a 2-in. pitch is permissible if the shingles are of the *seal-down* type—meaning that the tabs are glued to the surface underneath with daubs of asphalt cement applied at the factory.) Normal exposure (the distance from the edge of one butt to the next butt above) is 5 in.; but in windy locations this should be reduced to 4 in.

Asphalt shingles are sold by the *square* (100 sq. ft.). The number of shingles in a square varies slightly; the weight per square ranges from as little as 130 to as much as 320 lb. A good medium-grade shingle weighs 230 lb. per square.

ASPHALT TILE

A resilient floor tile, usually 9 x 9 in., made of asphalt. It is available in limited colors and patterns; is brittle, noisy, and hard underfoot; and is not very durable or easy to maintain. But it is outstanding for economical installations on concrete slabs laid on or below grade.

ASSUMPTION OF MORTGAGE

When the buyer of a property accepts personal liability for the payment of an existing mortgage acquired previously by the seller. However, a mortgage can be assumed only if the mortgagor agrees to it.

ASTRAGAL

A molding attached to the edge of one of a pair of hinged doors or windows to stop it from swinging past the other unit when it is closed.

ATRIUM

A terrace or court in the center of a house. It is surrounded on all sides by the house walls and therefore admits natural light into the adjoining rooms. It may be open to the sky or roofed with glass or plastic.

ATTIC

The space under the roof of a house. Louvers should be installed—preferably at opposite ends—to allow super-heated air to escape in summer and thus to prevent excessive buildup of heat in the rooms below. The louvers also help to carry off moisture which may enter the attic from the rooms below and condense on the rafters and roof sheathing.

If an attic is unoccupied, insulation is placed between the floor joists. But if it is intended to build rooms in an attic at a future date, the insulation is either installed between the rafters and between the studs in the gable ends or wrapped tightly around the framing for the future rooms.

An attic used for storage is obviously more useful if the joists are completely covered with a rough plywood floor. Articles to be stored are limited to those which are not affected by high heat or freezing cold.

Access to attics is usually gained by a disappearing stair installed above a hatch.

ATTIC, EXPANSION

An attic which may some day be finished off for occupancy. The cost of putting in rooms can be reduced if preparatory steps are taken at the time the house is built. These include installing windows and a permanent stairway to the attic, roughing in piping for plumbing and heating, and installing collar beams at proper ceiling height—at least 7½ ft. above the finish floor. Insulation should be installed in the attic roof or in the ceiling and wall framing for the future rooms.

AUSTRALIAN MAPLE

This is not a true maple. The wood is very strong, lustrous, and pinkish red in color. It is used in furniture and paneling.

AUSTRALIAN WALNUT

See Tigerwood.

AVODIRE

Used in cabinet making, avodire is occasionally called *African satinwood* because of its satiny surface. It has the color of a nicely done biscuit and is strong and light.

AWNING

Of the various ways used to keep the sun out of houses and off porches and terraces in summer, awnings are one of the best. They stop the sun outside the house—not after it has passed through windows which prevent the escape of heat. Because they project outward, they do not greatly interfere with the movement of air through windows and into porches. They give almost complete protection against rain. They admit some light.

Their main drawback—shared with other kinds of shading devices—is that they may detract somewhat from the appearance of a house.

Awnings are made either of fabric (cotton, duck, drill, canvas, or acrylic) or of rigid fiberglass or painted aluminum sheets. Fabric types are the most attractive, and are taken down and stored when not needed; but they deteriorate fairly rapidly and soil easily. Fiberglass and aluminum awnings, on the other hand, are durable and very easily cleaned; but current designs are ugly, and since the awnings are left up the year around, we are afflicted by them constantly.

AXMINSTER

A type of woven carpet identifiable by the ridged backing. It resembles a hand-knotted carpet.

BACK-BAND

An L-shaped molding which is "wrapped around" the outer edges of door and window casings to improve the appearance of the casings.

BACK-FILL

To fill in soil, rock, etc., against the outside of a foundation wall. Back-filling is one of the first steps taken when land is rough-graded following completion of a house.

Three precautions should be taken when back-filling is done:

1 / The trenches should first be raked clean of building rubble such as wood, plaster, BX cables, etc., which might attract termites or decay and cause settlement of the soil.
2 / The fill should be either compacted or, better, built up somewhat higher than the grade to allow for the settlement which will inevitably occur in the first month or two following back-filling.
3 / The fill must be graded away from the foundations so that water will run off rapidly.

Back-fill also means to build rough masonry behind or between the surfaces of a masonry wall.

BACKING

Any material used behind a surface. A drapery lining is a backing. A lining paper is the backing for wallpaper. A gypsum backer board is sometimes used as the backing for thin plywood paneling.

BACK SIPHONAGE

A dangerous phenomenon occurring when, for some reason, there is a vacuum in the water supply of a plumbing system. If a faucet happens to be open at the time and if the spout is immersed in a basin of water, water from the basin is sucked back into the supply lines where it may contaminate the fresh water.

To prevent back siphonage, modern plumbing fixtures are designed with an air gap between the sources of incoming water and water standing in the bowls or tub. But if an old plumbing fixture is used, care must be taken to mount the water inlets above the fixture rim.

BACKSPLASH

A vertical surface projecting upward from the back of a counter (usually a kitchen counter) to protect the wall against splashing and prevent things from rolling down behind the counter. The normal backsplash is 4 in. high and is an integral part of the countertop, but it frequently extends all the way up to the underside of wall cabinets.

BACKUP

The part behind the face of a wall. The word is most often applied to masonry walls but need not be restricted to them.

BAFFLE

A device for obstructing passage of air, light, etc. It can be made in various ways. A *louver* is a kind of baffle.

BALLAST

An electrical device required to operate a fluorescent tube. It is enclosed in the fluorescent fixture.

BALL FOOT

A furniture foot shaped like a ball—usually a rather big ball.

BALLOON BACK

A chair back with an open frame shaped like a woman's torso. It has a shaped horizontal splat just above the waist.

BALUSTER

One of the small uprights in a stair railing or balustrade. For security, they should be mortised into the bottom of the rail and top of the tread. Stock balusters are made in lengths of 30, 33, 36, 39, and 42 in.

BALUSTRADE

A horizontal railing supported on balusters or columns.

BAMBOO

This strong, smooth, oddly handsome material—a giant grass—has more potential than actual uses in the home. Americans have never done much with it except to make furniture—mostly for the terrace—and roll-down shades.

Large bamboo poles in many diameters and lengths are available singly. Slender strips are sold in bunches or bound together in mats or rolls.

BAND

A decorative border applied to or made an integral part of a piece of furniture, wall, etc. It is sometimes called *banding*.

A band is also a flat strip of fabric used for trimming or binding draperies, etc.

BANISTER

The entire railing on a stair or one of the turned splats of a banister-back chair. The word is sometimes applied—but incorrectly—to one of the balusters in a stair railing.

BANISTER BACK

A chair back with several vertical turned spindles resembling balusters. It belongs to the William and Mary period.

BANQUETTE

A long upholstered bench which may or may not be built in along a wall.

BAR

Home bars are built for serving and eating informal meals; mixing, serving, and drinking alcoholic beverages; and simply mixing and serving drinks. Only rarely is an eating bar used for drinking.

The eating bar—usually called a *breakfast bar*—is located in or very close to the kitchen. On the dining side, the counter is cantilevered to provide knee space. On the serving side, the space under the counter is—or should be—given over to cabinets, drawers, or shelves for storage of silverware, plates, etc. The counter height is usually 36 in. because it is built as an extension of the counter adjacent to the kitchen range, but it may be lower (usually not less than 30 in., however). Minimum depth of an eating bar is 18 in. At least 2 ft. of space should be provided along the front for each occupant.

Bars for mixing, serving, and drinking alcoholic beverages are normally located in the family room or recreation room. They are similar in design to eating bars, but they are often as much as 4 ft. high on the drinkers' side and usually 3 ft. on the bartender's side. The latter side incorporates a bar sink.

A bar used simply for mixing and serving drinks may be located in any part of the living area or kitchen. It is sometimes a counter in a wall between two rooms—frequently between the kitchen and family room. When not in use, the bar can be closed off from the family room. In other cases, this kind of bar is simply a small room or alcove with ample counters, cabinets, and a sink given over entirely to drink mixing.

BARBECUE

Barbecue grills for installation in kitchens or family rooms are heavy steel boxes with grilled tops. Most are built into masonry hearths or countertops and surrounded on all sides and the bottom by masonry. Others that are insulated can be built into a wooden framework. The grills burn charcoal, gas (in which case they must be connected to a gas line or canister of LP gas), or electricity (a 240-volt circuit is required).

All indoor barbecue units must be installed with an exhaust fan to carry off dense smoke, grease, and, in the case of charcoal grills, carbon monoxide. The fan should be sized for commercial installations (ordinary kitchen fans are too small) and built into a hood which extends several inches out beyond the front and sides of the grill. The distance from the grill to the bottom edges of the hood should be no more than 30 in.—preferably 24 in. The hood is connected to a duct—not exceeding 10 ft. in length and with no more than one bend—which leads through an exterior wall or roof to the outdoors.

BARGEBOARD

Also called a *vergeboard*, a bargeboard is a board nailed to the rake edge of a roof for ornament. In the past, it was often elaborately carved or cut out.

BARGELLO

A type of needlepoint stitch characterized by long vertical stitches. The designs are generally geometrical.

BARK POCKET

A wood defect in which a piece of bark is embedded in the wood.

BARN PAINT

An exterior paint made with a modified oil vehicle which is used on nonuniform or poorly prepared surfaces. The usual color is dark red, but other dark colors are available. The paint tends to fade badly and has a shorter life expectancy than conventional house paints.

BARN SIDING

Old siding boards salvaged from a barn. Rough new boards suitable only for a barn may also be called barn siding.

BAROQUE

A large, lavish style of design that swept Europe in the 16th and 17th centuries. Characterized by elaborate carvings, sweeping curves, and generally fanciful, bold designs, it was applied to both architecture and furnishings.

BARREL ROOF

An arched or vaulted roof. Barrel is a misnomer because the roof is actually shaped like half of a steel drum.

BAR STOOL

A small, high stool with or without a back. The frame is

generally of wood or metal. The seat may be padded and often swivels.

BASEBOARD
The wide wooden trim applied horizontally to the base of an interior wall just above the floor. It protects the wall against scuffing and blows, and conceals the base of the wall, which is usually ragged or has an open joint.

The baseboard, also simply called a *base*, may be nothing more than an ordinary board, or it may be specially shaped and used only as a baseboard. In the past, baseboards usually had decorative base-cap moldings along the top edges and base shoes at the bottom, covering the right-angle joint between the baseboard and floor. Today, to reduce cost and maintenance, baseboards are often very simple, smooth-surfaced boards with curved top edges so they don't collect dust and with nothing along the bottom edges.

BASE-CAP MOLDING
A decorative molding applied at the top of a baseboard to conceal a possibly ugly open joint between the baseboard and wall. In some specially milled baseboards the base-cap molding is an integral part of the board.

BASEMENT
The question most often asked about basements is, Is it cheaper to build a house without one? This cannot be given a clear-cut answer. Generally it is less expensive to build a one-story house on a concrete slab if the ground is relatively flat and the climate is moderate; and it certainly is less expensive to build without a basement if the ground is rocky or very wet. On the other hand, a house with a basement is economically justified if the house is two stories high (because the basement area is small in relation to the total house), if the lot is steep (because high foundation walls or piers will be needed anyway), and if the climate is severe (because very deep footings will be needed anyway).

Basement walls are constructed either of poured concrete or of concrete blocks. (*See* Foundation.) The former is stronger and rarely leaks, but the latter are generally used because they are cheaper. However, they frequently leak because the joints are not properly made; consequently, they should be parged (covered) with two ¼-in. layers of concrete followed by one or two coats of asphalt waterproofing compound. The parging need not extend above grade level, but the appearance of the walls is improved if it is carried all the way to the top.

The floor is a 4-in. reinforced concrete slab poured over a 6- to 8-in. base of crushed rock. A 1-in. open joint between the edges of the slab and walls is filled with asphalt. In wet locations, the slab is 6 in. thick and poured in two layers with a heavy polyethylene film sandwiched between.

For adequate headroom under girders and pipes hung below the ceiling joists, the height of the walls from the footings to sills should be equal to 11 courses of concrete block (88 in.) or, better, 12 courses (96 in.).

The basement should have an inside entrance, as well as an outside entrance either to the yard or to the garage. The latter should be at least 3 ft. wide and 6 ft. 4 in. high to permit carrying bulky articles to the basement.

Windows are installed in at least two of the walls to admit light and to ventilate the basement. The FHA standards call for a minimum window area equal to 1% of the floor area if the basement is open. If the basement is divided into rooms, each room should have a window with an area equal to 2% of the room area. Windows below grade level are surrounded by areaways with steel or masonry walls extending several inches above grade so water cannot flow in over them. (*See* Areaway.)

If the basement incorporates a family room or other living area, the walls may be painted on the interior. If covered with gypsum board or paneling of any sort, the covering is applied to 1 x 2- or 1 x 3-in. wood furring strips anchored to the walls with steel studs.

Although basements are usually uninsulated, installation of rigid foam insulating sheets or fiberglass batts down to below the frost line helps greatly to warm not only the basement but also the floor above.

BASE SHOE
        See Shoe Molding.

BASKETWEAVE
        A pattern often used in building, fabric construction, and, of course, basketry. The materials used are arranged in horizontal and vertical rows and are interlaced—or look as if they are interlaced.

BAT
        A piece of broken brick.

BATHROOM

Two widely accepted rules influence bathroom planning in new American homes and those undergoing modernization: There should be a bathroom on every floor of the house; the principal family bathroom—or bathrooms—should be as close as possible to the bedrooms. Beyond this, most American families are delighted to have as many bathrooms as can be squeezed into their home-building budgets—but they have fairly firm feelings that some bathroom locations are more desirable than others.

Good locations are: (1) opening off the front hall; and (2) opening off a downstairs study or family room.

Undesirable locations are: (1) opening off the living room, dining room, or kitchen; and (2) at the head of a straight stairway from the front hall to the second floor.

Also disliked are inside bathrooms (but not inside powder rooms). This prejudice, however, is breaking down as more families realize that if they want an extra bathroom, the only space they can find for it without enlarging the entire house is near the center of the house. Further contributing to the change in attitude is a relaxation of building codes to permit bathrooms without windows, provided they are equipped with ventilating fans which turn on automatically with the bathroom light.

Where possible, bathrooms should be grouped together so that all can be hooked directly into the same plumbing lines. This reduces plumbing cost. The ideal situation in a one-story house is to be able to place bathrooms side by side or back to back with one another or with the plumbing outlets in the kitchen or laundry. In a two-story house, the same results are obtained by placing one bathroom directly over another or over the kitchen or laundry sink.

The minimum space required for a conventional bathroom with either a tub or shower stall is approximately 5 x 6 ft. The space can be reduced to a little less than 5 x 5 ft. by installing a prefabricated bathroom with walls, floor, ceiling, tub, lavatory, medicine cabinet, towel bars, and paperholder molded out of two pieces of fiberglass which are bolted together to form a cube. (The toilet fits into the bathroom but is of conventional construction and is installed separately.)

The smallest space required for a powder room, or half bath, measures 2½ x 4 ft.

The dimensions and arrangement of bathrooms depend not only on the size of the fixtures installed but also on how much space is provided for the occupant. Although fixture dimensions are not standardized in the plumbing industry, the following are representative of the fixture sizes in commonest use:

Lavatory (free-standing)	22 x 18 in.
Lavatory (built-in)	36 x 21 in.
Toilet	21 x 30 in.
Tub	32 x 60 in.
Shower stall	36 x 36 in.

Floor space required by a bathroom user is based on the following minimum standards:

- Distance from front rim of lavatory to a facing wall or fixture—24 in.
- Distance from front of toilet to a facing wall or fixture—18 in.
- Distance from side of bathtub to a facing wall or fixture—24 in.
- Distance from center line of toilet to a wall or lavatory on either side—15 in.

Compartmenting is a way to increase bathroom useability without adding materially to its size. By dividing the bathroom into two or sometimes three compartments, two persons can use it at the same time with more or less complete privacy. Many arrangements are possible. For instance, the toilet or lavatory can be put in one compartment, the other two fixtures in the other compartment. Or the toilet and lavatory can be put in one compartment, and a second lavatory and tub can be put in the second compartment. Or a toilet and lavatory can be put in both compartments with a tub in one or the other. The exact arrangement depends both on the space available and on which fixtures are given most use during rush hours.

Once the location and general plan of a bathroom have been determined, numerous details must be worked out.

Storage • This is not limited to cabinets and closets but also includes facilities for hanging linens on the bathroom walls. Most bathrooms haven't enough of either.

In addition to a medicine cabinet over the lavatory, a bathroom should have a cabinet at least 1 ft. deep and containing at least 6 sq. ft. of shelf or drawer space for storing linens and other large articles. This can be provided in a cabinet under a built-in lavatory, in a floor-to-ceiling wall cabinet, or in a short cabinet hung over the toilet tank.

Minimum space required for hanging towels and wash cloths is 2 ft. of towel bar for each person, including guests, who uses a bathroom.

Ventilation • Windows can be installed anywhere in a bathroom but should be avoided over a tub because they are difficult to open and lose their finish under exposure to pelting water from the shower head. If necessary, however, a clerestory hopper window can be installed just below the ceiling line. Regardless of the number of windows or their placement, installation of a small exhaust fan is advisable—especially in cold climates—to carry off moisture in cold weather and to stop mildewing.

Lighting • A luminous ceiling gives maximum illumination. The alternative is to place lights on either side of the medicine cabinet and on the ceiling overhead. *See* Lighting.

Outlets and Switches • These must be installed so that no one can be electrocuted. They should be well out of arm's reach of the tub, shower stall, and lavatory. In a few communities, the building code stipulates that all bathroom switches must be installed outside the door.

Doors • Doors generally are hinged to swing into the bathroom but can be swung outward in tight situations. Recess sliding doors are even better because they take up no floor space. They are especially useful between compartments in a compartmented bathroom.

For privacy, doors should be of raised-panel design or flush doors with a solid core.

Also see Bathtub, Lavatory, Shower Stall, and Toilet.

BATHROOM ACCESSORIES

Towel rods, soap dishes, medicine cabinets, and other items which have no direct connection with bathroom fixtures.

BATHROOM CABINET

Bathroom, or medicine, cabinets are shallow units designed to be recessed in or surface-mounted on a wall above the lavatory. They are made of steel with baked-enamel finish and have mirrored doors which either swing outward on hinges or slide from side to side in tracks.

Recessed cabinets are generally preferred in custom-built houses because they make a neater installation; but surface-mounted cabinets are used in speculative and remodeled houses because they are easier and less costly to install. Another advantage of surface-mounted cabinets is that a bathroom occupant can rummage in them without disturbing people on the other side of the wall.

Both types of cabinet are made in roughly the same sizes. Widths are dictated by the fact that recessed units should fit into either a single or double stud space; and for economy of manufacture, surface-mounted units have the same dimensions. Heights range from about 18 to 36 in.

Installation of recessed cabinets must, of course, be made between studs, which means that the lavatory should usually be centered on a stud space so the cabinet can be placed squarely behind it. Surface-mounted cabinets can be placed anywhere. In both cases, the height at which a cabinet is hung depends on the height of the adults using the bathroom; but as a rule of thumb, the center of the cabinet is 60 in. above the floor.

BATHTUB

Interest in making bathrooms glamorous has triggered a proliferation of bathtub designs. The basic rectangular tub—made of cast iron or steel with a porcelain finish—still remains the most widely used design, but it no longer has the field to itself.

Tubs are made as small as 39 x 38 in. These are hardly useful for adult bathing but are more than adequate for children, and they also make an excellent base for a shower bath.

Standard-size tubs are 4½, 5, or 5½ ft. long and about 32 in. The 5-ft. tub is the commonest.

New tubs of conventional construction range upward to as much as 8 ft. in length. Many of these giant-size units are designed for recessing in the floor.

If tubs built of mosaic tiles are used, they can be built above or in the floor to any size and design.

The most radical new tub design is made of rigid fiberglass. The tub and the surrounding three walls are molded in one piece so the tub and shower recess can be completed together and so that leaks cannot occur around the tub rim. The unit is so lightweight that two men can install it with ease, thus lowering labor cost. But the base of the tub must be well supported so it doesn't sound ominously hollow when occupied. (Steel tubs must also be well supported for the same reason.)

BATHTUB ENCLOSURE
See Shower Door.

BATIK

A brightly colored fabric—usually of linen or rayon—produced by a Javanese dying process similar to *sarasa*. The material is used for such things as curtains, bedspreads, and wall hangings.

BATISTE

A fine, sheer or semi-sheer curtain fabric usually made of cotton, silk, or polyester. It often has a printed or sometimes an embroidered design.

BATT

A short length of blanket-type insulation. It is installed primarily in attic floors.

BATTEN

A narrow wooden strip used mainly to cover a joint between two other pieces of wood, plywood, etc. In board-and-batten construction, the battens are 2- or 3-in.-wide strips nailed over the joints between wide vertical boards.

A wooden cleat nailed across boards to prevent warping is also a batten.

BATTEN-AND-BOARD

A type of siding—the reverse of board-and-batten. In batten-and-board, the narrow battens are placed behind the wide vertical boards. The joint between the boards is about 1 in. wide.

BATTER

The backward slope of a wall or timber.

BATTER BOARD

When laying out a house, a stake is driven into the ground about 4 ft. out from each corner on a line that bisects the corner. Two additional stakes are then driven on either side of the first to form a right triangle, and these are connected to the first stake by horizontal batter boards. The boards should parallel the walls of the house. A taut line is then tied from the batter board at one corner to the parallel batter board at the other corner to mark the outside edge of the foundation wall. An additional line may be attached to mark the outer edge of the trench in which the foundation wall is built.

The purpose of this arrangement is to stabilize the corner stakes so they cannot shift position during excavation and construction of the foundations.

BAY

One of the series of similar spaces into which a building plan is divided.

BAY WINDOW

A window projecting from the wall of a house. It may be rectangular, rounded, or, more often, with a straight front and angled sides. Most bay windows are supported on foundations extending into the ground, but some are cantilevered from the wall.

BEAD

A small, rounded, projecting molding which is also called *beading*. Used for ornament in furniture and building, it may be smooth-surfaced or decorated.

A bead is also a small, smooth, convex strip carved into—and slightly below the surface of—a board. The tongue-and-groove boards used—especially in the past—to surface ceilings and interior walls have beads in the center and along one edge of each board.

BEADED BEVEL SIDING

A beveled board siding with a small, rounded, continuous bead cut in the surface just above the butt. It is installed horizontally.

BEAM

One of the principal structural members of a building. It is a heavy horizontal timber installed between posts, columns, or walls to support joists in the floor above. A beam is at least 5 in. thick and at least 2 in. wider than its thickness.

BEAM CEILING

A ceiling in which the beams are exposed. In ancient houses, the beams supported the floor or roof above; but today they are often false—used for effect only. False beams have become especially popular since they have been made in stock sizes out of light-weight, rigid plastic foam.

BEARING WALL

A bearing wall, or *bearing partition*, is a wall which supports any part of the structure above. All exterior walls of a house are bearing walls but are not known as such because their weight-supporting role is taken for granted. But only some of the interior walls or partitions are bearing walls.

Bearing walls are easy to identify when the skeletal framework of a house is exposed because the ceiling joists are at right angles to them and the ends of the joists rest on them. On the other hand, if ceiling joists stretch to either side of a wall underneath, the wall is nonbearing. And if the joists are parallel to the wall, it is nonbearing.

In an existing house, the only accurate way to identify a bearing wall is to bore a hole through the ceiling near the wall and peer into the space or fish into it with a wire to determine whether the joists are parallel or at an angle to the wall, and whether the ends of the joists rest on the wall or extend beyond it.

If a bearing wall is torn out of an existing house, a steel or wooden beam must be substituted for it; otherwise, the area once supported by the wall is likely to sag or collapse.

BED (1)

Until the early 19th century, beds were assembled by the homeowner out of four posts, four rails, and a headboard. Later, they consisted of a pair of wooden side rails, a headboard, and a footboard. Today, they are often nothing more than a box spring attached to four short legs, to which a headboard and footboard may or may not be added (this is called a *Hollywood bed*).

Along with the change in construction has come a change in bed height. Today, the top of the mattress on the average bed is 21 in. above the floor. But in the past the height was greater; in fact, some beds were so high that a step stool was needed to climb up into them.

The standard lengths and widths of the beds currently in general use in the United States are gauged by their mattresses as follows (actual bed sizes are a few inches greater in one or both dimensions):

Youth	33 x 66 in.
Twin or single	39 x 75 in.
Twin long	39 x 80 in.
Three-quarter or super-twin	48 x 75 in.

Double	54 x 75 in.
Double long	54 x 80 in.
Queen	60 x 80 in.
King	76 x 80 in.

Conventional beds are known by such names as *four-poster,* *spool* (with spool-turned posts), *brass, Hollywood, tester,* and *sleigh* (with slightly S-shaped headboard and footboard, giving the bed the outline of a horse-drawn sleigh). Special types of beds include the following:

Bunk Bed • With two or even three single beds in a tier.

Captain's Bed • A single bed with drawers and/or cabinets built in underneath.

Day Bed • Converts from a couch to a bed. *See* Day Bed.

Folding Bed • A cot on casters which folds up, end to end, into a bundle only about 16 in. thick.

Swing Bed • Twin beds attached to a single large headboard. They can be swung apart at the foot to serve as single beds or left side by side to form a king-size bed.

Trundle Bed • A single bed with a second single bed stored underneath. The latter can be pulled out at night and raised to standard height.

Wall Bed • Folds upright into a wall recess enclosed behind doors. It is a space-saving bed found mostly in apartments.

Water Bed • A bed with a mattress made of plastic and filled with water. Frame and mattress are sold together. In the best models, the bed also includes a plastic tub to catch the water in case the mattress leaks.

BED (2)

In building, a bed is any nonrigid base on which something is laid—a bed of gravel or sand, a bed of mastic, etc.

BED JOINT

The horizontal layer of mortar into which a brick, concrete block, or other masonry unit is set.

BED MOLDING

Any molding applied where two surfaces meet at an angle. However, a bed molding is most commonly considered to be the molding at the juncture of the eaves and side walls of a building.

BEDPLATE

A timber or piece of steel used to support a load on an existing surface. For example, if it becomes necessary to shore up a sagging floor in a house, the post used for the purpose is set on a bedplate in order to spread the load on the floor.

BEDROOM

In order to make a bed, at least 2 ft. of space is needed on both sides. The wall against which the head of a bed is placed should therefore have the following width:

Single	7' 3"
Double bed	8' 6"
Queen-size bed	9'
King-size bed	10' 4"
Two twin beds	12' 6"

Of course, this space can be reduced 2 ft. if a bed is jammed into a corner, but such poor planning should not be tolerated by any homemaker. If bedroom space must be limited for reasons of economy, savings usually are better achieved by building bureaus into closets.

BEDSPREAD

Although bedspreads are of various designs—plain, boxed, ruffled, pleated, etc—there are just two basic types: the *floor-length spread* and *short coverlet.* The former is particularly suited to modern low beds; on the higher beds of the past, it is a nuisance to put on and take off. On the other hand, the short coverlet is ideal for high beds and also suitable for low beds. It is usually used in conjunction with a dust ruffle or tailored skirt except on children's and youth beds.

Bedspreads are made of almost any material but preferably one which has sufficient body to lie smooth and resist wrinkling. It should also be soil resistant and easy to launder.

BEECH

A hard, tough, strong wood of pinkish brown color with innumerable tiny dark brown specks. It is used for flooring and furniture.

BELL PULL

A long, wide strip of fabric used in early days to sound a bell to summon servants. It now serves as a decoration and is particularly useful on narrow walls where little else can be hung. It is often made of petit point or crewel.

BELT COURSE

In masonry construction, a belt course, also called a *string course* or *sill course,* is a prominent horizontal row of building blocks dividing a wall. The course stands out because it either projects slightly beyond the wall surface or is fashioned of building blocks set on end. The course need not continue from one end of a wall to another; a brick windowsill, for example, is a belt course.

BENCH

A long seat without back or arms for several persons. Of simple design, it usually has a wooden seat but may be upholstered.

BENTWOOD

The name applied to a kind of furniture made by steaming and bending the wood—usually beech—of which it is made.

BERGERE

A commodious upholstered chair with closed arms extending only part way to the front. It also, as a rule, has a loose cushion and is in the Louis XV style.

BETA FABRIC

A fiberglass fabric which is very soft and pliable, yet strong and durable. Made of exceptionally fine fibers, it is used in draperies and curtains.

BEVEL

To cut the edge of a board, etc., at any angle except a right angle. An edge so cut is called a bevel. *Compare* Chamfer.

BEVEL SIDING

A general name given to any siding material which is thicker along the bottom edge than along the top, or is installed so that it appears to be thicker. Clapboards and shingles are bevel sidings.

BIBB

A faucet with a short spout angled toward the ground and threaded for easy attachment of a hose.

BIBLIOTHEQUE
A tall, shallow, usually wide, free-standing cabinet for books. It has doors with large glass panes.

BID
An offer to buy property, build a house, or do something else at a stated price. A bid, however, is not binding on the bidder until a contract is drawn up and signed by the parties involved.

Builders make two kinds of bid: *preliminary* and *firm.* The former is a rough estimate meant to give the prospective homeowner an idea about what his house or remodeling will cost. A firm bid is a carefully figured bid that the builder will stand by.

BIDET
A toilet-like plumbing fixture designed for thorough cleaning of the perineal area of men and women. The bowl holds water for washing, and also provides a spray. The water temperature is adjustable. The fixture measures approximately 15 in. wide by 30 in. long.

BIEDERMEIER
A German furniture style of the mid-19th century. It stemmed from classic forms but was heavy in appearance.

BILL OF SALE
A written deed evidencing the sale of property and conveying title to it.

BINDER
A small sum of money which a prospective buyer gives to the seller as evidence of his intention to buy a property. Binders— also called *earnest money*—were more widely used in the past than today. Currently, many lawyers feel that they have little meaning because if a buyer wants to back out of a transaction, he can do so; and the seller is obligated to return the binder. Consequently, in many part of the country, binders have been replaced by simple assurances that the buyers intend to buy.

BINDING
A strip of fabric used to finish raw edges.

BIRCH
A tough, hard, heavy wood widely used to make kitchen

cabinets, plywood paneling, and modern furniture, but with little beauty. It is a very pale brownish yellow.

BIRD'S-EYE MAPLE

See Maple.

BIRD'S MOUTH

The triangular cut made in a rafter near the low end so it can be fitted and nailed securely to the rafter plate.

BISCUITWARE

Unglazed, pinkish-tan pottery. These figurines and bric-a-brac were popular in the United States in the latter part of the 19th century.

BLEACH

To lighten the color of wood or eliminate discolorations which cannot be sanded out. Commercial bleaching agents are most effective, provided they are used according to the manufacturer's directions. Also good is oxalic acid, which is used by dissolving ½ cup of the crystals in 1 qt. of hot water and brushing on liberally. When dry, the crystals are removed and the process repeated again and again until the desired color is attained. The surface should then be neutralized and allowed to dry thoroughly before it is sanded smooth and finished.

BLEACHING OIL

A material applied to new exterior wood surfaces in order to produce an immediate weathered effect. The oil consists of a penetrating oil, a bleaching agent, and a little gray pigment. The pigment makes the wood look weathered. By the time it wears away in several years, the bleaching agent has also grayed the wood. The color is maintained thereafter by natural weathering processes.

BLEEDER VALUE

The small valve on the side of a plumbing valve. If the latter is turned off so repairs can be made in the pipe line, the drum-like cap on the bleeder valve is opened to drain the pipe.

BLEEDING

Bleeding occurs in wood when some substance in it penetrates and stains the paint or other finish applied to the surface. Bleeding is particularly troublesome in resinous woods such as pine and may occur not only at the knots but also sometimes in the sound wood. Other softwoods, notably cedar and redwood, exude soluble salts which cause blotching on a paint finish. And any wood which has been treated with a creosote stain or some old types of varnish may bleed.

Bleeding is not predictable, although it is generally safe to assume that pine and similar knotty softwoods will bleed; therefore, it is always wise to seal the knots with shellac or, better, a white-pigmented, shellac-base stainkiller before applying a final finish. Similar treatment should also be a matter of course when old creosote-stained or varnished woodwork is to be painted.

BLEMISH
An imperfection in wood which mars its appearance but does not affect its utility. *Compare* Defect.

BLIND
An adjective meaning concealed. In the blind mortise-and-tenon joint used in furniture construction, the mortise goes only part way through the wood and the tenon is completely concealed within it.

A blind is also a shutter.

BLOCK
A small chunk of wood. Blocks are used for innumerable purposes—as braces, spacers, bases to receive nails or screws, etc.

BLOCK FILLER
A very thick paint—usually latex—used to fill the voids in concrete blocks and other very porous or rough materials. By providing a smooth base for conventional paint, it reduces the quantity of paint required to give a good finish.

BLOCK FLOORING
See Flooring.

BLOCK FOOT
A furniture foot shaped like a square children's block. Also called a *Marlborough foot.*

BLOCK FRONT
A bureau front which is divided into three vertical sections—the center section recessed somewhat behind the end sec-

tions. Desks, secretaries, and chest-on-chests are also made with block fronts.

BLOCKING

Short lengths of 2 x 4s nailed horizontally between studs in a frame wall. When a wall is to be paneled with vertical boards applied directly over the studs, two rows of blocking equally spaced between the top and bottom of the wall are installed to serve as a nailing base for the boards. Blocking is also used to strengthen a wall which is covered with unusually thick ceramic tiles. And it is sometimes used to stop flames from soaring up inside walls (in which case the blocks are called *firestops*).

BLOND FINISH

A transparent or semi-opaque finish of a lighter color than the original wood. It is used on furniture, paneling, and woodwork. *See* Driftwood Finish, Heather-Mahogany Finish, Honey-Maple Finish, Limed-Oak Finish, Silver-Oak Finish.

Some people differentiate between a blond and a bleached finish, claiming the former is obtained only by applying a pigmented coating.

BLOWER

A large fan in a warm-air heating system or air conditioning system which circulates the air through a house. It draws in the stale air through the return ducts, and after the air is heated or cooled, it blows the air back into the house through the supply ducts.

BLUEPRINT

The white-on-blue photographic copies of the working drawings which show how a house, piece of furniture, etc., is constructed. Blue-on-white prints are actually used more often today. They are properly called *white prints* but are generally referred to as blueprints.

Several sets of blueprints are needed to build a house. Except for those given the building inspector, all should be returned to the owner of the house when it is completed, and he should then return all but one set to the architect (if any). *See* Working Drawing.

BLUE STAIN

An unsightly bluish or grayish stain sometimes encountered in unseasoned lumber. Caused by fungi, it does not affect the durability or strength of the wood.

BLUNT ARROW LEG

Fanciful name for a Windsor chair leg shaped like an arrow with a knob for a foot.

BOARD

A piece of lumber measuring at least 1 in. thick and 2 in. wide (nominal dimensions).

BOARD-AND-BATTEN

A siding in which the joints between wide vertical boards are covered with narrow battens.

BOARD-AND-BOARD

A siding made with vertical boards of the same width. The odd-numbered boards are nailed directly to the sheathing and are overlapped along the edges by the even-numbered boards.

BOARD FOOT

The standard unit of measure for all building lumber except moldings, interior trim, furring strips, grounds, and material under ½ in. thick. A board foot measures 1 x 12 x 12 in. To find the board feet in a piece of lumber, multiply the nominal thickness in inches by the nominal width in inches by the length in feet; then divide by 12. For example, to find the board feet in a 10-ft. length of 1 x 10:

$$\frac{1 \times 20 \times 10}{12} = 8\text{-}1/3 \text{ board feet}$$

Board measure can also be rapidly calculated by using the Essex Board Measure table on the back of a framing square.

BOARD MEASURE

The system for measuring lumber by board feet.

BOILER

The "furnace" for a hot-water or steam heating system. The best boilers are made of cast iron rather than steel, and should always be used if the water supply is corrosive or hard.

BOISERIE

Sculptured paneling.

BOLECTION MOLDING

A molding with a raised center strip and flat strips on either side. It is used for decoration and to cover joints in surfaces around fireplaces, doors, etc.

BOLSTER

A long, commonly cylindrical pillow. In carpentry, a bolster is a horizontal piece applied across the top of a post and used to lengthen the bearing of a beam.

BOLT

Nuts and bolts are used for joining metals and other materials which cannot be nailed or screwed, and also for joining wood when it is necessary to have a very strong union which can be broken easily without damage to the wood. Made of steel, brass, or aluminum, bolts of six types are available:

Stove Bolts • Most widely used bolts, these are threaded from end to end and have flat or round heads with slots for a screwdriver. They are made only in small sizes up to 6 in. long.

Carriage Bolts • Available in lengths up to 20 in., carriage bolts have smooth, oval heads with square collars underneath to keep them from turning in wood or metal. Below the collars are short smooth shanks, then threads. They are used in such things as garage doors, sleds and so on.

Machine Bolts • These have square or hexagonal heads which are turned with a wrench. The threads extend only about two-thirds of the way up the shanks. Maximum length is 39 in. They are used in heavy construction.

Lag Bolts • More commonly known as *lag screws (see below)*.

Continuous-Threaded Bolts • Three-foot rods threaded for their entire length and held with nuts at both ends. They can be cut to any desired length with a hacksaw and bent to any shape.

Handrail Bolts • These are specialized fasteners used to put together sections of stair rails and other wooden pieces which are joined in similar fashion end to end. The bolts are threaded and have nuts at both ends.

BOLT, LOCKING

A device for locking doors, windows, and cabinets. It has two parts—one containing a smooth-barreled bolt, and a strike into which the bolt slides to lock the door. Common types include:

Barrel Bolts • The simplest type most often used. The bolt slides in a long barrel-like sleeve with a C-shaped slot for the handle. The strike is usually barrel-shaped and mounted on the same plane as the bolt.

Square Spring Bolts • Similar to barrel bolts, but the bolts are held closed by springs.

Chain Bolts • Opened and closed by a chain. When the chain is released, a spring throws the bolt into the strike.

Foot Bolts • Installed at the bottom of doors to secure them to the floor or threshold. The bolt is closed by stepping on the cap and opened by stepping on a trip.

Cremone Bolts • Very long bolts installed vertically on doors to lock them simultaneously at top and bottom. The bolts are actuated by a central knob or handle.

Window Spring Bolts • Shaped like a fat pencil, these are set into a drilled hole in one side of a window frame. The spring-actuated bolt slides into a hole in the jamb, thus making it impossible to open a window.

Dead Bolts • *See* Lock.

BOMBÉ
A word applied to the bases of chests of drawers, desks, and secretaries which have swollen, rounded sides and fronts. Because of the resemblance to a kettle, a bombe base is also called a *kettle base.*

BOND
Something that fastens two things together. In building, materials are often bonded by adhesive or by cement mortar.

Masons use the word to describe the manner in which bricks and concrete blocks are arranged side by side in a wall or floor. The purpose of most wall bonds is to impart structural strength to the wall; and the bonds most often used are the *common bond* (also called *American bond*), *running bond*, *English bond*, *Flemish bond*, *English cross,* or *Dutch, bond.*

A pattern bond, on the other hand, has little or no structural strength and is used for ornament only. *Herringbone, basketweave, stack,* and *diagonal* are typical pattern bonds.

In paving, bonds are selected primarily for appearance. However, use of a bond with staggered joints helps to minimize cracking of paving.

BONHEUR DU JOUR
A small French lady's desk with a shallow cabinet at the back which is commonly topped with marble and a metal gallery. The writing surface pulls or folds out.

BONNETIERE
A tall, narrow French clothes cabinet or wardrobe.

BONNET TOP
A pediment on a piece of furniture, such as a secretary. It is shaped like a scroll pediment with slightly S-shaped sides which do not meet at the top.

BOOKCASE
Bookcases can be free-standing or built in. Both are arranged and constructed in essentially the same way, and there is very little difference in the floor space they occupy.

A free-standing bookcase is generally the more expensive; but it can be moved from room to room or house to house, and it can be used as a divider as well as being placed against a wall. Even though it is properly designed and placed on a level floor, it should usually be anchored to keep it from toppling forward.

A built-in bookcase is enclosed at the ends by boards which support the shelves. The bottom shelf is normally just above the top edge of the adjacent baseboards, and the space underneath is enclosed. The top shelf should be no more than 78 in. above the floor so books can be removed by an adult without standing on a stool or chair (but in a room with high ceilings, shelves may go higher if a step stool or ladder is used to reach the books).

Shelves made of 10-in. boards accommodate the majority of books. One-inch-thick boards are suitable if the shelves are supported at the ends and along the back edge and are no more than 5 ft. long; 1¼- or 1½-in. boards should be used, otherwise. The spacing between shelves depends on the height of the books to be stored, but if the shelves are fixed, standard spacing is 11 in. between the bottom and second shelves or between the bottom, second, and third shelves. Higher shelves are spaced 9 in. apart. Adjustable shelves which can be raised or lowered by 1-in. increments may be preferable.

Books can also be stored on cantilevered shelves, but since the shelves are open at both ends, they are not called a bookcase. The shelves should, however, be built of the same lumber and spaced in the same way. *See* Shelf.

BORE HOLE
A hole bored in a rock to mark a point in the boundary of a property. It is used instead of a pipe when it's impossible to drive a pipe into the ground.

BOSS
A rosette, keystone, or other small ornament applied to a surface.

BOUCLÉ
A nubby fabric made of various fibers with little loops on the surface. It is used in draperies, slipcovers, and bedspreads.

BOUNDARY LINE
The border of a property. If not actually marked out on the property by pipes, stakes, bore holes, fences, walls, or trees, it should be; otherwise, the owner has difficulty making full use of the property and defending it against trespassers.

A setback, or building line, is figured from the boundary line.

BOW BACK
A Windsor chair back with a bow-shaped top rail that is mortised at the ends into the arms. The bow is supported by slender spindles.

BOW FRONT
The front of a chest of drawers or other case piece which curves outward in a continuous line from the ends.

BOW WINDOW
A bay window with a bowed, or gently rounded, frong.

BOX
A small box-like device in which a switch, outlet, or other electrical device is mounted for safety. A junction box is a box in which cables are connected together. Boxes are most often made of rigid metal, but may be of plastic, and are rectangular, square, hexagonal, or round. The length and height vary, depending on the depth. The commonest boxes—used for switches and outlets—have a normal depth of 2½-in., but a 1½-in. depth is permissible in new construction in very thin walls. In remodeling, boxes only ½ in. deep may be used if another box would damage the structure.

Boxes are made with a variety of devices for anchoring them in a wall, ceiling, etc. So-called new-work boxes are used in new construction when the framing of the house is exposed. Old-work boxes are used in remodeling.

BOX COLUMN

A hollow column made of boards and usually square in shape.

BOX FRAME

A window frame with long boxes on either side to contain the cords and weights balancing the sashes which slide up and down. Since window sashes are now balanced by other means, box frames are no longer in use but are regularly encountered in old houses. Access to the weights and cords is provided through a pocket cover—a narrow, screwed-on trapdoor in the pulley stiles.

BRACE

A piece of wood or metal used to strengthen or hold something secure. Probably the commonest type of brace is a timber installed diagonally across two other timbers forming a corner to keep them from spreading apart or pinching together. In this use, the brace forms the hypotenuse of a triangle, and may be permanent or temporary. An example of a temporary brace is one of the long boards or 2 x 4s used to hold the frame walls of a new house upright until all can be joined together. An example of a permanent brace is the timbers installed in a Y or W form between the underside of a deck and the supporting posts.

Another kind of brace is a board wedged between opposite walls of a room to hold gypsum board or plywood panels while the adhesive with which they are applied dries.

BRACKET

A projection from a vertical surface. Some brackets are purely utilitarian—used to support shelves and handrails, for example. Others combine utility with ornament—such as the carved wooden brackets used under mantel shelves. Still others are strictly decorative—for example, the large carved brackets used under exterior cornices or the cut-out boards which are applied to stair stringers under the treads.

BRACKET FOOT

A foot on chests of drawers and other case pieces.

It is L-shaped and mitered to fit under a corner of the chest. The bottom edges of the sides of the corner are often cut out in pretty shapes.

BRAD
A small finishing nail between ½ and 1½ in. long.

BRAID
A plaited tape used to trim fabric articles.

BRASS
A heavy alloy of copper and zinc, brass is found in the home in hardware and decorative objects, in plumbing fittings, and as a base for chrome plate in top-quality plumbing fittings and bathroom accessories.

Brass tarnishes rapidly, and the only way to retain its natural soft luster is by frequent applications of brass polish. The alternative is to spray the surface with lacquer after thorough cleaning; but this produces a very glossy, bright finish.

BREAK
An interruption in a surface. A break in a wall may be an actual gap, a pilaster or comparable projection, or a jog or other change of direction.

BREAKFAST BAR
See Bar.

BREAKFAST ROOM
See Dinette.

BREAKFRONT
A tall cabinet or secretary with a front divided into three vertical sections—the center section projecting forward of the end sections.

BREAKING JOINT
The arrangement of building materials in a structure so that the crosswise joints in adjacent rows are staggered. In a brick wall, the joints in one course do not form a straight, continuous line with the joints in the adjacent courses. This gives the wall greater strength. Similarly, in a shingled wall the joints are staggered—in this case, to prevent leakage. Similarly, in a wooden floor, the joints are staggered to improve the appearance of the floor.

BREEZEWAY

A porch or terrace-like area connecting two parts of a house, such as the house itself and garage. It is usually open on two sides and has a floor and roof.

Breezeways are often screened in summer and glass-enclosed in winter. Many are enclosed year around with jalousies.

BRIC-A-BRAC

A collective noun meaning a group of small decorative objects.

BRICK

Bricks are durable building units made of baked clay in a variety of colors (but commonly reds and pinks) and textures. *Common,* or *building, bricks* are used for ordinary construction purposes. *Facebricks,* made of selected clays and/or treated to produce special colors or textures, are used to face walls. *Paving bricks,* called *pavers,* are especially suitable for use in pavements where resistance to abrasion is essential. *Fire bricks,* made of refractory ceramic materials which resist high temperatures, are used in fireplaces and chimneys.

The size of the original standard brick was 2¼ x 3¾ x 8 in., but bricks are now produced in a great many other sizes. Those used in walls range in height from a nominal 2 to 8 in.; in width from 3 to 8 in. and even 12 in.; and in length from 8 to 16 in. Most are solid, but some have hollow cores.

Paving bricks are even more variable since they are made not only in rectangles but also in hexagons and special shapes. In addition, there are bullnose bricks and bricks with nosings made for use as stair treads. Thicknesses range from ½ to 2½ in. Rectangular pavers are 3-3/8 to 4 in. wide (actual dimensions) and 7½ to 11¾ in. long. Squares measure from 4 to 16 in. on a side. Hexagonal units are 6, 8, or 12 in. across.

The mortar used in laying bricks is made of 1 sack of masonry cement and 2 to 3 cu. ft. of sand. Joints are 3/8 to ½ in. thick, depending on the dimensions of the bricks. In a wall the joints are contoured in several ways (*see* Mortar Joint). In a floor they are usually struck off flush with the face of the bricks.

The bonds, or patterns, in which bricks are most often laid are discussed above under Bond. Each horizontal row constitutes a *course.* Bricks running parallel with a wall are *stretchers;* those laid across the wall are *headers. Rowlocks, soldiers,* and *sailors* are names given to bricks laid in other positions.

In today's houses, exterior walls are generally veneered. In these a single tier of bricks (usually 4 in. thick) is built up in front of a framed and sheathed subwall with a small air space between. The veneer is fastened to the sheathing with metal ties but is otherwise independent of it.

Solid brick walls are usually built in two tiers (8 in. thick) which are tied together with mortar.

A well-constructed brick wall is watertight and requires no attention once completed. If it occasionally seeps moisture (but has no active leaks through joints), it can be dampproofed with a silicone water repellent. Painting to change the color is best done with latex, chlorinated rubber, or portland cement paint. Alkyd and oil paints can also be applied to completely dry walls.

Brick floors and outdoor paving can be laid in mortar, but they are more attractive if laid dry because the bricks are set tightly edge to edge and the joints are less obvious. In a floor, mortarless bricks are placed directly on a plywood subfloor. Outdoors, they are laid on a base made of 3 in. of gravel or crushed rock topped by 1 in. of well-compacted sand. To minimize staining, a masonry sealer can be applied to all floors and paving.

BRICK, CONCRETE
A gray brick made of concrete.

BRICK, SURFACE-APPLIED
A thin clay brick, similar in composition to conventional bricks, for application to any smooth, sound, clean subwall. Its purpose is to give the effect of solid brick masonry at a reduced installation cost. Two types are on the market:

Nail-On bricks • These are 1 in. thick, 2½ in. wide, and 7-5/8 or 11½ in. long, and made in several colors. They are applied indoors or out with nails. The interlocking edges form grooves which are pointed with concrete.

Glue-On Bricks • These measure ¼ x 2-1/8 x 8 in. They are made in several colors and are used only indoors. They are embedded in mastic spread on the subwall with a notched spreader. The joints are not filled.

Thin, surface-applied bricks are also made of plastic (*see* Masonry, Plastic). But whereas these are combustible, clay bricks are safe to use around fireplace openings and behind kitchen ranges.

BRICK VENEER
See Brick.

BRIDGING

The bracing installed between joists to stiffen them, hold them in alignment, and distribute the load upon them.

Bridging is usually made with 1 x 3- or 1 x 4-in. boards nailed between two adjacent joists to form an **X**. Prefabricated metal bridging of the same design, called *cross bridging*, is made.

Solid bridging consists of short lengths of 2-in.-wide timbers nailed between adjacent joists. The bridging is cut from the lumber used for joists.

All bridging is installed in straight rows perpendicular to the joists. The spacing between rows is usually 8 ft.

BRITANNIAWARE

A type of pewter made in the mid-18th century.

BRITISH THERMAL UNIT

Abbreviated *Btu* or *Btuh*, a British thermal unit is the amount of heat required to raise the temperature of one pound of water one degree Fahrenheit. The capacity of heating and air conditioning plants is stated in British thermal units.

BROADLOOM

A carpet made on a wide loom. It is not a special type of carpet such as an Axminster or Wilton.

BROCADE

A rich satin, silk, or velvet fabric with a heavy texture, with elaborate decoration, and often with metallic threads. It is used in upholstery and draperies.

BROCATELLE

An upholstery and drapery fabric. It resembles a stiff brocade with a high-relief design having an embossed effect.

BRONZE

A copper and tin alloy found in heavy decorative objects such as medallions and sundials. Bronze screenwire is also made. The metal is cleaned and finished like brass (*see above*).

BROWN COAT

The first cost of plaster on a wall or ceiling. Also called the *scratch coat.*

BTU
British thermal unit (*see above*).

BUBINGA
An exotic West African wood. It is heavy and hard, and has a deep, rich brown color with a purplish cast. It is streaked or mottled with a deeper purple-brown. Bubinga is used in furniture and paneling. Rotary-cut veneers are particularly beautiful and called *kevazingo*.

BUFFET
A sideboard.

BUILDER'S ALLOWANCE
Today, the usual practice of builders in bidding on a new house or remodeling job is to include in the bid price the cost of the work to be done according to the plans and specifications. The bid does not, however, cover the cost of work which is not specified but which is necessary to the completion of a house. For this work, the builder makes an allowance—an estimate of what the work will cost—and the actual cost of the work is added to the bid price when the house is completed.

Allowances are made on such things as kitchen cabinets, electrical fixtures, decorating, kitchen flooring—items which are not exactly described in the specifications because the owner isn't sure at the time he lets bids what he will use.

This system of bid'ding gives the owner a reasonably sound idea of what the total cost of the house will be. At the same time, it protects the builder in the event that the owner decides to put in more expensive kitchen cabinets and electrical fixtures, etc., than the builder might have figured on, had he included these in the bid.

The danger of the system is that an unscrupulous builder may make absurdly low allowances in order to lull the owner into thinking that he should award the contract to that builder. The owner then discovers too late what has been done, and he must decide either to go over his budget or to put in much cheaper equipment than he wants in order to hold the cost of the house down.

BUILDER'S HARDWARE
Locksets, latchsets, hinges, window locks, door tracks, and other hardware customarily installed by a builder as part of his contract. The installation of many other hardware

items—such as coat hooks, drapery hardware, knobs, and pulls—is made by either the owner or the builder, depending on their contract.

BUILDING AREA

The total area which may be occupied by buildings on a lot. Building area—sometimes referred to as *lot coverage*—may be restricted by zoning codes.

BUILDING HEIGHT

Zoning codes often restrict the height of a house in proportion to the size and zoning of the lot. The way it is measured depends on the code. For example, the code in one eastern suburban community defines building height as "the vertical distance measured from the average level of the ground along all walls to the highest point of the roof for flat roofs, to the deck line for mansard roofs, and to the mean height between eaves and ridge for gable, hip and gambrel roofs, and to the highest point of any other roof."

BUILDING INSPECTOR

The title ususally given to the head of the local building department as well as to various assistants who actually make inspections of buildings under construction to determine whether they comply with the building code and are safe.

In the name of the chief building inspector, the building department issues the building permit for a house (or other building) after it is satisfied that the house will comply with the building and zoning codes. When construction is under way, the assistant building inspectors make periodic inspections of the house. Such inspections are generally made when construction reaches a certain point—for example, before the footings are laid, when the framing is completed, when the plumbing fixtures are in—and at that time the contractor or owner calls the building department to request the inspection.

If an inspector finds anything wrong with a house, he can require that it be corrected; and unless he can be convinced that he is wrong, he can hold up construction until the necessary steps have been taken by the contractor.

BUILDING LINE

One of the lines on a lot behind which a building must be placed. It corresponds to a *setback (see below)*. Most properties have front, rear, and two side building lines.

BUILDING PAPER

A heavy paper used primarily to keep moisture from entering a house through the roof or side walls.

BUILDING PERMIT

Written permission given by a municipal building department to undertake construction of a house. The permit indicates that the department has inspected the plans for the house and approves of them.

If a house is to be built by a general contractor, he applies and pays for the building permit. If a house is built by subcontractors, the owner applies for the permit. The value given to the house on the permit has a rough relationship to the actual value. The cost of the permit is based on the permit value. The permit itself must be prominently posted on the building site.

In addition to the permit for the entire house, separate permits are usually required for the electrical and plumbing installations.

Issuance of a building permit does not automatically ensure that the building will be approved for occupancy when completed. On the contrary, it is inspected frequently during the course of construction and if any flaws or discrepancies are turned up at these times, construction may be halted until they are corrected. Then, when the building is completed, a final inspection is made before a certificate of occupancy is issued.

BUILDING SITE

The land on which a building is erected. The words may be used to describe the general area or the specific location of the foundations.

BUILT-IN

Made a permanent part of a building; or an object which is permanently built in. As an adjective, the word is broadly applied; as a noun, its use is circumscribed but in no clear fashion. Generally a built-in is considered to be a piece of furniture which is not traditionally built in—for example, a chest of drawers, bed, or dressing table.

The reasons for building anything in vary. Usually a built-in is thought to save space, though this is rarely true. However, it does help to organize space, tie the furnishings into the architecture, and reduce home maintenance by eliminating cracks and crevices that catch dirt. On the other hand, built-ins almost always permit less flexibility in the use and furnishing of a house than comparable free-standing objects.

BUILT-UP ROOFING
Roofing which is built up in layers of building felt and asphalt, and surfaced with gravel, slag, or stone chips. The resulting roof is without seams, resistant to fire and wind, and easy to repair. It has a life expectancy of about 20 years.

Built-up roofing is laid on dead-level roofs and those with a pitch of up to 3 in. per foot. It can also be laid on steeper roofs if special installation steps are taken. On sloping roofs, gravel stops are installed along the eaves to hold the gravel in place.

The color of the roofing depends on the kind of gravel used for surfacing. The white roofs which are common on air conditioned houses are covered, as a rule, with white marble chips.

BULKHEAD
The slanting or horizontal enclosure over the exterior stairway to a basement. It is designed to prevent flooding of the stairs and basement and to keep out intruders.

The bulkheads used in houses today are almost always prefabricated of steel. They are bolted to masonry walls surrounding the stairs.

BULLET
An incandescent light fixture shaped like a bullet. It can be surface-mounted on a ceiling or wall and aimed in any direction.

BULLNOSE
The descriptive name given ceramic tiles and bricks which are rounded along one edge or at one end. Bullnose tiles are used as the border tiles on wainscots and other partially tiled walls.

BUN FOOT
A furniture foot shaped like a hamburger bun.

BUNGALOW SIDING
Colonial siding (*see below*).

BURLAP
A rough-textured fabric of jute or hemp. Manufactured in various colors and a few patterns, it is used for bedspreads and draperies and also as a wallcovering. A vinyl-coated type is available.

As a wallcovering, burlap is available with and without a paper backing. The latter is easier to hang. Single rolls, produced in 26- and 45-in. widths, cover roughly 36 sq. ft.

Installation should be made over lining paper with a powdered vinyl adhesive. The burlap is hung like wallpaper.

BUSHING
A compact threaded pipe fitting used to connect a large pipe to a smaller pipe. It is internally threaded at one end to receive the small pipe and externally threaded at the other end. *Compare* Reducer.

BUTCHER BLOCK
A table with an extremely thick, laminated wooden top originally used by butchers for cutting meat and now often used in kitchens for food preparation.

BUTLER'S TRAY
A small rectangular table with narrow hinged leaves with handle holds on the four sides. The leaves fold up so the table can be easily carried. When folded down to horizontal position, the table top becomes oval or sometimes round.

BUTT
The thicker, bottom end of a shingle or piece of bevel siding. Also, a kind of hinge used primarily for doors. As a verb, butt means to place or fasten one thing against another.

BUTTER
To apply mortar to a brick, concrete block, or other masonry unit before setting it in place. In brick construction, for example, one end of the brick about to be laid is buttered and then pressed into place against the end of the brick previously laid.

BUTTERFLY ROOF
The opposite of a gable roof. The butterfly is V-shaped, with the ridge lower than the eaves. Water drains off either at the ends of the V or through a central drain.

BUTT JOINT
The simplest, commonest, and weakest type of joint used in building. The end of one piece is butted against the side of the other piece, and the two are fastened together with nails. In woodworking, fastening is also done with screws, dowels, glue, mending plates, wood blocks, or special fasteners.

Despite their deficiencies, butt joints are used almost exclusively in framing houses because they are quickly and easily made, and because there is ample bracing in a house to compensate for the weakness of individual joints.

BUTTRESS

An external support or structure which counteracts the outward thrust of a wall and holds the wall upright. A buttress may be a large masonry projection from a wall, as in the great medieval cathedrals, or simply a round timber permanently slanted against a wall as a shore.

BX CABLE

An electrical cable incorporating two or three insulated wires. The wires are encased in a ribbon of steel wound in a tight spiral to make the cable flexible. Almost all electrical codes permit the use of BX cable in house wiring (but not outdoors or underground). It is also called *armored cable.*

CABINET

The principal cabinets in a house are the kitchen cabinets (which are also used in laundries and pantries), and the medicine cabinet and any other special cabinets which may be built into a bathroom (as under a built-in lavatory). *See* Kitchen Cabinet and Bathroom Cabinet. All can be specially designed, and either built on the job by carpenters or fabricated to order by local cabinetmaking shops. But the common practice is to buy cabinets produced by a national or regional manufacturer. These cabinets are then shipped to the project and installed by the contractor.

CABLE

A large, sheathed, flexible "rope" containing electrical conductors. *See* BX Cable, Nonmetallic Sheathed Cable, and Plastic-Sheathed Cable.

CABOCHON

A smooth, convex, round or oval surface used for decoration on furniture.

CABRIOLE

A furniture leg with a gently rounded knee at the top, a reverse curve below, and a shaped foot. It was originally used in Queen Anne and Chippendale chairs, highboys, and other furniture pieces.

CALCIMINE

Also spelled *kalsomine,* this is an outmoded water-thinned interior wall and ceiling paint. It is still found in old houses, however. It must be washed off before new paint or wallpaper or other flexible fabric wallcoverings is applied.

CALICHE

Rock-hard calcium salts found in dense layers in the Southwest. They interfere with excavation.

CALICO

A simple, light, rather coarse cotton fabric that is generally printed on only one side. It is used in curtains.

CAMBER

The slight arch given a beam or similar horizontal support to keep it from bending under a load.

CAMEL BACK

A Hepplewhite chair back with a crest rail shaped like a single-hump camel.

CAMPAIGN FURNITURE

Furniture akin to that used by military officers which folds, collapses, or is generally easy to carry.

CANDELABRUM

A candleholder with several arms. It ranges in height from about 1 to 6 ft. or more and is usually made of metal but sometimes of wood.

CANDLESTAND

A little table on which a candlestick or lamp is set. It usually has three legs joined to a central post, and often has a tilt top.

CANDLESTICK

A single candleholder; however, some silver candlesticks today can be converted into candelabra and back again.

CANDLEWICK

A bedspread fabric made of cotton with little tufts of

threads on the front. The tufts are arranged to form a decorative pattern.

CANE
A slender, light brown, stiff, woody material used to make chair seats and backs and other furniture pieces. *See* Rattan.

CANOPY
In decorating, a canopy is a large piece of fabric which is draped over a piece of furniture (most commonly a bed) or over an entire room. The latter use has gained popularity with the increasing interest in decorating walls and ceilings in one fabric.

In building, a canopy is a roof projecting from a wall—over an entrance or driveway, for example.

CANT
To tilt or bevel. Also, an oblique angle.

CANTERBURY
A magazine rack. Originally—and still today—it was a rack for holding sheet music.

CANTILEVER
To build out from a vertical surface; or something which is built out from a vertical surface. A bookshelf projecting from a wall is a cantilever or is said to be a cantilever shelf. To install such a shelf is to cantilever it.

Many parts of buildings may be cantilevered: balconies, bay windows, steps, even the second floor of a house.

CANTONALE
A rather slender, tall, quarter-round, free-standing cabinet which fits into a corner.

CANT STRIP
A slanted or beveled wooden strip used to change the angle of a roof or to give a rounded contour to the junction between a sloping and flat roof surface. A cant strip is also the beveled strip placed under the butts of wood shingles to provide a smooth deck for new roofing.

CANVAS
A sturdy utility fabric usually made of cotton which is used

in sling chairs and awnings and as floor coverings. It soils and mildews badly, fades readily, and is hard to clean.

As a floor covering, very heavy deck canvas is often used to surface wooden porches and decks. The material is spread in a bed of white lead, secured around the edges with copper tacks, and then given two or three coats of oil-base deck paint.

Canvas is also used to make area rugs. Known as *floorcloths,* these are made by painting canvas with oil-base paints, usually in geometric designs. Originally used in 18th century American homes when rugs were scarce and expensive, floorcloths are today manufactured on a limited base.

CAP
The top of some things. The top of a column is the cap (or capital). Similarly, the cornice over a door or a coping on a wall is a cap.

A cap is also a pipe fitting with a solid end which is used to stop the flow of water.

CAPITAL
The very top part of a column (which is sometimes called a *cap* for short). *See* Order.

CAPTAIN'S WALK
A balustrade-encircled flat space on top of a roof from which sea captains and shipowners watched incoming and outgoing vessels. Also called a *widow's walk.*

CARCASE
The body of a chest of drawers, cupboard, or other case piece.

CARPENTER GOTHIC
Scornful name given the Gothic Revival style of architecture in the mid-19th century because of the elaborate, often raw ornamentation given houses by the carpenters who built them. The hallmark of carpenter Gothic was gingerbread.

CARPET
Carpets and rugs not only bring beauty to a room but also make floors more comfortable under foot, insulate them against cold, muffle noises within the room, and minimize the transmission of impact sounds to the rooms below.

Long before a homeowner is ready to settle on the color, pattern, and type of carpet he needs in a new house, he must decide whether the floors are to be covered with wall-to-wall carpet or with room-size rugs. If carpets are to be used, some money can be saved by laying them (together with rug cushioning) directly on a ½-in. plywood subfloor. In this case, however, the carpets are usually left behind when the house is sold.

If finished wood floors are installed, rugs are less expensive than wall-to-wall carpet and are less likely to require cutting if the owners move them to another house.

In all cases, however, wall-to-wall carpets are preferable to rugs for reducing home maintenance. For one thing, it is easier to clean a carpet with a single vacuum cleaner tool than to clean a rug plus a fringe of wooden or resilient floor with two tools. In addition, there is no need to turn back the edges of the carpet in order to polish the surrounding floor.

Carpets and rugs are made of the following fibers:

Acrylic • Resembling wool, acrylic is resilient, resistant to soiling and crushing, durable, easy to clean, and not bothered by moths or mildew. But new carpets tend to shed badly for a while.

Cotton • Durable and easy to wash, but soils and crushes easily.

Modacrylic • Similar to acrylic but not as resilient. It is often blended with acrylic because it increases fire resistance.

Nylon • The strongest and longest wearing of the man-made fibers. It is mildew and mothproof, and cleans well (but shows soil). Unless treated, it is subject to static electricity. *Staple nylon* (short lengths spun into yard) tends to pill and is only moderately resilient. *Continuous-filament nylon* (long strands) does not pill and has excellent resiliency.

Polyester • Soft, durable, mildew and mothproof, very resistant to crushing, washes well. But its stain resistance and resiliency are low.

Polypropylene • Used for indoor-outdoor and kitchen carpets, polypropylene (sometimes called *olefin*) is very tough and durable, resists soiling, and cleans very easily. But it is only moderately crush-resistant.

Rayon • Low cost, but generally a poor buy unless the pile is very dense. This improves its soil resistance, abrasion resistance, and resiliency considerably.

Saran • Has good soil and stain resistance and fair abrasion resistance, and does not burn (but melts at a low temperature). The color deepens with time.

Wool • Wool is the basic carpet fiber against which all others are judged. It is very resilient and resistant to crushing and soil. Durability is high and cleaning is simple. But the wool must be mothproofed.

Regardless of the fiber used, the quality of a carpet is best determined by the weight of the fiber in a square yard. For example, if the fiber in a given carpet weighs 24 oz. and the pile is ½ in. deep, the density is obviously twice as great as that of another 24-oz. carpet with a pile 1 in. deep. If the weight of the fiber is unknown, density of pile can be determined by bending a corner of the carpet back. The less backing that can be seen, the denser the pile.

The backing of carpets is usually made of jute or man-made fibers, and should be tight and firm. On tufted carpets, the backing is covered with latex to hold the yarns securely. A similar coating is used on many other carpets. Quality rugs have a double backing.

Most machine-made carpets are tufted. Hand-made Orientals are also tufted and then knotted to the backing. In tufting, needles punch the yarns through a woven fabric backing.

Surface textures produced in machine-made carpets include:

Plush • Straight yarns are sheared and used in a tight pile.

Chenille • A plush carpet with a deep pile.

Shag • Yarns are long and used in a loose pile.

Splush • A combination of plush and shag.

Frieze • Tightly twisted yarns in a rough, nubby, cut pile.

Loop • The yarns form loops.

Twist • A corkscrew, cut pile with a nubby texture.

Random-Sheared • The pile is a combination of sheared and looped yarns.

Sculptured • A plush surface cut at different heights to make a design.

Woven carpets are made on looms. The best known types are *Axminster, velvet, Wilton,* and *chenille.* The last is of outstanding quality and is usually custom-made.

In needlepunched carpets—made for indoor-outdoor use—webs of loose fibers are needled into the backing. In flocked carpets, which are also used indoors and outdoors and in kitchens, the fibers are stuck to the backing.

Carpets are also hand-embroidered by needlepointing.

CARPET TILE
One of a number of small pieces of carpet with adhesive backing which are used to cover floors. Tiles are made of polypropylene or acrylic in 9-, 12-, and 18-in. squares and in special shapes. They can be laid on any clean, dry floor on or below grade; and although they stick tight, they can be pulled up readily and put down elsewhere.

CARPORT
Carport advocates have maintained so long and so vehemently that carports are every bit as good as garages that garages should by now have disappeared from all newly built homes. The fact that they have not would seem to indicate the advocates are wrong. Carports are not as good as garages because

1 /   They are open to the world—and often ugly.

2 /   They often give inadequate protection to cars and drivers against weather.

3 /   They pile high with drifting snow and leaves.

4 /   They do not provide the storage space the average homeowner needs.

The only advantage of a carport is that it requires two or three fewer walls than a garage and is cheaper to build. But if the homeowner then turns around and constructs a big storage closet for mowers, tractors, etc., in the carport, his saving largely disappears.

Dimensions for carports can be 2 to 3 ft. less than those for garages (*see below*) but more drastic reductions in length or width expose the automobile and driver to the elements. The floor should be lower than the house floor and sloped away from the house toward the driveway or a central floor drain. If a storage cupboard is built in a carport, it should be raised off the floor several inches.

CARRIAGE
A stair stringer. *See* Stringer.

CARTOUCHE
A shield-shaped or oval, convex, scrollwork-framed surface which is carved or inlaid in a larger building or furniture

surface. The center of the cartouche may have a painted or low-relief design.

CARYATID

An architectural or furniture column in the form of a female figure.

CASED

Word used in reference to an exposed beam which is covered on the sides and bottom with boards.

CASEIN PAINT

A water-thinned paint which dries quickly to a flat, durable finish. Once widely used on interior walls and ceilings, it has been almost completely replaced by latex paint. However, modified casein paint is sometimes used to decorate wood furniture. In this case, the final finish is protected with flat varnish, shellac, or lacquer.

CASEMENT

A window hinged on one side so it swings out (or sometimes in) like a door. *See* Window.

CASEMENT CLOTH

A sheer fabric made of various fibers used for curtains and draperies—particularly on picture windows and window walls.

CASE PIECE

A piece of furniture shaped more or less like a box. A bureau is a case piece.

CASING

In building, a casing is the flat trim nailed to the wall around a door or window. It conceals the open joint between the back of the jamb and the adjacent wall.

In a drilled well, it is a steel lining which prevents the walls from caving in.

In decorating, a casing is a sleeve-like hem open at the ends through which curtain rods, cords, etc., are run.

CASTER

The wheel device which is attached to furniture legs to permit the furniture to be rolled around a room. It is made in several ways. The roller may be wheel-shaped or ball-shaped, and made of metal, hard rubber, or plastic in diameters up to 3 in. Casters are attached to legs either by a stem which is inserted in a metal socket in the leg or by screws driven through a flat metal plate into the base of the leg.

The larger the wheel or ball in a caster, the easier the furniture is to roll but the more ungainly it looks. As a practical matter, large casters are used only for very heavy furniture (or loads) or for movement over uneven floors or those covered with deep-pile rugs. Generally, the proper way to select casters is to determine the weight of the furniture piece and then follow the weight guides printed on caster packages.

CAST IRON

A heavy, coarse, brittle metal made into a variety of household objects as well as intricate benches and tables. Because it rusts rapidly, it must be well protected with paint—preferably a red metal primer followed by one or two coats of alkyd or oil paint.

CAST STONE

Building "stone" manufactured out of concrete.

CAT

A block of wood installed between studs to serve as a nailing base.

CATALYTIC COATING

A paint containing epoxy—or sometimes urethane—which dries and hardens through a chemical process rather than by evaporation of solvents and thinners. Applicable to all nonporus surfaces, it produces an exceptionally hard, durable finish but tends to chalk and fade upon exposure to weather. During its short drying period, it emits toxic fumes and should therefore be used only in a very well-ventilated location.

CATCH

A device for holding lightweight doors, such as those on furniture and kitchen cabinets, shut. Since it has no locking mechanism, the doors can be pulled open with a slight tug. Common types include:

Friction Catch • A very small device which is mortised into the edge of a door and the jamb. It consists of a rounded button which projects slightly from the edge of a door and slips into the strike in the jamb.

Magnetic Catch • The catch, mounted on the door, contains a magnet which holds it to a metal strike mounted on the jamb.

Roller Catch • Has one or two spring-controlled rollers which engage the strike.

Touch Catch • The only type of catch which does not require that a knob or handle be installed on a door so it can be pulled open. The device is similar to a double roller catch but releases automatically when the closed door is pushed.

Adjustable Spring Catch • A large catch for casement windows and doors. When a hook mounted on the window engages a spring-actuated arm on the jamb, the arm pulls the window shut.

Snap Catch • Used on screen doors, this is a one-piece catch mounted on the casing. As the door swings closed, it strikes the catch, which then folds around the edges of the door and clamps it to the jamb.

CATCH BASIN

A trough-like or bowl-like masonry pit or depression which collects rainwater and directs it into a drain or sewer.

CATHEDRAL CEILING

A high vaulted ceiling or a ceiling with steeply sloping sides that follow the roof lines.

CAULKING

A flexible material used to fill joints and cracks so moisture and air cannot enter. It is used primarily to seal the joints around window and exterior door frames, and between masonry and wooden walls. It is also commonly used around the rim of a bathrub where the joint at the wall opens. And it seals the large joints between cast-iron pipes in house sewers.

Caulking (except for pipes) is made of several thick mastics; but the best currently in use are silicone and polysulfide rubber. These are more expensive than older, usually oil-base materials, but they are more durable and retain their adhesiveness and flexibility for many years.

CAVITY WALL

A wall consisting of two fairly thin walls separated by a continuous air space but held together with metal ties embedded in the joints. Although rarely used in residences, such a wall improves water resistance and thermal insulation.

CEDAR, ALASKA
A tree belonging to the *chamaecyparis* genus. The decay-resistant, aromatic wood has a fine, straight grain. It is used in cabinet work and miscellaneous woodwork in the home.

CEDAR CLOSET
A closet lined with aromatic cedar boards to help repel moths. The boards are 3/8 in. thick, 2 to 4 in. wide, and 2 to 8 ft. long. They are tongue-and-grooved along the edges and at the ends. Installation is made over an existing wall or by nailing directly to studs.

For maximum protection, a cedar closet not only should be made with cedar on the walls and celing but also should have a cedar floor, cedar-lined door, and cedar shelves. The door should be weatherstripped.

CEDAR, INCENSE
Incense cedar is a very light, easily worked, dimensionally stable softwood with exceptional resistance to decay and an aromatic odor. The uniformly textured wood is adaptable to most rough construction purposes. The tree belongs to the *libocedrus* genus and grows in Oregon and California.

CEDAR, RED
The so-called cedars form a large and confusing clan. The most important is the western red cedar (botanically it belongs to the *thuja* genus), which is used to make practically all wood shingles, clapboards, and rough board siding. It is a very aromatic, uniform, and soft medium-brown wood with a straight grain. It works well; is easy to nail, paint, and stain; has outstanding dimensional stability; and is slow to decay.

The eastern red cedar (which belongs to the *juniperus* genus) is of less value because it contains many knots and is rather brittle. The heartwood is a beautiful red and extremely aromatic and decay resistant. The sapwood is white.

CEDAR, WHITE
One tree called white cedar belongs to the *chamaecyparis* genus, another to the *thuja* genus. The yellow-brown, decay-resistant, aromatic woods are used for shingles and miscellaneous purposes.

CEILING
The standard height of ceilings in today's homes is 8 ft. The

minimum height allowable by the FHA is 7½ ft.; and although ceilings in early houses were sometimes as low as 7 ft., the FHA figure is not very debatable.

Ceiling height has no maximum other than that dictated by practicality. Nine- to twelve-ft. ceilings are used to a limited extent to give spaciousness to very large living rooms. Sixteen-ft. ceilings are used when the homeowner wants a two-story living room in a two-story house.

Like interior walls, ceilings are usually surfaced with gypsum board. To prevent transmission of sound from a lower room to one above, the boards should be no less than 5/8 in. thick. For top-story ceilings, however, the board need not be more than 3/8 in. thick.

To reduce the level of sound in a noisy room, acoustical tiles are applied directly to furring strips nailed to the ceiling joists or are cemented to gypsum board. *See* Acoustical Tile.

Ceilings in the top floor of houses with unused attics should be insulated with materials having a resistance value of 19. Fiberglass or mineral-wool batts or fill insulation is most often used. Insulation is placed directly between the joists with a vapor barrier on the underside.

Also see Ceiling, Suspended, and Luminous Ceiling.

CEILING BOARD

To the lumber industry, this is a specially milled board used to cover ceilings. But any board applied to a ceiling may be called a ceiling board.

CEILING HEATER

See Space Heating.

CEILING PANEL

A wide ornamental molding nailed flat to a wall just below a ceiling or ceiling cornice.

CEILING, SUSPENDED

A ceiling which is hung below the ceiling joists. Suspended ceilings are almost always composed of large fiberboard tiles or panels placed in a lightweight metal framework which is attached around the perimeter to the walls and hung by wires from the joists. Light fixtures are set into the ceiling here and there.

CEILING TILE

A fibrous tile like an acoustical tile. It may or may

not have acoustical characteristics. Many units called tiles are more accurately described as boards or panels.

CEMENT

Although some glues are called cements, the commonest cement is a finely ground mineral used in masonry work. Many types are used:

Type I Portland Cement • The cement used in most masonry projects. Normally gray in color, it is also available in white. It is sold in sacks which contain 1 cu. ft. and weigh 94 lb.

Type IA Portland Cement • Called an *air-entrained portland cement,* this is used to produce concrete which is resistant to severe frost action and heavy applications of salt for snow removal.

Masonry Cement • A portland cement containing lime used for laying bricks, concrete blocks, and other masonry units.

Hydraulic Cement • A very fine, dark gray cement which hardens in the presence of water. It is sold in small packages for plugging leaks in foundation walls, etc.

Latex Cement • A cement which is mixed with liquid latex. Sold in small packages, it is used mainly for patching and for leveling uneven surfaces. Unlike conventional cement, it can be troweled to a feather edge about 1/16 in. thick and will not crack.

Epoxy Cement • Used for the same purposes as latex cement, epoxy cement consists of dry cement which is mixed with epoxy liquid.

Vinyl Cement • Another patching and leveling cement, this contains vinyl to which water is added.

Acrylic Cement • Similar to vinyl cement except that it contains acrylic.

CEMENTITIOUS COATING

Also called a *cement paint,* this is a heavy paint-like material used to waterproof basement walls which ooze moisture but do not leak actively. It comes as a dry powder which is mixed with water and applied with a whitewash brush to a damp surface. Two coats are usually enough, but more may be necessary. The coating is available in white and several pastel colors.

CEMENT, KEENE'S

A high-strength, white gypsum plaster used to produce a very hard, dense surface.

CEMENT, NEAT
Cement without any aggregate added.

CEMENT PLASTER
A cement mixture used to parge (cover) foundation walls to make them waterproof. It is made of 1 part portland cement and 2½ parts sand with sufficient water to give a plastic mix which will stick to vertical surfaces without sagging.

CENTER LINE
A line drawn to mark the center of something. On a plan, it is made up of alternate dots and dashes.

CENTER-MATCHED
A term describing tongue-and-groove boards in which the tongue and the groove are centered in the edges of the boards.

CERAMICS
Articles made of clay baked at high temperatures. The word is usually associated with decorative objects but is also properly applied to bricks, tiles, etc.

CERAMIC TILE
Ceramic, or clay, tiles are used in the home on walls, floors, counters, table tops, windowsills, and fireplace hearths and breasts because they are both beautiful and practical. Few other materials are as durable, tough, resistant to just about everything, and easy to maintain. Their principal drawbacks (though not in all situations) are that they feel cold, are hard underfoot, easily damage fragile articles which are set down on them carelessly, and are slippery when wet. In addition, the joints between tiles are dirt collectors and may be difficult to clean if exposed to water containing heavy concentrations of iron or maganese.

Walls • Although wall tiles are available in numerous shapes and sizes, the most popular are squares measuring 4¼ x 4¼ in. and mosaics, which are usually 1-in. squares sold in 1-ft.-square sheets.

Tiles used in the field of an installation—near the center of a wall—have square edges on all four sides. On the other hand, trim tiles—used around the borders of an installation—have specially shaped edges which do not require any sort of finishing. The commonest trim tiles are *bullnose tiles* with one rounded edge, *down-angles* with two adjacent rounded edges, and *cove tiles* with one outward curving edge.

Tiles are installed with portland cement or special adhesives. The latter are most often used because they simplify and speed installation. The base to which the tiles are glued must be level, sound, and rigid; and free of wallpaper and other flexible coverings, loose paint, grease, and dirt. In a shower stall or shower recess over a tub, a skim coat of adhesive is applied to the wall prior to tiling to increase its water resistance.

Standard size tiles are best installed from the center of a wall toward the sides. This assures that the vertical rows at each end of the wall will be of the same width. The height to which the tiles are carried above the floor depends on the effect desired and on whether it is necessary to protect the upper part of the wall. Generally, over bathtubs used for shower-bathing, tile is installed to a point 6 in. above the pipe to which the shower head is attached. Tiled wainscots behind lavatories and toilets and elsewhere in bathrooms are usually 4 ft. high. In kitchens, walls are tiled from the countertops to the bottoms of the wall cabinets.

The joints between tiles are grouted—usually with a dry cement which is mixed with water. For greater resistance to stains caused by grease, minerals in water, etc., mastic grouts packaged in cans ready for use are recommended. In either case, once the grout has started to harden, the joints between standard size tiles are tooled to a concave contour. Joints between mosaic tiles are struck off flush with the tiles.

Floors • The same tiles used on walls are used to cover floors in bathrooms and other areas. They are installed in the same ways—either with adhesive on a plywood base or with cement on a concrete base.

Larger tiles are also used—particularly in halls, family rooms, and other living areas. These are made in squares, rectangles, and special shapes. So-called patio tiles are up to a foot square and brownish red. Quarry tiles and pavers are smaller and available in a wide assortment of colors. Large tiles are usually laid in concrete and have ½-in. mortar joints. But they can be laid in adhesive.

Roofs • Roofing tiles are cruder in texture and finish than wall and floor tiles, but they are one of the most ornamental roofing materials and have been in use for centuries. They are made in flat rectangles, which are laid like slates or wood shingles, and in special shapes—usually with a barrel contour.

The tiles are laid on a solid deck covered with building felt. Minimum roof pitch is 4 in. per foot. For heavyweight tiles, additional framing is required.

In addition to being fire and wind resistant, roofing tiles do not accumulate the covering of moss which appears on many other types of roofing. They are very durable but hard to replace when broken.

CERTIFICATE OF OCCUPANCY

Approval issued by the local building department signifying that a new house or major addition to an old house is ready and safe to be occupied. Until the certificate is issued, the house cannot be legally occupied. However, issuance of a certificate does not necessarily mean that the builder has completed his contract.

CESSPOOL

A large covered hole in the ground used for the disposal of household wastes. It is lined on the sides with stones, bricks, or masonry blocks laid up without mortar. The solid wastes settle to the bottom, where they slowly disintegrate; the liquid part of the waste—effluent—seeps out through the sides into the surrounding soil.

Cesspools are banned in many parts of the country because they are unsafe and objectionable. Where permitted, they must be at least 15 to 20 ft. from any house and 150 ft. from all water sources. The ground must be porous.

CHAIR

It is doubtful if anyone except a person who devotes his life to the subject can sort out and label all the styles of chairs which have been made. For one thing, there are hundreds. For another thing, nomenclature has no rhyme or reason. Some chairs are known by their most distinctive feature, such as the shape of the back or legs or the materials of which they are made. Some are known by the names of their designers. Some are known by the use to which they are usually put.

In this vast and confusing array, however, it is possible to pin down two broad classifications of chair and several more or less basic types.

One classification comprises upholstered chairs. These are also called *over-stuffed* (perhaps a better word) because they have thickly padded, fabric-covered seats, backs, and arms. The other classification includes all other chairs. A great many of these have upholstered seats, and some have upholstered backs—but all are known simply as chairs.

Types of chairs are:

Side Chairs • Small, essentially straight-backed chairs without arms which are used along the sides of a dining table.

Straight Chairs • Similar to side chairs and sometimes difficult to differentiate from them—but they are not designed specifically for dining. Windsor chairs, for example, are straight chairs.

Arm Chairs • All chairs with arms. But since several of the types below have arms, the name is applied particularly to dining room chairs used at the ends of a table.

Wing Chairs • Upholstered chairs with wings which extend forward several inches and are roughly perpendicular to the back, thus forming a U. Both the back and wings extend approximately to the top of the occupant's head.

Club Chairs • Low-backed upholstered chairs with fairly low seats. Along with wing chairs, they are also known as *easy chairs.*

Reclining Chairs (Recliners) • A modern type of upholstered chair with a back which can be pushed back and locked in one or two positions. In most models, the upholstered front below the seat can also be raised to support the occupant's legs and feet.

Occasional Chairs • Arm chairs with fairly thickly upholstered backs and seats. They are used primarily in living and family rooms.

Corner Chairs • In these, the back forms a semi-circle around two sides of the chairs and the seat is diagonal to the middle of the back. The occupant straddles the front leg.

Swivel Chairs • Used primarily as desk chairs and also, to some extent, as bar chairs, these have seats which can be spun all the way around.

Rocking Chairs (Rockers) • All chairs designed to rock back and forth. Most have bent strips of wood or metal under the legs and resting on the floor; in *platform rockers,* however, the rockers are fixed to the top of a four-legged platform.

Folding Chairs • Very small straight chairs which can be folded up for storage. They are most often used at card tables. *Director's,* or *captain's, chairs* are folding chairs with arms.

Sling Chairs • Chairs with steel frames in which hang hammock-like seats of canvas, vinyl, or leather.

Bean-bag Chairs • Shapeless chairs, resembling a partially deflated ball, filled with polystyrene beads.

CHAIR RAIL

A horizontal molding nailed to walls to keep them from being marred by chairs and other furniture pieces which are pushed back against them. To be effective, the molding should be installed at the high point of the chair backs.

CHAISE LONGUE
A chair with a very elongated seat. Chaise longue is the French name for the original type of day bed.

CHALKING
Formation of a chalk-like powder on an exterior paint surface. Very slight chalking is desirable, because it helps to keep the surface clean (although the "chalk" may drip and discolor a surface below). But abnormal chalking is a problem which should be stopped by application of another one or two coats of paint. It generally results when paint is applied in too thin a coat or when only one coat is applied over a porous surface.

CHALKWARE
Figurines made of painted plaster of Paris in the 18th and 19th centuries.

CHALLIS
A fabric resembling soft, very lightweight wool. It was originally made of wool but is now also made of rayon or cotton. It is sometimes used in draperies.

CHAMFER
To trim the sharp corner along the edge of a piece of material to a 45° angle. The resulting surface is called a chamfer. *Compare* Bevel.

CHANDELIER
A big light fixture, usually with several lights, suspended from a ceiling. It is frequently of ornate design, and this makes it difficult to keep clean. In fact, in large metropolitan areas, some cleaning services specialize exclusively in cleaning glass chandeliers.

Another common problem with chandeliers is that to look attractive, they must be in almost perfect scale with the rooms in which they are installed, and they must be hung at exactly the right height.

CHANNEL
The metal box containing the ballast, starter, lamp-holders, and wiring for a fluorescent tube. Simple fluorescent

fixtures such as those built into lighted valances and luminous ceilings are commonly called fluorescent channels.

CHASE
A vertical recess in a wall or a slim, box-like structure applied on the outside of a wall to carry pipes, ducts, or wires.

CHATTEL
Any article of personal property except land and buildings.

CHECK (1)
A crack, caused by shrinkage, running with the grain of a piece of wood. If the end of the wood is examined, it will be seen that the crack extends down through the growth rings. *Compare* Heart Shake.

CHECK (2)
A fabric or wallcovering with a checkered pattern.

CHECKING
A paint problem characterized by small interlaced cracks which appear in the surface of the top coat. It results from use of poor quality paint. The area must be scraped smooth before it is repainted.

CHECK RAIL
See Meeting Rail.

CHECK VALVE
See Valve.

CHENILLE
A yarn made of several fibers that looks like a small, fuzzy caterpillar. It is used in making expensive rugs, bedspreads, and fringes.

CHERRY
A beautiful medium brown wood that is very popular for furniture and paneling. It is rather hard but light, and has a fine grain.

CHEST
A box with a hinged lid on top. Variable in size and interior

fittings, chests are made for storage of everything from jewels to firewood. They are usually identified by the objects they are made to store: jewel, toy, blanket, linen, sugar, silver, etc; but some are known by the title of the person for whom they were made (captain's chest) or by the name of the place where they were made (Ipswich chest).

Portable chests range from simple boxes to handsome furniture pieces. Almost all are made of wood. Chests are also built into houses—usually as the bases for built-in benches under windows, by the fireside, etc.

CHESTERFIELD
A large sofa.

CHESTNUT
A hard-to-find hardwood used for paneling. It is a soft, light, strongly figured, gray-brown wood.

CHEST OF DRAWERS
All chests of drawers—*bureaus*—are essentially large cabinets with two or more drawers in the front; but dimensions vary. They are roughly 38 to 48 in. wide; 18 to 22 in. deep; and 32 to 38 in. tall. There are, however, extra-wide chests with two tiers of drawers and tall chests to as much as 70 in. high. In most chests, drawers are of two depths, the shallower usually being at the top.

Chests of drawers are occasionally built in—sometimes in alcoves but most often in large storage walls. Complete chests of wood or metal are made especially for the purpose. There are also wood or steel drawer cases without sides, back, top, or bottom; wood stacking drawer frames which can be interlocked one on top of another; and wood or molded plastic drawers designed for building into frames constructed on the job.

CHEST-ON-CHEST
A two-piece furniture piece consisting of two complete chests of drawers. The slightly smaller chest without legs is placed atop the base unit with short legs. Also called a *tallboy*.

CHEST-ON-FRAME
A two-piece furniture unit with a chest of drawers which is set on a frame with legs.

CHEVAL GLASS

A heavy, full-length, framed mirror swinging between large posts set in a trestle.

CHEVRON

A V-shaped or sawtooth-shaped ornament. Also, the point at which rafters meet at the ridge of a gable roof.

CHIFFEROBE

To all intents and purposes, an armoire and chiffonier combined in one unit. In other words, the piece has a tall cabinet for hanging clothes and next to this a bank of drawers.

CHIFFONIER

A chiffonier was originally a tall narrow chest in which French women kept their sewing supplies, etc. Today it is simply a tall bureau with or without an attached mirror.

CHIMNEY

A chimney contains the flues needed to ventilate fireplaces; oil-, gas-, and coal-fired heating plants; and oil and gas-fired water heaters. A separate flue is required for each heating unit.

Chimney location is determined by the fireplace it serves and is usually either against an outside wall or behind an inside wall in the living or family room. The furnace and water heater are then tied into the chimney by horizontal runs of fluepipe. A separate chimney serving only the furnace and water heater is built only if those units must be at an unusual distance from the fireplace chimney.

Wherever it is built, a masonry chimney should not touch any wood. A 2-in. gap is required at all points, except the back of the fireplace where a 4-in. space is needed.

To prevent soot build-up, the flues must be as smooth as possible; and because they carry hot gases, they must be made of fireproof material and surrounded by additional fireproofing. The best flue lining is round or square clay tiles with walls at least 5/8 in. thick. These are surrounded on the outside by at least one course (4 in. thick) of common bricks, stones, or concrete blocks.

Chimney height depends on the slope of the roof and on surrounding buildings, trees, and hills. Generally the chimney top is at least 2 ft. above the peak of a sloping roof, 3 ft. above a flat roof. But it may be necessary to go higher if other things, such as tall trees, might play tricks with the wind and resulting draft.

Chimney caps to prevent fireplaces from smoking are most

easily made of slabs of flagstone laid across the top of brick piers placed on the corners of the chimney. The bricks are laid flat and cemented together. The total area of the four openings under the flagstone should at least equal the area of the flue. If a chimney incorporates two or more flues, each is separated from the others by *withes* (*see below*); but the area of the openings surrounding each flue should continue to equal the area of the flue.

Prefabricated chimneys are made of round lengths of large pipe which are fitted together and run up through a roof. They are so well insulated that they can be placed in direct contact with wood framing, floors, roof decks, etc. They are normally used in conjunction with prefabricated fireplaces when it is necessary to hold down the cost.

CHINA

Also called *chinaware* and *Chinese porcelain*, china is a mixture of clay and stone fired at high temperatures. It is used to make dinnerware and other objects of the highest quality and beauty. Despite its delicate appearance, it is nonporous and surprisingly resistant to cracking and chipping.

Until comparatively recent times, china was over-glazed (decorated after glazing); consequently, it had to be washed and handled gently to preserve the decorations. But most modern china (except that decorated with gold) is under-glazed (decorated before glazing) and can be washed safely in a dishwasher.

CHINA CABINET

A name which can be given to any tall, open or glass-enclosed cabinet in which china and glass are displayed.

CHINOISERIE

An 18th-century European style of decoration imitating Chinese decoration.

CHINTZ

A cotton fabric usually with, but sometimes without, a glazed finish. It is also usually colorful. It goes into slipcovers, curtains, and draperies.

CHIPBOARD

A type of particleboard made with somewhat larger bits of wood. *See* Particleboard.

CHIPPENDALE
A furniture style developed by Thomas Chippendale, who lived in England from 1718 to 1779. It is one of the most beautiful and certainly the most famous of all furniture styles. The strong forms were ornamented—at times almost lavishly—with details taken from classic, French, Gothic, and Chinese styles.

CHLORINATED RUBBER PAINT
A solvent-thinned rubber-base paint applied to masonry and asbestos-cement surfaces. It is highly resistant to moisture and alkalis in such surfaces, and has good durability. Two coats without a primer are used on masonry. Asbestos-cement is primed with an alkyd primer before the chlorinated rubber finish is applied.

CHORD
One of the main timbers in a truss. But the word is usually applied only to the long horizontal timber.

CHROME
The glossy, silvery coating applied to steel and brass. It is exceptionally tough, and easy to clean and polish; but its durability depends largely on its thickness. Thin chromium plate used on cheap furniture scratches easily.

CINDER BLOCK
A lightweight concrete block made with hard cinders and portland cement. It is the size and shape of a standard concrete block but is not strong enough to bear a heavy load.

CIRCUIT
The wires through which electricity flows from a fuse box or circuit breaker panel to the point or points of use. It is properly called a *branch circuit*. The number of branch circuits in a house depends on the size of the house and the number and size of the electrical devices in use. Lighting circuits and small appliance circuits serve several outlets, the exact number depending on the size of the circuit and the total wattage of the devices which are most likely to be used at the same time. Individual branch circuits are provided for devices using large amounts of power.

Circuits are composed of two or three wires, but the wires in any one circuit are bundled together in a single cable.

If too many lights and/or appliances are being served by a

circuit at one time, the circuit becomes overloaded and the fuse blows or the circuit breaker trips. A short circuit occurs when bare wires are crossed or a bare wire touches a piece of metal outside the circuit. This also causes the fuse to blow or circuit breaker to trip.

The following branch circuits are necessary in a well-wired house:

1 / One 15-amp, 120-volt lighting circuit for each 500 sq. ft. of floor space. In addition to supplying electricity to the lights, these circuits also serve all convenience outlets except those used for cooking and laundry appliances such as toasters and irons.

2 / Two two-wire, 20-amp, 120-volt circuits or one three-wire, 20-amp, 240-volt "split" circuit to supply power to the small cooking and laundry appliances as well as to a small refrigerator, ice maker, gas range, and gas dryer.

3 / Individual 20-amp, 120-volt circuits for an automatic washer, dishwasher and garbage disposer (the two use one circuit), food freezer, no-frost refrigerator, and workshop.

4 / One 15-amp, 120-volt circuit for the heating plant.

5 / Individual 20-amp, 120- or 240-volt circuits for each room air conditioner, water pump, and bathroom heater.

6 / One 30-amp, 240-volt circuit for an electric clothes dryer.

7 / One 40-amp, 240-volt circuit for a central air conditioner.

8 / One 50-amp, 240-volt circuit for an electric range.

9 / One 240-volt circuit for an electric water heater. The amperage varies.

10 / One or more 240-volt circuits of varying amperage for an electric heating system.

CIRCUIT BREAKER

A circuit breaker panel is the modern substitute for a fuse box in an electrical system. Each circuit is controlled by a switch-like trigger. When a circuit becomes overloaded or develops a short, the trigger automatically flips off and the circuit is inoperable. To restore power, the trigger is flipped to "on"; but if the overload or short has not been corrected, the trigger will immediately flip off again. *See* Fuse Box.

CIRCULATION

The ease with which people can move from one part of a house to another—circulate through it—without disturbing other people and without causing excessive wear of furnishings and building surfaces is a major concern of a good architect. His usual solution is to provide halls and stairs that permit walking from one room to another without passing through a third room.

The halls required for good circulation in the average house include the following:

1 / Between the front door and living room.

2 / Between the front door and bedrooms.

3 / Between the front door and kitchen.

4 / Between the garage or back door (wherever groceries are usually delivered) and the kitchen.

5 / Between every bedroom and a bathroom.

CIRCULATOR

An electrical device which circulates air or water through part or all of a house. Circulators are used in heating systems to assure that heat is delivered to all areas of the house and that the heating medium returns to the furnace for reheating and recirculation. Automatic blowers are used in warm-air heating systems, pumps in hot-water systems.

CISTERN

A concrete tank, usually below ground, in which water for household use is collected and stored. The water usually comes from rain and flows through pipes from the roof of the house into the cistern. In a well-designed system, the pipes are equipped with diverters which shunt aside the first rain that falls until the roof has been washed clean.

CLAPBOARD

An old but still popular form of bevel siding applied to exterior walls. It is ½ in. thick at the butt and 4 to 6 in. wide. Generally made of cedar, it has a very smooth finish on what is usually the front side and a rough finish on the back. But clapboards can be installed back-side to, in order to give texture to the wall. They are especially attractive this way when finished with an oil stain.

CLASSIC

Taken from or emulating the architecture or furnishings of the early Greeks and Romans.

CLAW AND BALL FOOT

A furniture foot carved to show a bird's claw clasped around a ball.

CLEANOUT

An opening in a house drain to facilitate cleaning of the drain with a snake. The opening is closed with a threaded plug.

CLEAR FINISH

Any transparent finish such as varnish, shellac, or sealer which protects the surface but does not conceal the grain or texture. The finish can be colorless or pigmented.

CLEAT

A wood strip or board nailed horizontally to a wall to support a shelf. Also, a board nailed across two or more boards to hold them together in a plane. The same kind of cleat may be used to straighten a single warped board or piece of plywood, or to stiffen it.

CLERESTORY

Sometimes spelled *clearstory*. An upper part of a wall containing windows. The most familiar clerestories are the high window walls in Gothic cathedrals. In speaking of houses, clerestory is usually used as an adjective to describe small windows installed close to the ceiling in walls which are usually blank underneath.

CLINCH

After driving a nail through a surface, it may be clinched by bending the exposed point at a right angle so it will not pull out.

CLOCK

Clocks have lost much of the decorative impact they once had because they are considerably smaller, they are designed to please mass tastes, and they have lost their tongues (except to emit nasty buzzing sounds calculated to jerk someone out of bed). This is not to say that handsome clocks are not made—but it is easier to find a handsome antique than a handsome contemporary design. Small wonder that at least one company is doing a thriving business selling kits for making one's own "antique clock".

CLOISONNÉ
A beautiful, intricate enamelwork in which the colored areas are separated by thin metal strips.

CLOSER
The last brick, concrete block, or other masonry unit laid in a course. A brick wall, for example, is built from the two ends toward the middle. The closer is the middle brick.

CLOSET
If the closets in a house are to be convenient and capacious, they must be planned as carefully as any other part of the house. The planning starts with determining exactly what has to be stored in closets and approximately how much space it will require. Then spaces for the closets must be found or made in the rooms where they are needed. Finally, the dimensions and designs of the closets must be worked out in the same way the proper arrangement of cabinets is developed for a kitchen.

Clothes Closets • The ideal clothes closet is 24 to 27 in. deep and as wide as the space allows. The closet doors should be wide enough to permit ready access to all corners of the closet; and if storage space in the house is at a premium, the doors should also be 8 ft. high to permit access to the otherwise unused space in the top of the closet. (The space can be put to use by installing two deep shelves above the closet rod rather than the single narrow shelf usually used.)

The closet rod is hung 5 to 6 ft. above the highest point in the closet floor. The shelf is placed 2 in. above the rod and should be at least 8 in. below the ceiling.

If a closet is more than 27 in. deep, wasted space can be held to a minimum if pull-out sliding clothes carriers are substituted for the closet rod. The carriers are installed perpendicular to the back wall and door of the closet. The number of carriers is limited only by the width of the closet door. Space at the ends of the closet can be put to good use by installing some of the many accessories, such as shoe racks and wall-mounted trouser hangers, available in department stores.

Bathroom Closets • Closets are needed in most homes to augment the grossly inadequate storage space afforded by the medicine cabinet and pipe-cramped cabinet under a built-in lavatory. Ideal is a 12-in.-deep cabinet 2 to 4 ft. wide and extending from floor to ceiling. If such a cabinet cannot be accommodated, space for a 3-ft.-high cabinet is almost always available above the toilet. (To provide headroom, the cabinet is hung 5 ft. above the floor.)

Linen Closet • The depth should not exceed 20 in. (the width of a standard pillow, which is the largest item stored in a linen closet). The width should be no less than 26 in. (the length of a standard pillow). The shelves are spaced 1 ft. apart. The closet door should be 8 ft. high to permit storing linens all the way to the ceiling.

Cleaning Closet • A cleaning closet which is perfect for one homemaker may be a total failure as far as another is concerned. But the dimensions which satisfy most people are: depth—12 to 16 in.; width—3 ft.; height—8 ft. The closet should have two doors—like French doors or Dutch doors—for easy access. The doors should be raised 1 in. above the floor to admit fresh air into the closet and to guard against spontaneous combustion.

CLOSING
The meeting at which the buyer of a property takes title.

CLOSING COSTS
Closing costs are extras that are paid by the home buyer when the deal for a house or mortgage is closed. They include such things as title search and title insurance, mortgage processing fee, appraisal fee, property survey, and escrow money for fire insurance and taxes.

CLOTHES DRYER
Standard-size dryers are 28 in. deep and 25 to 31 in. wide. The top is 36 in. high to align with a kitchen or laundry counter. Compact dryers range from about half the size of a standard machine downward.

The great majority of electric dryers require an individual 30-amp, 240-volt wiring circuit, but some can also be wired for 120-volt service. Dryers that use natural or LP gas for heat require 120-volt electrical service.

Because of the water vapor given off during operation, all dryers should be vented to the outdoors through a 4-in. metal or plastic duct connected to the back, side, or bottom of the appliance. The duct should be as straight as possible—no more than 20 ft. long if it has one elbow, and no more than 15 ft. long if it has two elbows.

CLOUD ON TITLE

Anything such as an encumbrance or claim which might impair the legitimacy of a title.

CLUSTER ZONING

Also known as *density zoning,* cluster zoning permits building houses unusually close together on a tract of land as long as the rest of the tract is left as open space. However, the actual number of houses allowed in a cluster development generally does not exceed the number allowed under normal zoning.

For example, if a builder has a 20-acre tract in a conventional half-acre zone, he can build 40 houses (not allowing for streets and easements), each with a half acre of land. The entire tract is developed. Under cluster zoning, on the other hand, he is able to group together 40 houses on only half of the tract. The remaining half is developed as a public space usable by all 40 homeowners.

The purpose of cluster zoning is to make it possible to build the maximum allowable number of houses on difficult terrain. Thus, land which might not be built on under normal zoning is put to use; the builder—hopefully—saves money and is able to sell the houses for less.

COCK

A plumbing valve similar to a faucet but installed in the pipe run (rather than at the outlet end) in order to permit shutting off the water or draining the pipe in cold weather.

COCK BEADING

A small, half-round, raised molding used to trim furniture, cabinets, etc.

CODE, BUILDING

A building code constitutes a law specifying the way in which a house or other building must be constructed. Despite many criticisms made of building codes and the people who draw them up and enforce them, their basic purpose is undeniably good: to assure that every house built is sturdy, safe, and healthy. They thus help to protect the homeowner against incompetent and dishonest contractors.

All larger communities have their own building codes, and all states have building codes. Many of these are modeled after or taken directly from one of the so-called national codes which are drawn up by various groups for the guidance of local building authorities. A small community without its own code is usually under the jurisdiction of the state code.

If a homeowner or his architect or builder feels that the requirements of a code are unnecessarily restrictive or out of date, he can appeal for relief to the local building department; but whether he is granted relief depends on the reasonableness of the appeal and the open-mindedness of the department.

CODE, LAND DEVELOPMENT

A national code without authority used to guide states and communities in establishing their own land-use codes.

CODE, LIFE SAFETY

A national code designed to make buildings safe against fire. Like the National Electrical and Plumbing Codes, it has no force of law in itself; and it does not have such wide acceptance as a model for local and state codes.

CODE, NATIONAL ELECTRICAL

A code specifying the way in which an electrical system should be installed in houses, commercial buildings, etc. It has no authority unless adopted as a part of a local or state code; but it serves as a model for the electrical sections of a great many local and state codes.

CODE, NATIONAL PLUMBING

A code similar to the National Electrical Code but applying to plumbing installations.

CODE, ZONING

See Zoning.

COFFER

A sunken panel in a ceiling or soffit used for ornament. It is also used to reduce the weight of a ceiling.

COLLAGE

A painting-like work of art composed by pasting miscellaneous items, such as cutout magazine illustrations, leaves, and ticket stubs, to a background to form a picture or design.

COLLAR

A projecting, collar-like band encircling a baluster, table leg, column, etc. It may be an applied molding or an integral part of the object.

COLLAR BEAM

A 2-in.-thick timber joining rafters on opposite sides of a roof. It is installed several feet below the ridge. If the space below is used as a room, the beam serves as a ceiling joist.

COLONIAL

America's most beloved architectural style. Houses were simple rectangular structures with medium-steep roofs, small windows, and balanced facades. New England Colonial homes built with wooden shingles or clapboards generally had large central chimneys to spread heat to all corners of the house. Southern houses were more often built of brick and had fireplaces and chimneys in the end walls. Dutch Colonial homes were generally low (although in many cases the first floors were raised well off the ground) and had gambrel roofs with flaring eaves covering gallery-like front porches. Country houses were often built in whole or in part of stone, those in cities of brick.

In the 1600s, American furniture was of Jacobean design, but this soon gave way to a simpler style now known as Early American, and then to Georgian.

COLONIAL SIDING

A bevel wood siding. The boards are 6 to 12 in. wide (*compare* Clapboard) and ¾in. thick at the butt.

COLOR CODING

The system of identifying wires in an electrical circuit by the color of the insulation. Black and red wires are hot; white wires, neutral; green wires, used for grounding.

COLOR SCHEME

Three basic color schemes are used in decorating:

Related Colors • These are the neighboring colors on a color wheel. (A color wheel is a disk divided into segments, each of which represents one of the primary or secondary colors. The colors are arranged in sequence: red, orange, yellow, green, blue, and purple.)

For example, blue and green are related colors. Similarly, orange and yellow are related, as are purple and red.

In a room with related colors, the selected colors are used on the walls, floor, and major furnishings. Nonrelated colors may be used in small spots for contrast.

Complementary Colors • These are the colors opposite one another on a color wheel: for example, red and green or blue and orange. A room decorated in this fashion is more vibrant than one using related colors.

Monochromatic Colors • In this color scheme, the entire room is done in different tones of the same color. Interest is gained by blending in a neutral color and/or a touch of a complementary color.

COLUMN

An exposed, upright, circular or square post or pillar supporting a load. It comprises three definite parts: base, shaft, and capital.

From early days columns have been treated as architectural elements of great beauty, and a number of more or less standard treatments have been developed. The most beautiful columns are the *Doric, Ionic,* and *Corinthian* of the early Greeks, and the *Tuscan* and *Composite* of the Romans. These are single, circular columns. *Clustered columns*—a much later development—are also single columns but look like an assembly of small shafts.

In the past, columns were made of wood or masonry. Today they are also made of aluminum sheets molded into hollow shafts. These have no structural value unless a timber or steel post is inserted in the center.

COMB BACK

A high Windsor chair back in which the crest rail supported on spindles resembles a woman's high comb.

COMMODE

In the Victorian era a commode was a low case piece with cupboards for storing a chamber pot, washbowl, pitcher, etc. It commonly had a marble top, so it could be used as a washstand, and one or more drawers.

To the French, who earlier named the piece, a commode was simply a low chest of drawers and/or a cabinet.

COMMON RAFTER
See Rafter.

COMPACTOR
An electrical appliance for compacting garbage and trash into small, solid blocks which require little storage space and are easily collected and disposed of. The unit is designed for installation under a kitchen counter, usually—but not necessarily—next to the sink. It is 15 in. wide and can be connected to a 15-amp lighting circuit or 20-amp appliance circuit.

Compactors, unlike garbage disposers, can dispose of all kinds of waste.

COMPLETION BOND
The same as a *performance bond* (*see below*).

COMPLETION DATE
The date agreed on in a contract when a house or other building project is to be completed. Because there are so many unpredictable problems and variables in building, a completion date should be considered only as a target which is difficult to hit. Nevertheless, if a builder is given ample time for a project, he should be expected to complete it almost on time.

Unfortunately, there is little an owner can do if a builder is badly behind schedule unless the building contract contains a clause stating that the contract can be terminated if the builder does not prosecute his work with diligence.

COMPRESSION
The state of being weighted or pressed. A lintel, for example, is under compression from the load it supports; consequently, it must be built thick enough to withstand the weight.

COMPRESSOR
The pump which circulates the refrigerant through an air conditioner.

CONCRETE
Concrete generally gets low marks for beauty but high marks for strength, durability, and general usefulness in construction. Almost anyone can mix and use it, but care is required to assure a fully satisfactory product.

Concrete mortar for masonry work is a mixture of portland cement, sand, and lime, or masonry cement and sand. Enough water is added to make a workable plastic mix. *See* Mortar.

Concrete which is poured to form a homogeneous structure is made of portland cement, sand, coarse aggregate, and a precise amount of water. Two basic mixes are used for almost all residential work.

For foundation footings, garden walls and retaining walls: 1 sack (1 cu. ft.) portland cement, 2¾ cu. ft. clean builder's sand, 4 cu. ft. clean pebbles or crushed stones between ¼ and 1½ in. in diameter. This is mixed with 6¼ gal. water if the sand and pebbles are damp, 5½ gal. if they are wet, and 4¾ gal. if they are very wet.

For watertight foundation walls, floors, terrace paving, steps, sidewalks, and driveways: 1 sack portland cement, 2¼ cu. ft. sand, and 3 cu. ft. coarse aggregate up to 1½ in. diameter. This is mixed with 5½ gal. water if the sand and pebbles are damp, 5 gal. if wet, and 4¼ gal. if very wet.

Ready-mixes, which are sold in bags ready for the addition of water, and completely mixed concrete, sold by the cubic yard and delivered in cement trucks, are also available for all purposes.

If concrete is poured in forms, the forms must be constructed of sound wood and plywood, and must be well braced to keep them from bulging. The surfaces are oiled to prevent sticking of the concrete.

If required for extra strength and to prevent cracking, reinforcing steel in the form of rods or coarse mesh is embedded in the center of the poured concrete. Rust does not impair the steel's usefulness.

As concrete is poured, it must be worked with a shovel and tamped to eliminate air pockets. After placement, it is struck off evenly with a straight-edged board, allowed to stand until the film of moisture begins to disappear from the surface, and then smoothed. Paving and other large horizontal surfaces are finished by striking off, tamping (but only if the concrete is quite stiff), darbying (further smoothing and leveling), and floating (smoothing with a board with a handle or with a steel tool). No further finishing is required if a nonskid surface is desired. For a very smooth (but less durable) surface, however, the concrete is troweled with a mason's steel trowel.

All concrete must be allowed to cure for at least seven days to give it maximum strength. Curing commonly is done by covering the concrete with wet burlap, canvas, or straw as soon as it is hard enough to resist abrasion. Other curing methods are to spray the concrete frequently with water or to flood it after it is hard.

Contraction, or control, joints are usually cut in exterior concrete slabs to minimize cracking. The job is done while the concrete is soft with a grooving tool up to ¾ in. deep or with a saw after the concrete is hard. In exposed-aggregate concrete pavements, redwood 2 x 4s are often used to separate sections of the pavement.

Colored concrete is generally made by mixing special powdered pigments into the concrete mix before water is added. The pigment should not exceed 10% of the weight of the cement; that is, no more than 9 lb. of pigment should be used per sack of cement.

In very hot weather, care must be taken to keep concrete from drying so rapidly that it loses strength and is difficult to finish. This is best done by using cool materials, wetting the forms and the base with water before placing the concrete, protecting the concrete against strong winds, and curing immediately.

In cold weather, freezing of concrete must be prevented by keeping the ground on which it is poured from freezing, by heating the water and sand before mixing, and by keeping the concrete insulated or enclosed during curing. An accelerator may be added to the concrete to hasten hardening, but it must be used in very small amounts.

CONCRETE BLOCK
A big, heavy building unit usually with a hollow core used for constructing walls. Concrete blocks have largely replaced poured concrete in foundation walls because they can be laid up so rapidly. They are also used in exterior walls and, to a lesser extent, interior walls, piers, chimneys, and garden walls. All-block walls are strong enough to support small buildings, and their strength can be increased by running reinforcing steel rods through the cores. But because of the numerous joints, they are not as watertight as poured concrete walls.

Standard concrete blocks have a semi-rough texture. The nominal dimensions of full-length units are 8 x 8 x 16 in. (actual dimensions: 7-5/8 x 7-5/8 x 15-5/8 in.). There are also half-length units, half-height units, and several other sizes. The most commonly used standard blocks are classified according to their design as *stretchers* (the blocks in the middle of a wall—with large vertical grooves in both ends), *corners* (grooved at one end, flat at the other), and *double corners* or *piers* (flat on both ends). *Cap blocks* are solid and only 3-5/8 in. high.

Heavyweight blocks are used in load-bearing walls; lightweight blocks such as cinder blocks are used in nonload-bearing walls.

Concrete blocks are also produced with a variety of texture and sculptured designs. Some are coated on one or both sides with a tough integral glaze in bright colors. Some, instead of being cored vertically, are pieced front to back in ornamental designs. These are used for dividers and screen walls.

Like bricks, blocks are laid up in several bonds (*see* Bond). The commonest used in foundation walls is the *running bond*. For exposed walls, the *basketweave* and *stacked bonds* are often used. In the latter, the blocks are placed in either horizontal or vertical position.

Standard thickness of a concrete block house wall is 8 in. (one block thick). The concrete mortar is made of 1 part masonry cement and 2 to 3 parts sand. The mortar is applied only to the ends and long edges of the blocks—not in the cores or to the divisions between cores. This is called *face-shell bedding*. As a rule, the joints are tooled to form a concave or V joint. Foundation walls should be covered on the outside with cement plaster and asphalt to make them water-tight. Latex or cement paint is used to decorate walls and other block structures.

CONCRETE, EXPOSED-AGGREGATE

A very decorative concrete used to pave terraces, walks, and other exterior areas. It is made by embedding small stones, gravel, or marble chips of uniform size in a wet concrete slab, and then brushing and washing away the concrete from around the top of the aggregate to produce a closely pebbled surface. The color of the surface depends on the color or colors of the aggregate. The paving is usually put down in large squares (about 5 x 5 ft.) surrounded by redwood timbers.

Exposed-aggregate concrete is sometimes used for interior floors, but in this case, the aggregate is exposed by grinding down the surface. The result is similar to terrazzo (*see below*).

CONCRETE, PRESTRESSED

An exceptionally strong building material made by pouring concrete around high-strength steel wires or rods under tension. It is used—but only rarely in residential construction—to form beams, slabs, shells, etc., which would be a great deal more expensive if constructed of conventional materials.

CONCRETE TILE

Tiles made of portland cement are used for roofing and flooring. They are not interchangeable.

Roofing tiles, which are used mainly in Florida and other warm climates, are thin, reinforced with steel, and coated with paint. They are laid like wooden shingles or slates on a solid deck with a minimum pitch of 4 in. per foot.

Floor tiles—often called *patio tiles*—are made in squares, rectangles, and several other shapes, and in a variety of colors and texture. They are 1½ in. thick. Installation is usually made without mortar on a 4-in. base of sand and gravel.

CONDEMNATION

Action of a public authority to take private property after compensating the owner or to order destruction of a building.

CONDENSATION

Condensation occurs in winter when the invisible water vapor in the air inside a house strikes a cold surface in an exterior wall. The film or beads of moisture which result discolor wood and other materials, loosen paint and putty, crack plaster, rot wood, and make insulation soggy and ineffective.

Condensation cannot be prevented if the occupants of a house use water—especially hot water—excessively in bathing, floor mopping, etc. But it can be minimized by taking several simple steps at the time a house is constructed:

1 / Keep basements and crawl spaces dry by the methods outlined under Foundation (*see below*). The ground in all crawl spaces should be covered with large sheets of heavy polyethylene film or a 2-in. layer of poured concrete.

2 / Install ventilating fans in the kitchen and bathrooms. Vent a dryer to the outdoors through a 4-in. duct. Screened ventilator openings should be installed in all crawl spaces. At least two are required. They are placed as high as possible in the foundation walls on opposite sides of the crawl space and left open the year around.

3 / Install vapor barriers on the inside of all exterior walls, top-story ceilings, and floors over unheated spaces. The barriers must form a complete envelope around the living space. In new construction, the best vapor barrier is made with polyethylene film which is stapled to the studs in the exterior walls and to the joists in the top-story ceilings, and which is laid between the subfloor and finish floor over unheated basements and crawl spaces. The alternative is to install insulating batts or blankets incorporating vapor barriers. The barriers must face into the house. Whatever is used, the edges of the barriers must be overlapped and stapled securely. In existing houses, alkyd or latex paint or varnish applied to inside walls and ceiling and floor surfaces serves as a vapor barrier. Vinyl wallcoverings and washable wallpapers are also effective.

4 / Insulate the house completely. *See* Insulation.

CONDENSER

The coil of an air conditioner which dissipates the heat from the refrigerant to the outdoor air. From the condenser the cooled refrigerant returns to the evaporator, where the cycle of extracting heat from the house air begins.

The condenser is either located outside the house or exposed to the outdoor air through a hole in an exterior wall.

CONDUCTIVITY

The degree to which a material transmits heat. Technically, the heat transmission value of a material is represented by a coefficient of thermal conductivity. This equals the number of Btu's which will pass through 1 sq. ft. of 1-in.-thick material in one hour, producing a one-degree difference (Fahrenheit) between the front and back surface. The coefficient is designated by the letter "k".

CONDUCTOR

A current-carrying electrical wire. The gauge (diameter) of conductors varies and is described by a number. The smallest used in a residential wiring system is No. 14. It is suitable only for lighting circuits. No. 12 wire is slightly larger and is used in most appliance circuits. It is also recommended for lighting circuits since it will carry a heavier load over a longer distance than No. 14. Still larger wires, such as No. 8, are used for appliances consuming large amounts of power.

CONDUIT

See Rigid Conduit.

CONFIDANTE
A roughly U-shaped sofa or settee.

CONNECTOR
One of several devices used for connecting cables or wires in an electrical system. One type is used to attach flexible cables and rigid conduits to electrical boxes. Another type, known as a *solderless connector* or *wire nut*, is an insulated, thimble-like device which connects two or more wires in an outlet, switch, or junction box.

CONNECTOR PLATE
A flat metal plate with numerous short prongs on one side used to connect timbers. Trusses are often put together with connector plates.

CONSOLE
A large television, radio, or phonograph cabinet which stands on the floor.
Also, a type of narrow, rectangular table. Originally it had two front legs and was supported at the back by brackets screwed to the wall. Modern versions have four legs but are otherwise similar.

CONTACT CEMENT
See Adhesive.

CONTEMPORARY
The style of architecture, decoration, and furniture which is currently in general favor. It is basically conservative—an adaptation and combination of many earlier styles—but it makes extensive use of the newest materials and methods.

CONTINUOUS AIR CIRCULATION
A system of continuously circulating heated or cooled air through the ducts in a house, even when the furnace or air conditioner is not operating. It is achieved by wiring the blower to operate independently of the thermostat. The purpose is to maintain more even comfort conditions throughout the house at all times. The system also makes it possible to cool an entire house with a single large room air conditioner.

CONTRACT
A written agreement signed by the persons involved and binding them to do or not to do certain things. When real estate

changes hands, a contract is drawn up by the seller setting forth the conditions of the sale and the amount of money to be paid. If the buyer approves, he signs the contract and gives the seller a deposit equal to about 10% of the purchase price. His lawyer then searches the title and makes sure that everything else about the transaction is in order. During this period—which usually lasts 30 to 60 days—the property is said to be under contract. The buyer takes title to the property at the closing.

A contract between a property owner and a builder, architect, or decorator is generally a lengthy document—best drawn up by a lawyer—giving a detailed description of the work to be done, when, and for how much; outlining the schedule of payments to be made by the owner; specifying what is to be done by the owner and contractor; describing the liabilities of the owner and contractor; and so forth. Before entering into a contract with a builder, architect, or decorator, the prudent property owner makes a careful check of the contractor's competence, performance, and reliability. He also asks for two or more bids from different builders and, in some cases, different decorators. (A professional code of ethics bars architects from making bids.)

CONTRACT BUILDER

A builder who puts up individual houses on contract with the owners. Generally the houses are built to a special design.

Developer builders may build houses on speculation or on contract, but when building on contract for a specific buyer, they use the same plans as for other houses in the development.

CONTRACTOR, GENERAL

A builder who performs all the work in the construction of a house. *Compare* Subcontractor.

CONVECTOR

A heating outlet used in place of a radiator in a hot-water or steam heating system. It heats rooms almost entirely by convection. The usual design is a cabinet resembling a radiator containing copper tubes to which dozens of thin copper fins are soldered. As hot water or steam circulates through the tubes, the fins are heated and heat the air which passes through the cabinet.

CONVERSATIONAL

Also called a *tete-à-tete*, a conversational is an S-shaped Victorian settee with two seats, one facing forward and the .

other backward, so that two people can sit facing each other. Because of its design, it must be placed well out from the walls of a room.

CONVERSATION PIT

An area that is several inches to several feet lower than the main floor of the room—commonly the living room or family room—of which it is a part. It is designed to make a cozy setting for conversation. The area usually incorporates a fireplace and is surrounded with a built-in bench or sofa units, the backs of which serve as a railing protecting people on the higher level.

CONVEYANCE

The transfer of property from one person to another. Also, the document by which this is accomplished.

COOLING TOWER

A device installed outdoors and used to cool and recirculate the water used in a water-cooled air conditioner. Thus, it reduces water consumption. Early residential air conditioners used cooling towers, but modern units are air-cooled and do not require them.

COPED JOINT

A type of butt joint most often used in joining two pieces of molding at a corner. The end of one piece is cut out with a coping saw to fit against the contoured side of the other piece.

COPING

The finished top course of a masonry wall. Designed to keep water out of the wall below, it usually projects slightly beyond the sides of the wall and/or is beveled on top. It is sometimes called the *cap course*.

COPPER

As a basic building material, copper is losing out because of its high cost; but in most cases it is being replaced by inferior materials. Its principal remaining uses are for wiring (because it is an outstanding electrical conductor) and piping (because it resists corrosion, scaling, and clogging). Other uses—today minor—are for flashing, roofing, gutters and leaders, and fireplace and range hoods.

Copper is best joined by soldering. Because it is malleable, it should be laid over a rigid base if denting is to be avoided. The natural color can be retained only by frequent polishing and/or lacquering; but the color is not popular. The brown coloration resulting from tarnishing is preferred.

If the metal is exposed to sun and rain, as on a roof, it develops a soft green oxide. This is unusual and very attractive, but unfortunately the film is generally uneven and streaky. Water washing over the oxide stains surfaces below green.

COPPER NAPHTHANATE

A wood preservative. It is available as a green or clear liquid.

CORBEL

Strictly speaking, a corbel is any kind of projection, such as a timber or stone, which directly supports a weight. More commonly, it is considered to be a wall, chimney, column, etc., which is given a projection shaped like an upside-down stairway. For example, in order to give mass to that part of a chimney projecting above a roof, the chimney may have corbels (or be corbeled out) on four sides just below the roof. Corbeling may also be used to increase the size of the load borne by a wall.

CORDING

Cotton cord covered with fabric to make welting.

CORDUROY

A sturdy cotton fabric with closely spaced, soft pile cords. It is used in bedspreads, draperies, and upholstery.

CORK

Cork is used as a floor or wall covering. In addition to its attractive color and texture, it is comfortable and quiet underfoot, and does an excellent job of absorbing sounds within the room in which it is used. Its primary faults are fading and poor resistance to dirt and stains.

Solid cork is available in several forms:

One-Foot-Square Tiles, 3/16 In. Thick • These are made for flooring but are also used on walls. They are sold with a wax or urethane finish.

Thick, Rough-Textured Cork • This material is available in various rectangular shapes up to 2 x 3 ft. and in thicknesses up to 2 in. Used to cover or decorate walls, it can be left natural or stained and finished.

Bulletin-Board Cork • This is smooth, fine-textured cork ¼ in. thick and produced in rolls of great length up to 6 ft. wide. It is available natural and in several colors. The colored materials are mounted on a burlap backing.

All cork products are installed with linoleum cement on a clean, sound base.

CORK WALLCOVERING

A wallpaper-like material made with small pieces of wafer-thin cork bonded to a paper backing. The backing is often colored red, orange, gold, or black, and shows through cracks in the cork and spaces between the slices of cork. Some coverings are also printed with a pattern.

The material is put up in 30- and 36-in.-wide rolls up to 45 ft. long. Installation is made over lining paper.

CORNER BEAD

A long L-shaped strip of wood or steel which covers an outside corner in an interior wall. Wooden corner beads are moldings nailed over a corner. Metal beads are made of thin steel nailed over a corner and then covered with plaster or gypsum board joint compound. Only the molded arris is exposed.

The purpose of all corner beads is to strengthen and protect the corner. The metal beads also assure that the corner is straight and smooth.

CORNER BOARD

One of the two vertical boards sometimes used to trim corners of exterior walls. The siding butts against the edges of the boards.

CORNER CABINET

A cabinet fitting into the corner of a room. A number of stock designs are sold. Some cabinets—stock or specially designed—extend only part way to the ceiling; others are built in completely. Antique walls cabinets are often free-standing.

Sizes and designs are variable. The usual practice is to close in roughly the bottom third of the cabinet with a single or double door;

the upper two-thirds is open to view, although it may have glass doors.

CORNICE (1)
The exterior trim at the eaves. It helps to keep moisture from entering the framework of the house between the roof overhang and exterior wall, and also serves to ornament the building.

In a simple cornice—not often seen—the rafters end at the rafter plates and are concealed by the exterior walls; and there is only a very slight roof overhang. In an open cornice, the rafters overhang the exterior walls and are left exposed. In a boxed cornice, the rafters and underside of the roof are completely enclosed. In traditional architecture, boxed cornices are often elaborate and handsome.

CORNICE (2)
A prominent horizontal structure projecting from an interior wall at or near the ceiling. It is usually installed over windows to conceal the tops of draperies or a fluorescent lamp.

A window cornice consists of a long 6- to 8-in.-wide face board with short returns at the ends. It may or may not have a solid top. It is cantilevered from the wall on angle irons or by other means. Drapery hardware is usually mounted on the wall or window trim behind the cornice.

A lighted ceiling cornice is similar except that it is installed flush with the ceiling. The channel for the fluorescent light fixture can be mounted on the wall or on the back of the cornice.

A cornice may be of very simple design—nothing more than painted or stained boards with slender moldings around the edges—or it may be elaborately contoured along the bottom edges. Cornices are also frequently padded and covered with fabric.

Another name for this type of cornice is *valance.*

CORNICE MOLDING
A molding applied to a cornice or at the top of interior walls.

COROMANDEL
A method of decorating English furniture in the early 18th century. The wood was covered with lacquer—often black—and then given an incised design which was filled with gold

and color. The method originated in the Far East and has a distinctly Far Eastern look.

CORONA

The projecting slablike member of a cornice. It is supported by the bed molding. Its purpose is to direct dripping or falling water away from the surface below.

COTTAGE FURNITURE

Simplified furniture mass produced in the Victorian period. It often featured decorative painted designs and spool turnings.

COTTON

The world's most important textile fiber, cotton is used alone or in blends to make a great variety of household articles. Its usefulness is extended by treating it with special finishes.

In addition to its versatility, cotton is strong, easily dyed, and holds color well; but it deteriorates in sunlight.

COUNTER

In effect, a counter is a horizontal built-in table top serving as a work surface in the kitchen or laundry or a surface on which to place things elsewhere.

In some situations, the base on which a counter rests is thought of as part of the counter. For example, a breakfast counter is the entire structure down to the floor—similar to a breakfast bar.

COUNTERSINK

To recess slightly below the surface. Finishing nails and flat-head screws are countersunk so they will be less noticeable and will not snag or scratch anything that slides across them. Nailheads are covered with a filler after countersinking.

COUNTERTOP

A word used in building to differentiate between the surface of a counter and whatever base it is resting on. The top can be made of any durable, easy-to-clean material. Sheets of 1/16-in.-thick laminated plastic bonded to plywood or particleboard are most popular in the kitchen, laundry, and bathrooms because the tops have few (if any) joints, and are very tough, scratch and heat resistant, easy to maintain, and available in many colors and patterns.

Ceramic tile is often used. It is durable, scratch and heat resistant, and colorful. The joints, however, are difficult to clean, and the tile may chip glasses and china set down on it carelessly.

Glass ceramic (*see below*) is a new material with characteristics similar to tile. Made in larger pieces, it has fewer joints; but it is available in only a limited color range.

Also new is a heavy methacrylate panel made in sheets large enough to cover most counters in one piece. It is an excellent imitation of marble but easier to maintain.

Wood is used for cutting blocks in kitchen counters and for countertops for bars and counters not receiving heavy wear. It should be given a durable finish to resist damage.

Dimensions of countertops vary. But kitchen and laundry counters are usually 25 in. deep. Bathroom counters into which lavatories are recessed are 21 in. deep. Kitchen counters are often equipped with built-in backsplashes which extend up the wall 4 in. or more.

COUPLING

A pipe fitting used to join two lengths of pipe in a straight end-to-end line. The pipes are inserted in the coupling.

COURSE

A horizontal row of bricks, stones, shingles, etc.

COURT CUPBOARD

A rare furniture piece used for storage but wasteful of floor space. It forms a wide, flat-topped rectangle. The upper section is a cupboard with shelves and hinged doors. The bottom section—which may be a separate unit—is supported on rather tall legs and consists of a single row of drawers with a large shelf several inches above the floor.

COVE

An integral part of a house with a concave contour: for example, a rounded corner between a ceiling and wall. Also, a small niche, such as the toespace under a kitchen cabinet. Also, the inverted concave or L-shaped shelf for an indirect fluorescent light (*see* Lighted Cove).

COVE MOLDING
A concave molding used to round off inside corner joints—for instance, under the nosing of a stair tread.

COVENANT
An agreed-on clause in a deed. In some instances, it limits the buyer of real estate as to what he can do on or to his property. He may, for instance, be prohibited from building a house or adding to an old house without having his plans approved by a designated person. Or he may not be allowed to park a boat on his property. And so forth.

Deed restrictions of this sort are not common but home buyers must watch out for them.

COVERAGE
The area covered by a building material. Builders speak of the coverage of a gallon of paint or bundle of shingles, for example.

COVERLET
A bedspread (*see above*).

CPVC
Chlorinated polyvinyl chloride. A plastic used to make plumbing pipe for indoor and outdoor use. The pipe will carry hot and cold water. *See* Pipe.

CRASH
A durable, soft but rough-textured fabric sometimes used in bathroom linens, draperies, and upholstery. It is made with various fibers.

CRAWLING
A paint problem. The paint draws itself up into bubbles soon after application. The problem is usually caused by poor preparation of the surface, inadequate mixing of the paint, or very cold or humid weather.

CRAWL SPACE
A shallow, not fully excavated space under a house.

It should be at least 18 in. deep so a person can get under the house to inspect pipes, insulation, foundation walls, etc.

The floor of the space should be covered with a 2-in.-thick continuous concrete slab or with overlapped sheets of heavy polyethylene film or asphalt building paper to keep moisture in the earth from entering the house. Ideally, the space should also be ventilated the year round with fixed screened openings high in the foundation walls.

Floors over a crawl space should be insulated with material having an R value of 13. Heating and plumbing pipes and ducts should also be insulated to prevent excessive heat loss. The alternative is to leave the pipes and ducts uncovered, omit the ventilator openings, and cover the foundation walls rather than the floor above the crawl space with insulation.

CREDENZA
A sideboard or buffet of Renaissance style. It usually lacks legs.

CREOSOTE
The best preservative for wood which is constantly exposed to moisture and need not be painted or finished. It is excellent for piers and fence posts.

CREPE DE CHINE
A soft, lustrous silk fabric with a crinkled surface used for curtains.

CREST RAIL
The top rail of a chair or other furniture piece used for seating.

CRETONNE
A firmly woven cotton, linen, or rayon fabric usually with a big bright pattern. It is used for slipcovers and draperies.

CREWEL
Embroidery in wool on almost any fabric. Many kinds of stitches are used. Crewel work is used for upholstery, bedspreads, pillows, valances, wall and bed hangings, etc.

CRIB

Most cribs for children take mattresses measuring 24 x 42 or 27 x 52 in. Actual crib sizes are slightly larger.

CRICKET

A little wooden footstool with splayed legs. Also, a small roof area specially shaped to divert rainwater around an obstruction such as a chimney.

CRIPPLE

A stud of less than normal wall height; also, a short rafter.

CROMWELLIAN

Severe, rectilinear furniture made in England during Cromwell's regime (1649-1660) and later made in America. The seating pieces often had leather seats and turned legs with ball feet.

CROWN

The uppermost part of a cornice.

CROWN MOLDING

A molding at the top of a cornice.

CUBE

A piece of furniture used for storage. Made of rigid plastic or wood, it is a square or rectangular box open on one side. Some cubes may be fitted with shelves, drawers, or doors. Ready-made units measure from about 12 x 12 x 12 to 15 x 15 x 15 in., but they can be built to any size.

In normal usage, several cubes are assembled to form a bookcase-like unit, divider, or storage wall. When joined together, they can be arranged in ceiling-high stacks and in rows of indefinite length.

CUP

A lengthwise, bow-shaped bend in a board.

CUPBOARD

Today a cupboard is usually considered to be a reasonably small free-standing or built-in cabinet with a door or doors and usually with shelves. In earlier days, a cupboard was any closet with shelves.

CUPOLA

A structure built on a roof (usually of a traditional house) for ornament, but it can also be used to ventilate the roof space below. Most cupolas are small—about 2 ft. square by 3 ft. high, but on many old houses they are large enough for a person almost to stand up and turn around.

CURIO CABINET

A narrow, tall, glass-enclosed cabinet for the display of decorative objects. It stands on the floor or is hung on a wall.

CURTAIN

See also Drapery.

Among the several materials used in curtains, permanent press fabrics, fiberglass, cotton organdy, and ninon are outstanding. Linings are needed only to improve the hang of curtains, protect them against sunlight, and/or make them look better from outside.

The width of *draw curtains* equals the length of the rod plus the returns (if any). Extra fabric should be allowed to give the curtains fullness. In the case of sheer, ruffled curtains, each panel should equal the length of the rod. And if curtains crisscross, each panel should be twice the length of the rod.

Glass curtains made of sheer fabric are stretched tight between rods installed just above and below the glass. They extend 1 in. beyond each side of the glass and about 2 in. beyond the top and bottom. To allow for fullness, the curtain should be twice the width of the glass.

Cafe curtains cover only part of a window. The usual arrangement is a double cafe with one curtain extending from the top of the frame to just below the center of the window, and the other curtain extending from the center of the window to the sill. A single cafe covers either the bottom half or bottom three-quarters of a window. It may also extend to the floor. A triple cafe divides a window into three equal parts. A quadruple cafe also divides a window into three equal parts, and a fourth part equal to the other three in length hangs between the sill and floor.

CURTAIN ROD

See Drapery Hardware.

CURTAIN WALL

A wall which encloses a building but doesn't support it. It is made of large panels which are inserted between the posts that support the building or are hung in front of the posts. The walls of the glass- and metal-walled office buildings put up in the 1950s and 1960s are curtain walls. But relatively few houses have curtain walls.

CYLINDER FRONT

A desk or secretary front resembling a quarter segment of a water heater tank which is laid on its side. The front is pivoted so it covers the writing surface when closed, and slides back into the carcase of the desk when open.

CYPRESS

The wood called cypress is cut from the bald cypress found in the swamps of the Deep South. It has outstanding resistance to decay and is used in its native country in almost all parts of houses. The sapwood is creamy-colored, the heartwood red to brown.

DADO
A rectangular groove cut across the grain to receive the end of a board. Also, a wainscot (*see below*).

DAMASK
A beautiful fabric, made from various fibers, into which the design is woven. It is used in upholstery, draperies, bedspreads, and table linens.

DAMP COURSE
A course or layer of waterproof material used to keep moisture from entering a wall or floor. In good construction, a basement floor is poured over a layer—or damp course—of polyethylene film.

DAMPER
A cast-iron, lid-like device in the throat of a fireplace. It is used to regulate the draft and close the flue when no fire is burning.

DAMPPROOF
To prepare a surface so that moisture cannot seep through. However, dampproofing is not the equivalent of waterproofing because it does not stop active leaks. A commonly used dampproofing material is silicone water repellent.

DART

A tapered seam made in a fabric article to take up excess fullness and improve the fit. Darts are often made in the arms of slipcovers, for example.

DAVENPORT

A late 19th-century American name for a sofa that was sometimes convertible into a bed. Also, an English name for a small desk with a sloping, lift-up lid.

DAY BED

A sofa which can be converted into a bed. Originally it was a long cushioned bench with a back.

DEACON'S BENCH

A long wooden bench with open, spindled arms and back. It is similar to some early settees and may be called a *settee.*

DECAL

Decal is the shortened form of *decalcomania.* It is a picture which is transferred from specially prepared paper to wood or other materials. Once applied, it is difficult to remove without damaging the base.

DECORATIVE BEADS

Strings of large, bright-colored plastic beads which are hung like curtains at windows or doors, or used as room dividers or wall hangings. They come in long strands which can be cut to any measurement, and they are usually hung in a grooved rod so they can be slid from side to side.

DECOUPAGE

A technique of decorating furniture, walls, etc., with cutout pictures. These are pasted to the surface and then covered with innumerable coats of clear lacquer.

DEED

A written instrument conveying title to a property. The deed passes from seller to buyer at the closing. There are several kinds:

Warranty Deed • The seller guarantees the title is clear of defects. If it isn't, he is liable for damages.

Bargain-and-Sale Deed • The seller warrants that he himself has done nothing to becloud the title.

Quit-Claim Deed • This conveys the seller's title to the buyer. It does nothing more; it guarantees nothing.

DEED RESTRICTION

A covenant (*see above*) restricting the buyer's use or development of a property.

DEFECT

As applied to wood used for any kind of building, a defect is an imperfection which affects the wood's utility, strength, or durability (whereas a blemish affects only its appearance). As applied to anything else, however, defect has a much less precise definition. It is any imperfection.

DEHUMIDIFIER

A free-standing electrical appliance which lowers the humidity of a house by passing the air over refrigerating coils and collecting the condensate. Most units can be plugged into a 120-volt, 15-amp lighting circuit.

All air conditioners automatically dehumidify the air when they are used to lower air temperature.

DELAMINATE

What happens when the laminations (plies) of a piece of plywood separate. Delamination is generally a problem only if an interior-grade plywood is used outdoors or in a damp location.

DEN

A study. The two words are interchangeable.

DENIM

Originally this was a heavy, tough cotton twill fabric, but it is now also produced in blends of cotton and synthetics in lighter weights and many colors. It is used in draperies, bedspreads, slipcovers, etc.

DENSITY ZONING
See Cluster Zoning.

DENTIL
A rectangular, tooth-like projection used for ornament. A dentiled cornice has a series of closely spaced dentils.

DESK
With the advent of the typewriter and the increase in the amount of paperwork necessary to run a household, desks have undergone a drastic change in shape and size. Early desks, made of wood, were rarely more than about 4 ft. wide and 2 ft. deep, and had a cubicled storage cupboard at the back of and above the writing surface. They were designed for placement against a wall. A writing shelf pulled or folded out to make space for hand-writing letters.

By contrast, modern desks are large, flat tables with all storage space provided in drawers and occasionally a cabinet underneath. Also under the top is a deep kneehole which allows the user to sit close to the top when working. The desk is placed against a wall or set out from it so the user can face the room and have a window or standing lamp at his back.

Modern desks of stock designs are made entirely of wood, of wood with a laminated plastic top, or of steel with a laminated plastic or linoleum top. Steel units are strictly functional and lacking in beauty, despite excellent paint finishes. The best wooden desks combine beauty and functionalism.

Also see Secretary.

DESK-ON-FRAME
An early desk made in two parts—one a supporting frame, the other a large, shallow box with sloping lift-up lid.

DETAIL DRAWING
A plan for a small part of a house, furniture piece, etc.: for example, a plan for a bookcase or the capital of a column. It is generally drawn to a fairly large scale and may even be drawn to actual size. *See* Working Drawing.

DIFFUSER
Translucent plastic or glass used to diffuse the light from a light fixture and shield the eyes from the bulb. Of the plastics used

in diffusers, acrylic is best because it is least discolored by exposure to light. Glass is completely resistent to discoloration but is less desirable than plastics in big diffusers because of its weight and breakability.

DIMENSIONAL STABILITY

Ability to resist changes in size. Hardboard and particleboard, for example, have much better dimensional stability than plywood and solid wood.

DIMMER

An electrical switch with a revolving knob which adjusts the intensity of the light controlled. Dimmers are made for both incandescent and fluorescent lights, but installation of a fluorescent dimmer is rather complicated.

DINETTE

A room or alcove adjacent to the kitchen in which meals are eaten. As usually designed, dinettes are so small that, even with tiny furniture, a person cannot get up from the table without disturbing others. The situation is aggravated when a bench is built in across the end or side of the room.

DINETTE SET

A table and chairs for a dinette. The furniture is small in scale and generally made of metal with a plastic table top and cushioned, plastic-covered chair seats.

DINING ROOM

A four-walled room which is designed specifically to incorporate a large table at which the family can sit down to eat meals. Although the room was also used prior to World War I as a family living room, it has always been meant primarily for dining and today is rarely used for anything else. Because of this, dining rooms are generally cramped in size.

Dimensions should be based on the size and amount of furniture to be used. The following are minimum table and chair dimensions:

- Rectangular table for three or four persons—30 x 36 in.
- Rectangular table for five or six—36 x 48 in.

- Rectangular table for seven or eight—38 x 72 in.
- Square table for six to eight—48 x 48 in.
- Round table for four—31 to 37 in. diameter
- Round table for six—46 to 52 in. diameter
- Round table for eight—61 to 68 in. diameter
- Side chairs—16 x 16 in.
- Arm chairs—22 x 22 in.
- Chairs when people are sitting in them at the table—allow 24 in. from back of chair to table edge.
- Space for passing behind occupied chairs—18 in.

Based on these dimensions, the minimum size of a dining room with a rectangular table seating eight persons is 10 ft. 2 in. wide by 13 ft. long. Adding a buffet or sideboard on one wall increases the width or length approximately 2 ft.

A dining alcove off a living room or dining area with a living room, family room, or kitchen requires only slightly less space.

DINING TABLE

When man started to eat from a table top is lost in history; but it wasn't until the 17th and 18th centuries that tables made and labeled specifically for dining came into widespread use (along with dining rooms). In part, this may be attributable to the table designs of the great cabinetmakers of that era.

Selection of a dining table is subject to several influences:

1 / The appeal of its design and the material of which it is made.

2 / The shape—rectangular, square, round or oval.

3 / The basic size and how much it can be expanded to accommodate guests. A minimum of 24 in. of space along the edge of the table should be allowed per person. Table expansion is usually accomplished by pulling out the ends and filling in between them with one or more leaves. Other methods have been used but are almost always complicated.

4 / The arrangement of the table's underpinnings. This should be examined carefully to make sure that there are no legs, stretchers, or aprons which interfere with comfortable seating for the diners.

DIP-AND-RUB FINISH

A simple shellac finish used on wooden furniture. The first coat, applied by brush, is a mixture of 1 part white shellac and 2 parts turpentine. The two final coats are applied with a cloth pad dipped first in turpentine and then in white shellac and rubbed on the surface with a rotary motion.

DIRECT CURRENT

Electric current which flows continuously in one direction.

DIRECTOIRE

An early 19th-century French furniture style with classic motifs. It succeeded the Louis XVI style and preceded the Empire style.

DISHWASHER

An automatic dishwasher is a built-in or roll-around electrical appliance which in one operation rinses, washes, and dries almost all the dishes, glasses, silverware, and utensils used by a small family in a single day. Thus, it simplifies a tiresome chore. In addition, it reduces breakage of dishes, washes them cleaner, and destroys most of the bacteria on them.

Built-in dishwashers are 24 in. wide and fit under a standard kitchen counter. They are usually installed next to the sink so they can be connected into the same water supply lines and drain. An individual 120-volt, 20-amp wiring circuit is required unless the sink is equipped with a garbage disposer, in which case both appliances are connected into the same circuit. In some communities, the electrical code requires installation of a wall switch in addition to the switch built into the dishwasher.

Roll-around dishwashers, known as portables, are also 24 in. wide and about 36 in. high. Most units have a top-opening lid, but several are front-opening like a built-in unit. When in use, it is rolled close to the sink, plugged into a 20-amp appliance circuit, and connected to the sink faucet by a hose. Dirty water is pumped back into the sink through another hose. After dishes are washed, the dishwasher is rolled back into an out-of-the-way corner for storage.

Although all dishwashers contain electric heaters which raise or maintain the water temperature and dry the dishes, the temperature of the water heater which supplies the entire house should be set at between 140° and 160° to compensate for loss of heat in the pipes to the dishwasher.

DISPOSAL FIELD

The tiled field through which effluent from a septic system is dispersed. *See* Septic System.

DISTRESSED FINISH

A clear or paint finish used to make wood look old. The clear finish can be applied to unfinished wood or over old varnish, shellac, or lacquer. First, slight random scars are made in the wood. Dark brown or black paint is rubbed into these. And the surface is overcoated with a glaze, shellac, or varnish.

A distressed paint finish consists of a base coat covered with a thin coat of a second color. When dry, the surface is sanded with coarse sandpaper to cut through the top coat into the base coat here and there.

DISTRIBUTION PANEL

The point from which the branch electrical circuits in a house arise—in other words, the fuse box or circuit breaker panel.

DIVAN

A sofa without visible framework and usually without back or arms. In motion pictures, the sheiks of the Near East are invariably shown reclining on divans.

DIVIDER

A nonload-bearing partition used to divide a room into two small areas—for example, to separate the dining from the living area or to screen a kitchen partially from the dining area.

One type of divider is nothing more than a built-in screen with large panels of translucent glass, sculptured plastic, or pierced metal or hardboard set into a decorative wooden frame.

A second type of divider consists of shelves which are cantilevered from posts wedged between the floor and ceiling. As sold in department stores, the dividers are usually made with specially slotted metal posts into which shelf brackets may be inserted at any height on one or both sides of the posts.

A third type of divider is a storage wall made up of closets, cabinets, and shelves. *See* Storage Wall.

DOG-EAR
Undulating in a manner suggestive of the flap of a dog's ear. Cornices and bed canopies often have a dog-ear outline.

DOLLY VARDEN SIDING
A bevel siding with a rabbet in the back edge of the butt. The top edge of the board below fits into the rabbet.

DOMED ROOF
A roof shaped like a mushroom or sphere. It is readily built with prestressed concrete.

DOOR
Many considerations enter into the selection and use of doors in a house.

Location • As a rule, there is little choice in positioning a door. But when possible, those between halls and rooms should be placed near corners so the largest possible wall area is left available for use in the rooms. This position also allows doors to be swung back into the corners out of the way.

Doors into and out of kitchens should also be located near corners, but in this case a space of 26 in. or more should be provided between the edge of the door opening and the corner. Thus, a base cabinet can be installed all the way into the corner, and there is a loss of only about 30 in. of base-cabinet storage. (By contrast, if the door were installed all the way in the corner, the loss of cabinet space would be doubled.)

Size • All doors should be at least 6 ft. 8 in. high. Eight-foot doors are often used on closets to permit maximum use of the closet space. *See* Closet.

Minimum door widths are as follows:

Front door	36 in.
Outside basement door	36 in.
Other exterior doors	30 in.
Interior doors (except as noted	30 in.

Bathroom door	24 in.
Closet door	6-12 in. less than actual closet width

Interior doors are 1-3/8 in. thick, exterior doors 1¾ in.

Types • *Hinged doors* are the most common type. They must be used in exterior openings because they are the only doors which can be made waterproof and draftproof without elaborate weather-stripping. In addition, they operate easily, and things can be hung on the front and back, which increases their usefulness on closets. But they take up floor and wall space when open.

Bifold doors look like hinged doors which are split vertically and then folded together backwards and fastened with butt hinges. They are hung in door openings like hinged doors but are swung on pivots rather than hinges. The result is like a telephone booth door, but it swings out. Bifolds are used because they take up half as much floor space as hinged doors when open, and because they can be used in pairs (as well as singles) to close openings as wide as 9 ft. Further-more, they can be made in the same styles as hinged doors. On the other hand, they do not fit tightly into door jambs, so dust and air can get through. And if used on closets—for which they are well suited—nothing can be hung on the back.

Folding doors are made of rather narrow vertical strips fastened together along the edges. Open, they form a lot of W's set together side by side; closed, they collapse into a small bundle. They are used primarily on closets because they take up virtually no floor space and absolutely no wall space when opened or closed. But they do not give a tight seal around the edges, and nothing can be hung on front or back.

Accordion doors are similar in appearance and operation to folding doors, but they consist of a complicated metal frame covered with vinyl, and they fold accordion fashion rather than serpentine fashion. Since they are costly and made in large sizes, their main use in the home is to divide rooms into small areas—for example, a dining area off a living room, or a playroom into two small children's sleep-ing rooms.

Bypass sliding doors the commonest type of sliding door, have lost ground to folding and bifold doors as closet closures. The doors consist of two or three rigid slabs sliding in parallel tracks. They take up little space—the main reason for their popularity—but they permit access to only one half of a closet at a time. In addition, they don't fit tightly, often come off the tracks and are useless for hanging things on.

Recess sliding doors are the ideal space-saving doors because, when opened, they are pushed back into a pocket in a wall and are completely out of the way and almost out of sight. Single doors are used in halls and bathrooms—wherever there isn't space for hinged doors. Double doors are used in large entrances to rooms and also on closets. Since the doors slide in the same track, they produce a smooth, flush surface when closed. They fit more tightly in their frames than most doors (with the exception of the hinged type). But they are costly and can have nothing attached to their faces.

The huge glass doors which open onto terraces are a form of recess sliding door although they do not disappear into a recess. Such doors are especially weatherstripped against rain, wind, and dirt. The glass must be shatterproof.

Swinging doors are, in effect, hinged doors except that there are no stops on the jambs to keep the doors from swinging right through the opening, and they move on double-action hinges or pivots. Their main use is in openings between kitchen and dining room or between kitchen and pantry. The doors should have a small window so users can see if anybody is coming from the other side.

French doors consist of a pair of hinged doors swung from opposite jambs so they meet in the center of a door opening. They are used indoors and out for decoration more than utility; even so, each panel should be at least 20 in. wide so a person can walk through without opening the opposite panel.

Dutch doors are hinged exterior doors cut in two horizontally just above the latch. Although mainly decorative, Dutch doors do allow ventilation while keeping people out. Dutch doors are also called *cottage doors.*

Styles • Except for folding and accordion doors, most doors are made in the following styles:

Raised panel is a traditional style in which the door is separated into panels held in place by stiles and rails. The edges of the panels are recessed, but the centers are raised to approximately the same level as the stiles and rails. The great majority of raised panel doors are made of wood, but some for exterior use are of steel or urethane while many interior doors—especially those in speculative homes—are surfaced with molded laminated plastic.

Recessed panel is a similar but much less attractive design in which the panels are completely flat and sunk below the rails and stiles.

Flush doors are a popular modern design, not because they are good looking—which they aren't—but because they are economical. The door is a flat slab. Most flush doors in residential use have hollow cores and have no sound-stopping ability whatever. Solid-core doors are superior in all respects (except appearance).

Louvered doors have their entire front made of closely spaced horizontal louvers. The design is useful for ventilating rooms and closets while shutting off the view. But painting is tedious.

Installation • Doors generally are hung on the job by carpenters. In a well-designed custom house, about one hour is needed to frame a door opening and then to hang the door itself.

For speed and economy, however, prehung doors can be bought from lumberyards. In these, the doors (of any selected style) are hinged to jambs ready to be tilted into place in the door openings. The trim, cut to size, comes with the doors. In some cases, the doors are already fitted with locks and latches.

DOOR BELL

The modern door bell—and door chime—is a low-voltage electrical device connected into a 120-volt circuit. The low voltage is provided by a small transformer installed in the basement or utility room. The wiring is done with small, lightly insulated "bell" wires which can be run through the walls, tucked behind trim, or stapled to baseboards. The circuit is made by running a wire from the transformer to the door button, another wire from the button to the bell, and a third wire from the bell back to the transformer.

DOOR, CABINET

Bypass sliding doors (two or more doors sliding in parallel tracks) are used on cabinets of all kinds but have the same grave flaw as bypass sliding closet doors: They permit access to only half of the cabinet at one time. Hinged doors are more common. The types in general use are the flush, overlay, and lipped.

A *flush door* is installed inside the door opening so that the front surface is on the same plane as the jambs. An *overlay door* is installed over the facing strips that frame the door opening. In some designs, the edges of the door extend all the way to the outside edges of the facing strips, thus concealing the strips and resulting in a completely smooth, level surface. In other designs, the door overlaps the strips only a fraction of an inch. In a *lipped door,* the door edges are rabbeted so that the door fits partly inside the door opening and partly overlaps the facing strips.

DOOR CHAIN

A device for holding a door shut against an intruder.

It is not very reliable since it can be snapped or loosened from the door. Mounted on the inside of a door, it consists of a chain which locks into a metal receptacle screwed to the casing. When the chain is in place, the door can be opened just wide enough for the homeowner to see who is at the door.

DOOR CHIME

See Door Bell. The devices are similar except for the sounds they make. Chimes are usually decorative enough to be hung on a wall in a hall or living area.

DOOR CLOSER

A device which pulls doors firmly shut by means of a spring, but cushions the shock by means of a chamber filled with liquid or air. It is used in homes on storm doors and can also be used on heavy doors which are supposed to be kept closed.

The type installed on storm doors is a lightweight cylinder, usually installed horizontally but in a few cases vertically. Liquid closers are more expensive but more powerful and durable than pneumatics.

Standard closers, which are larger, are used on heavy doors—mainly in public buildings. The shock is taken up by a liquid.

Coiled door springs perform the same function as closers, but because they are not shock-absorbing, they are used only on screen doors.

Hinges on doors equippped with closers should incorporate anti-friction bearings.

DOOR HEAD

Door head can be used as the name for any trim over a door, but it normally refers to a large, ornamental arrangement of moldings and panels—similar to a fireplace mantel. Such treatments are generally used only in traditional architecture. If the design of the head is triangular, it is called a *pediment.*

DOOR HOLDER

A device screwed to the bottom of a door to hold it open. One type of holder resembles a vertical plunger; the other works like the leaf of a hinge.

DOOR JACK

A carpenter-built device to hold doors steady and upright while they are being fitted for door openings.

DORMER

A framed structure which projects from a sloping roof and incorporates one or more windows. Its principal purposes are to increase the headroom—hence the usable floor space—under the roof of the house and to provide light and air. Thousands of houses which are essentially one-story houses become story-and-a-half houses because they have dormers which make the attic space livable.

Dormers vary greatly in size. Most are fairly small, taking only a single window, and there are usually two or more strung out in a row across a roof slope. They can have gable roofs (the commonest), hip roofs, barrel roofs, or shed roofs. The cost of construction is rather high because special framing and extra flashing are required.

Dormers with shed roofs (called *shed dormers*) are also made very large—in some cases stretching from one end of a roof to the other. They provide much more headroom of uniform height than a series of small dormers, yet cost less.

Unfortunately, shed dormers are almost without exception ugly; and any kind of small dormer can be ugly, too. Consequently, they should be designed by an architect who can proportion and place them properly and give them contour and texture which add to rather than subtract from the appearance of the house.

DOUBLE-COURSE

To install wooden shingles and sometimes other sidings on walls in two courses, one directly over the other. The purpose is to deepen the shadow lines at the butts. Double-coursing also usually permits greater exposures than single-coursing.

DOUGLAS FIR

Douglas fir is a heavy, dense, straight-grained softwood more widely used in structural timbers than any other wood because of its great strength. It is also the most popular wood for making structural plywood.

As long as it is used structurally, the wood gets high marks on almost every score except two: It is hard to work with hand tools (but is readily worked with machine tools), and it does not hold paint well.

DOVETAIL JOINT

A complex joint used by furniture- and cabinet-makers to lock two pieces of wood together securely, as in drawers and frames for chair seats. The joint is made by cutting teeth in the pieces and interlocking them. The name dovetail comes from the fact that the teeth are wedge-shaped like a dove's tail.

DOWEL
A short cylinder of wood or metal used to fasten pieces of wood together or to reinforce joints.

DOWNLIGHT
A light fixture with a single bulb which directs light downward in a concentrated spot. Downlights can be square or round, and are designed for surface mounting or recessing in a ceiling. In some units, the light is diffused through metal louvers or baffles, in others through a glass lens. A so-called *high-hat fixture* is shaped like a man's high hat and has an aperture 3 to 6 in. across. A *pin-hole light* has an aperture of 1 to 2½ in.

DOWNSPOUT
See Leader.

DRAIN
Just as large communities have sanitary sewers and storm sewers, well-built houses are equipped with sanitary drains and storm drains. The former carry plumbing wastes from the house into the community sanitary sewer or a septic tank; the latter dispose of storm water accumulating in the ground around the foundation walls.

Storm drains are made with 4-in. perforated plastic pipes which are laid in a trench beside the footings and covered with 12 to 18 in. of crushed rock or gravel. The pipes are slightly pitched and lead into a line of solid drain pipes which carry the accumulated water away to a community storm sewer or to a dry well, stream, pond, or other disposal area.

On many properties, the footing drain's only purpose is to dispose of the water in the ground next to the foundation walls. By thus relieving water pressure against the walls, they help to assure that the basement is dry. However, footing drains can also be used to carry off rainwater falling on the house roof. To achieve this end, the water collecting in the house gutters is piped down through the leaders into 4-in. drain pipes which are connected into the footing drains.

A residential sanitary drainage system consists of large pipes which carry wastes to the house sewer, from whence they are discharged into the community sewer system or a septic tank. The entire system is ventilated through the roof of the house in order to get rid of noxious gases and to maintain atmospheric pressure within the system. Every sanitary drainage system incorporates the following parts:

Waste Pipes • These are the small pipes (approximately 2 in. in diameter) which carry waste water from lavatories, sinks, bathtubs, and shower stalls into the soil branches or house drain.

Soil Branches • Large 4-in. cast-iron or 3-in. copper pipes discharging wastes from toilets into the soil pipe.

Soil Pipe • The soil pipe is the large drain (3 or 4 in.) into which all household wastes are discharged. At the bottom it empties into the house drain; at the top, it is extended through the roof where it serves to ventilate the system.

House Drain • The horizontal drain line into which the soil pipe empties and which discharges the household wastes into the house sewer.

House Sewer • The drain line extending from the house drain to the community sewer or a septic tank. It is connected to the house drain just outside the foundation wall.

Traps • U-shaped devices which are installed below all plumbing fixtures. Because they are full of water, they prevent sewer gases from backing up into the house. Traps are built into the base of toilets. The traps for all other fixtures are sections of pipe. The house trap is a large U-shaped pipe installed in the house drain where it discharges into the house sewer.

Vents • These are the pipes which remove gases from the drainage system and simultaneously maintain atmospheric pressure within the system. The main vent is the upper part of the soil pipe extending through the roof. Individual vents are installed on the sewer side of each fixture trap and are connected into the main vent.

DRAKE FOOT

A furniture foot with three toes. Also called a *trifid foot.*

DRAPERY

If there was ever a definite distinction between draperies and curtains, it has become muddied by time. Draperies are generally considered to be to-the-floor hangings of heavy material, curtains to be window-length hangings of light material. However, draperies are made to hang only to the bottom edge of window aprons and are also made of thin material; while curtains are made to hang to the floor and are also made of fairly heavy material (but never of the very heavy material sometimes used in draperies).

Both draperies and curtains are used alone at windows. When they are hung together, the curtains are inside the draperies. (In this case, the draperies are sometimes called *over-draperies,* or—to confuse matters—the curtains may be called *under-draperies.*)

Draperies hang from the top of a window casing, from a little above it, or from the ceiling. Curtains, on the other hand, always hang from the top of the casing.

One of the distinct differences between the two hangings is that draperies—but not curtains—are also hung at the sides of interior and exterior doors and on bare walls. Another difference is that cafe and glass curtains are never called draperies.

Draperies can be made of almost any fabric appropriate to the decorative scheme and the functional requirements of the draperies. In stores today, however, the emphasis is on permanent press fabrics and fiberglass because they are easy to wash and require little, if any ironing. In addition, fiberglass is flameproof and not damaged by sunlight.

Except for fiberglass and open-weave fabrics which are used to filter sunlight, drapery materials are usually lined to protect them from the sun and fading, and to make the draperies hang better and look better from outside. Common lining materials are sateen and cotton twill. Acrylic foam and metallized fabrics are also used if one of the purposes of the linings is to keep out cold and hold in warmth.

On a conventional window, the width of the draperies equals the length of the rod plus the returns (elbows at the ends) plus 3 in. to permit overlapping if draw draperies are hung on traverse rods. To allow for pleats or folds in tailored draperies, actual fabric width is double this figure; and if the material is very light, fabric width is tripled.

To make a window look wider than it is, draperies are extended far enough beyond the casings so that, when open, they come just to the edges of the casings. Draperies for sliding glass doors and those made of very heavy fabric should also be extended beyond the casings; otherwise, they overlap the windows or doors too much when open.

If full-width draperies are used on a wall-to-wall window, the rod should bend back along the adjacent walls so that when the draperies are open, they do not block off the ends of the windows.

DRAPERY HARDWARE

The rods and accessories (such as tie-backs and festoons) used to hang draperies and curtains. The choice of rods is dictated by the style of drapery or curtain, whether it is to be hung within the window opening or overlapping, and whether it is to be drawn and how.

The simplest rods are essentially flat steel strips which are curved at the ends and hook over brackets screwed to the window casings or wall. Made in two interlocking pieces, they can be extended to almost twice their collapsed length. The largest sizes extend to 10 ft.

So-called brass rods (actually made of steel coated with brass or enamel) are slender round rods which must be cut to the desired length. They are held in brackets which are made in various shapes for mounting on the casings or on the outside.

Spring-tension rods are small, round or oval extension rods which are held in place inside casings by spring tension.

Larger rods up to 1¼ in. in diameter are made of wood or steel in ornamental designs. Unlike smaller rods, which are run through the casing of the curtains or draperies, the larger rods are fully exposed, and the curtains hang from them in big rings.

Traverse rods permit operation of draperies and curtains by means of cords running over pulleys. The draperies hang from slides that move back and forth as the cords are pulled. Most rods are designed to hold a drapery panel at both ends, but there are one-way rods which pull a single drapery to left or right.

Traverse rods are mounted in brackets on the window casings or wall. Some rods hold only a pair of draperies; some hold a pair of draperies and a pair of curtains or a valance; some hold draperies, curtains, and valance. In a combination traverse-and-curtain rod, the draperies are cord-controlled, and the curtains are adjusted by hand. In a double traverse rod, both the draperies and curtains are cord-controlled.

All traverse rods can be extended somewhat beyond their collapsed length. The largest extends to 26 ft. The rods are usually straight. But curved rods are made for bow windows; and right-angle rods are made for corners.

Because of the weight of the fabric they must carry, all types of curtain rod must be securely mounted. Long rods usually should be supported at the middle by an extra bracket. If the end brackets are not screwed to the casings, they should be attached to the wall with toggle bolts or hollow-wall screw anchors. The alternative is to install wooden blocks in the walls while a house is under construction and screw the brackets through the wall surface into these.

DRAWER SLIDE

A metal rack with rollers used to improve the operation of drawers in kitchen and other cabinets, built-ins, etc. The track is mounted on the bottom or each side of a drawer.

DRAWING-BOOK CHAIR BACK

A chair back copied from Sheraton's "Drawing Book". It features a draped urn in the center of a three-section back.

DRESSER

In the United States, a dresser is a chest of drawers; in England, it is a cupboard with open shelves built in above.

DRESSING CHEST

A small chest of drawers in which the top drawer is compartmented to hold cosmetics and toilet articles. The center section of the top, with a mirror fixed to the underside, folds back so the user can look at herself.

DRESSING GLASS

A small mirror usually swiveled between a pair of uprights which are mounted on a flat base containing several small drawers. It is set on a chest of drawers or table. It is also known as a *shaving stand.*

DRESSING TABLE

Any small table with knee space and a mirror which may or may not be attached to the top. Old dressing tables were of refined design and made of choice woods, but modern units are commonly unfinished pieces. These are fitted with a two-piece snap-on skirt attached to the sides of the table and to a pair of arms that swing out from the front. The top is covered with a plate-glass mirror or fabric.

DRIFT PIN

An enormous steel pin up to 26 in. long used for fastening large timbers together. It is driven into a drilled hole of slightly smaller diameter.

DRIFTWOOD FINISH

A blond finish for furniture and woodwork. The bare wood is first stained a dark color. Then it is covered with white enamel undercoater which is worked into the pores and wiped off. Finally, it is given a protective coat of white shellac or varnish.

DRILL

A strong, closely woven cotton twill fabric similar to denim. It is used in upholstery, slipcovers, curtains, awnings, and porch shades.

DRIP

A projecting edge designed to make water fall clear of the wall or other surface below. Modern wooden windowsills, for instance, have a small groove in the bottom just back of the front edge. The tooth-like projection thus formed is a drip. Similarly it is customary to installed L-shaped strips of aluminum along the edges of asphalt-shingle roofs to force water flowing off the roof to drop straight to the ground. These are also drips, or drip edges.

DRIP CAP

A molding designed to prevent leaks by directing water away from the wall surface below. Drip caps are used primarily over exterior windows and doors. The back edge, in effect, locks into the siding to stop leaks along the top of the cap, and the front edge projects beyond the casing almost an inch.

DRIPLESS PAINT

An interior paint with jelly-like consistency which is not supposed to drip.

DRIVE ANCHOR

A device for fastening heavy objects to masonry walls. It is a spring-steel rod split at the point into two bowed legs. When hammered into a predrilled hole, the legs press against the sides. The head of the anchor is flat, rounded, or threaded to receive a nut.

DROP

A carved ornament hanging down from a beam, overhang, table top, etc. *Compare* Finial.

DROP LEAF

A section of a table top or countertop which can be folded down out of the way when not in use. When open, it is usually locked into a horizontal position by a hinged drop-leaf support roughly similar to the support on a card-table leg.

DROP SIDING

A horizontal, flat board siding in which the boards are separated by rather deep concave grooves in the top edges of each board. The boards interlock to keep out moisture.

DRY ROT

Dry rot is a misnomer because wood decays only in the presence of moisture. Wood with dry, decayed areas might be said to have dry rot, but it would be more proper to say simply that it is rotten.

DRY SINK

An Early American kitchen cabinet with a rectangular, rather deep, zinc-lined sink set in the top and a cupboard below. The sink had a drain, but water was poured in by a bucket or a hand-driven pitcher-spout pump.

DRY WALL

A stone wall laid up without mortar.

DRYWALL

An interior wall surfaced with gypsum board. *See* Gypsum Board.

DRYWELL

A large, usually round hole in the ground used to collect and dispose of rainwater piped into it from the roof of a house or other building. It may also be used to dispose of laundry water or rainwater collecting in a swale.

Drywells should be located in reasonably porous soil at least 8 ft. from a building. The top is a foot or more below ground to allow grass to grow over it. The well is lined on the sides with masonry blocks or stones laid up without mortar, and is then filled with rocks.

DUCK

A sturdy cotton fabric very similar to a lightweight canvas. It is used in slipcovers, upholstery, and awnings.

DUCT

A rectangular or round tube which carries air. Ducts for warm-air heating and air conditioning systems are formed of galvanized sheet steel. They should be laid out with just as few elbows as possible (because elbows slow the air flow), but there should be enough of them to muffle the noises traveling from the furnace to the registers. For strength and rigidity, the ducts should be hung by metal straps rather than wires. The connection between the ductwork and the furnace or air conditioner is made with a flexible canvas sleeve to further minimize the noise of the blower. Ducts used for both air conditioning and heating should be insulated to prevent condensation on the metal in summer.

Ducts are also used to ventilate kitchen and bathroom fans and automatic clothes dryers. These are usually 4-in. rounds made of steel or plastic. Installation is less critical because they move a much smaller volume of air and any sound they transmit goes to the outdoors. Nevertheless, the runs should be as short and straight as possible.

DUST RUFFLE

A short, ruffled curtain surrounding the base of a bed just above the floor to conceal the space under the bed. It is hung on brass curtain rods or by fastening it to a box spring with hooks or snaps. It can also be stitched to muslin which covers the top of the box spring. The only basic difference between a dust ruffle and a skirt for a bed is the appearance. *See* Skirt.

DUTCH FOOT

See Pad Foot.

DUTCHMAN
> A piece of wood used to plug a hole or opening.

DWARFWALL
> A wall extending only part way to the ceiling.

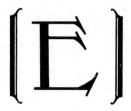

EAGLE-HEAD FOOT
An outcurved furniture foot resembling the beak and head of an eagle.

EARLY AMERICAN
The first furniture made in America was Jacobean; but when Cromwell came to power in England, the New England Puritans, approving of Cromwell's government, began turning out chairs, tables, etc., in the simple, sturdy Cromwellian style. This is the beginning of Early American furniture. Later, when the Dutch settled in New York, Dutch and New England styles were combined. The furniture, however, continued to be simple and practical—made from native woods such as pine, maple, oak, and ash (several woods were often combined in one piece of furniture).

EARNEST MONEY
A binder (*see above*).

EARTHENWARE
Dinnerware and miscellaneous ceramic objects made of semi-coarse clays. Easily chipped and semi-vitreous, earthenware soaks up and is stained by liquids when the glaze is cracked.

EASED EDGE
A slightly rounded corner at the edge of a piece of material.

EASEMENT

A legal right to make some use of another person's land. For example, the right one property owner has to pipe water from his neighbor's well constitutes an easement. Or the right a neighbor has to enter his property via a next-door driveway is an easement—which in this instance is normally called a *right-of-way*.

An easement is an encumbrance on the title of the person granting the easement, and is therefore undesirable because it limits the grantor's right to do with the property as he wishes.

EASING

A short, slightly curved section of stair rail which connects a straight stair rail to a newel post that is offset to right or left. It is also called an *easement*.

EASTLAKE

A furniture style developed by Charles Locke Eastlake, an English designer, which was popular from 1870 to 1890. The style was supposed to be simple and honest, characterized by straight lines. But the furniture turned out by most manufacturers was over-ornamented like most Victorian furniture.

EAVE

That part of a roof overhanging the side walls. The width of the overhang is dictated by the design of the house and also by the relative importance of shading the windows against the sun and protecting the walls against rain.

ECLECTIC

Architecture, decoration, or furniture adapted from several styles of the past.

EDGING

Anything used to cover a raw edge. Kitchen countertops, for example, have edgings made of stainless steel or plastic. Plywood and other wood-base composition materials are edged with strips of wood tape. When an edged piece and the edging are of the same material, the piece is said to be *self-edged*.

EFFLORESCENCE

A whitish, sometimes crusty powder which often forms on masonry surfaces. Caused by moisture dissolving salts in the masonry, it is particularly common on brick walls. Washing the surface with a weak solution of muriatic acid removes the efflorescence but does not prevent its return. However, as masonry ages, it usually stops efflorescing.

EFFLUENT

The liquid part of household wastes. In a septic system, it flows from the septic tank into the drain tiles composing the field. In a cesspool, it seeps through the sides of the pool.

EGGCRATE

A piece of openwork divided into small, deep, open squares. Eggcrates are frequently used as diffusers under fluorescent lights. On a larger scale, they are used to shade terraces against the sun.

EGGSHELL FINISH

See Flat Finish.

ELBOW

An elbow-shaped plumbing fitting used in a run of rigid pipe where it turns a corner. Elbows are generally made for 90° or 45° bends. They may be called *els.*

ELEVATION

A plan showing a wall or other vertical part of a house. *See* Working Drawing.

EMINENT DOMAIN

Governmental right to take private property by condemnation.

EMPIRE

A style of furniture derived from classic forms which originated during Napoleon's reign and which was popular through the better part of the first half of the 19th century. The furniture was massive and elegant, yet severe. It was made of fine woods and featured metal mounts, eagles, animal-paw feet, stars, and wreaths.

EMULSION PAINT

A paint made by emulsifying, or mixing, various elements in water instead of dissolving them in a solvent. *See* Paint.

ENAMEL

A usually small decorative object or piece of jewelry made by bonding colorful enamels to metal or glass at high heat.

Also, a paint containing varnish which produces a very smooth, hard coating. Enamels are made for interior and exterior use in gloss, semi-gloss, and flat finishes. Most have an oil or alkyd base, but latex enamels are on the market. Enamel should be applied over an enamel undercoater by brushing or spraying.

ENAMELWARE

Correctly speaking, any metal object which has been coated with hard, semi-gloss porcelain enamel is enamelware; but the name is usually applied only to utensils and similar objects used for cooking and, frequently, for display. The color and luster are beautiful; the finish is very durable but will chip when struck a sharp blow with something very hard. It cannot be touched up satisfactorily.

The toughest enamelware has a cast-iron base. Aluminum and steel are also used.

ENCROACH

To trespass. Both people and buildings can encroach; but only people are said to trespass.

ENCUMBRANCE

Anything which constitutes a claim or burden on a property. Easements and mortgages are encumbrances.

END-MATCHED

Boards with tongue-and-groove joints at the ends as well as along the sides. Wooden flooring strips and the boards used in cedar closets are end-matched.

ENGAWA

A small Japanese terrace ordinarily raised off the ground and used for sitting, walking, or displaying plants. In the United States, it is often incorporated into a conventional terrace and is constructed largely of wood.

ENGLISH REGENCY

An early-18th-century furniture and decorating style inspired by classic motifs and architecture. Furniture became heavier, less delicate, and more complicated than in the preceding Chippendale-Hepplewhite-and-early-Sheraton period. Rich woods, black lacquer, and gilt were widely used. Green was a particularly popular color.

ENTABLATURE

The upper part of an order (*see below*). Supported by columns, it comprises the *architrave, frieze,* and *cornice.*

ENTASIS

The outward swelling of a column. It is used to counteract the illusion of curving inward characteristic of tall columns which are the same diameter from top to bottom.

ENTRANCE

The entrance of a house may be thought of as the entire front outdoor-indoor area used by people who are paying a visit, as only the outdoor part of this area, or as only the door itself. Most homeowners use the second definition: The entrance includes the front door and any adjacent exterior structure such as a porch, stoop, or canopy.

If it is to fulfill its purpose—which is more than simply letting people into a house—an entrance should be visible from the street and identifiable as the entrance, well-lighted for the benefit of both visitors and homeowners, and free of hazards. There should be a roof or canopy to give protection against bad weather. The door bell should be clearly visible.

Most Americans undoubledly prefer the general atmosphere of entrances to be friendly and welcoming, but their feelings in this regard are influenced by the person who happens to be ringing the door bell at any given moment. In the 1970s, entrances tend to be less friendly than they were in the 1940s. Doors flanked by windows or lights which allow visitors to look into the front hall are rare today.

Minimum width of a front door is 3 ft. If a double door is installed, the total width should be no less than 4½ ft. so a person can enter readily if only one of the doors is opened.

Steps to the door should be the width of the front walk, but never less than 3 ft. The risers should be no more than 7½ in. high and can be a great deal less. Tread depth should be a minimum of 11 in. The height of a single riser plus the depth of a single tread should total 17 to 18 in. *See* Stair.

Any porch, terrace, or stoop more than 10 in. above the ground should have a railing.

Also see Front Hall.

ENTRE DEUX
A narrow, openwork band used as trim between seam edges in fabric.

ENTRY
A small enclosed area just outside the main entrance where people take off rubbers and other wet clothing before stepping into the house. It may be called a *storm entrance* or *mud room,* and in some climates—particularly those that are very cold or stormy—there are entries at the back as well as at the front door.

Front halls or vestibules are also called entries. The area defined in this way, however, is usually not a distinct room but merely a part of the living room which is screened by a partial partition.

EQUITY
The interest a person has in the property he owns.

ESCRITOIRE
Also called *scrutoire,* an enclosed desk or simply a box holding writing materials with an inner lid which forms a writing surface when opened.

ESCROW
A deed or other written agreement deposited with a third person until the grantee, who is to receive it, completes his part of the bargain.

ESCUTCHEON

A metal plate used partly for ornament and partly to conceal a hole. For example, the plate around a keyhole, at the base of a door knob, at the base of a faucet, or under some types of drawer pull.

ESSEX BOARD MEASURE

A figure table on the back of a framing square blade. It tells at a glance how many board feet are in a board or timber of given dimensions.

ETAGERE

A tall, rather shallow, usually fairly narrow framework with shelves used to display decorative objects. It may be placed against or hung on a wall, or set out from a wall like a small display case in a store.

EVAPORATIVE COOLER

A little-used electrical appliance which lowers temperature in a house as much as 10° by blowing dry air through a wet pad. It is most effective in arid areas, where it originated.

Evaporative coolers are made for installation outside a window or on a windowsill. Some are portable devices used entirely inside a house.

EVAPORATOR

The cooling coil in an air conditioner. It absorbs the heat from the air which is drawn into the air conditioner from the rooms in a house.

EXHAUST FAN

See Fan, Exhaust.

EXPANSION BOLT

See Drive Anchor.

EXPANSION JOINT

A joint built into something to absorb movement caused by the contraction and expansion of the materials. In constructing wooden and concrete floors, for example, it is customary to leave an open expansion joint around the perimeter of the floor.

EXPANSION TANK

A tank installed near the boiler in a hot-water heating system which allows the water to expand and contract as the temperature changes. Thus, it protects the system against abnormal pressures.

EXPOSURE

The direction, as determined by a compass, in which a house faces.

Also, the size of the surface of a material which is exposed to the weather. When an overlapping siding or roofing material is used, the exposure is the area between the butts and the next butts above. For example, if a 5-in. exposure is used on a wood shingle roof, the distance from the butt of a shingle in the first course to the butt of the next shingle above is 5 in. The amount of exposure is dictated by the overall size of the siding material (for example, maximum exposure of a 16-in.-long wood shingle is 7½ in.; of a 24-in. shingle, 12 in.); but it also depends on the effect that is desired.

EXTERIOR TRIM

The cornices, rakes, casings, quoins, etc., on the outside of a house. They are made of softwoods which are easily worked, take a good finish, and resist splintering and decay.

EYEBALL

A light fixture with a rotating shield having a small hole in the center. It is used to concentrate a spot of light on a table top, art object, etc. The shield may be turned downward in any direction.

EYEBROW

A flat, horizontal structure built out over the top of a large window or window wall to keep out the sun. Usually made of wood, it may be louvered, eggcrated, or solid. Some eyebrows have hinged or sliding flaps which can be extended outward and downward.

FABRIC FINISH

A special treatment applied to a fabric to give it a quality it does not naturally possess. The most important fabric finishes in current use are:

Permanent Press • A factory-applied finish which makes a fabric wrinkle and crease resistant, and helps it to hold its shape. No matter how grimy and mussy a permanent press article may be, it will return to its original shape after proper laundering and will require little, if any, ironing.

Soil-Release Finishes • Factory-applied finishes which help to retard soiling and simplify removal of bad stains. They are used primarily on permanent press articles.

Soil and Oil Repellents • Colorless, odorless liquids which are applied to fabrics—particularly upholstery fabrics—to repel water and resist staining by oil and watery substances. They are most effecitve when applied at the factory or by trained applicators. They may, however, be applied at home with an aerosol.

Shrinkage-Control Finishes • Used mainly on cotton, wool, and some types of rayon which require frequent laundering.

Hygienic Finishes • Retard growth of bacteria and fungi, and thus stop mildew and prevent the spread of diseases. Such finishes are applied mainly to blankets and other fabrics which come in close contact with the body; but in humid climates, where mildew is a serious problem, they can be used on furnishings as well.

Flame-Retardant Finishes • These are used mainly on clothing but may be applied to any fabric.

Insect-Repellent Finishes. • Used to protect fabrics against moths and carpet beetles primarily.

FABRIC WALLCOVERING

Any fabric which is used to cover interior walls. Burlap, felt, grasscloth, and shiki silk are so commonly used for this purpose that they are described under their own names. This entry deals with silk, velvet, moire, linen, and similar beautiful fabrics which are applied in preference to wallpaper and other conventional wallcoverings because of their texture, color, patterns, and general suitability, and because they unify the walls with draperies of the same material.

Installation is made in several ways:

Lath and Staple Method • In this, the strips of fabric are sewn together and the entire sheet is then stretched and stapled over a framework of ¼-in. wood lattice strips nailed to the wall around its perimeter and around all doors and windows. The main advantage of the method is that the wall to be covered need not be in good repair. But the fabric can be easily snagged and torn.

Double-Faced Tape Method • Each strip of fabric is stuck to the wall with double-faced adhesive tape applied under all edges of the strip. The resulting wall surface is less subject to snagging and tearing; but the base must be smooth, sound, and clean.

Adhesive Method • The fabric strips are pasted to the wall like wallpaper with vinyl adhesive. The wall must first be covered with lining paper.

Paper-Backed Fabric Method • This method makes use of fabric which is laminated at the factory to a paper backing. Installation is similar to that for wallpaper.

Self-Adhesive-Fabric Method • The fabric used is coated on the back with contact cement. It is hung much like wallpaper after a protective paper backing is peeled off.

FACADE

The whole exterior side of a building. But normally the word is applied only to the front—what is seen from the street.

FACE

The surface seen when a person looks at a wall, column, timber, etc. Note that the face is not just any exposed surface; rather, it is the one first seen. For instance, in an unfinished frame wall, the face of the stud is the narrow edge seen by someone standing in front of it.

FACEBRICK

This can be any brick that is used on the surface of a wall or floor, but generally it refers to a brick of superior appearance. *See* Brick.

FACING

A wide strip of fabric used to finish a raw edge when a binding is impractical. In building, a facing may be used for the same purpose. For example, the exposed edges of the side members of a built-in bookcase or wood cabinet are customarily covered with facing strips.

Also in building, facing is used interchangeably with *veneer* to describe a veneered wall. For instance, a brick veneer wall is faced with brick or has a brick facing.

FAIENCE

High-quality glazed earthenware.

FAILLE

A soft silk, rayon, or acetate fabric with crosswise ribs. It is used in draperies and curtains.

FALL FRONT

A desk or secretary with a front panel which is hinged to open outward to form a writing surface. It is vertical when closed.

FALSE FRONT

A facade applied to a building to make it look larger and more elaborate than it is. Buildings in early Midwestern and Western towns were notable for the variety of false fronts.

FALSE RAFTER

An extension nailed to a main rafter over a cornice. It is used primarily when there is a change in the slope of a roof.

FALSEWORK
A temporary framework erected to aid in construction of a building.

FAMILY ROOM
An informal room used by the entire family—together or separately—as a place to relax, watch television, play games, etc. It is commonly located in the basement or next to or actually in the kitchen; but in many houses, it is a completely separate room on the first floor. In all cases except when it is designed purely for recreation, its purpose is to provide a more casual setting than the living room for family life and to minimize wear and soiling of the living room.

Family rooms tend to be large—often larger than living rooms—and because of the hard usage they get, they should be finished and furnished to withstand this. But often because of their size and informality, they completely take the place of the living room, which then becomes expensive waste space.

FAN BACK
A Windsor chair back shaped like a slightly opened lady's fan from which the joint has been removed.

FAN, EXHAUST
Conventional fans for ventilating kitchens are made for installation in exterior walls or ceilings, where they are connected to ducts that carry off to the outdoors the odors, smoke, grease, and water vapor generated in cooking. Hood fans—so called because they are built into rectangular hoods—are installed over the range. One type is ducted through an outside wall or ceiling to the outdoors. A second type, which is not ducted, is used only to filter odors, smoke, and grease from the air; consequently, it is not an exhaust fan, although it may be substituted for one when installation of a duct is impossible.

The efficiency of an exhaust fan depends on its capacity to move air and its placement in relation to the range. Capacity is rated in cubic feet per minute (cfm), and should not be less than 2 cfm per square foot of floor area.

The ideal placement for a wall fan is about 1 ft. above the backsplash or side of a range. A ceiling fan should be centered directly over the range cooking surface. Because of the greater distance from the cooking surface, it is less efficient than a wall fan.

A ducted hood fan is slightly more efficient than a wall fan because almost all the rising smoke, etc., is sucked directly into it. The closer the bottom edges of the fan are to the cooking surface, the better. However, they must be high enough—about 21 to 24 in.—so the cook can see into the utensils on the back burners. The edges of the hood must be shaped so the cook cannot be cut on them.

Regardless of the design of a fan, the duct to the outdoors should be as short and straight as possible. This is the reason why a range should, if possible, be placed against an outside wall. If located elsewhere, so that the fan must be ducted through the ceiling, the duct should not be more than 10 ft. long.

If a barbecue is built into a kitchen, it must be served by a separate fan. *See* Barbecue.

Exhaust fans are also desirable, and may be required, in bathrooms, laundries, basements, and recreation rooms. Conventional wall or ceiling fans are used. Bathroom fans may be about half the capacity of a kitchen fan, and are most often incorporated in a ceiling unit which also contains a light and sometimes an electric heater. Fans for laundries, basements, and recreation rooms should be intermediate in size between kitchen and bathroom fans.

FANLIGHT

A fan-shaped window usually installed over a door or in the gable end of a roof. It is generally of decorative design and fixed so it cannot be opened.

FASCIA

A board set on edge, parallel with the wall, forming part of the exterior trim under the eaves. In a cornice, the fascia is installed just below the crown molding. It is often used to conceal the ends of rafters.

Fascias are also parts of entablatures.

FAUCET

In the name of progress, plumbing fixture manufacturers have chosen to replace the universally used compression faucet with improved designs of their own. Progress has not been served. The new faucets cause as many problems as compression faucets. And whereas anyone can stop a drip in a compression faucet simply by purchasing a washer of the appropriate size at a hardware store, it is possible to fix a new faucet only after determining the brand (not easy), taking it apart (not easy without directions—which are rarely provided), finding the wholesale distributor who has the right parts for sale, and making the repairs (which differs from one brand of faucet to the next).

Since faucets and other plumbing fittings are sold separately from fixtures, the homeowner need not accept those suggested by the fixture manufacturer. And although the appearance of faucets must be considered in making a selection, it is far less important than the durability of the faucets and the ease of maintaining them.

The two best rules to follow in buying faucets and other plumbing fittings are:

1 / Stick with a design which has been well tested by time. In addition to compression faucets, this includes single-lever faucets of the type used in kitchen sinks.

2 / Buy quality faucets of conservative styling. Inexpensive faucets are made of second-rate metals which disintegrate rapidly. Fancy styling, such as gold plating and carved spouts, is more likely to be found in second-rate than first-rate faucets (the high price notwithstanding).

FAUTEUIL
An upholstered armchair with openings under the arms. *Compare* Bergere.

FEATHER
To shape to a very thin edge. When joints in gypsum board are taped, the joint compound is smoothed to a feather edge to make it invisible when painted or papered.

FEDERAL
The American architectural style which flourished from the last decades of the 18th century until about 1825. It coincided with and was influenced by the Adam style.

Buildings of Federal design were inspired partly by classic architecture, but they have an air of extreme lightness (and were commonly painted white inside and out). They are strongly horizontal in proportion (despite high ceilings) with slightly sloping roofs. Walls are broken up into several planes. Windows are often down to floor level. Balconies are surrounded by delicate ironwork. And much use is made of sculptured ornamentation.

Outstanding buildings of the period include the White House, U.S. Capitol, Monticello, and the Gardiner-White-Pingree house in Salem, Mass.

FEDERAL HOUSING ADMINISTRATION

Better known as the *FHA,* a U.S. government agency which insures mortgages issued by approved lenders and establishes minimum standards for houses eligible for such loans. Though the standards are not binding on anyone putting up a contract-built home, they serve as useful guidelines for him.

FELT

A dense, rather thick, nonwoven fabric made by bonding together wool fibers (which are occasionally combined with rayon or cotton). It has little strength, is easily soiled and hard to clean except by dry cleaning, and should be mothproofed. But it has good acoustical qualities and helps to deaden noises in a room. It comes in 54-in. widths in long rolls.

Felt can be used in decorating in places where it is not subjected to wear or soiling. If hung as a wallcovering, it should be laminated to a paper backing; otherwise, it stretches and is difficult to handle.

FELT PAPER

Building paper applied over sheathing or a roof deck. Often called *building felt.*

FEMALE

A plumbing or electrical fitting with an orifice into which a male fitting is inserted.

FENESTRATION

The arrangement of windows in a house.

FESTOON

In architecture and furniture, a festoon is a carved or molded ornament of flowers or leaves arranged in a drooping curve.

In decoration, a festoon is a drooping curve of fabric, such as a drapery.

FIBERBOARD
A rather soft panel formed of cellulose fibers pressed together. Acoustical tiles are made of fiberboard; but the word is most generally associated with large panels (roughly 4 x 8 ft.) used either as sheathing or to surface interior walls. As a surfacing material, fiberboard has some thermal insulation value; but it is easily damaged by blows or scrapes. The joints between panels should be either left open or covered with battens. Today the panels usually come prefinished.

For fiberboard used as sheathing, *see* Sheathing.

FIBERGLASS FABRIC
A fabric made of very fine glass fibers which is widely used in curtains and draperies. Produced in many lovely colors and patterns, it hangs straight and holds its shape, is resistant to the sun's rays and does not need to be lined, and is heat resistant and fireproof. Its main disadvantage is that it attracts soil, but it releases it rapidly when dunked in warm detergent solution. Most stains can be removed by sponging with detergent.

Beta fabric is a type of fiberglass fabric made with ultra-fine fibers.

FIBERGLASS, RIGID
This material is actually made of polyester reinforced with fiberglass. It is fabricated in large, translucent, colored, corrugated or flat panels roughly 1/16 in. thick. Strong, durable, and shatterproof, it is widely used in terrace roofs and dividers. It also goes into garage doors and sliding doors for cabinets, bathtub enclosures, etc. It is easily sawed and installed with nails driven through pre-drilled holes. In a roof, joints are overlapped and sealed with mastic.

For roofing a terrace, rigid fiberglass is economical and requires only a light, open supporting framework. Because it transmits light, the terrace is bright, but much warmer than a terrace with an opaque roof. Debris and dirt on top are visible from underneath the fiberglass.

FIDDLE BACK

A Queen Anne period chair back with a center splat shaped like a violin.

FIELD

The principal large, central area of a design. In an Oriental rug, the field is the area surrounded by the border. In a tiled wall, the field is also the area surrounded by the border.

The tiled area beyond a septic tank is also called a field.

FIGURE

The wavy grain, streaking, or mottling in wood. Some woods have a pronounced figure; others have none. Frequently, a wood which shows little figure when sawed in one way has a distinct figure when sawed in another way.

FILIGREE

Delicate, ornamental openwork done with fine wires. It is used in furniture and room dividers.

FILLER

Any material such as spackle, putty, or shellac sticks used to fill holes and cracks in wood, gypsum board, plaster, metal, etc. Cement-base materials used for patching concrete and masonry are about the only fillers not known as such. *Also see* Filler, Wood.

FILLER STRIP

Also known simply as a *filler*, a filler strip is a 1- to 3-in.-wide strip of wood or metal finished to match kitchen wall cabinets and used to fill gaps in rows of cabinets. Base filler strips are used with base cabinets, wall filler strips with wall cabinets. Strips used with metal cabinets are made separately from the cabinets and then attached to them with bolts. Strips for wooden and plastic-covered cabinets may be separate or made integral parts of the cabinets. The latter are called *extended stiles.*

Filler strips have three specific functions:

1 / To piece out a row of base or wall cabinets in order to fill a wall space. The filler may be inserted between two of the cabinets but is usually installed between an end cabinet and a wall.

2 /   To fill an ugly gap between an end cabinet and a slanting or crooked wall. In this case, the filler strip is scribed to the wall.

3 /   To allow opening of the drawers and doors of cabinets which are installed on opposite sides of an inside corner. The filler strip, in effect, pushes the cabinets far enough away from the apex of the corner so that a drawer on one side of the corner can be pulled out without striking the cabinet handle on the other side of the corner.

FILLER, WOOD

A paste used to fill the pores of open-grain woods such as oak in order to secure a smoother final finish. It is available in various colors. Application is made to wood after it has been stained but before it is given a final finish of varnish, shellac, etc.

Fine-grain woods are generally not filled. If they are, a couple of coats of white shellac are used instead of paste filler.

FILLET

A slim, concave strip used to round off an inside corner joint.

FILL-IN LIGHT

Supplementary light which eliminates dark areas in a room. A basic principle of good lighting requires that the illumination of a room be more or less uniform in order to prevent the eyestrain caused by sharp contrasts between dark and light areas.

FILTER

A device for filtering air, light, or water. Filters are often used in warm-air heating systems to remove dust, dirt, and pollen from the incoming air; in light fixtures to change the amount and/or color of the light; and in water systems to remove objectionable elements in the water supply.

FINIAL

A carved upright ornament atop bedposts, cupolas, etc. The opposite of a drop.

FINISH GRADE

The land around a house after it has been brought to the proper contour by raking. *Also see* Rough Grade.

FIR

An almost white, straight-grained, lightweight softwood used mainly for construction lumber. It is also used in doors, sashes, and millwork but is less desirable here than white pine. The wood comes from the white fir growing in California.

FIRE ALARM SYSTEM

A complete system which can be counted on to sound an alarm if fire breaks out anywhere in a house. It incorporates the following things:

1 / Heat detectors which are mounted on the ceiling in all danger areas.

2 / A smoke detector in each sleeping area and another in the living area.

3 / A loud alarm.

4 / An individual 15-amp, 120-volt wiring circuit plus batteries in case the power fails.

5 / A means by which the system can be tested weekly without damaging the detectors.

The system should be approved by either Underwriters Laboratories (UL) or Factory Mutual Laboratories (FM). Installation should be made only by a reliable, experienced firm which has done business in the area for a long time.

Various simple nonelectrical fire alarms are made for use in specific parts of the house—but none is an adequate substitute for a complete system. They are actuated only by heat, not by the odor of smoke.

FIREBACK

A usually decorative cast-iron plate used to cover and protect the back wall of a firebox.

FIREBOX

The central fireplace opening which contains the fire. It is built of solid masonry or reinforced concrete at least 8 in. thick (12 in. thick if stone is used). The entire firebox should be surfaced with firebrick, although stone or hard-burned brick may be used on the back and sides of the opening.

The back of the firebox is narrower than the front opening. The lower 10 in. are perpendicular to the hearth; then the back is slanted forward to throw the maximum amount of heat into the room.

The sides of a firebox are set at an angle of 30° to 45° to the back and rise straight up.

FIRE CLAY

A type of cement mortar used to construct those parts of fireplaces and flues which are directly exposed to heat.

FIRE DOOR

Doors which control the spread of fire are often surfaced on both sides with steel; but while these stop flame, they do not stop heat, which may reach such a point that it causes fire to burst out on the other side of the door. The most effective fire door, therefore, is one made of noncombustible material sandwiched between steel or plywood panels. This stops both heat and flame, and is more attractive to boot.

All fire doors must be of the hinged variety and closely fitted into the door jambs so that fire cannot penetrate through the cracks.

In homes, fire doors are most likely to be required between the house and an attached garage or a utility room.

FIREPLACE

Development of prefabricated fireplaces has taken most of the guesswork out of fireplace building. If the home builder doesn't settle for a single Franklin-stove-type of free-standing fireplace, he can choose between a circulating fireplace and a prefabricated insulated unit that builds right into the framing and requires no foundations. Conventional built-from-scratch fireplaces are still common, however—especially in better houses.

A fireplace can be located on an outside wall, on an inside wall, or in the middle of a room. An outside location saves money and space whereas a location against an inside wall makes it possible to cluster the furnace and water heater close to the center of the house, thus reducing pipe runs and improving efficiency. Furthermore, heat escaping through the chimney helps to warm the surrounding rooms.

A free-standing fireplace in the middle of a room generally has a prefabricated chimney, which cuts cost substantially; and since the firebox is open on four sides, heat is radiated to all corners of the room. But the principal reason for installing this kind of fireplace is for drama and decoration.

A fireplace can be almost any size, but if it is very big, it loses efficiency because it requires more air than it may get in a tightly insulated house. It must also be fed with proportionally larger logs which are often difficult to come by.

Although dimensions vary widely, the average single-face fireplace (open on one side only) has an opening between 30 and 40 in. wide. For this width, a good height is 30 to 31 in.; a good depth, 16 to 18 in.

The size of the opening determines the area of the flue. An old rule of thumb called for a flue area equal to 10% of the area of the fireplace opening. But since chimney height must be taken into consideration, a more accurate rule calls for a flue area equal to 12% of the fireplace opening if the chimney top is less than 17 ft. above the hearth; 10% if the chimney is 17 to 25 ft. above the hearth; and 8% if the chimney is more than 25 ft. above the hearth.

Multi-opening fireplaces are more complicated, and should be designed by a true expert—even though he may not be able to guarantee the fireplace against smoking.

Fireplaces have various parts, some of which are familiar to the layman and some of which are not:

Foundation—essential to support a masonry fireplace and chimney of any type.

Ash pit—a pit under or in the hearth in which ashes are dumped. It is omitted from many fireplaces.

Hearth—the stone or brick floor of a fireplace.

Firebox—the large hollow space containing the fire.

Jambs—the exposed edges of the firebox.

Lintel—an iron bar supporting the masonry over the fireplace opening.

Throat—the connecting area between the firebox and smoke dome. The damper closes the top of the throat.

Smoke shelf—one of the most important parts of a fireplace. The shelf is a wide, flat space at the base of the smoke dome just behind the damper. It deflects air blowing down the chimney upward so that it does not affect the fire.

Smoke dome—a more or less triangular space above the smoke shelf which funnels smoke into the flue.

Chimney—the structure through which smoke and fumes from the fire escape to the outside.

Mantel—the facing around and projecting shelf above the fireplace.

FIREPLACE, CIRCULATING

A fireplace with ducts which carry heat from the smoke dome to outlets located some distance away. Thus, the fireplace heats like a standard fireplace by radiation and also by convection, and less heat from the fire is wasted up the chimney.

The fireplace is a steel shell which is set on a prepared foundation and then surrounded with bricks or stones. This simplifies construction for the mason and virtually assures a fireplace which works well.

FIREPLACE HOOD

A canopy-like device usually made of sheet metal which is built in or hung over a fireplace to funnel the smoke into the flue. The simplest kind of hood resembles a shallow valance which is attached to the top of the fireplace opening. It is installed as an afterthought on fireplaces which smoke.

Another kind of fireplace hood is a large unit built as an integral part of the fireplace to serve as the connecting link between the fire and the chimney flue. Such hoods are most commonly used on fireplaces which are open on two, three, or four sides because they are much simpler and lighter to build than a masonry structure. However, hoods are sometimes used in contemporary houses over conventional fireplaces for purely decorative purposes.

FIREPLACE TOOLS

The poker, shovel, broom, tongs and their holder; fender; wood basket; andirons or dogs; grate, firelighters, etc., are a prominent feature of every fireplace; and they have been considered as more than mere utilitarian articles for centuries. Because of their durability, luster, and color, brass tools are generally the first choice, but many handsome articles are available in black iron.

FIRE-RETARDANT PAINT

Properly called an *intumescent coating*, this is a paint which, when exposed to heat, foams up to form a barrier between the painted surface and source of heat. It thus delays ignition of the surface but does not prevent it.

Fire-retardant paints are available in limited colors, usually in a flat finish. They are less attractive than other paints.

FIRE SCREEN

Early fire screens were ornamental devices—often covered with embroidery—designed not to contain sparks but to shield people from the heat and glare of the flames. Modern firescreens, of course, are the reverse, and their value is judged mainly by their ability to keep sparks from scorching carpets and setting fire to a house.

From this standpoint, the best screen is a flat, upright unit which is built permanently into the fireplace opening or overlapping its edges, and has draw curtains of metal mesh. Free-standing units of the same type are available, but these are somewhat less safe because there are usually cracks around the edges through which sparks can escape.

Other free-standing screens consist of three folding mesh panels or of a large, rigid panel shaped something like a giant coal shovel.

Fireplaces with tempered glass doors which are built into fireplace openings are the equivalent from the safety standpoint of built-in mesh screens. Their particular value, however, is in permitting better control of the draft in fireplaces with several openings.

FIRE STOP

A piece of material set into a wall between studs to stop fire from spreading from a lower to a higher floor. The simplest kind of fire stop is a 2 x 4 wooden block. However, fire stops are rarely required in today's houses because the plates block off the stud spaces between floors.

FIRE WALL

A wall designed to slow or stop the spread of fire. The construction depends on the building code. In a two-family house, for example, a fire wall between the dwelling units may be of masonry construction. On the other hand, a fire wall between an attached garage and a single-family house may be a conventional frame wall surfaced on the garage side with 5/8-in. gypsum board or the equivalent.

FISHED SPLICE

The simplest way to connect timbers end to end. The ends of the opposing timbers are squared, butted, and held in place by fishplates, or scabs, that are nailed, screwed, or bolted to the sides. A fished splice is a *compression splice.*

FISHPLATE

A short metal plate or board nailed or bolted over joined pieces of wood to hold them together. It is the same thing as a *scab.*

FISH WIRE

A flexible but stiff, flat wire with a small hook in the end. It is used to pull (snake) electric wires through conduits and flexible cables through the framework of a house.

FITTING

A small device which joins parts of a plumbing or electrical system, or is fitted into a plumbing system. For example, couplings, elbows, and unions are pipe fittings. Faucets, shower heads, and pop-up drain stoppers are plumbing fittings.

FIXTURE

A toilet, lavatory, sink, bathtub, shower stall, or permanently installed light. Bathroom soap dishes, towel rods, toilet paper holders, etc., are also called fixtures, or accessories.

FLAGSTONE

A gray, blue, or brown sandstone cut into thin, flat slabs and used for paving outdoors and flooring indoors. It is durable, strong, and skidproof without being objectionally rough.

Flagstones are available pre-cut into squares and rectangles of many sizes, and they can be ordered specially cut to any size or shape. They are also sold in uncut irregular shapes. Standard thickness is 1½ in.

Flagstones are generally laid in mortar with ½-in. joints between stones; but for terraces they may be laid without mortar on a sand and gravel base, and indoors they may also be laid without mortar on a plywood subfloor. In the latter cases, the joints are made as tight as possible. For walks, the stones are frequently set directly into holes scooped out of the soil.

FLAKEBOARD

A type of particleboard made with large, flakelike bits of wood. *See* Particleboard.

FLAME STITCH

A variation of bargello *(see above)* with a jagged design resembling flickering flames.

FLANGE

A projecting part of an edge. Paper-backed rolls of insulation, for example, have flanges along the edges for fastening to studs and joists.

FLARING EAVE

A pitched roof which is curved gently upward—like a ski jump—just before the eaves. It was a characteristic of many Dutch Colonial houses.

FLASHING

Sheets of metal, asphalt roll roofing, plastic, or rubber used to waterproof joints which are particularly likely to leak. Of the three metals used, aluminum is currently the commonest because it is relatively inexpensive, and is generally resistant to corrosion (although it is quickly eaten out in seacoast areas and some industrial atmospheres, and cannot be placed in direct contact with concrete). Copper is an older and better flashing material, but it is priced too high for widespread use. Galvanized steel is also used, but it rusts out too quickly to be given serious thought.

Fifty-five pound asphalt roll roofing can be substituted for metal only for flashing valleys and eaves. Plastic and rubber flashing is used only around plumbing vents.

The main use for flashing is on roofs. It is installed in the following ways:

In Valleys • In an open valley (the roofing on the adjacent roof slopes is separated by an open space), wide strips of metal or roll roofing are laid in the valley in a single strip from top to bottom. The roofing overlaps the edges of the strips at least 4 in. and is fastened with roofing cement—not nails.

In a closed valley (in which the roofing comes together at the center of the valley), the flashing is made of short pieces of metal which are bent diagonally and interleaved with the shingles.

At the Juncture of a Roof and Exterior Wall • If the roof slope is perpendicular to the wall, a continuous strip of metal flashing is forced up under the siding material and lapped down over the top of the roof. This same installation may be made along the joint at the juncture of a wall and a roof with a slope which parallels the wall; but the flashing is done with small squares of metal which are folded in half, inserted under the siding, and interleaved with the roof shingles.

Around Chimneys • This is the most complicated flashing installation and should be made with metal by an expert. In essence, the flashing encases the entire lower section of the chimney and is bent down over the surrounding roof to form a large skirt. At the top, the flashing is inserted in joints in the chimney and held in place with mortar or caulking. All joints in the flashing are soldered.

Around Vent Stacks • Plastic or rubber "jackets" designed specifically to fit down around the stacks and spread out over the roof are used.

Eaves • Eaves flashing is not essential and is usually omitted in new houses; but it is the best way to prevent water from backing up a roof and dripping down into a house in winter when ice dams form in gutters and along the edges of the roof. The flashing is done with 3-ft.-wide strips of asphalt roll roofing which are laid on the roof deck parallel with the eaves. The lower edge of the roofing overlaps the edge of the roof a fraction of an inch. The upper edge should extend up the roof to a point at least 1 ft. inside the inside wall line.

In the past, flashing was also installed over the tops of window and door frames to keep water from dripping through the joints. The metal used was sandwiched between the siding and sheathing and bent out and down over the casings. However, wooden drip caps usually perform the same function today.

FLAT FINISH

A dull, lusterless paint finish. It soils more readily than a semi-gloss or gloss finish, and is more difficult to clean. It should therefore be used only on surfaces that are not generally touched by hand or otherwise exposed to soiling—walls and ceilings in living and sleeping areas, for example.

A flat finish is also called a *matte* or *eggshell finish* when reference is to paint or enamel, a *dull finish* when reference is to varnish.

FLAT ROOF

Flat roofs are easy and inexpensive to build, but they require extra framing in areas with very heavy snows. The roofs are pitched just enough to permit drainage. Suitable roofing materials are limited to built-up tar and gravel, silicone, and metal.

FLATWARE

Silver, stainless steel, or pewter cutlery as well as larger pieces, such as meat dishes and trays, which are more or less flat. They are often displayed in racks or cupboards, on shelves, etc.

FLIGHT

A continuous run of steps. If a stair is interrupted by a landing, it is made up of two flights.

FLITCH

A log which has been rough-sawn on two opposite sides or sometimes on all four sides.

FLOAT VALVE

See Valve, Plumbing.

FLOCK

Finely powdered, velvety wool or other material applied to the surface of wall coverings in a decorative design to give texture. Flock collects dust, soils easily, and is difficult to clean; but some flocked wallcoverings are washable.

FLOOR

Except in slab houses, where the floor is made of poured concrete overlaid with the finish flooring, most residential floors are built—though not necessarily finished—with wood.

The floor joists are made of 2-in.-thick timbers, 6, 8, 10, or 12 in. wide. The width used depends, among other things, on the length and spacing of the joists. Normal spacing is 16 in. center to center, but this is sometimes reduced to 12 or increased to 24. The joists are braced with rows of bridging spaced not more than 8 ft. apart.

If the joists are spaced 16 in. apart and the finish floor is to be made of wooden strips 25/32 in. thick, the subfloor can be made of 1 x 4, 1 x 6, or 1 x 8-in. boards laid diagonally or at right angles to the joists. Normal practice, however, is to use ½-in. plywood sheets laid with the outer plies at right angles to the joists. The end joints must be staggered. The plywood is put down with nails spaced 6 in. on center along all edges and 10 in. through the middle. The subfloor is covered with building paper.

Under resilient flooring, 5/8-in. plywood covered with ¼-in. hardboard, plywood, or particleboard underlayment is used. However, if the resilient flooring is to be level with wooden flooring, ¾-in. plywood should be used as the base.

Ceramic tile cemented down with adhesive is laid over a subfloor consisting of 5/8-in. plywood covered with 3/8-in. exterior grade plywood.

When thicker materials such as bricks or slates are used for flooring, the joists should be dropped or made of narrower timbers to bring the finish floor flush with adjacent wood floors.

FLOORCLOTH
An area rug made of canvas (*see above*).

FLOOR DRAIN
A grated opening through which water accumulating on a basement or garage floor—or wherever the drain is installed—is carried away. It should be connected only to a storm sewer, not to a sanitary sewer or septic system. To be of any value, it must, of course, be located at the lowest point of the floor.

FLOOR FURNACE
See Space Heating.

FLOOR PLAN
A plan for one floor of a house, showing the location of walls, stairs, windows, etc. *See* Working Drawing.

FLOOR SINK
See Sink.

FLORAL
A fabric or wallcovering patterned with flowers.

FLOUNCE

A strip of fabric like a ruffle, but wider, used to decorate a bedspread, slipcover, etc. It is stitched to the body of the article along the top edge and hangs loose along the bottom edge.

FLUE

A large clay pipe which exhausts the products of combustion to the outside air. Each fireplace has its own flue. In addition, gas-fired and oil-fired furnaces and water heaters also have flues. No flue should serve more than one heat source; but all flues are ordinarily installed together in a single chimney and separated by mortar. At the top, if the chimney is capped, withes (*see below*) are built between the flues.

FLUORESCENT PAINT

An exceptionally bright paint with high visibility which glows at night upon exposure to light. It is used for safety purposes inside and outside a house, and also for decorating. Several formulations are sold. They are applied in a thick, even layer with a brush.

FLUORESCENT TUBE

As opposed to incandescent bulbs, fluorescent tubes cost much more but last seven to ten times longer, provide three to four times as much light per watt, and produce less heat.

The majority of fluorescent tubes are straight tubes used in large, heavy metal fixtures, often called *channels*, which incorporate a ballast that controls the current. Some tubes which require a starter—a small metal can inserted in the fixture—are known as *preheat tubes.* These take several seconds to start. Other types of tubes, which light almost instantly, do not require starters. These are called *rapid-start* or *trigger-start tubes.* Preheat tubes are made in more sizes than rapid-start or trigger-start tubes.

Circular and U–shaped fluorescent tubes are also made but not widely used. The former are called *circline tubes*, the latter *mod-u-lines*. Neither requires a starter. Sizes are limited.

The straight fluorescent tubes in most common use in homes are 15, 20, 25, 30, and 40-watt T-12 tubes. (T stands for tubular; 12 means the diameter of the tube measures 12 eighths of an inch.) Fifteen-watt tubes are 18 in. long; 20 watt, 24 in.; 25 watt, 33 in.; 30 watt, 36 in.; and 40 watt, 48 in. If more than one tube is used in a light fixture, all should be of the same color and same diameter; but they need not be the same length.

Although fluorescent fixtures are wired into the household electrical system like incandescent fixtures, their installation presents two slight complications. Because of the weight of the ballast, extra care must be taken to anchor the fixture securely through the wall or ceiling surface into the studs or joists. And the fixture must be separated from a combustible surface such as wood or plywood by a layer of fire-resistant material or an air space.

FLUSH

Forming a level, smooth surface. A wall made of boards installed edge to edge is a flush wall composed of flush boards.

FLUSH DOOR

See Door.

FLUSH VALVE

See Valve, Plumbing.

FLUTE

A fairly large, concave groove used to decorate columns, pilasters, and trim. Such things are said to be fluted.

FLUX

A material used to clean oxides from metal which is to be soldered. It is made of a rosin paste or an acid liquid. When solid solder is used, the flux is brushed on the metal first. Some wire solder contains a core of flux which cleans the metal as the solder melts.

FOAM

Latex, or rubber, foam and urethane foam have become the basic cushioning materials in today's furniture because of their ready availability and economy, and because they spring back to their normal shape after they have been compressed.

FOLDING SCREEN

A screen comprised of two or more vertical panels hinged together, usually with double-action hinges so the panels can be swung in a 360° circle. Most screens are roughly 5 ft. tall or more so they can be used as dividers or to hide things in corners.

FOLK ART
Arts and crafts which originated among common people. Quilts made by Kentucky mountaineers are an example.

FOOD PREPARATION CENTER
An electrical kitchen appliance used for mixing, blending, grinding, shredding, juicing, etc. Most food preparation centers are portable appliances with a general similarity to a mixer. One make, however, has a motor which is built into a kitchen counter—usually near the sink. The attachments are plugged into this.

FOOTCANDLE
The unit for measuring light. One footcandle equals approximately the light produced by a candle measured at a distance of 1 ft.

FOOTING
A footing is a thick, rectangular, below-ground concrete slab required to support foundation walls and piers. Because of its size, it distributes the weight of the structure above over a greater area and helps to prevent settlement. It also adds stability to the structure.

Footings should be laid below the frost line in cold climates and at least 2 ft. deep in frost-free climates. They should project at least 4 in. to both sides of the wall or pier and should be twice as deep as one of the projections. For a typical 8-in. wall, the footing is 16 in. wide and 8 in. deep.

Most footings are made of poured concrete consisting of 1 sack portland cement, 2¼ cu. ft. sand, and 4 cu. ft. coarse aggregate.

FOOTLAMBERT
The unit for measuring the brightness of light. The brightness of a perfectly white, diffuse surface placed 1 ft. from a candle is approximately one footlambert.

FOOTSTOOL

A small, low, stool-like furniture piece for resting the feet on. It generally has a padded top which may be covered with petit point or crewel. An *ottoman* is a large footstool.

FOUNDATION

The foundations of a house support and stabilize the entire above-ground structure. All houses, even those built on floating slabs, require them. In the great majority of houses, the foundations consist of concrete walls and footings; but in a few houses—mainly small vacation homes—they consist of concrete, steel, or wooden piers anchored to concrete footings.

The footings are made of poured concrete laid below the frost line or at least 2 ft. below grade in frost-free climates. *See* Footing. Eight-inch-thick foundation walls are built up from these to the height of the sills. In very early houses, the walls were constructed of stone or brick. Then came poured concrete, which is still used to a limited extent. Today concrete blocks are almost always used because of their economy and the speed with which they can be put up.

Even though the area enclosed by the foundation walls may not be used for a basement, three steps should be taken to keep the area dry:

1 / Four-inch drain pipes are laid around the entire house beside the footings. The pipes may be perforated plastic tubes or clay tiles laid with open joints (which are covered with asphalt building paper to keep out soil). The pipes are sloped very slightly toward a drain which carries water away to a storm sewer or other disposal area. Crushed rock is piled over the pipes to a depth of 12 to 18 in.

2 / Foundation walls built of concrete block are parged with two ¼-in. thicknesses of cement plaster and one or two coats of asphalt waterproofing compound.

3 / After the trenches in which the foundations are built have been back-filled and the soil has settled, the ground is graded away from all walls for at least 6 ft.

FRAME

To construct the basic framework, or skeleton, of a building. This involves cutting and fastening together the studs, joists, plates, headers, beams, rafters, etc.

FRAMING

The framework of a house. It is built in two ways:

Balloon Framing • This is no longer widely used but had many adherents among two-story home builders before World War II. The system was characterized by the use of two-story-high studs in outside walls and interior load-bearing partitions. Joists for the second floor rested on ribbon boards nailed to the studs.

A balloon-framed house has more rigidity than one framed by the platform method, and there is less shrinkage of materials. Pipes and cables can be run from one floor to another without cutting the plates. But the installation of firestops between studs is required.

Platform Framing • Almost all houses are framed this way today. After the foundations are completed, the first floor is constructed. Then the framework for each exterior and interior wall is laid out and put together on the floor, and tilted upright into place. Then the second floor is constructed, and the walls for the second story are erected on this. Platform framing—also called *western framing*—is faster and safer than balloon framing and permits maximum use of short lengths of 2 x 4 for studding.

FRANKLIN STOVE

A free-standing iron stove developed by Benjamin Franklin for heating rooms. The design has been somewhat variable, but the stove has always been popular—mainly because of its efficiency—and is still made today. It should be installed, like other free-standing fireplaces, on a fireproof base set out about a foot from all walls.

FREE FORM

A shape which does not conform to the conventional. The lines are usually curving and flow into one another. Some furniture is of free-form design; but the most popular current use of free-form design is in pools.

FREE-STANDING

Not permanently built in.

FREEZER

Food freezers for freezing and storing food at zero temperature are designed as upright, front-opening cabinets closely resembling refrigerators and as top-opening chests. The average upright, with 12 to 15 cu. ft. of storage space, is almost exactly the same size as the most popular sizes of refrigerator. Some units are small enough to fit under a kitchen counter, while the largest are roughly twice the size of the average refrigerator.

Chest freezers are about the same height as kitchen counters and several inches deeper. A 12-cu.-ft. model is about 4 ft. long; a 22-cu.-ft. model, about 5 ft.; and the largest sizes, about 6 ft.

Chest freezers take up more floor space and, when the lid is raised, more wall space than uprights. On the other hand, it is necessary to allow deeper floor space in front of an upright to accommodate the swinging door.

A freezer should not be installed in the kitchen work area because it takes up more space than is warranted by the infrequency of use. But it usually should be close to the work area so the homemaker doesn't waste time and steps going to and from it.

FRENCH FOOT

A bracket foot (*see above*) which is curved slightly outward. It is always combined with a valanced apron in furniture pieces.

FRENCH POLISH

A beautiful but tedious-to-apply clear finish for fine furniture. It consists basically of eight or more coats of thinned white shellac which is rubbed on the surface with a cloth pad, allowed to dry, and then smoothed with fine steel wool and pumice.

FRENCH PROVINCIAL

Under the French monarchs of the 18th century—Louis XIV, XV, and XVI—furniture designed for members of the court was successively baroque, rococo and classic. French provincial was the ordinary man's less elaborate interpretation of these styles. In this, rococo curves were simplified and classic lines softened. The result is charming and somewhat feminine, although many pieces were large. The most characteristic feature of the furniture is the moderately complex curves given to the aprons of upholstered chairs, sofas, and case pieces.

FRETWORK

An ornamental pattern of interlacing lines which are carved in relief or silhouetted by cutting out the material between the lines to form a screen.

FRIEZE

A wide, horizontal band often decoratively carved or molded on an outside wall or the side of a piece of furniture. In houses the frieze is most commonly the horizontal trim board nailed to the wall immediately below the cornice. In classic architecture, it is the middle part of an entablature.

Frieze is also a heavy wool fabric used in upholstery because it is durable. But it is stiff and scratchy. The pile is made of loops of varying height.

FROG

A recessed panel in the face of a brick, tile, etc.

FRONTAGE

The distance between the side lines of a lot measured along the front line. If the front of a lot is curved or irregular, the frontage may be figured as a straight line between two designated points on the side lines.

Road frontage, lake frontage, river frontage, and ocean frontage are terms obviously descriptive of specific types of frontage. Some properties have two or even more kinds of frontage.

FRONT HALL

Also known as a *vestibule*, a front hall is a room just inside the main entrance through which people must pass to reach the principal rooms of a house. Although it is sometimes considered waste space—and therefore omitted from houses—a front hall actually gets heavy usage and serves a number of important purposes:

1 / It serves as a buffer to keep unwanted visitors from disturbing occupants of adjacent rooms and even from seeing into those rooms.

2 / It is a place to greet and say goodbye to guests.

3 / It is a place to collect delivered parcels and guest luggage prior to distribution elsewhere in the house.

4 / It provides space for taking off and hanging up outer clothing. Thus, it keeps clutter and dirt out of the rest of the house.

5 / It is a connecting link between rooms and areas, and facilitates circulation through a house. The stairway

to the second floor usually originates in the front
hall.

In palatial homes the front hall is sometimes enormous; but in
small homes it is commonly so cramped that two people can hardly
turn around. Actually, because of its many uses, it should have an
area of at least 40—preferably 50—sq. ft.; and its minimum
dimension should be 6 ft.

FROSTED
Given a finish resembling heavy frost: for example,
frosted glass.

FROST LINE
The depth to which the ground usually freezes in
winter. To provide stability, the footings of a house must be laid
below the frost line. Metal pipes carrying water should also be laid
below the frost line to prevent freezing and bursting.

FRUITWOOD
Pearwood (*see below*). In low-cost furniture, fruitwood
is any close-grained hardwood such as gum which is given a
grayish-brown finish.

FUNCTIONAL
Made to serve a purpose of the user. A house and
furniture can be strictly functional, but since they feel cold or even
crude, the designer generally gives them aesthetic values, too.

FUR
Animal furs used for rugs, throws, or wall hangings are
inevitably central features of the decorating scheme in which they
are used; but they require care to keep them worthy of attention.
Exposure to too much sunlight or heat is likely to dry out and
crack the leather and precipitate loss of hair. In some cases, fading
may occur. Equally troublesome are moths, which should be warded
off by semi-annual moth treatment and regular cleaning by a
qualified fur cleaner.

FURNACE

The central heating unit in a warm-air heating system. (The corresponding unit in a steam or hot-water system is a *boiler.*)

FURNITURE ARRANGING

Furniture is arranged in rooms to meet the requirements of the occupants. But the arrangements are also dictated by the sizes and shapes of both the furniture pieces and the rooms.

In most rooms of a house, the furniture arrangement goes unchanged once it has been worked out satisfactorily because activities in the rooms rarely change. In the dining room, the table and chairs are centered in the room. In bedrooms, the beds are placed against the largest available wall space and the bureaus are arranged near the closets because most traffic is between the closets and bureaus and the entrance to the room.

Furniture arranging in a living room, on the other hand, is never set because too many different things happen in the room: People read by themselves and write by themselves; they converse in groups of varying size; they watch television and listen to music by themselves and in groups; they play the piano for people who sit back and listen and for those who gather round and sing; and so on.

To accommodate to this milling about, the homemaker's best approach is to arrange the room for a large group of talkers and, if the room is big enough and so shaped, to set up secondary areas for the piano and television set. But generally the fireplace is the center around which the sofa and related chairs and tables are grouped.

One happy aspect of the whole situation is that no furniture arrangement is ever the last word. It can be—and often is—completely changed a couple of times a year just because change seems like a good idea. It can also be changed temporarily and piece-meal when a change in guests or activities demands it.

FURNITURE CHECK

A checkered fabric occasionally used to cover the backs of upholstered chairs and sofas, thus reducing the amount of expensive fabric needed to cover the fronts.

FURRING

Rough 1 x 2- or 1 x 3-in. boards which serve as a nailing base for rigid interior wall or ceiling surface materials such as gypsum board, plywood, hardboard, or solid board paneling. The boards, commonly called *furring strips*, may be used in several ways:

1 / They are nailed directly to an old wall or ceiling which is not level enough or in good enough repair to permit direct application of a new surfacing material.

2 / They are applied to masonry walls to simplify attachment of a surfacing material and/or to protect the material from dampness in the masonry.

3 / They are nailed directly to a stud wall to serve as a nailing base for vertical board paneling.

The process of applying furring to a wall is known as *furring out* the wall. When furring is used on a ceiling, the ceiling is said to be *furred down*.

Furring is applied horizontally when a wall is to be paneled with 1-in.-thick boards. One strip is installed at a bottom of the wall, another at the top, and two more equally spaced between. But when an existing wall is to be covered with gypsum board, plywood, or any other thin sheet material, the furring strips are applied vertically, with one strip directly under each vertical edge of the surfacing material and usually with two strips between.

FUSE

A safety device which is designed to "blow" and shut off the flow of electricity when a circuit has a short or becomes overloaded. Fuses have been largely supplanted in today's homes by circuit breakers because fuses must be replaced when they blow—and this is a more troublesome little job than resetting a circuit breaker. On the other hand, a fuse is as safe and efficient as a circuit breaker, and a fuse box filled with fuses is less expensive to buy and install than a circuit breaker panel.

Two basic types of fuse are used. *Plug fuses* are screw-in devices used for most lighting and appliance circuits. They are made in 10, 15, 20, 25, and 30-amp sizes. The conventional plug fuse is screwed directly into a socket in the fuse box. In a nontamperable fuse, often called a *Fustat*, the fuse consists of an adapter which screws into the fuse box and the fuse itself, which screws into the adapter.

Cartridge fuses resembling firecrackers are made in 10- to 60-amp sizes but are used primarily to protect circuits serving appliances which use large amounts of power.

Both plug and cartridge fuses are also available with a time-delay feature which permits a momentary overload without blowing the fuse. These are used only in circuits serving large motors which require a higher current when they start than when they are running normally.

In the home, lighting circuits made with No. 14 wire are fused at 15 amps. Lighting and appliance circuits made with No. 12 wire are fused at 20 amps.

FUSE BOX

The box in which fuses are installed. Most houses have a single fuse box (or circuit breaker panel) installed on the house side of the master switch. But in a large house, several fuse boxes may be installed near the points at which electricity is most heavily used.

GABLE

The triangular wall area under a sloping roof. Although gables are usually associated with gable roofs, a house with a gambrel room or a shed roof also has gables.

GABLE ROOF

A roof shaped like a pup tent.

GADROON

Ornamentation consisting of repeated curves and flutes used on edges of furniture and silver.

GAIN

A notch or mortise cut to receive a piece. The mortise for a hinge is called a gain.

GALLERY

In architecture, this is a very imprecise word which is best restricted to a long, rather narrow area with a roof or ceiling, a wall on one side, and glass or no wall at all on the other side. In other words, a gallery is a narrow porch or lanai.

In furniture, a gallery is a small ornamental railing around the top of a table, desk, etc.

A gallery is also a huge concrete-block-lined hole in the ground used to dispose of the effluent in a septic system.

GALLOON

A flat, wide braid used to trim draperies and upholstered furniture. *Compare* Gimp.

GALVANIC CORROSION

Corrosion which occurs when two dissimilar metals are in contact in the presence of moisture. To prevent it, the metals should be insulated from one another. Better still, only one metal should be used. For example, aluminum flashing should be installed with aluminum nails, not steel nails.

GALVANIZED STEEL

Steel coated with zinc. It is used wherever there is moisture which might rust ordinary steel; but in time the zinc coating wears off, and the steel starts to rust. All nails in the exterior of a house should be galvanized. Galvanized steel is also used for gutters and leaders and for screen wire.

If galvanized steel is painted, it should be primed with a zinc-dust primer and overcoated with an alkyd or oil house paint.

GALVANIZED STEEL ROOFING

Flat or corrugated steel sheets which are laid up and down a roof. They measure approximately 2 ft. wide and 6 to 12 ft. long. Edges of corrugated sheets are overlapped; those of flat sheets are interlocked or soldered.

Galvanized steel roofing is used mainly in rural homes because it is fire and wind resistant, and if kept painted, it lasts many years. But it is noisy and unattractive.

Installation can be made over a solid deck, spaced boards, or—if corrugated steel is used—widely spaced purlins. A minimum roof pitch of 3 in. in 1 ft. is required.

GAMBREL ROOF

A rather steeply pitched roof sloping in two directions. The two sides of the roof are, in effect, bent slightly outward like a partially raised leaf on a drop-leaf table. The lower half of the slope is steeper than the upper half.

GAME ROOM

A game room today is the same thing as a recreation room, but in large houses of earlier eras, it was used only by adults—mainly men—for billiards and cards.

GARAGE

Garages have continually grown in size, not just because more families own more cars and because cars have grown larger but also because they are called on to store just about everything else for which there is no space indoors. (This requirement has been greatly aggravated by the trend away from basements and attics.) Even so, the average garage is not as large as it should be.

Today no garage should be built for less than two cars or measure less than 20 x 20 ft. This size permits the homeowner to squeeze into and out of the cars but provides no space for storing lawnmowers, wheelbarrows, lawn furniture, bicycles, etc. Consequently, the true minimum size for a garage is 25 x 25 ft.

Whether attached to or separate from the house, a garage should, if possible, be placed so that the doors open toward the side or rear lot line, not toward the front. Aesthetically, a garage has little to offer, and when the doors are open—as they are most of the time—it is hideous. It follows that there is no sense in letting it spoil the appearance of the property from the street any more than is necessary.

Single garage doors are easier to operate than double doors, are more attractive, and permit opening only half of the garage at once. They are usually 8 ft. wide, but installation of a 9- or 10-ft. width makes it easier to drive into a garage—especially when there is a turn-around in front of the garage. Normal width of double doors is 15 to 16 ft., but an 18-ft. width is preferable.

Garages are constructed on slabs with foundations extending below the frost line. The floor should be several inches lower than the house floor and sloped toward the door or a central floor drain. Interior walls are generally left open. If covered, 5/8-in. gypsum board should be installed on the wall between the garage and house for fire safety. The door in the wall should be of fire-resistant design also.

A hose bibb is usually installed in the garage for washing cars, filling radiators, and watering the garden, and it can be made even more useful if a laundry tub or sink is installed underneath. This can be allowed to drain directly onto the garage floor.

Lights in the garage should be controlled by three-way switches next to the garage doors and the door into the house. In a two-car garage, one light is positioned on the ceiling above the engine of each car, and a third light should be between the cars near the garage door.

GARAGE DOOR

Overhead garage doors—the only type now in use—are made of wood, steel, aluminum, hardboard, or fiberglass in flush and panel designs. Metal and fiberglass are the most durable; wood is the most attractive but should be saturated with wood preservative to prevent rotting.

The doors operate in several ways. Sectional doors, made in several horizontal panels, slide up and back in a curved metal track. They are the most popular type in cold climates because they fit tight against the jambs, thus keeping out rain and snow. Because they slide straight up for several feet (before curving backward), their operation is not impeded by snow drifting against them.

Other doors are made in one rigid piece. These are slightly easier to open if properly balanced; but because they swing outward at the bottom, snow interferes with their movement. Some fit tight against the jambs; others do not.

Width of garage doors is discussed above (*see* Garage). A point which must be considered in selecting the type to be used is the clearance required between a door and the garage ceiling when the door is opened. This varies from about 6 to as much as 18 in.

GARAGE DOOR OPENER

A 120-volt electrical device which automatically raises and lowers a garage door and locks it. The unit is controlled by a small radio transmitter in the homeowner's car and also by an electrical switch in the garage or house.

GARBAGE DISPOSER

Fitted under the drain opening in a sink, a garbage disposer grinds food into small particles and washes them down the drain into the sewer. It is effective with virtually all food matter except occasionally corn husks and similar fibers and fruit pits. It also gets rid of paper and cigarette butts if these are mixed with food waste, but it should not be used for other materials.

A disposer requires an individual 20-amp, 120-volt wiring circuit, or it can share a similar circuit with a dishwasher. It is approved for use on the great majority of municipal sewer systems, and is required in some communities (but banned in a few others). It is also approved for houses with septic systems (but not cesspools) of specified capacity (*see* Septic System).

Two types of disposer are sold. The *batch-feed* unit which handles one load at a time is turned on and off by a special stopper-like cover in the sink opening. The *continuous-feed* unit is controlled by a wall switch and will continue to grind up food wastes as long as these are dropped into the grinding chamber.

GAS
Natural gas is supplied to a house through an underground main installed by the utility at no expense to the homeowner. It terminates at the meter outside the foundation walls. From there 1- to 1¼-in. feeder lines are run into the house to each gas-burning appliance by the gas utility or a plumber. The cost is borne by the homeowner. The piping is usually exposed but may be concealed in a raceway which can be opened for servicing.

GATE LEG
A swinging leg supporting a table leaf.

GATE VALVE
See Valve, Plumbing.

GATHERED
A fabric which is drawn up into informal folds by running a thread through it for a short distance, then stitching in place. Gathering is done to give fullness to a curtain, dressing table skirt, etc. *Shirring* is a form of gathering.

GAUGE
To measure. Also, to mix plaster with water.

As a noun, gauge is the diameter or thickness of a material. For example, the thickness of metal is the gauge; the diameter of a screw is the gauge.

As applied to knitted fabrics, the gauge is the number of loops per 1½ in.

GAUZE
Also called *theatrical gauze*, an open, crisp cotton or linen fabric used for curtains.

GEORGETTE
A sheer silk crepe fabric with a pebbled effect used for curtains and bedspreads.

GEORGIAN
Georgian architecture and furniture flourished in England and America in the 1700s. They exhibited a classic elegance and formality which have made the style popular with almost everyone, even though the houses were generally much larger than a family of modest means could aspire to.

Outstanding examples of Georgian homes in the United States include Gunston Hall and Kenmore in Virginia, Hammond-Harwood house in Maryland, and Longfellow house in Massachusetts. The furniture of the period was designed by Chippendale, Hepplewhite, and Sheraton.

GESSO
A mixture of plaster of Paris, glue, and water applied to wood to produce a very smooth base for paint or gilt.

GILT
The gold leaf, gold coating, or gold-colored substance applied to furniture, ceramics, silver, etc.

GIMP
A narrow, ornamental braid used to trim draperies and furniture. *Compare* Galloon.

GINGERBREAD
The elaborately cut-out or carved trim on the exterior of many 19th century houses. Gingerbread is gaudy, whimsical, rococo—often charming but lacking the elegance of classic trim.

GINGHAM
A fabric made of crisp cotton or a blend of cotton and synthetic printed in checks, stripes, and plaids. It is used in curtains.

GIRANDOLE
An ornate wall bracket with one or more arms for candles. A mirror is often centered in the bracket. Girandoles are also designed for placement on tables, mantel shelves, etc.

GIRDER
A large, horizontal wooden or steel beam supporting joists or walls. If made of wood, it is usually a single timber, but it may be

made of thin timbers spiked or bolted together. A so-called *spaced girder* is made of thin timbers joined in such a way as to provide an open channel in which to run pipes and cables.

GIRTH
Circumference of a round timber, etc.

GLASS
Flat glass for windows, doors, shelves, table tops, shower stalls, etc., is available in many forms.

Sheet Glass • This is ordinary window glass. *Grade B*, called *common*, has most imperfections; *Grade A* has fewer; *Grade AA* has least. Sheet glass is available in *single-strength* thickness (3/32 in.), *double-strength* (1/8 in.), and *heavy* (3/16 and 7/32 in.). Single-strength is safe in openings up to about 2 x 2 ft., double-strength in openings up to 3 x 5 ft. Heavy sheet is for large openings or shelves.

Plate Glass • Plate is ground and polished glass used mainly in mirrors to provide an undistorted view and in very thick shelves. Common thicknesses are 1/8 and ¼ in., and for most jobs the grade known as *glazing* is satisfactory. Heavy plate glass, used mainly for shelves, table tops, and wherever it is subject to considerable weight or pressure, is made in thicknesses from 3/8 to 1¼ in.

Float Glass • Very similar in appearance to plate but not of quite the same quality. Thicknesses of ¼ in. and less are commonly used in medium-grade mirrors.

Tinted Glass • Plate glass used in large windows to reduce glare. Gray and bronze distort colors least and reduce glare almost 50%; blue-green both reduces glare (about 25%) and absorbs heat.

Tempered Glass • This is plate glass which has been given a special heating and cooling treatment to increase its strength four or five times. If broken, it breaks safely into fragments like rock salt. It is required in sliding doors and should also be used in one-pane floor-to-ceiling windows, hinged and swinging doors, and shower doors.

Patterned Glass • Any glass which is textured, molded, frosted, etc., to make it translucent. It is available in a great many patterns and in several thicknesses. It is used primarily for dividers, for shower stalls, and in windows exposed to the street or neighbors.

Wire Glass • Glass in which fine wire mest is embedded to give it strength and resistance to breaking.

Laminated Glass • Similar to the glass in automobile windows, this is made with a thin transparent sheet of plastic sandwiched between glass layers. The plastic may be colored or printed with designs.

Insulating Glass • An expensive window and door glass consisting of two layers of glass with a hermetically sealed air space between. It reduces heat loss as much as 50%. Although usually made with clear glass, it is available with patterned, tempered, tinted, etc., glass.

Picture Glass • Very thin sheet glass used for covering framed pictures.

Nonreflecting Glass • A heavier picture glass with a finish which permits view of a framed picture even when light shines on it. However, the glass is not favored by many artists because it may distort colors and/or obscure a picture which is viewed from the side.

GLASS BLOCK

A hollow cube of glass used to build nonload-bearing interior walls and panels in exterior walls. Some blocks are transparent, but most are patterned or textured to transmit light while obscuring vision. The latter are made simply to diffuse light or to angle it toward the ceiling.

Because they are thick and incorporate a sealed air space, glass blocks have good sound and thermal insulating characteristics. They resist impact but are not strong enough to support a load.

Glass blocks are 3-7/8 in. thick and made in 5¾-, 7¾-, and 11¾-in. squares (the most popular sizes). They are laid up in a stacked bond with cement mortar reinforced with special metal strips and wires. The exposed concave joints are ¼ in. thick (at the center of the blocks, the mortar is much thicker). Partitions can also be constructed with a rather elaborate wooden framework.

GLASS CERAMIC

A new man-made material closely related to glass and ceramics. It is used in household articles which must be very strong and heat resistant. One type goes into cooking utensils, another into tableware.

GLASSWARE

Objects made of glass for holding liquids or food. They may be made of ordinary glass or of crystal, but in either case, they play an important role in the decoration of dining tables, sideboards, etc. Glasses with stems are also known as *stemware*.

GLAZE
A fast-drying clear coating applied over a painted surface to produce special effects. It is made of 1 part linseed oil, 3 parts turpentine, and colors in oil.

GLAZE COATING
Sometimes called a *tile-like coating*, this material is made with plastic resins to produce an extremely hard, dense, abrasion- and stain-resistant, easily cleaned interior or exterior wall finish. Some types of finish resemble smooth paint or varnish; others have a texture; and still others are surfaced with sand, pebbles, or marble chips.

Depending on the formulation, glaze coatings can be applied to masonry, plaster, gypsum board, plywood, or hardboard. But the work tends to be difficult, and many manufacturers insist that it be done only by professionals.

GLAZIER'S POINT
A small, triangular- or diamond-shaped piece of flat metal. It is used to hold window panes in the frames.

GLAZING COMPOUND
A plastic, putty-like material smoothed around the edges of window panes to help hold them in place and to seal out air and moisture.

GLIDE
A small, stainless steel dome which is tapped into the end of a furniture leg to permit easy sliding.

Swivel glides are designed with a swivel connection between the base and the stem which attaches to the furniture leg. The base rests flat on the floor, regardless of the angle at which the furniture leg is set.

GLOBE VALVE
See Valve, Plumbing.

GLOSS FINISH

A very shiny paint, varnish, or other finish. It is more washable than any other finish, but it is so glossy that it is not particularly recommended for walls and ceilings, even in kitchens and bathrooms. It is better suited to woodwork which gets very hard wear and to furniture. Even so, gloss varnish is so mirror-like that it should be dulled with fine steel wool or pumice.

All floor paints have a gloss finish because they require frequent washing.

GLUE

See Adhesive.

GODET

An inset, usually pie-shaped, sewn into an article to give it fullness and to add to its decorative effect. Godets are often used in bedspreads, for example.

GOLD LEAF

Gold in extremely thin sheets which is applied to an object, such as a mirror frame or piece of furniture, for ornament. Gold-leaf work is prized not only because the material is expensive and intricate to apply but mainly because it has an elegant beauty not equalled by other gilding methods.

GOOSENECK

Anything curved roughly like a goose's neck. A stair rail often incorporates a gooseneck to join the bottom end at the newel post to the straight rail above.

GRAB-BAR

A projecting bar anchored to and parallel with a wall which a person holds on to as he pulls himself up, lets himself down, or supports himself in an upright position. It is installed in shower baths and also next to toilets in bathrooms used by the elderly or handicapped.

GRADE

The level of the ground. The grade can usually be raised or lowered to accommodate a new house; but the less filling or excavating that is done, the lower the cost of the house.

Concrete slabs used as floors in houses are said to be *on grade* if they rest directly on the ground, *below grade* if they are in a basement, and *above grade* if they are suspended above the ground.

GRAIN

The direction in which wood fibers run. Several terms are used to describe grain more fully:

Straight Grain • The grain runs in straight lines nearly parallel to the edges of the board.

Cross Grain • The grain runs at an angle to the edges of the board.

Spiral Grain • The grain follows a spiral pattern around the board.

Fine Grain • Wood with small cells producing a dense, smooth texture.

Open Grain • Wood with large, open cells giving a rough, porous texture.

Close Grain • The growth rings are closely spaced.

Coarse Grain • The growth rings are widely spaced.

End Grain • The grain exposed when a board is cross-cut.

Edge Grain • This term describes softwood lumber which is cut from a log in such a way that the growth rings cross the end of a board at a sharp angle and the grain on the face of the board is close and uniform. Edge-grain lumber is superior because it shrinks, warps, and splits little, and it wears evenly.

Flat Grain • This term describes softwood lumber cut so that the growth rings cross the end of a board at a shallow angle and the grain is open and variable. Flat-grain lumber is less desirable than edge-grain but cheaper.

Mixed Grain • A board with a mixture of edge and flat grain.

GRAND RAPIDS

Furniture mass-produced first in Grand Rapids and then in other American cities from the mid-19th century on. The style of the furniture changed with the times and followed popular tastes, but it is often sneered at by interior designers.

GRANITE
A hard, heavy stone containing feldspar and quartz crystals. It is usually gray but is sometimes almost white, pink, brownish-red, yellow, or green. Although not as easily cut as sandstone or limestone, granite is one of the handsomest stones available in the United States and has been used in the walls of many beautiful homes. It is also used for fireplaces and paving.

GRASSCLOTH
A fabric made of vegetable fibers or synthetics with a pronounced texture ranging from loosely woven linen to burlap to straw matting. The colors are muted and usually fade in sunlight.

Grasscloth is used as a wallcovering. It is laminated to a paper backing and put up in rolls 3 ft. wide by 24 ft. long. It is hung almost exactly like wallpaper, but the edges must be trimmed.

Other fabrics very similar to grasscloth are on the market. They are loosely known as grasscloth even though they are not the same.

GRASS RUG
Grass rugs are informal, attractive, durable rugs used indoors and out. They are produced in various sizes out of several types of grass; they may be a natural brown or straw color, or dyed. The rugs are usually laid directly on a floor but are sometimes cushioned with several thicknesses of newspaper or thin rubber padding.

GRAVEL STOP
An L-shaped metal strip installed at the edge of tar-and-gravel roofs to keep loose gravel from falling to the ground.

GREEK REVIVAL
Of the many architectural revivals, the Greek Revival period was the most important in the United States because it influenced the design of so many houses, churches, and public buildings. The period ran from about 1820 to 1850. Examples of the style are easily identified by the columns and colonnades which were used.

GREEN WOOD
Wood which has not been seasoned or which has been seasoned but still has a moisture content in excess of 19%.

Green wood is not only harder to work with and less stable than seasoned wood but also a little weaker.

GRILLE
A piece of openwork or grating used to cover an opening. Grilles serve various purposes such as obstructing vision, diffusing light, barring entrance to the opening, etc. For some purposes, the selection of the grille is critical; in other cases, it makes little difference.

GROSPOINT
Needlepoint made with large stitches. It is best used in pillows and wall hangings where it will not get heavy wear or be easily damaged.

GROUND
One of the wooden strips or metal beads nailed to the framework of a wall to ensure that plaster which is later applied is of the proper thickness. The grounds are applied around all wall openings, at the base of walls, and at outside corners. The plasterer smooths the plaster off level with the grounds.

GROUND FAULT CIRCUIT INTERRUPTER
Abbreviated *GFI*, this electrical device detects leakages of current—called *ground faults*—and cuts off the power before they can do any harm. It is designed to prevent accidents in case something goes wrong with the conventional grounding system (*see below*). GFIs today are required by the National Electrical Code to protect electrical equipment near swimming pools. They are also recommended for workshops and laundries.

GROUNDING
Connecting an electrical system to the earth in order to minimize danger of shocks and protect against lightning damage. In a grounded wiring system the cables contain three rather than two wires. The green ground wire runs from the exposed metal housing of, say, a water pump motor to a copper rod or steel pipe driven 7 ft. into the earth below the fuse box. In the case of a convenience outlet, the ground wire runs from the grounding terminal on the outlet to the metal rod. When an appliance with a three-prong plug is

plugged into the outlet, it is then grounded. In the event that the housing of the appliance or water pump becomes energized, the ground wire allows the current to flow to the ground; the circuit becomes overloaded, and the fuse blows.

GROUT
A very wet mortar usually made of cement and water. The degree of fluidity depends on the purpose of the grout. For example, when flagstones or ceramic tiles are laid for a floor on a concrete base, the base is brushed with a very soupy grout before a thick mortar layer is troweled on and the stones or tiles are laid. On the other hand, the grout used in filling (grouting) the joints in a ceramic tile wall or floor has more body but is still wet enough to apply with a sponge or squeegee.

GROWTH RING
One of the rings visible in the end grain of lumber or the butt of a log. It represents one year's growth. Each ring is divided into two parts—one composed of the *springwood* (*See below*), the other of the *summerwood* (*see below*). A growth ring is also called an *annular ring.*

GUERIDON
A small table or candlestand, usually round.

GUM
Cut from sweet gum trees, gum is very widely used in moderate- and low-cost furniture because it is strong, hard, and takes stain and paint well. The heartwood is reddish brown, the sapwood pinkish white. The grain is inconspicuous.

GUSSET
A piece of lumber or plywood used to hold together a truss at a juncture of the principal timbers. It is nailed or bolted in place. In mass-assembling trusses, fabricators usually use steel gussets rather than wood. These are flat plates with numerous projecting teeth on the underside.

GUTTER
Although gutters detract from the appearance of a house to a certain extent and are therefore omitted from many architect-

designed houses, they do several useful things simply by collecting
and disposing of the water which would otherwise drip and cascade
directly from the eaves.

1 / They direct water away from the foundations and
thus prevent leaky basements.

2 / They keep plants under the eaves from being battered
by falling water and ice.

3 / They keep wind from blowing falling water against
the side walls and windows.

4 / They protect people who are waiting to come in the
front or back doors.

Gutters are made of copper, aluminum, galvanized steel, vinyl,
and wood.

Aluminum with a durable baked-enamel finish is most widely
used today. The various gutter sections—troughs, elbows, end caps,
outlets, etc.—are held together by friction; the entire assembly is
hung from the edges of a roof by flexible straps, L-shaped hangers, or
spikes driven through ferrules.

Vinyl gutters are installed in the same way and are basically
comparable in performance. Their main advantage is that they never
need to be finished. On the other hand, tight joints are difficult to
make.

Copper and galvanized steel gutters are assembled by soldering,
and are much stronger and less likely to leak than aluminum or vinyl.
But galvanized steel is little used because it rusts out fairly rapidly.
And copper—the best of all gutter materials—has been priced off the
market.

Wooden gutters are occasionally used on custom-built traditional houses because they look more like integral parts of a house
than metal gutters. Nailed directly to the rafter ends, they are heavy
and strong, but are prone to splitting and rotting unless they are
treated with wood preservative and kept painted inside and out. The
joints are also hard to keep sealed.

Gutters are sloped 1/16 in. per foot. As a rule, only one leader
is needed for each 35 ft. of gutter. This can be installed at either end
or in the middle. If a gutter is over 35 ft. long, it is generally sloped
from the middle toward the ends, where the leaders are attached.

The leaders are ordinarily attached to gutters by two 45°
elbows which, in effect, push the leaders back against the house walls
to make them as invisible as possible. At the bottom of each leader,

another elbow is installed to direct the water away from the foundations. An alternative—and superior—arrangement is to extend the leader directly into a 4-in. drain pipe which carries the water down to the footing drains and then away from the house.

GYM SEAL
A very durable penetrating sealer for wooden floors.

GYPSUM BOARD
Also called *drywall* and *Sheetrock*, gypsum board is far and away the leading material for building interior walls and ceilings. It produces a durable, smooth, generally maintenance-free surface which is easy and economical to install. And because it is put up dry, it does not cause construction problems like plaster. On the other hand, because speculative builders try to cut costs by using thin gypsum board, the material can be blamed for the bad acoustical problems encountered in so many houses built in the past 25 years.

Consisting of a plaster core sandwiched between layers of strong paper, gypsum board is produced in panels 4 ft. wide and 6 to 16 ft. long. The panels are classified by thickness and type (not all types are available in all thicknesses):

Standard Board • The type a person is given when he asks a lumberyard simply for a sheet of gypsum board.

Superior Fire-Rated Board • With greater fire resistance than a standard board.

Special-Edged Board • The actual name applied to the board depends on the maker. As opposed to standard boards, which usually have square edges, these are shaped in various ways to increase the strength of joints when application is made to badly framed walls.

Foil-Back Board • Aluminum foil is glued to the back of the board to serve as a vapor barrier and as thermal insulation. The board is used only on the inside of exterior walls.

Backer Board • A low-cost gypsum board used in multi-ply construction of walls or ceilings.

Water-Resistant Backer Board • Used as a base for tile and plastic panels in bathrooms.

Vinyl-Faced Board • Gypsum board with a sheet of colored, patterned, or textured vinyl glued to the front to serve as a finish wall surface. A wall made of it is slightly cheaper than a conventional wall made of standard gypsum board which is then surfaced with a vinyl wallcovering, but the choice of colors, etc., is extremely limited.

Available thicknesses of gypsum board are:

- ¼ *in.*—should be applied only over an existing wall surface or backer board.
- 3/8 *in.*—used for multi-ply construction of walls and in a single layer on the ceilings of upper floors.
- ½ *in.*—normal thickness used on walls and ceilings.
- 5/8 *in.*—used to improve fire resistance of walls and/or to reduce noise transmission.

In new construction, gypsum panels are nailed directly to studs and joists. To prevent loosening of the nails, only annular-ring nails should be used. The joints between panels are then covered with a paper tape embedded in a cement-like joint compound and covered with three coats of compound. Inside corners are made in the same way; outside corners are covered with metal corner beads which are concealed with joint compound.

Gypsum board can also be applied to furring strips over masonry surfaces or old walls, and directly over an existing wall if it is sound and level.

Multi-ply construction is used primarily to deaden the transmission of sounds from room to room. First, a 3/8- or ½-in. backer board is nailed to the studs or joists. This is covered with ½- or 5/8-in. standard board which is either glued to the backer board or nailed through the backer into the studs. (Backer board is used in the same way to reduce noise transmission through walls which have a finished surface of plywood, hardboard, or plastic sheets.)

A well-built wall or ceiling of gypsum board serves as an excellent base for paint, wallpaper, or other flexible wallcoverings. If paint is used, the board should be primed with latex and then given a final coat of latex or alkyd paint. Surfaces which are to be covered with a flexible material of any kind must first be given a prime coat of latex paint; otherwise, if the wallcovering should ever be removed, the paper surface on the gypsum board would peel off with it, weakening the board.

GYPSUM-COATED WALL FABRIC

A new wallcovering resembling a loosely woven burlap with color in the pores. It is impregnated with gypsum, and when hung on a wall like wallpaper, the fabric becomes as hard as ordinary plaster. The resulting surface is strong, durable, and fire resitant, but readily stained.

Although gypsum-coated wall fabric is made especially for application to concrete block and other smooth masonry surfaces, it can be hung on plaster, gypsum board, and wood. Because it is thick and rough-textured, it does an excellent job of concealing imperfections in a wall.

It is available in 30-yd. rolls 4 ft. wide.

H

HAIRCLOTH

A furniture upholstery fabric used in the mid-19th century. Made of cotton or linen and horsehair, it was stiff, glossy, and usually black.

HALF-ROUND

A wooden molding shaped like half of a broom handle after it has been split down the middle. It is used to conceal joints, to hold down the edges of screen wire, and for many other purposes.

HALF-STORY

See Story.

HALF-TIMBERED

A house with exterior walls built of exposed posts and beams. The open spaces between them are filled with bricks or stones. The original Tudor houses were half-timbered.

HALL

A passageway between different parts of a house. In a well-planned house, it is essential to good circulation through the house. A front hall is necessary for additional purposes (*see* Front Hall).

Halls used mainly as passageways should be at least 3 ft. wide to permit furniture to be moved through them. If closets open into a hall, the width should be increased another foot so a person can walk by an open door. (Doors to rooms off a hall should open into the rooms, not into the hall.)

Every hall should have at least one light. Two or more spaced at 10-ft. intervals are needed in long halls. The light or lights should be controlled by switches at both ends of the hall; and in large or long halls, additional control should be provided next to all other doors through which traffic passes.

HALL, FRONT

See Front Hall.

HALVED SPLICE

A halved splice is a compression splice made by notching the ends of the timbers to half their depth so they interlock, and nailing or screwing them together. For added strength, fishplates can be nailed or bolted over the splice to the sides of the timbers.

HANDRAIL

The top rail of a stair railing, balustrade, etc. The normal height of a sloping rail is 30 in.; of a horizontal rail, 34 in.

HANGER ′

A strong steel strap bent into a U and nailed to the side of a beam or joist to support the end of another beam or joist at the same level.

HANGING

Any fabric hung on a wall or from a ceiling for decoration: for example, a tapestry, rug, or flag.

HARDBOARD PANELING

Hardboard is a man-made sheet material concocted of small wood fibers which are bonded together under heat and pressure. The result is a very dense, strong, durable board that is dimensionally stable, does not split or crack, and has good resistance to moisture. It is also easy to work and to fasten to other materials, and takes paint well. It can be bent to conform to curving walls.

Hardboard panels for covering interior walls are made in 1/8-, 3/16-, and ¼-in. thicknesses, 4 ft. widths, and 7-, 8-, 9-, 10-, and 12-ft. lengths. While unfinished panels are available, most are textured and painted at the factory so that no final finishing is required in the house. The panels are most often made to resemble board paneling, marble, ceramic tiles, wallpaper, etc. Some panels are heavily embossed to resemble wicker, shutters, prismed glass, etc. Others are pierced in a decorative way for use as dividers. Probably the best known of all hardboard designs is *pegboard*, which is perforated at 1-in. intervals.

In new construction, ¼-in. panels should be used. These can be nailed or fastened directly to studs and joists; but to improve the acoustical qualities of the wall, the panels should be applied over ½-in. gypsum backer board. In remodeling, 1/8- and 3/16-in. panels can be installed over existing walls, provided these are smooth and level. In all cases, installation is made with small finishing nails or annular-ring hardboard nails which are colored to match the panels, or with adhesive applied to the backs of panels in wiggly stripes.

Hardboard is generally installed with butt joints between panels. The joints are left open or covered with moldings. Corner joints are usually covered with moldings made by hardboard manufacturers to match their panels.

HARDBOARD SIDING

The hardboard used for siding is like that for interior paneling. It is fabricated into large panels (standard size: 4 x 8 ft.) as well as narrow strips which are overlapped like clapboards. The material is approximately 3/8 in. thick.

Installation is best made over sheathing, although this can be eliminated in some instances. The newest types of siding do not need painting since they come from the factory with durable plastic finishes with long-term guarantees. Unfinished siding is given a prime coat of linseed-oil-base primer followed by two coats of oil-base house paint.

HARDPAN

Extremely dense, heavy clay that is very difficult to dig through.

HARDWARE

The metal pieces used to put together a building, close doors and windows, hang clothes and curtains, etc. *Rough hardware* includes the nails, screws, hangers, etc., which are largely hidden in a building. *Finish hardware* includes locksets, latchsets, window locks, kickplates, and other exposed items.

Finish hardware is made in three grades. The *commercial grade* is the best and most expensive, and is rarely used in homes. The *medium,* or *light-commercial, grade* is second best. Because it combines durability with moderate price, it is the type recommended for homes. The *builder's, lightweight,* or *budget grade* is the cheapest in price and quality, and should be avoided—especially in locksets and latchsets.

HARDWOOD

A tree, or the wood of a tree, which has broad leaves: for example, oak, maple, and birch. Many so-called hardwoods actually have softer wood than softwoods, however.

HASP

A simple locking device consisting of a long, hinged metal strap with a slot in the end and a staple. After the strap is slipped over the staple, a padlock or peg is inserted in the staple.

HASSOCK

A thick, firm cushion placed on the floor and used as a footstool or for kneeling. Electric fans shaped like squat steel drums are called *hassock fans.*

HATCH

Also called a *hatchway*, an opening in a floor or ceiling providing access to the adjoining space. It is usually covered with a trapdoor.

HEADBOARD

Headboards were once as much a part of every bed as the rails and springs. In fact, the headboard and footboard supported the bed above the floor. But a great many beds today are made without headboards (and even more are made without footboards); consequently, these must be bought separately if the homeowner wishes to improve the appearance of a bed and to keep pillows from falling off the end.

Headboards are made in sizes to fit all beds and are also available in many styles and materials.

HEADER

When an opening is made in a floor or roof, a large timber called a header is installed across the end (or ends) of the opening to support the ends of the joists or rafters. The timber may be a single 4-in. thickness of wood or made up of two 2-in. thicknesses spiked together. The joists are toenailed to the sides of the timber or hung against it in metal hangers.

The large timber across the top of a window or door 'is also referred to as a header, but it is properly called a lintel.

In masonry, a header is a brick, concrete block, or other masonry unit laid at right angles to a wall. Its principal purpose is to tie the tiers together securely.

HEADING

The topmost part of a curtain, drapery, dust ruffle, and similar hangings. In normal construction, the heading is the part above the casing. But casings are often eliminated as, for example, when a drapery is hung with pins inserted in pleated heading tape or when a curtain is hung below rings sewn into the top seam.

HEAD JOINT

A vertical joint between two bricks, concrete blocks, etc. The same as a *cross joint*.

HEAD LAP

The point at which the top edge of a shingle in one course is overlapped by the bottom edge of the shingle in the next course above. Head lap also refers to the amount of the overlap.

In addition to shingles, a number of building materials such as clapboards and roofing tiles are installed with a head lap.

HEADROOM

Vertical space which is high enough to permit a person of normal height to walk through without ducking. Minimum headroom in a house is as follows:

In rooms	7 ft. 6 in.
On stairs	6 ft. 6 in.
Under doorways	6 ft. 8 in.

HEARTH

The floor of a fireplace that extends from the back of the firebox into the room. It is usually level with the room floor but is often raised. In either case, it must be supported on a masonry base, not on joists. The area within the firebox is constructed of firebricks or other fireproof material; that outside must also be fireproof but need not be so resistant to heat as firebricks. Ordinary bricks, slates, ceramic tiles, and marble are popular materials for this area.

The forward part of a hearth is at least 16 in. wider than the firebox opening and projects at least the same distance into the room.

HEART SHAKE

A split through the center of a log. It is usually caused by decay in the heart. The split may form a single, more or less straight line; a pair of crossed lines; or a whole series of lines radiating out from the center in a star shape. *Compare* Check.

HEARTWOOD

The old wood in the center of a tree. It is usually darker in color than the surrounding sapwood, a little harder, and a little stronger. In many woods, but not all, it is also more resistant to decay and is therefore selected for use when it is to be exposed to dampness.

HEAT GAIN

The amount of heat, measured in Btu's per hour, that enters a house from outdoors. The rate of gain depends on the construction of the exterior walls, roof, and windows, and on the temperature differential between indoors and outdoors.

HEATHER-MAHOGANY FINISH

A blond finish for mahogany furniture or paneling made by bleaching the wood, working a white paste filler or enamel undercoater into the pores and wiping it off, and overcoating with white shellac or varnish.

HEATING

Probably the first question home builders ask themselves when it comes to designing the heating system for their houses is which of the three leading fuels—gas, oil, and electricity—they should use. In times past, the usual answer was to use the fuel which sold at the lowest price in the area; but since the energy crisis began in 1973, no fuel has had a clear-cut advantage over another.

Lacking price as a criterion, a home builder may then wonder whether one fuel has any important advantage over another. But despite claims by fuel distributors, all fuels are about on a par. All are reasonably safe. All heat efficiently—if the heating system itself is efficient. All are clean—if the heating system is properly designed and maintained. All can be knocked out by storms (although a modern gas-fired heating system, which uses electricity to run the blower and thermostat, can be made to limp along).

In other words, the choice of heating system should be based on the advantages and disadvantages of the system itself—not on the fuel it burns.

Forced Warm-Air Heating • This is the most popular central heating system because it costs relatively little to install, responds rapidly when the thermostat calls for heat, and heats a house evenly—especially if the blower is set for continuous air circulation (*see above*). In addition, the system can be readily adapted to humidifying and/or cleaning the air and to air conditioning. On the minus side, it may be fairly noisy, and if improperly designed, it is hard to correct.

The system uses all three major fuels (as well as LP gas) and can be installed in houses of any size. The center of the system is a furnace and large blower. Air heated in the furnace is circulated by the blower through supply ducts installed under the first floor and in the walls. The exact arrangement of the ducts depends on how the house is built. In cold climates, the registers through which the heated air enters rooms are placed low in the walls or floors under windows so that the air is blown upwards over the glass. In warm climates, where air conditioning is more important than heating, the registers are placed high in the walls or ceilings.

After the air gives up its heat, it flows back to the furnace through return registers located on the inside walls.

Forced Hot-Water Heating • In the heating trade, this is known as a *wet system* to differentiate it from a system using air. Popular primarily in the East, it is fast and reliable, takes up less space than a warm-air system, and is easier to put in properly. The boiler can be equipped with an indirect water heater to heat the domestic water supply at low cost. But the system is more expensive to install than warm-air heating; it cannot be used for cooling, air-filtering, or dehumidifying; and it must be drained if the house is vacant in winter.

When the thermostat calls for heat, the water filling the system is heated in the boiler and pumped out through pipes leading to radiators installed in the outside walls. After the water loses much of its warmth, it flows back to the boiler where it is reheated. As in warm-air heating, the pump can be set to operate continuously—even when the boiler isn't operating—so that semi-warm water circulates through the radiators constantly.

The arrangement of pipes in a hot-water heating system varies. In small houses, the system is often built with a single pipe line which supplies the heated water to the radiators and returns the cool water. In another system adaptable to large as well as small houses, a single pipe runs from one radiator to the next—all the way around the house until it returns to the boiler. Yet another system—for large houses—has two pipelines: one supplying heated water to the radiators, the other returning cool water to the boilers.

Electric Heating • There are several systems for heating houses with electricity. The least popular are the central systems like those just described. They differ from gas- and oil-fired systems only in that the air in the furnace or water in the boiler is heated by electricity. In other types of central system, a centrally located circulator carries air or water to the rooms where it is heated by small heaters under the control of individual room thermostats. Yet another central system—using air to heat the house—is built around a heat pump (*see below*).

The commonest type of electric heating system is designed to heat the rooms in a house individually—not all to the same temperature as from a central source. Each room has its own heater and thermostat. Thus, some rooms can be kept hot, some cool, and some turned off completely. This flexibility is the greatest advantage of electric heating, but there are others: It is economical to install because there is no need for ducts, pipes, or a chimney to carry off the gases and particles produced in an oil or gas system; the heat comes up fast and is subject to unusually exact control; the system is easily expanded if an addition is made to the house. On the other hand, there is no central system for cooling, filtering, or dehumidifying the air.

To heat a house electrically, it must be equipped with a very large service entrance operating at 240 volts. Thick insulation is required to reduce heat loss and hold down operating costs.

Six types of room heater are used:

Baseboard—long, slender heaters installed in the place of wooden baseboards along the exterior walls of rooms. They are more widely used than any other type of electric room heater.

Recessed Floor Heaters—also called *floor inserts*. These are similar in shape to baseboard units but are recessed in the floor. They are used primarily in rooms with large floor-to-ceiling window walls.

Valance Heaters—long, slender heaters which are mounted on exterior walls near the ceiling. They warm the ceiling by convection, and heat is then radiated to the room below.

Wall Heaters—smallish heaters which are usually recessed in walls of small rooms.

Ceiling Heaters—small units which are recessed or surface-mounted on the ceilings of small rooms. Some models have fans to circulate the heated air; others have exhaust fans and built-in lights.

Ceiling System—designed to convert the entire ceiling—or a major part of it—into an invisible radiator. The heater consists either of a cable which is embedded in the ceiling in rows or of big, pre-wired panels which are cemented to the ceiling surface.

Gas Wall Furnaces • These are used to heat very small, compact, one-story houses in mild climates. They are tall, slender, gas-fired units which are installed in or against a wall in the center of a house. Heated air is blown from the top of the furnace into surrounding rooms through wall grilles or openings above interior doors. Ducts are used to carry the air to more distant rooms.

Other Central Heating Systems • These include gravity warm-air, gravity hot-water, and steam systems. All were widely used in the past and are still found in old houses, but they are rarely installed in new houses because forced warm-air, forced hot-water, and electric heating systems are so much better.

Also see Radiant Heating, Solar Heating, and Valance Heating and Cooling.

HEAT LOSS

The opposite of heat gain: the amount of heat that escapes from a house to the outdoors. Obviously, heat loss affects the selection and design of a heating system, while heat gain affects the selection and design of an air conditioning system.

HEAT PUMP

A large electrical appliance which extracts heat from air or water, and uses it to heat buildings in winter and cool them in summer.

The commonest type of heat pump, known as an *air-to-air unit*, operates exactly like an ordinary air conditioner in summer. It sucks in the hot air from the house, extracts the heat and pumps it outdoors, and returns the cooled air to the house. In winter, the unit reverses itself, pulls in the outdoor air from which it extracts heat (all air contains some heat), and circulates the heat through the house.

In a second type of heat pump, heat from the house is pumped into the water in a well in summer, and pumped out of the well and into the house in winter.

Central heat pumps are designed to heat and cool entire houses. Installed in a basement or utility room, they pump the conditioned air into the house through supply ducts. Air returns from the rooms to the heat pump in return ducts.

Smaller heat pumps are also made for installation in windows like ordinary room air conditioners.

Air-to-air heat pumps are used in all parts of the United States but are most economical in warm climates, where the winter temperatures rarely fall far below freezing. In colder climates, electric resistance heaters must be installed in heat pumps to raise the heat of the incoming air high enough to maintain comfort in the house.

HEEL
The end of a timber.

HEM
A twice-turned fabric edge of the same width from end to end.

HEMLOCK
The wood of the eastern hemlock is used to some extent in building, but it is undesirable because it is low in strength, coarse-grained, and splintery. Western hemlock wood, on the other hand, is even-textured and reddish colored, and has good weight-to-strength ratio. It is used mainly in framing and also goes into doors, sashes, and millwork.

HEMP
A tough vegetable fiber which is woven into small squares which are, in turn, sewed together to make informal, durable rugs—especially for porches.

HEPPLEWHITE
A furniture style developed by George Hepplewhite, an English cabinetmaker, and depicted in his book, *The Cabinet-*

Maker and Upholsterer's Guide. The style was at its height in the last quarter of the 18th century, following the Chippendale style. It was characterized by delicate, graceful classic lines; shield or heart-shaped chair backs; slender legs; curved fronts; and motifs featuring wheat sheaves, urns, fans, etc.

HERRINGBONE

A pattern used in building, embroidery, and fabric manufacture. It resembles a group of fish skeletons laid side by side with the heads alternating from left to right.

HIGHBOY

A two-piece chest of drawers. The legless upper chest is taller, narrower, and shallower than the bottom one, on which it is placed. The bottom chest usually has only two drawers and stands on legs that are approximately as high as the two drawers. (*Compare* Chest-on-Chest and Tallboy.) The total height may be as much as 8 ft.

Highboys are, for the most part, very handsome, and are used more often in the living room or other living area than in bedrooms. The design reached its height in Chippendale.

HINGE

Hinges outnumber other pieces of hardware in the house, and because they are used to open and close so many different kinds of doors and windows, they are made in many more types and styles than other hardware pieces. Their selection is based, among other things, on the material of the door and frame; the size, thickness, and weight of the door; the clearance required; the frequency of use; the exposure (indoors or outdoors; to sea air, corrosive atmospheres, etc.); the desired appearance of the door; and the amount of work the installer is willing to do.

On interior doors, which are 1-3/8 in. thick, it is customary to use two hinges, but three are better. The hinges are 3½ in. high on doors up to 32 in. wide, 4 in. high on wider doors. On exterior doors (1¾ in. thick), three hinges are always used. Those for doors up to 36 in. wide are 4½ in. high. Five-inch hinges are used on wider doors. Loose-pin hinges are used in all cases so the doors can be taken down easily when necessary.

On all doors over 7½ ft. high, one extra hinge is required.

Types of hinge used in the home include:

Butt Hinges • These are commonest because two or three are required on most house doors. They have rectangular leaves which are joined at the knuckle by a loose (removable) or fixed pin. Most hinges are swaged (the leaves are slightly offset at the knuckle) so that there is a hairline clearance between the leaves when closed. This makes for a tighter fit between the door and jamb.

Full-Surface, Half-Surface, and Half-Mortise Hinges • One or both leaves are exposed on the door, on the jamb, or on both.

Concealed or Semi-Concealed Hinges • Made in various ways, these are used primarily on cabinet and furniture doors.

Parliament Hinges • Similar to butt hinges but made with wide leaves so that there is adequate clearance between the door and the casing or adjacent wall when the door is open.

Pivot Hinges • For flush, recessed, or overlay doors.

Offset Hinges • Used on lipped cabinet doors.

Olive Knuckle, Paumelle, and Fische Hinges • Substituted for butt hinges when a very small, ornamental knuckle is desired.

Double-Acting Hinges • Used on folding screens so they can be opened in either direction.

Piano Hinges • Long, slender hinges which run from one end of a piano top or heavy table leaf to the other.

Ornamental Hinges • Include H and H-L hinges, butterfly hinges, Chippendale hinges, and rustic strap hinges. They are surface-mounted.

Cabinet Hinges • This is a loose name applied to various types of small hinges.

Hinges (but not all styles) are made of steel, stainless steel, aluminum, brass, and bronze. Some are chrome-plated. Hinges made to be painted by the user are primed and designed with a slight clearance between the leaves and knuckle so they will operate freely after the final coat of paint is applied.

HIP
One of the slanted timbers at the angle of a hip roof.

HIP RAFTER
See Rafter.

HIP ROOF
A fairly steep roof which slopes upward from all four walls. The front and back slopes form trapezoids which meet at the

ridge; the end slopes form triangles which just touch the ends of the ridge.

Some hip roofs have flat tops which are surrounded with a railing and used as a captain's walk.

HOG

To lay up a brick wall with more courses at one end than the other, even though the wall is the same height throughout. Such a wall is also said to have a hog in it. Usually it is a mistake and should be torn down and rebuilt.

HOLDING POWER

The ability of wood or other material to keep nails and screws driven into it from pulling loose. Hardwoods generally have more holding power than softwoods.

HOLLOW TILE

A red clay tile made in various shapes and sizes for different purposes. The tiles are sometimes used (but rarely in houses) as the cores of walls and floors. Simple, round, tube-like tiles are more often used around a house in footing drains and sewer lines.

HOLLOW WALL

A wall with an open space between the front and back surfaces, but in which the surfaces are tied together. For example, a stud wall or a wall made of concrete blocks. *Compare* Cavity Wall.

Most house walls are hollow because they save materials. In given circumstances, they may also have other advantages as well as disadvantages.

HOLLOW-WALL SCREW ANCHOR

A hardware item used for fastening objects to hollow walls. It consists of a metal sleeve and a slender bolt. The sleeve is first inserted in a hole drilled in the wall. As the bolt is screwed in, the sleeve splits and mushrooms out against the hidden inside surface of the wall, thus anchoring the bolt firmly. The device is also called a *Molly screw* or *Molly bolt*. *Compare* Toggle Bolt.

HOLLOWWARE

Silver, pewter, and stainless steel of a deep concave shape or actually hollow. Bowls, pitchers, coffee pots, and candlesticks are hollowware. Knives with fat handles are called hollow-handled, although they are classified as flatware.

Of all silver pieces, the most beautiful usually are hollowware, and they frequently have a prominent part in the decorative scheme of dining rooms.

HOMES-ASSOCIATION DEVELOPMENT

A housing development with recreation areas, parks, and other open spaces and facilities which are privately owned by a neighborhood association of the homeowners in the development. In such a development, the houses are grouped in clusters; the remaining open land is the common property of the association.

HOMESPUN

A rough, moderately heavy, loosely woven fabric with an informal, irregular texture and plain color. Usually made of cotton or wool, it is used for draperies, bedspreads, and slipcovers.

HONEYCOMB

Tiny white pockets in wood. They are caused by a fungus but do not impair the strength of the wood.

HONEY-MAPLE FINISH

A blond finish for maple or birch furniture and woodwork. The wood is first given a very thin coat of white lacquer mixed with clear lacquer. This is followed by two coats of clear lacquer.

HOOD FAN

See Fan, Exhaust.

HOOD, FIREPLACE

See Fireplace Hood.

HOOK AND EYE

A familiar two-piece device for locking doors and windows.

HOPSACKING

A coarse, heavy, durable fabric usually made of cotton or rayon. It is used in draperies and slipcovers.

HORSEPOWER

One horsepower equals 746 watts. Electric motors in the home are rated by their horsepower. The horsepower of a clock motor is infinitesimal; that of a deep-well submersible pump may be as much as 1½ hp.

HOT SPOT

An area of incompletely cured plaster which is destructive to any paint or wallpaper applied on top. Most such spots disappear after plaster has aged half a year.

HOT WIRE

In an electrical circuit, the hot wire is the one carrying power. It is covered with black insulation in a two-wire circuit and with black or red insulation in a three-wire circuit. In all cases, the neutral wire is usually white.

A hot wire should always be connected to a gold terminal in a switch or outlet.

HOUND'S TOOTH

A fabric with a pattern of jagged checks.

HOUSE DRAIN

The large drain into which all household wastes are discharged. It, in turn, carries the wastes to the house sewer.

The house drain is commonly made of cast-iron, copper, or occasionally plastic pipe. Depending on the elevation of the house and city sewer, the drain may be run under the basement floor or through the basement or a crawl space. If for some reason it is necessary to install a house drain below the city sewer, an ejector pump is used to lift wastes into the sewer.

HOUSED STRINGER

See Stringer.

HOUSE MAIN

The pipe which brings water to a house from the city main, a well, or other private water supply. It is usually made of plastic or copper tubing laid below the frost line, and should be ¾ to 1½ in. in diameter, depending on the water needs of the family, the water pressure, and the distance from the source to the house.

HOUSE SEWER

That part of a sanitary drainage system running from the exterior side of the foundation wall to the main sewer at the street or to a septic tank. It may be made of cast-iron, vitrified clay, or plastic pipe, depending on the local building code and the particular soil conditions.

HOUSE TRAP

A U-shaped pipe in the house drain just inside the foundation wall. It prevents gases in the public sewer from entering and circulating through the house plumbing system.

HOUSE WRECKING

Having a house knocked down by a house wrecker is generally more expensive than homeowners assume. The cost depends on the location, size, and construction of the house; local laws; whether there is a local dump and how much it charges for dumping of the materials; and the value of the salvageable materials. Demolition of only part of a house costs considerably more than demolition of the whole thing.

HUMIDIFIER

A device which introduces water vapor into the air of a house in order to make it more comfortable, keep furniture and other wood from drying out and cracking, protect house plants, and minimize static electricity. In houses with warm-air heating, humidifiers are generally built into the system at the furnace. The best type, powered by a 120-volt electrical circuit and connected to a cold-water supply line, is fully automatic in operation. Other types are less expensive and also less efficient.

In a house heated by hot water, steam, or electricity, humidifiers are separate units which blow water vapor directly into the house air. Some are portable or roll-around devices. A few can be built into a wall and plumbed in. All operate on a 15- or 20-amp, 120-volt wiring circuit.

HUMIDISTAT
A device comparable to a thermostat which controls the humidity in a house.

HUNT BOARD
A simple, large, rectangular sideboard with one or two drawers and/or cupboards supported on long legs. The top is 42 to 52 in. high. They were built in the first half of the 19th century, mainly in Virginia and Kentucky.

HUTCH
A word ascribed almost indiscriminately to small cupboards, chests, or bins.

I BEAM

A steel beam, so called because it is shaped in cross-section like a capital I. Used in place of a wooden beam when the space to be spanned is very wide, it helps to support the joists for the floor above.

ICEMAKER

In addition to the small icemakers in refrigerators, there are separate units which do nothing but make and store ice cubes. The largest, designed for under-counter installation, is 18 in. wide and 24 in. deep. Others are also made for under-counter installation or are small devices which can be placed anywhere. All are connected into a cold water supply line by a ¼-in. copper tube, and all can be plugged into a 20-amp appliance circuit.

IDEAL WALL

A wall made with bricks laid horizontally on their thin edges. (Such bricks are called *rowlocks*.) Each course is laid with alternate stretchers and headers in a Flemish bond. An ideal wall uses fewer bricks than a conventional brick wall.

IMITATION LEATHER

Imitation leathers used for furniture upholstering and covering tables are currently made of vinyl and urethane. Both are more durable and pliable than leather and easier to maintain.

INCANDESCENT BULB

Incandescent bulbs have been the standard residential light source for many years. The relatively inexpensive standard bulb has a light output of about 1750 lumens and a life of about 750 hours; the more expensive long-life bulb lasts about three times longer but produces only about 80% as much light. Both bulbs produce a warm light which enhances warm colors (orange, red, brown, etc.) and subdues cool colors (blue and green).

One of the advantages of incandescent bulbs over fluorescent tubes is that the majority of bulbs in homes use a medium screw-base; consequently, it is easy to change the light output of a fixture or lamp at any time. In recent years, however, growing use has been made of bulbs with smaller intermediate or candelabra bases. Two other base sizes which are used to some extent are the large mogul and small miniature.

The shapes and wattages of incandescent bulbs are extremely variable. The shape is indicated by a letter or letter combination (for example, an A bulb is the standard shape; PS, pear-shaped; F, flame-shaped). In all cases, the standard color is white, but several tints are available.

Special types of incandescent bulb used in homes include the following:

Three-Light Bulbs • Also called *three-way bulbs*, these provide three levels of lighting.

Silvered-Bowl Bulbs • Standard bulbs silver-coated at the rounded end. They are used base up so all light is directed upward.

Tubular Bulbs • These are finger-shaped. The *show-case bulb* has a screw base. The *lumiline bulb* has bases at both ends and requires special sockets.

Reflector Bulbs • Large mushroom-shaped bulbs used indoors for floodlighting or spotlighting. They are designated by the letter R.

PAR, or Projector, Bulbs • Somewhat similar in shape to reflector bulbs and used for the same purposes. However, since they are made of tempered glass, they are not damaged by rain or snow, and can be used outdoors as well as in.

INDIAN HEAD

Trade name for a smooth cotton fabric of plain weave. It can be used for bedspreads, draperies, and curtains.

INLAY
A small piece of wood, stone, etc., set into a surface for ornament.

INSERT
A small piece set into a large surface for decorative effect. A ceramic tile set into a concrete wall is an insert. An insert might also be an isolated inlay in a table top.

INSIDE CORNER
A 90° corner. *See* Outside Corner.

INSULATION
Insulation which slows the passage of heat and cold has become a standard part of every American home. It is used in the South to keep homes cool just as much as it is used in the North to keep them warm. Types of insulation in common use are:

Fiberglass and Mineral Wool • Soft, thick fibrous materials made in long rolls or batts (6 to 8 ft. strips) or as loose fill. The rolls are constructed with a strong paper backing on one or both sides to facilitate stapling to studs and joists, and to keep the insulation from sagging. In many cases, one of the paper surfaces is treated to serve as a vapor barrier. Occasionally, aluminum foil is substituted for this. Batts are usually made in the same way, but sometimes the backing is eliminated.

The loose fill comes in bags and is poured between the joists in attic floors. It is also blown into walls of existing houses by professional applicators.

Mineral Pellets • Made of vermiculite and similar materials, the pellets are put up in bags for pouring between joists in attic floors.

Urethane • A liquid which is sprayed on the back of roof and wall sheathing, where it foams up to form a thick, highly efficient thermal barrier. Urethane has greater insulating value than fiberglass but must be applied only by professionals. It is banned in many communities on the grounds that it may constitute a fire hazard.

Vegetable Fiber Boards • These are 4 x 8-ft. and larger panels which are used for sheathing or as an interior wall finish. Extra-thick boards are also made to serve as the deck for roofing materials. The undersurface serves as the finish ceiling, and a vapor barrier is sandwiched into the boards to prevent the escape of moisture from the house.

Polystyrene and Urethane Boards • Rigid, waterproof boards used primarily to insulate foundation walls and concrete slabs laid on the ground. The boards are either glued to the outside surfaces, or sandwiched between them and extended under the slabs. The same boards may be used to insulate basement walls on the inside.

Reflective Insulation • Made of several layers of aluminum foil with air spaces between. To be effective, an air space at least ¾ in. wide must be provided between the insulation and the back of the wall or ceiling. The aluminum serves as a vapor barrier.

Whichever kind of insulation is used, it should be installed wherever heat can escape from or enter a house—in the roof, outside walls, and floors over unheated spaces. The optimum amount of insulation is measured in terms of its resistance, or R, value. Since the energy crisis began, the recommended R values are as follows:

- In the roof or top-story ceiling—R-19
- In all exterior walls—R-11
- In floors over unheated spaces (crawl spaces, unheated basements, porches, etc.)—R-13
- Under or around concrete slabs laid on the ground—R-13

The R values required are the same, regardless of the kind of insulation; however, the actual thickness varies. In other words, to insulate a roof calls for roughly 6 in. of fiberglass or mineral wool, 8 in. of vegetable fiber board, or 3½ in. of urethane foam.

Unless the insulation has a built-in vapor barrier (as in blanket and batt insulation), a vapor barrier must be installed on the warm side so that moisture in the house cannot penetrate the insulation. *See* Vapor Barrier.

INSURANCE

The several kinds of insurance that are of particular interest to homeowners are:

Homeowners' Insurance • Gives protection against fire, theft, and damage suits, and thus takes the place of separate fire, theft, and liability policies.

Glass Insurance • Covers damage to large windows.

Flood Insurance • Available only in certain parts of the country under a program run by the U.S. Department of Housing and Urban Development. Insures against water damage caused by overflowing streams or hurricane-driven waves—damage not covered by homeowners' policies.

Earthquake Insurance

Fine Arts Insurance • Insures paintings, sculpture, antiques, etc., specifically designated by the owner.

Mortgage-Protection Insurance • A form of term life insurance which assures that a mortgage will be paid off in case the mortgagee dies.

Workman's Compensation Insurance • This insurance is carried by building contractors to cover claims for damages suffered on a project by their employees or subcontractors. The homeowner should make sure that the contractor has such insurance; otherwise, he may become liable.

Title Insurance • Protects the homeowner against financial loss in the event it is found he does not possess clear title to his property.

INTAGLIO
A carving which is recessed slightly below the surface.

INTERCHANGEABLE WIRING DEVICE
Small switches, outlets, or pilot lights which can be used interchangeably or in any combination in one standard-size outlet box. They eliminate the necessity for installing two or three separate boxes or a single over-size box in order to provide equivalent switching and outlets.

INTERCOAT PEELING
A paint problem characterized by peeling between coats rather than down to the bare wood. It may develop shortly after paint is applied, after several months, or even after a year. Usually only the top coat is involved.

The problem can be prevented in new construction by applying the second coat within less than two weeks after the first. In old work it is avoided by cleaning and sanding the existing coat thoroughly before the second is applied.

INTERCOM

A communications system used primarily so home-owners can talk or hear sounds between rooms and can pipe music throughout the house. Some systems also serve as fire alarms.

One type of intercom operates on 120 volts and is installed by a contractor. Another type is connected into the telephone system and installed by the phone company. Installation of both systems is best made before interior walls and ceilings are surfaced.

INTERIOR DECORATOR

See Interior Designer.

INTERIOR DESIGNER

An interior designer, or decorator, is a professional qualified by education and experience to plan the decoration of a room, and to assemble and put together all or part of the furnishings and materials required. Unfortunately, interior designers are not licensed like architects, consequently, there is nothing to prevent anyone from claiming to be one.

In addition to seeking the opinions of previous clients, the best way for the homeowner to determine whether an interior designer is indeed qualified is to check whether he is a member of the American Institute of Interior Design (AID) or the National Society of Interior Designers (NSID). Membership in both organizations is fairly well restricted to those who meet certain schooling and training requirements; however, it is no assurance that a particular member is a good decorator or is well versed in the style the client may favor.

The role of the interior designer varies. He may serve simply as a consultant, recommending what should be done to improve a room or house, and perhaps drawing up plans for the owners to follow. Or he may help the clients find and buy the materials and furnishings they need. (In some cases, he actually supplies materials and furnishings himself.) Or he may also hire and/or supervise the painters, paperhangers, upholsterers, and others required to execute the decorating project.

Some interior designers work entirely on a fee basis; some take a commission on the materials, furnishings, and work purchased by the client; and some do both.

INTERIOR FINISH

The total effect of the woodwork, paint, wall-paper, etc., with which the interior of a house is finished.

INTERNATIONAL

The first successful modern style of architecture and decoration. It flowered in the 1920s.

INTUMESCENT COATING

See Fire-Retardant Paint.

IROKO

A West African wood sometimes called *African teak* because of its resemblance to true teak. It is of medium brown color with irregular yellowish bands, and is used in furniture and paneling.

IRONING BOARD CABINET

A tall, shallow, narrow, recessed wall cabinet with a built-in ironing board which folds out when the door is opened. Although a space-saver, it is one of the worst ideas ever perpetrated on homeowners, because the board is almost impossible to work at.

IRONSTONE

A type of stoneware (*see below*).

IRONWORK

Decorative pieces of iron used inside and outside a house. Porch columns and railings are often elaborately shaped ironwork. Actually, much ironwork today is made of aluminum.

IVORY

Once plentiful, ivory has become a scarce commodity and is used almost entirely for small decorative objects. It turns yellow with time, but to a lesser degree if exposed to sunlight.

JABOT

A curtain with pleat-like vertical folds and a sharply angled bottom edge. It is usually used with a swag at the top of a window.

JACK POST

A steel post with a screw jack in the upper end so the height can be adjusted. It is most often used for jacking up sagging floors. The posts are made in 3- to 8-ft. lengths. *Jack screws* are similar but shorter.

JACK RAFTER

See Rafter.

JACOBEAN

An English furniture style popular during the early 17th century in England and America. Pieces so styled were simple, solid, and heavy, and usually had large turned legs.

JALOUSIE

A window with numerous narrow, horizontal panes which swivel up or down and overlap at the edges when closed. It is installed in doors as well as in window openings. *See* Window.

JAMB

One of the boards lining a door or window opening. The vertical boards on each side of the opening are *side jambs*. That to which the hinges are screwed is the *hinge jamb*; the other is the *latch jamb*. The horizontal board at the top of the door opening is the *head jamb*. In a window, the jambs include the *stops*, *stiles*, and *parting strips*.

JAPANNED

Decorated with paint and varnish in the manner of early Oriental lacquer work. In the 16th, 17th, and 18th centuries, everything from bread boxes to Chippendale chairs was japanned. The pieces were decorated with lovely pictures of weeping willows, pagodas, Chinese men and women, etc., which were often raised above the surface.

JASPÉ CLOTH

A hard, firm, durable cotton or rayon fabric with multi-colored vertical stripes on a solid, monochromatic background. It is used in draperies and upholstery.

JOINT

The point at which two or more pieces of material are joined. In carpentry and woodworking, joints are considered to be the connections between pieces that meet at an angle. By contrast, splices (*see below*) are connections between pieces of material that are joined end to end.

JOIST

A horizontal timber supporting a floor or a roof with little pitch. A ceiling may be nailed to the underside. A joist is described according to its primary function as a floor joist, roof joist, or ceiling joist; but many joists serve as both roof and ceiling joists or floor and ceiling joists.

Joists are normally 2 in. thick and no less than 6 in. wide. The width depends on the wood of which they are made, how closely they are spaced, their span, and the weight of the load they support. Normal joist spacing is 16 in. center-to-center.

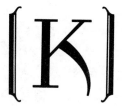

k
Coefficient of thermal conductivity. *See* Conductivity.

KAKEMONO
A Japanese scroll picture which is hung vertically on a wall. It is rolled up and stored when the owner wants a change of scene.

KAPOK
A silky fiber used to fill cushions.

KAS
A massive, free-standing, wood-paneled cupboard made by Dutch colonists in the eastern United States in the late 17th and early 18th centuries. It is usually painted with flowers and fruits, and is surmounted by a large cornice.

KETTLE BASE
See Bombé.

KETTLE CLOTH
A cotton and polyester fabric suggesting a firm, crisp, grainy-textured gingham. It is used in bedspreads.

KEVAZINGO
See Bubinga.

KEY

To roughen a surface so that plaster or paint will adhere better.

KEYSTONE

The wedge-shaped piece at the very top of a masonry arch. It serves to lock the other pieces into place.

KICKPLATE

A metal plate screwed to the face of a door to protect it against scuffing.

KILN-DRIED LUMBER

Lumber dried in an oven. This speeds up the seasoning process and presumably produces more controlled results—meaning better lumber. In actual fact, however, kiln-dried lumber (abbreviated *KD lumber*) may be no better than air-dried lumber.

For the moisture content permitted in lumber seasoned by either method, *see* Air-Dried Lumber.

KILOWATT-HOUR

One thousand watt-hours. Electrical bills are based on the number of kilowatt-hours (kwhr) used in a month.

KING POST

The vertical timber in the center of a truss.

KITCHEN

As the major work center of the home, the kitchen not only should include all the mechanical servants that are available to simplify the homeowner's work but also should be planned with more attention to detail than any other room. Careful planning is especially important now that the kitchen has become a major living center for the family, too.

Location • When remodeling an existing house, normal practice is to keep the kitchen in its original location. But in a new house, the following points should be considered in settling on the kitchen's location:

1 / It must be close to the dining room, and it should also be close to the garage since groceries are generally brought in from that point.

2 / If there are small children in the family, the kitchen should be placed where one can keep an eye on them while working. This location is also desirable so that children can have access to the refrigerator and sink, and can shake off dirt on an easily cleaned floor rather than the front hall rug.

3 / The kitchen should be near the terrace if the family enjoys eating outdoors. But a second door—from the living room, family room, or hall—should be provided so people can reach the terrace without walking through the kitchen, where they interfere with the cooking operations.

4 / To prevent unpleasant build-up of heat, the kitchen should not be oriented to the west.

5 / Although street noises are less disturbing in the kitchen than other rooms, a kitchen which is out of view of the street and front walk allows one to work without feeling on display before the world.

6 / In large, one-story houses, a central kitchen location is ideal because it is often the hub of activities in the house. Such a location also makes it possible to use the kitchen as a buffer zone between the adults at one end of the house and the children at the other.

Basic Planning Precepts • Once kitchen location is settled, actual planning of the room can get under way—but only after several questions have been answered:

1 / How is the kitchen to be used? Will it be used for more than simply cooking family meals; and if so, what other activities will it encompass?

2 / Who will use the kitchen and when? If two or more persons help in preparing meals and cleaning up, the size of the kitchen should be increased.

3 / Do family members have any physical characteristics, handicaps, or habits that affect kitchen design?

4 / Which appliances and which types and sizes are desired?

The work area of a kitchen is the area in which meals are cooked and utensils and dishes washed. It incorporates the range, refrigerator, sink, and dishwasher (if any) plus counter space and cabinets for storage. In many houses, the kitchen is so small that the whole room is a work area. In large kitchens, however, the work area is frequently separated in some way from the rest of the room.

Whatever the size or arrangement of a kitchen, the work area is the critical area from the planning standpoint. This does not mean it should be planned without reference to whatever else the room is used for, because they are interdependent. But the work area should be given priority.

The plan is dictated—not by magazine articles on the supposed merits of U-shaped kitchens, L-shaped kitchens, island kitchens, etc.—but by the following facts:

1 /   The work area should be small enough for efficient, relatively effortless work; but at the same time, it must be big enough to provide ample counter space and storage and to permit the occupants of the room to move around easily, without bumping into things and one another.

2 /   Kitchen work is easier and less messy if the counter is continuous from the range to the sink to the refrigerator.

3 /   Maximum efficiency is gained when the range, sink, and refrigerator are arranged in a triangle with 4 to 6 ft. between each appliance.

4 /   The sink is best placed between the range and refrigerator in the continuous run of counter. The range, however, may occupy center position—but not the refrigerator because it breaks the counter space and stops the flow of work.

5 /   Of the three main appliances, the range should be closest to the dining room or wherever most meals are eaten; the refrigerator should be closest to the door through which groceries are delivered.

6 /   When appliances are installed on parallel walls, the floor space between them should be at least 42 in. wide to permit opening appliance and cabinet doors and looking inside. A 48- to 60--in. space is better.

7 /   Traffic through the kitchen should be routed around the work area by relocating the back door into the kitchen and the door from the kitchen to other parts of the house. If this is impossible, the work area

should be laid out or located so the traffic does not pass through the center.

8 / Minimum storage space in a kitchen work area should be 6 running feet of base cabinets and 12 running feet of wall cabinets at least 30 in. high. Cabinets less than 30 in. high, cabinets under sinks, and open shelves do not count. As many additional cabinets as possible should be provided in the work area to store all foods, utensils, china, and glass that are used there regularly. Cabinets outside the work area are for items which are used less often and for foods, such as cookies and soft drinks, which are consumed between meals.

For specifics about the sizes and placement of appliances, *see* Compactor, Dishwasher, Garbage Disposer, Sink, Range, and Refrigerator. *Also see* Countertop; Fan, Exhaust; Kitchen Cabinet; Lighting; and Wiring.

Remaining Kitchen Space • If the work area occupies only part of the kitchen, the remaining space can be used for a multitude of purposes including:

A second sink—can be used for washing dishes, glasses, and silver after meals while the sink in the work area is used for washing utensils. It is also used for flower arranging, drink mixing, preparing meals for pets, etc.

A second range—useful for families that do a great deal of entertaining or food preserving.

A barbecue.
A freezer.
Laundering.
Eating area.
Planning desk.
Television viewing.

KITCHEN CABINET

In the long run, the size, interior arrangement, and location of kitchen cabinets are far more important to the homeowner's happiness than the construction of the cabinets. This does not mean that cabinet construction should not be considered at the time a kitchen is built or remodeled—but it should not be such a source of concern as it is. The fact is that one type of construction is about as good as another if all the cabinets under consideration are of equal quality. None is perfect.

Cabinets are made entirely of wood, entirely of steel, particleboard surfaced with laminated plastic, or with a steel shell and a wooden door. Steel construction is the sturdiest and holds an enamel finish better than wood. Plastic cabinets are most resistant to the wear caused by cleaning. Natural-finish wooden cabinets are the most beautiful.

All kitchen cabinets are produced in standard sizes. Base cabinets are 24 in. deep and 34½ in. high (addition of countertops brings the total height to 36 in.). Widths start at 12 in. and range upward in 3-in. increments to 60 in.

Wall cabinets are 12 in. deep and are produced in the same widths as base cabinets. Standard height is 30 or 33 in. Additional heights which are made—but not in all widths—are 15, 18, 21, 27, and 42 in.

Standard base cabinets have three shelves, three drawers, or one drawer and two shelves beneath. Wall cabinets have shelves only; these are usually adjustable.

A wide variety of special base and wall cabinets is also available, although no one manufacturer produces all. These include corner cabinets with revolving shelves, built-in oven cabinets, cabinets with doors on front and back for use as dividers between a kitchen and an eating area, small space-making cabinets which are installed under wall cabinets, tray cabinets, linen cabinets, utensil cabinets, four and five-drawer cabinets, 7-ft.-high pantry cabinets for bulk storage of packaged foods or china, and off-the-floor base cabinets which stand on legs.

Special accessories for use in cabinets include racks, cup hooks, half shelves, and storage turntables.

Standard 30- or 33-in. wall cabinets are normally hung 18 in. above the countertops (or 4½ ft. above the floor), but this space can be reduced to 15 in. in low-ceilinged rooms. The tops of all wall cabinets, regardless of their height, are aligned. The space above the cabinets is sometimes left open, but unless the ceiling is very high, the result is a dark, unattractive horizontal niche which collects dust and grease; consequently, the usual practice is to close in the space with a plywood or hardboard soffit which is secured between the ceiling and cabinet tops, flush with the cabinet doors.

KLISMOS

A side chair inspired by an old Greek design. The front legs are in-curved like a saber. The back legs and rail uprights are made in one piece and also in-curved.

KNEE
A timber bent or cut to knee shape. It is used to take the strain off another timber. A knee is also the curved upper section of a cabriole leg in furniture.

KNEE WALL
A short wall under a pitched roof. It closes off the hard-to-get-into triangular space under the low side of the roof. Knee walls are common in the upper story of story-and-a-half houses.

KNOB-AND-TUBE WIRING
Knob-and-tube was the first wiring system used and is still encountered in old houses. If properly installed, it is as safe and efficient as any system, although it is a little more readily damaged.

In the system, individual insulated wires—one hot and one neutral—are run through the house in parallel lines at least 2¼ in. apart. They are held in place with porcelain knobs and cleats which are nailed to joists, etc., and are run through studs, etc., in porcelain tubes.

KNOCKOUT
A circular tab in an electrical box which can be knocked or pried out in order to connect a cable to the box.

KNOT
A defect in lumber which mars its appearance and weakens it somewhat. The remnant of a branch covered over by the growing tree trunk, it is usually more or less round but may form a long oval. The latter is called a *spike knot.*

Knots are said to be *loose* if they are so weakly held in lumber that they may fall out, *fixed* if they are firm but will give way under pressure, and *tight* if they are permanently held in place.

Knots are also classified as *pin knots* if less than ½ in. in diameter, *small knots* if between ½ and ¾ in. in diameter, *medium knots* if between ¾ and 1½ in. in diameter, and *large knots* if more than 1½ in. in diameter.

In some softwoods knots contain resin which will bleed through a coat of paint unless they are first sealed with shellac or stainkiller.

KNURL FOOT
See Whorl Foot.

LACE

A beautiful and valued netlike fabric with an ornamental design. It is made of silk, nylon, acetate, or cotton. Once used in curtains, it is now restricted mainly to table linens and bureau scarves.

LACQUER

A very fast-drying clear or pigmented finish used mainly to produce a hard, tough, glossy protective coating on furniture. It is applied to bare wood, old lacquer, or shellac, but it should never be used over other finishes since it may act as a paint remover.

Because ordinary lacquer is very runny and dries so rapidly, it is difficult to apply by brush. Spraying is preferred. However, so-called brushing lacquers dry more slowly and are somewhat easier to brush on.

Lacquer is thinned with lacquer thinner.

LADDER BACK

A chair back with several horizontal slats which may be shaped or pierced. Also called *slat back*.

LAG SCREW

Also called a *lag bolt*, this is a very large screw with a square head which is turned with a wrench. It is used to fasten big timbers or to anchor objects in masonry into which lead shields have been set.

LALLY COLUMN
A hollow steel post filled with concrete. Without ornamental value, it is used in basements, garages, etc., as a center support for girders and beams.

LAMBREQUIN
A short drapery hung across the top of a window or door or under the front edge of a shelf. Also, a decorative wood frame around the top and sides of a window. This projects several inches from the wall and laps over the edges of the window trim several inches.

LAMÉ
A silk or rayon fabric with metallic threads in the background and/or design. It is used in draperies.

LAMINATED BEAM
A rather new development, laminated beams are made by gluing two or more timbers together side by side. They are normally used when solid wood beams of adequate size are unavailable or to form supporting timbers of unusual shape, as for an arch. They are very strong and are often given a fine finish when left exposed.

LAMINATED FABRIC
A two-thickness fabric made by bonding one fabric to another or to thin foam rubber. Used in draperies, the fabric-to-fabric type obviates the need for a lining. The fabric-to-foam type is used in throw covers.

LAMINATED PLASTIC
See Plastic, Laminated.

LAMINATED WOOD VENEER
A wallcovering made of paper-thin wood veneers bonded to a flexible backing. It is produced in sheets 0.015 in. thick, 10 to 24 in. wide, and up to 12 ft. long. These are glued directly to any smooth, sound, dry wall surface. The technique is similar to wallpapering.

Laminated wood veneers are available in over 80 native and exotic woods ranging from ordinary knotty pine to rare zebrawood. They are produced in matched strips to give a definite pattern on the wall and also in unmatched strips (the effect is similar to a wall paneled with solid boards).

Although the veneers are used primarily in commercial and public buildings, they have three uses in homes:

1 / When a large wall is to be covered with perfectly matched wood paneling.

2 / When a curving or contoured wall is to be surfaced with wood.

3 / When it is desirable to eliminate horizontal joints on an exceptionally high wall. This is made possible by the fact that end-matched veneers are available on special order.

LAMP

Portable lamps with extension cords either are purely decorative or combine attractive design with functional light for seeing. Almost every home has a few of the first type, but they should never be depended on to provide light for critical seeing tasks. On the other hand, it is perfectly possible to provide all illumination in a room with lamps that combine function and appearance. About five are needed in a room of average size because the light spread of each lamp is limited to approximately 40 to 50 sq. ft.

Lamps should be selected on the basis of size, construction, and lighting quality.

Size is measured from the bottom of the lamp base to the bottom of the shade. The required table-lamp height depends on the height of the table. Added together, the two figures should equal the eye height of the seated person, which averages 40 in. above the floor. In other words, if a table is 26 in. high, the lamp-base should be 14 in. high. If a table is 20 in. high, the lamp-base should be 20 in. high.

Since floor lamps are usually placed at the back corner of a chair, the lamp should be high enough for the light to clear the head of a seated person. Recommended height from floor to the bottom of the shade ranges from 47 to 49 in.

Wall lamps are smaller but are hung to the same dimensions— that is, 47 to 49 in. above the floor if placed behind a chair, 40 in. if placed to the side of a chair.

If a lamp contains a single bulb, the socket should be in line with the bottom edge of the shade in order to deliver the maximum amount of downlight. When there are several bulbs, their positions may vary somewhat, but all should be low behind the shade.

To soften and spread light, functional lamps used for lighting surfaces underneath should incorporate a bowl- or dish-shaped diffuser of translucent glass or plastic under the shade. This should surround the bulb or be placed directly below it. Bureau and dressing-table lamps do not need diffusers since their purpose is to light the face. The shades, however, should be of translucent material.

Single-socket lamps require a minimum bulb size of 150 watts. Generally, three-light bulbs in 50/100/150, 50/200/250, or 100/200/300 watt sizes are used. Multiple-socket lamps require a minimum of three 60-watt bulbs.

The most effective and efficient lamp currently on the market is the Better Light-Better Sight study, or desk, lamp using a 200-watt incandescent bulb. This combines a special diffuser and a translucent plastic shade with baffles in the top. It not only produces more glarefree light per watt than ordinary lamps but also spreads the light more evenly over a larger area.

Also see Lampshade.

LAMPHOLDER

A device into which electric bulbs are inserted. All lamps and light fixtures have lampholders, or sockets. Lampholders made of porcelain with screw-in sockets for incandescent bulbs are commonly used as light fixtures in basements, attics, garages, and closets, where more elaborate fixtures are unnecessary.

LAMPSHADE

Just as a portable lamp must be properly designed to serve as a functional light source, so must the lampshade used on the lamp.

Lampshades for table and floor lamps should be at least 16 in. across the bottom. The same diameter is required for wall lamps except when they are used in pairs, in which case the diameter can be reduced to 12 in. Bureau and dressing-table lampshades can be as small as 9 in. across.

Shade depth is variable but should be sufficient to keep a person standing from looking into the top of the shade. If a shade is shallow, a diffusing or perforated disc should cover the top.

Shades which are very narrow at the top or completely enclosed are undesirable because the heat given off by bulbs hastens deterioration of the shade material. In addition, the difference in brightness between the areas above and below the lamp is annoying and unattractive.

In lamps used for downlighting, the shades should have a nearly white inner surface to diffuse and reflect the light, and should also be translucent to transmit light without revealing a bright spot marking the location of the bulb. Dense or opaque shades are used only in rooms with very dark walls. Ideally, all shades in a room should have a similar brightness.

For bureau and dressing-table lamps, the shades should be made of extremely translucent material such as thin plastic, fiberglass, or silk—not laminated fabrics.

Except for opaque shades, which may be of dark or strong colors, shades should have outer surfaces of off-whites or neutral tints. Because these do not distort the color of the light, they permit surrounding furnishings and people to be seen in their true colors.

LAMP STAND

A small table on which a lamp is placed. It is the antique equivalent of an end table.

LANAI

A roofed terrace forming an integral part of a house. It is usually rather long and narrow.

LAND CONTRACT

Also called a *land sales contract*, this is a contract under which a piece of land is purchased on the installment plan. The buyer can take possession of the land when the contract is signed, but title remains with the seller until most or all of the installments are paid.

LANDING

A horizontal, usually rather small platform used at turns in stairs or to interrupt long flights of stairs. The platform at the top of exterior stairs is also a landing.

LAND-USE LAW

A law controlling the development of land for building purposes. Land-use laws are new in the United States but are spreading rapidly. Most are state laws.

LAP JOINT

A joint made by laying one piece over another and fastening them together with nails or screws or bolts. The result is crude looking and weak.

A *half-lap joint* is preferable in every way. In this, identical notches to half the depth of the wood are made in the pieces being joined; the pieces are fitted together and fastened with screws or glue.

LARCH, WESTERN

Larch is a very heavy, straight-grained softwood prized in construction because of its great strength. It is rated ahead of Douglas fir in many respects but shows more surface defects.

LATCH

Although a few latches are called *catches*, the devices differ in that a latch cannot be opened until a knob is turned or a handle is lifted, whereas a catch releases automatically when the door is pulled or pushed. Neither has a locking mechanism. Most latches are designed for use on interior doors in houses. Types on the market include the following:

Mortise Latch • The type used to close interior doors in old houses. The latch mechanism is incorporated in an iron box which is mortised into the edge of a door.

Cylindrical Latch • Modern version of a mortise latch and considerably easier to install. The latch tongue is enclosed in a small sleeve which is set into a hole drilled in the door edge.

Sliding Door Latch • Made for doors which slide back into a pocket in the wall. The latch fits into a rectangular cut taken out of the side of a door and has an L-shaped tongue which hooks into the strike in the jamb.

Thumb Latch • A rustic latch used in early houses and still used on gates. The latch tongue is a strap of iron, fastened to one side of the door with a screw, which is raised or lowered into a slot cut in the top edge of a strike that projects beyond the door casing. The tongue is operated by an L-shaped handle which extends through the door and ends in a scooped-out thumb depresser.

Bar Latch • Another old-style iron latch for cupboard and cabinet doors that are opened only from the pull side. The tongue, or bar, is pivoted on the doors and slides up or down into a hook in the strike mounted on the casing.

Other latches are made for use on screen or storm doors, gates, transoms, cupboards, and cabinets.

LATEX PAINT

An emulsion paint in which water is used as the vehicle. It is the most popular type of paint now in use because it dries so fast that two coats can be applied in a day. It is also almost odorless, and because it is soluble in water, splatters are easily wiped up and painting tools quickly cleaned. The paint can be applied to a damp surface or one containing alkalies. The finish produced is attractive, durable, and washable.

Latex paints are used indoors and out. They are particularly adapted to plaster, gypsum board, and masonry; they are also used on wood, although they do not seem to wear as well as solvent-base paints.

Although many water-base emulsion paints are called latex paints, not all contain rubber. Two of the best "latex" paints are actually made with acrylic or vinyl.

LATH

The base to which plaster is applied. Originally, it was a narrow, rough strip of wood nailed diagonally or horizontally to the framing and spaced 3/8 in. from the next lath. Today laths are applied in large sheets. One type is a gypsum-board panel 3/8 or ½ in. thick. It is economical, saves plaster, and increases the sound resistance of walls. Another type is an expanded steel mesh which can be bent or curved to conform to any wall or ceiling.

LATTICE

Openwork made of thin wooden strips arranged usually in squares or diamonds. It is used as a partition or roof or to support vines.

LAUAN

One of several Philippine woods sold as Philippine mahogany, lauan is a light, soft, rather loosely grained hardwood ranging from reddish brown to grayish brown and with dark and light striping. Because of its ready availability, it is much used in inexpensive plywood paneling. It also has a limited use in furniture.

LAUHALA

A glossy, yellow-brown material made by folding the leaves of a Hawaiian tree into 1-in strips. These are plaited into mats which are used for screens and floor coverings.

LAUNDRY

The ideal location for a laundry is on the first or second floor because almost all articles needing washing accumulate there; consequently, the tedious, foot-wearying job of collecting dirty clothes and distributing clean clothes is minimized. A basement laundry is less desirable, even though a laundry chute is installed from the floors above. On the other hand, the basement usually affords much more space for laundering operations; and if it is in disarray—as it generally is—no one is offended by it.

Finding space for a washer and dryer on the main floors of a house is generally not difficult because the standard automatic washer and dryer, set side by side, measure only about 5 x 2 ft. And a combination washer-dryer which washes and then dries each load automatically is only half as large. This means that the two machines can be located in the kitchen, utility room, large bathroom, or closet used for nothing else. But what is often overlooked by architects is the fact that a deep sink or tub is required for hand-washing certain articles, a 6 x 6-ft. floor space is required for ironing at a board, and a large cabinet is required to store a hand iron and the myriad laundering supplies in vogue today. This is why the ideal laundry is a rarity in a small- or medium-size house, and, like it or not, the laundry usually winds up in the basement.

Given space, a laundry should be laid out so that the work progresses logically from a sorting counter to the tub to the washer to the dryer and finally to the ironing board and a second sorting counter. If the sorting counters, washer, dryer, and tub are arranged in a straight line, they require a space approximately 13 ft. long. To allow for easy operation, the space in front of this lineup should be 2 to 3 ft. deep except at the ironing area, where it is 6 ft. deep.

Because of the need for a high level of illumination to inspect the laundry, two 25-watt fluorescent tubes should be installed in a surface-mounted ceiling fixture over the washer, dryer, and tub, and a similar fixture should be centered over the ironing board.

LAUNDRY CHUTE

A chute used to deliver soiled clothes and linens from the bedroom area to a laundry on the floor below or in the basement. Clothes are loaded into the chute through a small door in a wall and are usually deposited in a cabinet or bin at the bottom.

In addition to eliminating the necessity for carrying a heavy load downstairs, a laundry chute saves soiled-clothes storage space in the bedroom area. Its most serious drawback is that it becomes a flue through which fire can spread upward unless it is kept tightly closed at both ends.

LAUNDRY TUB
See Sink.

LAVATORY
Lavatories—bathroom basins—are free-standing or built in. The free-standing ones are actually anchored to the house in one way or other, but the space underneath the bowl is open to the floor.

Built-in lavatories, sometimes called *vanities*, have boomed in popularity because they provide more counter space than free-standing lavatories, there is cabinet space underneath for storage of bathroom supplies, and since they are built to the floor, cleaning under them is unnecessary. This, at least, is the theory of built-in lavatories. The truth is that many of them have no more counter space and no more usuable storage space than many free-standing lavatories. Their advantages, in other words, are a figment of the imagination unless they are properly sized and designed to the needs of the people using the bathrooms.

Cabinets for built-in lavatories are available in stock sizes and designs, and can be made to order. The average height is 31 in.; depth, 21 in. Width ranges from 30 in., which offers little counter space, to 6, 8, or 10 ft. The positioning of the lavatory in the counter affects not only the amount of useful counter space but also the amount of useful storage space underneath.

Free-standing lavatories are usually designed for installation about 1½ in. out from the wall so the wall can be cleaned. But some lavatories are hung tight to the wall. This is true particularly of those designed for corner placement.

Both free-standing and built-in lavatories are made of porcelain enamel on cast iron, porcelain enamel on steel, and fiberglass. The cast-iron type is the most durable as well as the most expensive.

LAWN
A light, sheer curtain fabric of fine cotton or linen. It is soft but has a certain crispness.

LEACHING FIELD
The disposal field in a septic system.

LEAD
In masonry work a lead is an end of a wall which is built up ahead of the middle. During construction, every masonry wall has two leads.

LEAD ANCHOR
A small cylinder of lead used to fasten things to masonry and other surfaces which do not hold screws or nails. The anchor is tapped into a predrilled hole of the same size. When the screw which holds the object being fastened is driven into the anchor, the anchor expands and grips the sides of the hole.

Lead anchors are also known as *lead shields.*

LEADER
A downspout which carries water from a gutter to the ground. Leaders should be made of the same material as the gutters to which they are connected (but if the gutters are wooden, the leaders can be of any material). They come in 10-ft. lengths.

Ordinarily, the gutter outlet empties into a leader elbow which is bent back toward the house wall. This is connected to a reverse elbow. Then comes a straight run of leader pipe. And at the bottom is an elbow directing water away from the house.

In houses with unusually shallow eaves, the two upper elbows are omitted, and the leader is connected directly to the gutter outlet.

Leaders are fastened to the house walls with flexible metal straps. Two straps are needed on leaders less than 15 ft. long, three on others.

LEAN-TO
A rather low structure with a shed roof. The design is used occasionally for very simple, economical vacation homes; and in the country's early days, it was frequently used for additions to existing homes.

LEATHER
Other needs for leather, combined with the development of imitation plastic leather, have cut into the use of this handsome, durable material for furniture upholstery and table tops. It will

always be prized, however, even though it needs frequent treatment with neatsfoot oil to keep it soft and crack resistant and with special coatings to prevent rapid soiling.

LEATHERETTE

An imitation leather made by applying an opaque coating to a cloth or paper backing. The material is less durable and less attractive than imitation leathers made of vinyl or urethane.

LECTERN

A reading stand. Lecterns in the home are not necessarily shaped like those used by speakers and clergymen, but may be small tables with flat or slanted tops just large enough to hold an open dictionary or Bible.

LEDGER

A horizontal timber nailed to an open stud wall or directly to a finished wall to support the ends of joists or beams. It is generally cut from a 2 x 4. The joists or beams can be placed on top of the ledger or hung at the side in metal hangers.

LENS STRIP

A long, narrow light fixture similar to a lighted cornice (*see below*) but incorporating incandescent bulbs which direct light downward through glass lenses.

LEVEL

Absolutely horizontal. The level of a floor, shelf, etc., is checked with a tool called a level, or *spirit level* or *carpenter's level.*
The word is also used to describe the height of something. Grade level, for instance, is the height of the ground.

LIBRARY

A large room with numerous bookcases used for reading, writing, and similar work. Only big houses have libraries.

LIEN

A claim against a property. Subcontractors and suppliers who have not been paid by a general contractor place most liens, and until their claims are settled, the owner's title to the property is in jeopardy. For this reason, a contract with a builder should always contain a clause to the following effect:

> Contractor agrees to indemnify and save harmless owner from all mechanics liens and claims upon the building or premises upon which the building covered by this contract is located, arising out of the labor and materials furnished by the contractor or any of its subcontractors under this agreement, provided that owner shall have paid to contractor all amounts due hereunder. Before final payment, contractor shall prepare and cause to be executed a complete waiver of any and all liens by all who have rendered any service or furnished any materials in connection with the fulfillment of this contract. Such waiver shall be executed in favor of the owner of the premises.

LIGHT
A pane of glass in a window. A window with eight panes is said to have eight lights. *Sidelights* are the vertical window strips on either side of some front doors. *Fanlights* are semi-circular windows installed over front doors.

LIGHTED CORNICE
A built-in fluorescent fixture consisting of a row of fluorescent tubes installed on a ceiling just out from a wall and shielded from view by a 6- to 8-in. board hanging from the ceiling. All light is directed onto the wall below. Most lighted cornices extend the full length of a wall.

LIGHTED COVE
This can be likened to a lighted cornice turned upside down. A row of fluorescent tubes is mounted on a shelf projecting from a wall at least 1 ft. below the ceiling. Because all light is directed upward on the ceiling, the fixture produces only about half as much illumination as a cornice light, and loses efficiency as it collects dust. The effect, however, is soft and relaxing.

The fluorescent tubes are shielded from the room by a board or strip of translucent plastic.

LIGHTED SOFFIT
A built-in fluorescent fixture used to give a high level of illumination on a horizontal surface, such as a dressing table or kitchen sink. It consists of fluorescent tubes installed in two or

three short, parallel rows on a ceiling between a wall and a wide shielding board. The bottom of the fixture is enclosed by a sheet of diffusing glass or plastic.

LIGHTED VALANCE

A large built-in fluorescent fixture used for general lighting. It consists of a single row of tubes mounted on a wall above a wide picture window or bank of small windows. The tubes are shielded from the room by a topless cornice (*see* Cornice), or valance, made of 6- or 8-in. boards. Light is directed upward on the ceiling and downward on the window and draperies. However, in cases where the fixture must be installed less than 10 in. from the ceiling, the top is covered (to prevent objectionable glare on the ceiling), and all light is directed downward.

LIGHTED WALL BRACKET

A built-in fluorescent fixture similar to a lighted valance (*see above*) except that it is installed on a blank wall rather than over a window. Large brackets are used for general lighting of a room. Small brackets are often used for local lighting over tables, headboards of beds, range tops, etc. In such cases, the brackets are hung much lower than those used for general lighting. The actual mounting height must be checked carefully to make sure that the shielding board shields the fluorescent tube not only from a person sitting down but also from one standing up.

LIGHT FRAMING LUMBER

Lumber used in light construction. It is no more than 4 in. wide or thick. The most common size is 2 x 4 in.

LIGHTING

The primary purpose of lighting in the home is to help the occupants see what they are doing without straining and walk through the house safely. Secondarily, it should accent the colors and textures of the rooms and their furnishings. And it may also be used for decorative effects.

Good lighting, combining built-in fixtures for general illumination and portable lamps and/or built-in fixtures for illumination of specific areas, provides a glareless, more or less uniform-throughout-each-room, but controllable light level. It should not distort colors objectionably or make large windows look like black mirrors.

Efficiency depends not only on the choice of fixtures, lamps, and bulbs but also on the reflectance values (*see* Reflectance) of walls, ceilings, floors, counters, and furnishings.

Incandescent bulbs, fluorescent tubes, or a combination of both may be used. *See* Incandescent Bulb and Fluorescent Tube.

General lighting is provided by lighted valances, lighted brackets, lighted cornices, lighted coves, luminuous ceilings, and luminous walls (all of which are described elsewhere) as well as by conventional fixtures attached to the ceiling or walls.

Surface-mounted ceiling fixtures are the commonest source of general illumination—especially in bedrooms, dining rooms, halls, bathrooms, kitchens, and utility areas. They should be equipped with translucent diffusing bowls and hung 3 to 12 in. below an 8-ft. ceiling. In rooms under 250 sq. ft., one centrally located fixture is adequate. In large rooms or rooms which are 60% longer than they are wide, two fixtures are required. In most cases, the fixtures should provide 1 watt of incandescent light or slightly less than ½ watt of fluorescent light per square foot of floor area. However, kitchens and laundries need twice as much light.

If fixtures are recessed in the ceiling, light spread is reduced; consequently, the number of fixtures should be increased to provide approximately 2 watts of incandescent light or 1 watt of fluorescent light per square foot of floor area. The fixtures should be of a nondirectional type.

When wall fixtures are installed for general illumination, their total wattage should equal that of surface-mounted ceiling fixtures; but for uniform light, fixtures must be placed on two or more walls.

Local lighting for specific areas or tasks is done with lighted brackets similar to but generally smaller than those used for general lighting, lighted soffits (*see above*), track lights (*see below*), directional recessed ceiling fixtures, wall fixtures (for bathroom mirror lighting only), and floor and table lamps. All should be equipped with diffusers or shades which shield the bulbs from the eyes. The fixtures and lamps should be placed so that most of the light given off is concentrated on the desired spot. The wattage required is variable but generally higher than that needed for general lighting. (For example, a 100- to 150-watt incandescent bulb is used for a reading light.)

In areas where good lighting is of critical importance, the following installations are recommended:

Over Kitchen Counters • One 20-watt fluorescent tube for every counter less than 3 ft. long, one 40-watt tube for counters 4 to

6 ft. long, and one 20-watt tube every 4 ft. on counters more than 6 ft. long. The fixtures should be mounted on the bottom of wall cabinets over the counters. If there are no wall cabinets, two 25-watt fluorescents are mounted on the ceiling behind an 8-in. vertical board which shields the bulbs from view.

Over Kitchen Sink • Two 25-watt fluorescents mounted on the ceiling 12 in. out from the wall. An 8-in. vertical board shields them from view.

Over Kitchen Range • The same arrangement as for a sink. Or one 25-watt fluorescent tube is installed in a wall bracket 22 in. above the range cooking surface. (Ranges are also illuminated— usually inadequately—by lights built into hooded ventilating fans.)

Over Laundry Tub and/or Washer • Two 25-watt fluorescent tubes in a surface-mounted ceiling fixture centered overhead.

Over Ironing Board • Same as for a laundry tub.

Bathroom Mirror • If the mirror is of average size, one 20-watt fluorescent tube or one 60-watt incandescent bulb is mounted in a shielded fixture on either side of the mirror, and a third similar fixture is centered over the mirror on the ceiling 12 to 18 in. out from the wall. The wall fixtures are spaced 30 in. apart and centered 5 ft. above the floor. If the mirror is unusually wide, a fluorescent fixture with two rows of tubes extending the width of the mirror is installed on the ceiling 1 ft. out from the wall.

Over a Workbench and Large Power Tools • An individual fixture with two 25-watt fluorescent tubes is hung from the ceiling 4 ft. above the work surface of the bench and each power tool.

At Front Door • Two 50-watt incandescent wall fixtures located on either side of the door, close to the casings, 66 in. above the sill. The alternative is a 100-watt incandescent fixture centered above the door on the wall or overhang.

LIGHTNING PROTECTION

A system of metal rods installed on roofs and connected by wires to other rods driven into the ground. With this system, lightning bolts strike the roof rods rather than the house itself and are diverted harmlessly to the ground.

Lightning protection is more necessary in rural than built-up areas. Since a system is difficult to design, it should be planned and installed only by a firm specializing in the business.

LIMBA

A pale yellow or very light brown West African hardwood with straight grain and fine texture. Its primary use is in plywood paneling.

LIME

One of the materials used in making mortar for laying up brick and other masonry structures. The type most often used is called *hydrated lime* because it has been slaked (mixed with water) before packaging and is ready for immediate use. *Quicklime* is unslaked lime. It can be used only after mixing with water and storing for about two weeks.

Lime is normally mixed into a mortar in the proportion of about 10% lime to 1 sack of cement.

LIMED-OAK FINISH

A blond finish for oak woodwork and furniture. After the wood is bleached, it is sealed with a thinned white shellac. The pores are then filled with white paste filler, and the wood is given a protective coating of white shellac or water-white lacquer.

LIMESTONE

Sedimentary rock of uniform structure. It is rather soft and easy to cut. Because it was laid down in layers, it tends to split into flat-sided blocks and is therefore very easy to build with. But it deteriorates rather rapidly in industrial atmospheres. The color ranges from white to gray and tan.

Some types of limestone make interesting paving materials because of the fossil impressions they contain.

LINEAL FOOT

The standard unit of measure for interior trim, moldings, furring strips, and grounds, regardless of their width and thickness. The term *running foot* is used interchangeably with lineal foot.

LINEN

A strong, durable fabric woven from fibers of the flax plant. Its quality depends on the length and fineness of the fibers. White linens tend to revert to their natural grayish-tan color unless bleached occasionally.

LINEN PRESS

A tall, two-piece furniture unit consisting of a chest of drawers on which rests a cupboard with hinged doors. The cupboard is equipped with shelves or sliding trays.

LINING PAPER

An inexpensive, yellowish wallpaper used as a base for hand-printed and other very fine wallpapers. It can also be used under ordinary papers to conceal a rough wall texture which would otherwise show through the finish paper.

LINOLEUM

One of the first resilient flooring materials and still one of the best. It is sold only in sheets and in very limited colors and textures; but it has excellent durability and grease resistance, and is easy to maintain. It must be laid above grade only since it is damaged by moisture if laid on or below grade.

LINSEED OIL

An oil made from flax seed which is used as the vehicle in oil paints and varnishes. It is also applied to wood as a transparent finish. Although it protects the wood well, it gradually darkens it, and it tends to mildew badly when used outdoors.

Two kinds of linseed oil are made: *raw* and *boiled*. They are essentially similar and used pretty much interchangeably, but boiled oil dries a little faster and is of more brownish color.

LINSEED OIL FINISH

An old but excellent clear finish for wood furniture. Either raw or boiled linseed oil can be used. It is warmed slightly in a double boiler, swabbed on the wood, and rubbed in with clean rags for 20 to 30 minutes. The excess is then removed, and the oil is allowed to dry for a week. Then the process is repeated at least twice. The resulting finish has a warm, mellow look; does not require waxing; and tends to conceal scratches—but is not very resistant to water-marking. If it becomes worn, it can be renewed at any time with another application of oil.

LINTEL

The horizontal timber over a window or door required to support the studs and wall directly above. A lintel is normally made of a pair of 2 x 4s nailed together, but it may be made of a single 4-in.-thick timber. The width varies from a minimum of 4 in. upward, depending on the span of the opening.

LIP

Where the edge of one surface overlaps another surface, it forms a lip. Many cabinet doors are lipped.

LIVING ROOM

Because the living room is the place where the family relaxes, reads, drinks, watches television, listens to music, plays games, and entertains (among other things), it should be located where it does not serve as a heavily used trafficway to other parts of the house. It should also be screened—or only partially visible—from the front door so that those knocking at the door need not disturb occupants of the room.

If the room is oriented to the east or north, it is cool in the late afternoon and evening, when it is usually occupied; and the furnishings (which are probably the most expensive in the house) are not subjected to fading by the hot southern or western sun.

Unless a living room is built for show or frequent large-scale entertaining, its size should be limited—for reasons of economy—to the number of people who ordinarily occupy it and the things they do. Anything less than about 200 sq. ft. is likely to feel cramped, however.

The shape of the room is more critical. Long, narrow rooms are difficult to furnish and unsuited for all but the smallest gatherings. The ideal room for conversation is a square or a rectangle in the proportions of 3:4 or 4:5. If this is not more than 300 sq. ft. in area, it feels spacious but permits people to talk across it without raising their voices.

An additional advantage of an almost-square room is that a fireplace—to which people naturally gravitate—can be placed on any wall without upsetting the way the room is used. By contrast, if a fireplace is placed on one of the narrow walls in a long room, people tend to cluster around it and leave the opposite end of the room unoccupied. (For this reason, a fireplace in a long room is better placed on one of the long walls.)

LOAD

The weight supported by a post, beam, joist, floor, wall, or other supporting member or structure. The *design load* is the total load which a wall, etc., is designed to support. *Static*, or *dead load* is the weight of the building itself plus that of more or less stationary objects such as pianos and safes. *Live load* is the weight of variable and moving loads, such as people walking, wind, ice, etc.

LOCK

Locks are designed to make doors and cabinets secure against intruders. Once locked, they can be opened only with special keys or by other means.

Door locks in wide use include the following:

Mortise Lock • In this, the locking and latching mechanism is enclosed in a steel box which is mortised into the edge of a door. Locks for exterior doors should incorporate a dead-bolt operated by a key or thumb screw separate from the snap lock. A top-quality mortise lock is the most reliable, durable, and burglar-proof type of lock.

Key-in-Knob Lock • Properly known as either a *cylindrical lock* or a *tubular lock* (there are two slightly different kinds), this is the lock which is most widely used in homes today because a carpenter has to bore only two holes in a door to install it. Exterior locks should have a dead-locking latch bolt which prevents jimmying.

Rim Lock • A lock which is mounted on the face of a door and the casing. It is used today primarily to supplement other locks on exterior doors. One kind of rim lock has a dead-bolt which slides horizontally. In another kind, the bolt slides vertically through interlocking "teeth". The latter is the more difficult to pry open.

Cross-Bar Lock • This is centered on the back of a door and controls two long bars which slide into large steel strikes mounted on both sides of the door frame. It is used on doors which open outward from wooden frames and have hinges on the outside.

Chain Lock • A surface-mounted device similar to an ordinary door chain but incorporating a lock for extra security.

Cabinet Locks • These are much smaller than door locks. Controlled as a rule by a key, some are mortised into a cabinet or furniture piece; others are surface-mounted.

LOCK BLOCK

A solid block of wood in a hollow-core flush door through which the lock or latch must be fitted. Each door has a lock block on both edges.

LOG CABIN
The earliest log cabins were built by cutting deep notches in the ends of the logs and interlocking them at the corners. Later cabins and those built today have vertical corner posts which are squared on two adjacent sides. The horizontal logs are butted to the posts and spiked.

When whole logs are used, they are stripped of bark to discourage attack by carpenter ants. The chinks between logs are stuffed with insulation (moss in bygone days) and then usually covered with triangular wood battens nailed to the logs.

Cabins are also built with logs which have been squared with saw or adz. The spaces between the logs are filled with lime mortar, thus producing walls which are more or less level, if not smooth.

Precut log cabins are widely available in numerous plans and sizes.

LOGGIA
A porch or gallery with a roof supported on columns and generally of classic design.

LOOKOUT
One of the short timbers forming the nailing base for the soffit under an eave. It is installed horizontally between the lower end of a rafter and the exterior wall.

When prefabricated soffits are installed, lookouts are often eliminated, and the soffits are hung from metal channels.

LOOP BACK
A Windsor chair back with a frame which forms a well-rounded U and is supported by slender spindles.

LOT LINE
The boundary line of a lot.

LOUVER (1)
The word louver is applied to several closely related things, all designed to permit movement of air from one space to another. In building, the word is most often applied to an opening in an attic, basement, exterior wall, or soffit which is used for ventilation. The opening may be covered with slanted louvers, a coarse screen, or both.

A louver is also a thin, slanted board used in shutters, doors, fences, etc. It is usually horizontal but sometimes vertical.

A louver is also the entire louvered section of a shutter, door, etc. This type of louver is often used more for its decorative than utilitarian value. Its principal drawback in any case is that it collects dirt and is hard to clean. It is also very hard to paint.

LOUVER (2)

A device used in lighting fixtures or lamps to restrict the view of the bulb or to absorb unwanted light. It is slatted like a building louver, but the slats are aimed straight outward instead of being slanted.

LOUVERED ROOF

A hip roof with louvers in small gables at both ends of the ridge. The roof is usually rather steep. It is found mainly in tropical climates.

LOVE SEAT

An uphostered sofa seating two persons.

LOWBOY

A drawer unit usually made as a companion piece to a highboy. It consists of one or two rows of drawers standing on legs roughly 18 in. off the floor.

LOW-VOLTAGE WIRING

Wiring which provides power at 12 to 25 volts for the operation of lights. The main purposes are to reduce the danger of shock and to lower installation cost; but the system is not widely used.

LP GAS

LP—standing for *liquified petroleum*—gas is also known as *bottle gas, tank gas, butane gas, propane gas,* or *LPG.* Stored in a steel tank, it is a liquid which turns into gas when a gas burner in the house is turned on.

LP gas is used like natural gas for heating, water heating, cooking, and clothes drying. Some equipment can burn LP gas only; other equipment can burn either natural or LP gas.

Principal customers are homeowners living in the country beyond the gas mains. Their storage tanks are installed either in or above ground and are filled periodically by tank trucks comparable to oil trucks. The gas can also be purchased in small prefilled cylinders which are stored outdoors in a rack.

LUGGAGE RACK

A knee-high folding piece with wooden legs pivoted in the middle and held together, when open, with three or four wide fabric strips that form the top on which a suitcase is set.

LUMBER

Wood after it has been cut from logs and is ready for use by carpenters, woodworkers, etc.

Most lumber is cut from softwood trees such as pines and firs, but millions of feet of oaks, maples, and other hardwoods are also used. The lumber is called *flat-grain* or *edge-grain, plain-sawed* or *quarter-sawed*, depending on how it is sawed from the logs and on whether it is a soft or a hard wood.

Lumber is further classified as follows:

Rough Lumber • Has not been planed after sawing.

Surfaced, or Dressed, Lumber • Has been planed but not necessarily on all sides or edges. A code is used to indicate the extent of planing. For example, if S4S is printed on lumber, the lumber has been surfaced on all sides and edges. S2S means surfaced on two sides but not on the edges. S2S1E means surfaced on two sides and one edge. S2E means surfaced on two edges only.

Lumber which has been surfaced is smaller than its stated size. For example, if a carpenter orders a 1 x 4-in. board from a lumberyard, he receives one which is ¾ x 3-9/16 in. This is the *actual size*; 1 x 4 is the *nominal size*.

The actual size depends on whether the lumber is green or dry. Green lumber is very slightly larger after it is dressed than dry lumber. For instance, the actual thickness of a 1-in. board is ¾ in. if the lumber is dry and 25/32 in. if it is green. Board widths vary in the same way:

Nominal width	4	6	8	10	12	14
Dry lumber	3-9/16	5½	7½	9½	11½	13½
Green lumber	3-5/8	5-5/8	7-5/8	9¾	11¾	13¾

The minimum length of lumber is usually 6 ft., and it goes up from this, usually in 2-ft. multiples.

Yard Lumber • Light construction lumber. Most softwood lumber in a lumberyard is yard lumber.

Dimension Lumber • Yard lumber 2 to 5 in. thick and of any width.

Finish Lumber • Yard lumber that has a good finish.

Structural Lumber • Softwood lumber used in heavy construction. The smallest dimension of any piece is 5 in.

Factory, or Shop, Lumber • Lumber which is to be used for the manufacture of doors, cabinets, etc.

Milled Lumber • Factory or shop lumber after it has been processed. Also called *millwork*.

Softwood lumber is sorted into eight grades, the three best are known as *select* and the five lowest as *common*. The specific grades are:

B & Better or 1 & 2 Clear • Used for the finest cabinetwork. Virtually free of blemishes.

C Select • A few blemishes.

D Select • A few small knots, checks, and other blemishes.

1 Common • Has some fairly large knots, but they are sound and tight. (This grade is usually available only on special order.)

2 Common • Close to No. 1. Used for exterior trim and knotty pine paneling.

3 Common • More and larger knots, but the lumber is amply good for shelving, paneling, siding, etc.

4 Common • Used in subfloors, sheathing, and other concealed places.

5 Common • Suitable only for the roughest uses.

Hardwood lumber is similarly graded. The best grades are *A Finish* and *B Finish*; those for everyday use are known as *No. 1, No. 2*, and *No. 3 Construction Boards*.

LUMEN

The unit for measuring the light output of an incandescent or other type of bulb. The lumens, wattage, and life of all incandescent bulbs of 15 to 150 watts are printed on the jackets in which the bulbs are packaged. The higher the lumen rating, the shorter the life of the bulb.

LUMINAIRE

An illuminating engineer's name for a light fixture.

LUMINOUS CEILING

A large to giant-size fluorescent lighting fixture used—especially in kitchens, bathrooms, and family rooms—to provide a very high level of illumination throughout an entire room. It consists of parallel rows of fluorescent tubes mounted on a white surface above a plastic or glass diffuser or a wood, metal, or plastic grille.

Luminous ceilings are sold in prefabricated assemblies which are suspended below ceiling joists, or they are especially designed and put together on the job piece by piece. In the latter case, the installation can be of any size (ranging from a relatively small panel to a unit covering a whole ceiling) and any shape (square, rectangular, round, oval, free-form, etc.).

For maximum effectiveness, a luminous ceiling should be installed with the diffusing panel or grille at least 7½ ft. above the floor. There should be a 10- to 12-in. space between the diffuser and the center lines of the fluorescent tubes, and the rows of tubes should be spaced 15 to 18 in. center to center. The surface on which the fixtures are mounted must be painted flat white.

The best diffuser is made of a rigid sheet of acrylic because it is lightweight and unbreakable, has good resistance to color change, and transmits light well. Because of its texture, a grille is more attractive than a diffuser; but since it does not completely conceal the bright tubes, it should be used only if a diffuser is placed above it.

LUMINOUS WALL

Similar to a luminous ceiling, a luminous wall is an entire wall or section of wall lighted from within by fluorescent or incandescent bulbs. It is surfaced on one or both sides with translucent plastic or glass.

Such a wall is used to give the effect of natural light filtering through a thinly curtained window, to balance the light in a deep room that has windows in only one wall, to emphasize structural features, and to silhouette decorative objects displayed in front of the wall.

LUSTERWARE

Pottery given an overall metallic film or decorated with metallic designs.

LYRE

A furniture motif representing the stringed musical instrument called a lyre. It is used in the backs of chairs and for table supports—this usage having been popularized by Duncan Phyfe. Lyre clocks are wall or shelf clocks with lyre-shaped cases. Lyre sofas have S-shaped arms resembling one half of the frame of a lyre.

[M]

MACHINE-SCREW ANCHOR

A device for attaching very heavy weights to masonry walls. It is made in several ways, but the operation is the same in all cases. A bolt-like machine screw is inserted in a lead sleeve, and as it is tightened, it jams the sleeve tight against the sides of the hole drilled for it.

MAGAZINE RACK

A narrow, boxlike frame on legs which holds magazines standing on edge.

MAHOGANY

Mahogany is the aristocrat of furniture and cabinet woods, and a room paneled in it is a sight to behold. The true mahogany available today is cut from a tree named *swietenia macrophylla*. Known as Honduras, Tropical American, Peruvian, or Brazilian mahogany, it is a medium-deep brown and has a soft glow when sanded and polished. The grain is straight and not too pronounced, but when logs are sliced into veneers, it is curly and wavy. The wood is strong, extremely stable, and durable; not very heavy or hard; and easy to work.

African mahogany comes from the tree named *khaya ivorensis*. It is not considered quite as good as Honduras mahogany but is very similar in all respects and often hard to distinguish from it. The principal discernible difference is in the pores, which are usually clustered rather than scattered.

MAHOGANY, PHILIPPINE
See Lauan.

MAJOLICA
Earthenware with a lustrous enamel glaze in rich colors. The ware was first produced on the island of Majorca in the late 15th century. Objects made of it include vases, pitchers, bowls, cups, etc.

MALE
A plumbing or electrical fitting which is inserted in a female fitting. For example, an electrical plug is a male fitting; the outlet into which it is inserted is the female fitting.

MANSARD ROOF
A compound hip roof popular in French architecture. The lower slopes above the eaves are very steep—almost vertical—and have dormers set in. The upper slopes are almost flat.

MANTEL
The decorative trim or facing on a fireplace breast. It includes the horizontal trim above the fireplace opening and also the vertical trim (if any) at the sides. Its purpose is primarily ornamental, but in many cases it also serves to conceal the joints between the fireplace and surrounding wall.

Mantels are commonly made of wood and, like most residential woodwork, are available in stock designs and sizes; but they may also be specially made of other materials, such as stone. For safety, wood mantels must be set back from the edges of the fireplace opening at least 8 in. The mantel shelf should be at least 12 in. above the opening. The masonry surfaces exposed within the mantel are called *jambs* and are often covered with marble or ceramic tile.

Mantels are also called *mantelpieces*. And to some people the flat shelf above the fireplace is the entire mantel, but it is actually only a part and should be identified as the *mantel shelf*.

MAP CRACK
A tiny crack in a plaster wall. Usually such cracks appear in groups and cover an area like the lines on a road map.

MAPLE
The maple in greatest use for lumber is known as *hard*, or *rock, maple* and is cut from the sugar maple. It is hard, heavy, strong,

and tough, with excellent resistance to abrasion and denting; consequently, it is one of the best woods for flooring and cutting blocks in kitchens. It is also used in paneling and furniture. The color is creamy to light reddish brown. The pores are scattered, the grain subdued and uniform. But some maple is highly figured and is especially prized; *bird's-eye* and *curly maple* fall into this group.

MARBLE

A stone valued for its many beautiful colors and the natural patterns in which it is found. Marble actually is a fine-grained, crystalline limestone which is easy to cut and polish to a glossy surface; but it is readily scratched and etched by acids.

Marble is used for flooring, wall surfacing, hearths, fireplace breasts, windowsills, table tops, countertops, etc. After installation, it should be given a couple of coats of penetrating sealer to prevent soiling and staining.

MARBLE FINISH

A furniture finish which is supposed to resemble marble. It is usually made with three paint colors. The first is applied as a base coat. The other two are applied with a brush, feather, cloth, or any other tool to give a marbleized effect.

MARBLEIZE

To apply a paint finish resembling marble.

MARBLE TILE

A solid piece of marble ½ in. thick and cut into 8- and 12-in. squares. It is available in several colors and with a gloss or satin finish. Application is made with adhesive or by setting in concrete.

MARLBOROUGH FOOT

See Block Foot.

MARQUETRY

A decorative inlayed design made in furniture with choice wood veneers, ivory, mother-of-pearl, etc. *Boulle* is an especially elaborate form of marquetry named for a French cabinetmaker.

MARQUISETTE
A fine, sheer fabric with a lacy effect used for curtains. Generally made of polyester, it can be soft or crisp.

MASONRY
A structural element made of or bonded together with cement mortar.

MASONRY, PLASTIC
Plastics molded to resemble bricks or stones are laid up in a wall. They are fair to good imitations of real masonry, much less expensive, light in weight, very cleanable, and reasonably durable. But they are damaged by fire and heat.

All the materials must be installed with adhesive to a smooth, sound, clean subwall. Some of the coverings are made in panels up to 4 x 8 ft.; others are the same size as individual bricks or stones. All have molded-in "mortar joints", but joints between panels or pieces must be filled by the installer.

MASONRY SEALER
A transparent liquid used to penetrate and seal the pores of masonry to help prevent staining and to simplify cleaning. Brick, stone, and other masonry floors are often given a couple of coats of sealer. The floors can then be waxed or left as is.

MASTER SWITCH
The large switch between the fuse box and the electric meter which controls the flow of current to the house. It is also called the *main disconnect switch.*

MASTIC
A thick, gooey adhesive.

MATCHED
Boards which are designed to be fitted together by means of tongue-and-grooved or rabbeted joints. Board panels, plywood, and furniture veneers which have similar grain or figure are also said to be matched.

MATELASSÉ
A double fabric with a quilted or crinkled effect resulting from the way the surface is joined to the back fabric. Difficult to clean but durable, it is used in draperies and upholstery.

MATTE FINISH
See Flat Finish.

MEDALLION BACK
An oval-shaped chair or settee back. The oval is framed in wood with the center upholstered.

MEDITERRANEAN
A currently popular decorating and furniture style featuring dark woods, elaborate carving, arches, leather, etc. Also called *Spanish style.*

MEDULLARY RAY
One of the bands of cells which extend from the heart of a log across the grain to the bark. They are inconspicuous in most woods but prominent in others such as oak.

MEETING RAIL
On a double-hung window, the meeting rail is the top rail of the lower sash and the bottom rail of the top sash. It is also called the *check rail.*

MENDING PLATE
A rigid strip of steel or brass used to reinforce joints in wood and sometimes other materials. It is usually attached with screws but may be attached with nuts and bolts.

All metal strips used for making connections are mending plates. These include angle irons (*see above*) and T plates (*see below*). But the device to which the name is usually applied is a straight strip up to 4 in. long with four screw holes.

MERCURY-VAPOR BULB
A very efficient type of light bulb with a high light output and long life. However, it is at present rarely used

in homes because it gives a very cool, unflattering blue-white light and takes several minutes to attain full brightness.

MERIDIENNE
A French day bed with arms of unequal height connected by a sloping back.

METAL FOIL WALLCOVERING
A material consisting of very thin sheets of metal laminated to a paper or cloth backing. Most coverings are of plain design, but some are hand-printed or flocked or are produced in a raised pattern. All come in rolls covering 36 sq. ft. and are hung more or less like wallpaper. Lining paper is required under paper-backed foils.

METAL-HALIDE BULB
A long-life, high-output light source which is presently of little value to homeowners because of the unnatural color of the light and the slow start-up time. Lamp manufacturers, however, expect that it will become more widely used for lighting the grounds around houses.

METALLIC FIBER
Any manufactured fiber composed of metal, plastic-coated metal, or metal-covered plastic. When used in decorations or furnishings, metal fibers treated with plastic are generally preferable to pure metal fibers because they are lighter, stronger, and more resistant to tarnishing.

METALLIC PAINT
An oil paint containing tiny particles of metal. It is used as a decorative finish. Aluminum paint is also used as a sealer and to reflect heat.

METAL TILE
Wall tiles made of 4¼-in. squares of aluminum with a baked-on enamel finish or of solid stainless steel. Applied to a smooth wall base with adhesive, they are best suited for use in kitchens behind ranges, sinks, and counters.

METER

A device for measuring the amount of electricity, gas, or water consumed by a household. In the past, meters were installed in houses or garages, but today electric and gas meters are almost always mounted on an exterior wall. Water meters are usually in the basement.

METHACRYLATE PANEL

See Plastic Paneling.

MEZZANINE

A theater-like gallery which is part of and overlooks a room with an unusually high ceiling.

MILDEW

Mildew, a fungus, is almost certain to be troublesome in all houses built in humid or semi-humid climates; and in dry climates, it can also cover the interior surfaces of tightly constructed houses in which a lot of water is used. Prevention, in all cases, is difficult, but the thin, dirty deposits can be minimized if houses are designed so that air flows through freely in warm, damp weather and if all paint used contains a mildew-retardant additive.

Additional steps which will stop mildew include those used to keep basements and crawl spaces dry.

MILLWORK

Millwork includes lumber which is milled to special shapes, such as moldings, and also assembled building materials, such as doors and windows. Most millwork today is produced to stock designs in a limited number of sizes. This helps to hold down cost but makes it difficult to achieve a special effect except by having millwork produced to order.

MINERAL-FIBER SHINGLE

See Asbestos-Cement Shingle.

MINERAL SPIRITS

An almost odorless liquid for thinning alkyd and oil-base paints and varnishes, and for cleaning up after application.

Mineral spirits are also called *petroleum spirits, petroleum distillates,* and simply *paint thinners.*

MINERAL WOOL
        A fibrous insulating material made by blowing molten rock or furnace slag into fine filaments or fibers. It can be used interchangeably with fiberglass insulation. It is also called *rock wool.*

MIRROR
        Although a mirror is just a mirror to many people, it is a utilitarian and decorative object with many variations.

    Most mirrors are made of glass. The best—because they are strong and free of distortions—are made of ¼-in. plate glass. Those made of ¼-in. float glass are only slightly inferior. But the drawbacks of mirrors made of 1/8-in. sheet glass are obvious: They are not only fragile but also give a distorted, wavy appearance to the image; consequently, they should be used only in small sizes.

    All types of glass mirror are available in the usual silvered form as well as in special patterns (veined, antiqued, stenciled, etc.) and colors. None of the patterned or colored mirrors is as fully reflective as a silver mirror.

    Two-way mirrors are made so a person can see a reflection in one side and see through from the other side. For best results, the reflecting side should be brightly lighted, the other side dim.

    Glass mirrors are produced in innumerable sizes. It is possible to get them big enough to cover the average bedroom wall in one piece. Because of the weight and fragility of large mirrors (which are always made of ¼-in. glass), installation should be left to the professional. Small mirrors are usually framed and hung on picture hooks. Unframed small mirrors of plate or float glass can also be mounted directly on flat walls. The easiest installation is made with plastic mirror clips screwed around the edges. A somewhat neater installation is made with straps screwed to the wall under the top and bottom edges of the mirror. The mirror is then set into clips mounted on the straps. A third method of installation, which should be used only if a mirror is never to be taken down, is to spread beads of silicone-rubber adhesive over about 25% of the mirror back and stick it to the wall.

    Acrylic mirror is unbreakable and only half as heavy as plate-glass mirror. It also costs less than plate-glass mirror but is as combustible as wood and reflects a slightly distorted image. It is made in silver and several solid colors in sizes up to 6 x 9 ft.

Acrylic mirrors are mounted directly on any level, smooth, clean wall with double-faced adhesive tape, silicone-rubber adhesive, or mirror clips. Tape or adhesive should be used only for permanent installations because they pull the reflective film off the back of a mirror which is taken down from a wall.

Acrylic mirrors can be bent to conform to curved walls. They can also be painted on both sides with acrylic-base enamels or decorated by stenciling, engraving, or appliqueing.

MIRROR TILE

A 12 x 12-in. or larger square of mirror made of acrylic or of sheet, float, or plate glass used to cover interior walls in a tiled pattern. The tiles are available in a variety of colors and patterns. So-called flexible mirror tiles are 1-ft. squares divided into 1-in. squares mounted on a backing and used to cover furniture, cabinets, or interior house surfaces.

The walls on which mirror tiles are installed must be strong, sound, level, smooth, and clean. The tiles are applied with double-faced adhesive tape stuck to the backs in strips or small squares.

MISSION

An early-20th century style of American furniture which was usually made of oak. It has a heavy, square-shaped, medieval look with little beauty.

MITER

To cut at an angle other than 90°. Also, a surface cut at an angle.

MITER JOINT

A joint made by mitering the pieces to be joined to corresponding angles and fastening them together with nails, screws, dowels, glue, or special fasteners such as corrugated nails or angle irons.

In a more elaborate miter joint, the mitered edges are tongue-and-grooved and then glued. In a splined miter joint, both edges are grooved and held together by a glued spline.

MIXING VALVE

A plumbing valve which blends hot water with cold to a desired temperature. It has a single handle.

MOBILE

A piece of sculpture made up of several balanced parts which is suspended from a ceiling, roof, tree, or other overhead structure by a wire or cord so that it will move freely in a breeze or even a slight air current.

Mobiles can be made out of any material, although the best are generally metal or wood. They vary from small, lightweight sculptures to enormous pieces weighing hundreds of pounds. *Compare* stabile.

MODACRYLIC

A modified acrylic fiber with many of the same properties. The fibers are used in carpets because they help to reduce flammability. They are also used in draperies and fur-like pile fabrics.

MODERN

An ever-changing style of architecture, furniture, and decoration. What is called modern today bears only slight resemblance to the moderne of 1925. The single constant is a dedication to pure, clean lines.

MODILLION

A bracket (*see above*) supporting the upper members of a cornice.

MODULAR UNIT

A box-like furniture piece used for storage. *See* Cube.

MODULE

A unit of measure serving as the basis for standardization of building materials. As a result of this standardization, houses are less costly to build than they would be otherwise.

The accepted building module is 4 ft. or any easily divisible fraction thereof, such as 8 in. Materials which are supplied in this module include plywood, gypsum board, bricks, concrete blocks, etc.

Modular planning and modular construction mean to plan and build a house in multiples of 4 ft.

MOHAIR

The lustrous hair of Angora goats. It goes into a smooth, durable, resilient fabric used for upholstering furniture.

MOIRÉ
A fabric with a wavy or watery appearance used in draperies and bedspreads. The walls of the Green Room in the White House are covered with it. It is woven from silk, rayon, or cotton fibers.

MOLDING
A specially shaped wooden or sometimes urethane strip used in many places inside and outside a house. Its purpose is occasionally strictly decorative, but usually it has a practical purpose, such as concealing joints or for hanging pictures.

MOLLY SCREW
See Hollow-Wall Screw Anchor.

MONK'S CLOTH
A loose, coarse cotton fabric with a basketweave which is used for draperies and slipcovers.

MONTAGE
A picture made by combining a number of photographs.

MORTAR
A mixture of water, sand, and portland cement or lime (or both) used to bond together bricks, stones, and other masonry units. For most work, the mortar consists of 1 sack masonry cement and 2 to 3 cu. ft. sand, or of 1 sack portland cement, 3 cu. ft. sand, and 10% hydrated lime (approximately one small shovelful of lime to each sack of cement). Enough water is added to produce a workable plastic. If the mixture is too wet and sticky, it is said to be *fat*; if it is more or less nonadhesive and hard to spread, it is *lean.*

All concrete mortar joints (except those made with special cements) are about ½ in. thick.

MORTAR JOINT
Joints between bricks, concrete blocks, and other masonry units must be filled with mortar to keep out moisture. The joints also give texture and color to walls.

A mortar joint should be finished soon after the bricks, etc., have been laid, while the mortar is still workable. Six types of joints are commonly used:

Flush Joint • The mortar that squeezes out from between the bricks is cut off flush with the face of the bricks. It may be smoothed or left rough.

Weathered Joint • The mortar is beveled backward and upward so that the top brick overhangs it.

Struck Joint • The reverse of a weathered joint. The mortar is beveled backward and downward so that a shallow ledge is formed along the top of the bottom brick. This is less weatherproof than a weathered joint.

Concave Joint • The mortar is given a concave shape with a special rounded tool or simply the end of a pipe.

V Joint • The joint is formed into a shallow V with a special tool.

Raked Joint • The mortar is raked out to an even depth to a flat surface parallel with the face of the bricks but recessed behind the face about ¼ or ½ in.

Forming a joint with a mason's trowel is called *striking* the joint. When a special tool is used, the joint is *tooled.*

MORTGAGE

Whether they can afford to buy a house outright or not, most Americans prefer to buy on mortgage. To get a mortgage they depend on five sources: savings and loan associations, mutual savings banks, commercial banks, life insurance companies, and private individuals. The interest rates charged by these sources, the duration of the mortgage, and the special conditions attached to the mortgage vary with the state of the money market.

Types of mortgage which are generally available include:

Conventional Mortgages • Mortgages which are secured only by the value of the mortgaged property and the integrity of the borrower. For this reason, the lender usually requires a substantial down payment. The interest rate paid by the borrower is determined by the money market at the time the mortgage is written. Once set, it does not change.

Variable Rate Mortgages • A new kind of mortgage under which the borrower pays a higher interest rate when interest rates in general go up. Similarly, he pays a lower rate when rates in general go down.

FHA Mortgages • Mortgages issued by a lending organization which the Federal Housing Administration accepts as a qualified lender. The FHA insures the lender against loss in case the mortgage is foreclosed. The down payment required is generally low. The interest rate is established by the government.

VA Mortgages • Mortgage loans made only to a qualified military veteran or his widow. The loan is made by a private lender who is guaranteed by the government against loss if a mortgage is foreclosed. The mortgage is liberal and the interest rate, set by the government, low.

Open-End Mortgages • Conventional mortgages which contain a provision allowing the homeowner to borrow additional money to make improvements in his house. The additional money becomes available only as the principal is paid off.

Second Mortgages • Short-term, high-interest mortgages secured and recorded after the first mortgage. They are, in other words, additional to the first mortgage but subordinate to it.

Under the terms of most mortgages, the monthly payments made by the homeowner cover both principal and interest. But flexible mortgages are written which allow the homeowner to pay only the interest on a loan for the first five years; repayment of principal doesn't start until the sixth year.

MORTISE
A hole made in wood or other material into which something is inserted.

MORTISE-AND-TENON JOINT
A wood joint used in making furniture, cabinets, doors and windows, etc. A mortise is cut in one of the pieces to be joined; a tongue-like tenon is made in the other. The tenon is then inserted in the mortise and glued.

In a *blind mortise-and-tenon joint,* the mortise extends only part way through the wood and the tenon is completely concealed in it. In a *through mortise-and-tenon joint,* the mortise extends through the wood so that the end of the tenon is exposed. When the tenon protrudes beyond a through mortise, the tenon is also mortised to receive a wooden wedge, called a *key*. The result is a *keyed mortise-and-tenon joint.*

Other mortise-and-tenon joints are called *haunched* and *mitered.* The first is used to join a rail to a stile in a paneled door. The latter is used in furniture.

MOSAIC
A picture or decoration composed of small pieces of tile, glass, stone, etc., set in mortar or adhesive. Mosaic tiles are 1-in. square (usually) ceramic tiles mounted on a flexible backing in 1-ft. squares. *See* Tile, Ceramic.

MOUCHARABI
A pierced wooden panel made in Africa.

MOUNT
A decorative piece of hardware or metal on the face of a furniture piece.

MUD ROOM
An entry or small room between the back door and the rest of the house where people take off and hang up their outer clothing. Its purpose is to prevent unnecessary dirtying of the living areas.

In farm houses, the mud room—called a *wash room*—often has a lavatory and shower so the farmer and others can clean up before entering the house.

MULL
A soft, sheer, lustrous cotton, rayon, or silk fabric used in draperies.

MULLION
One of the slender bars between panes of a multi-paned window sash. It is sometimes called a *muntin.* A mullion is also the vertical framing member in the middle of a paneled door.

MULTI-COLORED PAINT
A paint containing two or more colors used to produce a multi-tone effect on walls, woodwork, and furniture. It also helps to conceal imperfections in surfaces.

Application is usually made with a sprayer, but several types of paint can be brushed on.

MUNTIN

A mullion (*see above*).

MURAL

A large picture painted on a wall or painted on canvas and mounted on a wall. A scenic wallpaper is a kind of mural.

MURIATIC ACID

A strong, dangerous chemical used to etch masonry and metal surfaces before painting. It is also used to clean masonry—especially to remove mortar stains and efflorescence. Muriatic and hydrochloric acids are the same thing.

MUSLIN

A sturdy, inexpensive cotton fabric, usually rather coarse but sometimes sheer. It is sometimes made into curtains, simple bed-spreads, and table skirts. It is also used as a lining under scenic wallpapers which the owner may want to take down and rehang on another wall.

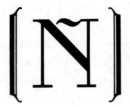

NAIL

Almost all nails in residential construction are made of steel. Those used indoors are of bright steel which quickly rusts if exposed to moisture. Nails for exterior use should always be galvanized, although builders frequently ignore this requirement.

Steel nails with special finishes are used to some extent for special purposes. Aluminum nails are occasionally used outdoors, particularly in the application of aluminum flashing, etc.

The sizes of most nails are described by the word "penny" or the letter "d". Standard sizes are as follows:

2d	1 in.	10d	3 in.
3d	1¼ in.	12d	3¼ in.
4d	1½ in.	16d	3½ in.
5d	1¾ in.	20d	4 in.
6d	2 in.	30d	4½ in.
7d	2¼ in.	40d	5 in.
8d	2½ in.	50d	5½ in.
9d	2¾ in.	60d	6 in.

The types of nail most often used in and around houses include the following:

Common Nails • Standard construction nails with flat, round heads and thick shanks. They are used for framing a house, applying sheathing and subfloors, applying wood and plywood siding, etc. In concealed work, the heads are left exposed, but in siding they are usually countersunk and covered with putty.

Spikes • Common nails over 6 in. long. They are sold by the inch rather than by the penny.

Box Nails • Like common nails but with thin shanks. They are used where common nails might split wood.

Wire Nails • Tiny common nails for fastening thin materials such as lattice strips. They are sold by the inch.

Finishing Nails • Thin-shanked nails with very small globular heads which are easily countersunk. They are used to apply interior and exterior finish.

Casing Nails • Almost identical to finishing nails and used more or less interchangeably with them. The shanks are a trifle thicker.

Brads • Tiny finishing nails.

Shingle Nails • Short common nails always galvanized and with very sharp points.

Roofing Nails • Even shorter galvanized common nails with very wide heads.

Annular-Ring Nails • Common nails with concentric grooves in the shanks so they will hold better in wood. They should always be used to apply gypsum board to walls and ceilings. Also called *ring-grooved* or *ringed-shank nails.*

Screw Nails • The shanks have steep spiral threads to increase holding power. The heads are small. They are used for laying wooden floors.

Cut Nails • Also used for laying wooden floors. The shanks are rectangular and tapering, the heads rectangular and flat.

NEEDLE

A horizontal steel girder used to hold up a wall temporarily while a permanent supporting structure is built underneath. Needles are used, for example, when an old building with inadequate foundations is being remodeled.

NEEDLEPOINT

A hand embroidery made on mesh canvas usually with wool yarn. It is used to upholster furniture and to make pillow covers, rugs, and wall hangings. Three basic stitches are used: *petit point, grospoint,* and *bargello. Flamestitch* is a form of bargello.

NEOCLASSIC

A style of architecture and furnishings which makes a return to the straight lines, geometric curves, and regulated rhythms of the ancient classic style. Neoclassicism thrived in France, England, and America from roughly 1750 to 1850.

In France, the Neoclassic era can be subdivided into Louis XVI, Directoire, and Empire periods. In England, the early Neoclassic period corresponded to the Late Georgian period; the Late Neoclassic period corresponded to the Regency period. In the United States, the Federal and Greek Revival periods comprised the Neoclassic era.

NEUTRAL WIRE

The white wire in an electrical circuit. It is always connected to the silver terminal in a switch or outlet.

NEWEL CAP

The part of a stair railing or balustrade supported on top of a newel post.

NEWEL POST

One of the large posts at the bottom and top of a stair railing or at the ends of a balustrade. Similar posts are also installed at sharp turns in railings and balustrades.

NICHE

A small, usually vertical wall recess used to display an art object such as a piece of sculpture or handsome vase. It may extend all the way or only part way to the floor; usually it has a clamshell top.

NIGHT STAND

A bedside table. *See* table.

NINON

A chiffonlike fabric, but harder and heavier. It is made of various fibers and is used for curtains and draperies.

NIPPLE

A short threaded piece of pipe. Nipples are used in plumbing systems and also to attach light fixtures to outlet boxes.

NOMINAL SIZE

The stated size, although the actual size may be smaller. For instance, the nominal size of a 12-in. board is 1 x 12 in., although the actual size is ¾ x 11½ in. Similarly, the nominal size of a standard concrete block is 8 x 8 x 16 in., although the actual size is 7-5/8 x 7-5/8 x 15-5/8 in. On the other hand, the standard panel of plywood or gypsum board has a nominal and actual size of 4 x 8 ft.

NONBEARING WALL

A wall or partition which does not support the structure above. *See* Bearing Wall.

NONMETALLIC SHEATHED CABLE

An electrical cable with two or more insulated wires inside and covered on the outside by a tough, braided jacket or sheath. The least expensive type of electrical cable, it is permitted by some communities for residential wiring, and prohibited by others. Even where permitted, it should never be used outdoors, underground, or in masonry.

NOSING

A rounded wooden edge. The word is applied primarily to the rounded edges of stair treads. The front nosing is usually an integral part of a tread, but if a stair is exposed along the sides, separate nosings are nailed to the ends of the treads.

NURSERY

Although young families very often designate one room in their houses—usually the smallest bedroom—as a nursery, almost no houses are built with a room specifically designed for use as a nursery. It can be argued, of course, that such specificity is unnecessary and unwise economically in these times. But if a room is meant to serve two purposes—first as a nursery and then as a bedroom or study—the requirements of a good nursery should at least be given more thought.

The principal need is to locate and/or arrange the room so that the crib and dressing table can be placed where they do not interfere with entrance and egress, and where there is full headroom so one can dress the baby, make up the crib, etc., without bending double.

Space for a bassinet should be large enough to accommodate at later dates a crib, then a junior bed, and perhaps even a full-size bed. Free floor space should be large enough for a play pen.

NUT

A threaded device for tightening and holding a bolt in place. *See* Bolt.

NYLON

The strongest of all commonly used man-made fibers, nylon has good dimensional stability, resiliency, and abrasion resistance, but poor resistance to sunlight and soiling. It has various uses in home furnishings but is especially popular as a carpet fiber.

As a solid material, nylon is usually used in small parts such as gears and faucet seats.

NYLON ANCHOR

A small cylinder of nylon which expands and grips the sides of a hole drilled to receive it. The nearest thing to an all-purpose anchor, it is used to fasten things in masonry walls and also to thin surfaces such as ¼-in. hardboard.

OAK, ENGLISH

All oak is heavy, hard, curable, strong, and tough. English oak is more definitely brown in color than red or white oak and sometimes has black spots. The grain and figure are of such character that the wood is much used as a veneer.

OAK, RED

Red oak is an American wood somewhat less durable than American white oak because of its coarser grain and large open pores. It is a little redder and more uniform in color than white oak. Most flooring is made of it. Other uses are in furniture cabinets and paneling.

OAK, WHITE

The outstanding oak for flooring, furniture, and paneling. It is more decay resistant than red oak; also, it is a little tougher and of somewhat more refined appearance. It is the most important American hardwood.

OBJET D'ART

A small artistic or decorative object. In conversation the term is often abbreviated to *objet*.

ODOR CONTROL

Most homeowners take care of unpleasant odors by simply opening windows, turning on ventilating fans, or spraying with an aerosol air freshener. Automatic year-round odor control can be had, however, by installing a new electrical appliance which distributes through the house a chemical that neutralizes odors and adds a slight scent to the air. The device is installed in a warm-air heating or air conditioning system or by itself on a wall in the center of the house.

OFFSET
Any surface in a different plane from a more important adjacent surface. A sunken panel in a wall is an offset. A small alcove may also be called an offset.

OGEE
A molding with a curve shaped something like an S. The word is also used to describe an S-shaped curve.

OIL
A painting done with oil paints applied to stretched canvas or stiff composition board. It needs no protection but should be professionally cleaned every few years. The canvas should be kept taut but not drumhead tight.

OIL PAINT
Properly called an *oil-base paint*, this is a paint in which the pigment is suspended in oil. *See* Paint.

OIL TANK
Tanks used for storing fuel oil on residential properties range from 250 to 1000 gal. in capacity. They are commonly buried in the ground outside a house, but in many communities they may be installed in the basement (in some cases, however, these must be walled off behind masonry).

Generally oil tanks should be located within 60 ft. of the burner and 100 ft. of the point of delivery, and they should not be less than 8 ft. lower than the burner. But by use of pumps, the distance from the burner and the depth can be increased.

OLEFIN
A group of plastics including polypropylene and poly-ethylene. The olefin fibers often discussed in carpet advertisements are polypropylene.

ON CENTER

A term used to describe the spacing between studs, joists, and rafters. The space is measured from the center line of one timber to the center line of the next. In conventional construction, the timbers are spaced 16 in. on center. This may be written 16 in. o.c.

ONE-COAT HOUSE PAINT

A heavily pigmented oil or latex paint which gives good coverage with only one coat. However, it does this only if applied over previously primed or painted surfaces which are in sound condition. It is not applied to bare wood.

OPEN FLOOR PLAN

A house with few interior partitions. This increases the spacious feeling, but it also makes for a very noisy house and minimizes privacy.

OPEN STRING

A stair without walls on the sides or with a wall on only one side.

OPENWORK

A surface with openings which can be seen through. Room dividers frequently contain openwork. So do cabinets, radiator covers, and parts of furniture. Openwork is usually made of a solid panel which is stamped, cut, or pierced; but it can be made by applying strips over one another at an angle, as in a lattice.

OPTION

In real estate, an option is a right to buy a piece of property. The option is usually secured with money. If the option holder exercises his right, the grantor is obligated to sell the property to him (if the price is agreed to). If the option holder does not exercise his right, he is not liable for damages, although he usually loses whatever money he has put up.

ORANGERIE

Also spelled *orangery*, a greenhouse or simply a glass-enclosed room in which orange trees—along with other tropical plants—are grown.

ORDER

A column with its base (usually), shaft, and capital and the entablature it supports.

In classic Greek architecture there were three orders of column—the Doric, Ionic, and Corinthian.

The *Doric order* has a fluted shaft without a base. The capital consists of a circular cushion topped with a plain square plinth. The entablature consists of the architrave, decorated frieze, and projecting cornice.

The *Ionic order* has a more slender fluted shaft with a base and is topped by a capital adorned with large volutes. The entablature comprises two or three flat bands and a decorative molding, a simple frieze, and a very beautiful cornice, often with rows of dentils.

The *Corinthian order* also has a slender fluted shaft with base, but the capital is more elaborate. It consists of a bell-shaped cone surrounded by several rows of acanthus leaves and, above these, pairs of branching scrolls which meet at the corners in spiral volutes. The entablature is much like that of the Ionic order.

Roman designers borrowed the three Greek orders and added two more—the *Tuscan* and *Composite*. The former is a rudimentary Doric; the latter has a capital combining parts of the Ionic and Corinthian capitals.

ORGANDY

A stiff, translucent cotton or nylon fabric used for curtains. Since organdy is rather difficult to launder, these should be hung only where they are subjected to little soiling.

ORIEL

A window projecting beyond the face of a wall. A bay window, for example.

ORIENTAL

A rug produced in the Near East in which each tuft of wool, silk, or silky animal hair is hand-knotted to the backing.

ORMOLU

Ground gold or an alloy of copper and zinc used to gild furniture and ornaments. Ormolu decoration was popular in the 19th century and was applied particularly to fussy candelabras festooned with prisms.

OSNABURG

A strong, durable, rough-textured cotton fabric with an open weave. It is used for informal curtains and coverings.

OTTOMAN

A large footstool with an overstuffed top. It is sometimes made as a companion piece to and sold with an upholstered chair—in which case the ottoman is the same height as the chair seat.

OUTLET

In electric wiring, an outlet is the point at which electricity is used. Although most people think of it only as a plug-in receptacle in a wall, it is also the box into which a light fixture is permanently wired (*lighting outlet*). A switch is not an outlet because it does not use current—it simply controls it—but when an electrical contractor gives a price on wiring a house, he counts each wall switch as an outlet.

Plug-in outlets—more often called *convenience outlets*—are made in various designs. The commonest is a duplex outlet with two receptacles into which light and appliance cords are plugged. But single, triple, and four-plug outlets are made, and there are also specialized outlets for clocks, exterior installation, etc.

In houses built before about 1968, each receptacle in an outlet had two holes to receive plugs with two prongs. Since then, most outlets have three holes. The third, centered near the bottom of the receptacle, is U-shaped. This is a grounded outlet and is designed to make the use of tools, appliances, lights, etc., safer. Most electrical codes now require installation of grounded outlets.

In a house with adequate wiring, outlets used mainly for the connection of lamps should be provided in all principal rooms on the basis of one outlet per 150 sq. ft. of floor space. They should be installed wherever a furniture arrangement calls for a floor or table lamp. In all cases, however, they should be located so that no point along the floor line is more than 6 ft. from an outlet. Normal height above the floor is 1 ft., although this can be varied. In front of a large window wall, the outlets are usually installed in the floor.

In halls, outlets are placed where portable lamps are to be used. In long halls, they are spaced 15 ft. apart; in big, wide halls, they are placed so that no point along the floor line is more than 10 ft. from an outlet.

In a dining room or breakfast room, one outlet connected to an appliance circuit is advisable behind the buffet or other piece of furniture on which a toaster, etc., may be used.

In bathrooms, if the light fixtures beside the medicine cabinet do not incorporate outlets, there should be one outlet near the mirror.

On terraces, patios, or decks, there should be one outlet per 15 ft. of solid wall. These and all other outdoor outlets should be of weatherproof design and installed at least 18 in. above the paving or ground.

Appliance outlets in the kitchen should be provided for every 4 running feet or work surface. No counter should be without an outlet. Installation is made 44 in. above the floor. One or more outlets for appliances should also be installed in a laundry room.

OUT OF TRUE

Not plumb or level. A wall which slants even slightly is out of true.

OUTSIDE CORNER

In an ordinary packing box, the outside corners are the four corners on the exterior of the box; the inside corners are those in the box. The same terms are used to describe the corners of a house, wall, or furniture piece.

An outside corner is normally a 270° corner; an inside corner, a 90° corner.

OVERHANG

Today an overhang is usually thought to be that part of the roof which extends out over the exterior walls. In early days, the second floors of New England Colonial houses often overhung the first floors about a foot. Modern-day replicas of such houses have similar overhangs.

OVERLAY

Anything which is applied or laid directly over something else. For example, some exterior plywood panels are made with an overlay to assure a tight, long-lasting paint bond. An overlay door is one which overlaps the jambs or casings slightly.

OVERLOAD
To use more lights, appliances, and other devices at the same time than an electrical circuit can carry. For example, a 15-amp, 120-volt wiring circuit made with No. 14 wire has a capacity of 1800 watts; a 20-amp, 120-volt wiring circuit made with No. 12 wire has a capacity of 2400 watts. If, in either case, the wattage of the equipment in use exceeds these amounts, the circuit becomes overloaded, and the fuse should blow or the circuit breakers should trip to prevent dangerous overheating of the wires.

OVERMANTEL
The space over a mantel shelf. It is usually paneled or outlined with moldings.

OVERMANTEL MIRROR
A mirror made specifically for hanging over a mantel shelf. Victorian overmantel mirrors were elaborately carved and often had little shelves for the display of art objects.

OXALIC ACID
An acid used to bleach color. Available in crystalline form, it is mixed with water before use.

OXBOW FRONT
The undulating front of a case piece, such as a chest of drawers. It is concave at the center and convex on either side. Also called a *yoke front,* it is the opposite of a serpentine front.

[P]

PADAUK

A distinctive furniture wood of a rich reddish color with darker streaks and large open pores. It is exceptionally strong, hard, and heavy. It comes from Burma and the Andaman Islands.

PAD FOOT

A furniture foot shaped like a dog's pad at the base of a cabriole leg. Also called a *Dutch foot.*

PAINT

The paints and related paintlike finishes used in and around the house fall into seven broad groups: oil-base paints, alkyd paints, emulsion paints, portland cement paints, catalytic coatings, clear finishes, and stains.

1 / *Oil-base paints* are interior and exterior paints made with a pigment suspended in oil and thinned with a solvent—usually turpentine or mineral spirits. Because they are slow drying and have a strong odor, they are not as popular today as they were, but are still widely used outdoors.

2 / *Alkyd paints*, made with a manufactured resin called *alkyd* and thinned with mineral spirits, are the principal replacements for oil-base paints. Used indoors and out, they are easy to apply, nearly odorless, and fast-drying, and they produce a very tough coating which can be washed repeatedly.

3 / Emulsion paints are made by mixing pigments and chemicals in water instead of dissolving them in solvents. One of the newer types is a *linseed-oil emulsion* used for house painting. But the most important is *latex paint*—the most popular paint for application to interior walls and ceilings, and fast becoming the most popular paint for outdoor use, too. It has reached this point because it is very quick-drying, almost odorless, and easy to touch up, and it makes for easy after-job cleanup. In addition, it produces an excellent durable, washable finish; is unlikely to blister if water is trapped behind it; and can be applied to a damp surface or one containing alkalies.

4 / Portland-cement paint is sold as a dry powder which is mixed with water and applied to masonry surfaces—to which it sticks tenaciously, even in the presence of moisture. One type, called a *cementitious coating*, is a very thick paint used to waterproof interior basement walls.

5 / Catalytic coatings are paints which dry through a chemical process. The most popular kind—made with epoxy—produces one of the toughest finishes available to house painters. It can be applied to most materials.

6 / Clear finishes include varnish, shellac, lacquer, sealers, and water repellents. The first three (which are also made in pigmented finishes) are used indoors more than out. They build up a hard film on the surface. The last two are penetrating finishes that seal the pores of the material to which they are applied and change the surface appearance only slightly, if at all. They are used indoors and out.

7 / Stains are transparent or semi-opaque finishes which change the color of wood and plywood, but do not conceal the texture. Those in commonest use are made with oil. Long applied to furniture, cabinets, floors, paneling, and woodwork, they have recently become very popular as an exterior finish—especially on shingles and other wooden sidings with a rough texture.

House Painting • Latex paint is generally used on masonry walls and is often recommended for wooden walls; but because its wearability is subject to doubt, linseed oil paint and semi-opaque oil stains are still the first choice on wood. Alkyd enamel is used on trim. If a clear finish is desired, a transparent oil stain is used to change the color of wood; a water repellent is used to retain the natural color of wood.

Most exterior finishes last four or five years and then need to be redone. The most durable pigmented finish is produced by a transparent oil stain. This lasts approximately eight to ten years on rough wood. Water repellents also have a long life in dry climates, but may need to be renewed every few years in humid climates.

Fall is usually the ideal time for painting a house in most parts of the country, but the work can be done whenever the temperature ranges between 50° and 80°. There should be little wind and few insects.

Unless wood or plywood is to be given a clear finish, there is no need to hurry to get a new house painted. Several months of weathering help to let moisture escape from both wood and masonry. When painting is started, the priming coat should be followed within no more than two weeks by the finish coat. If there is a longer time lag, a phenomenon known as *intercoat peeling* may damage the top coat.

Interior Painting • Flat latex paint is almost always used to finish plaster and gypsum board walls and ceilings in living and sleeping areas. Semi-gloss alkyd paint, however, is generally recommended for kitchens and bathrooms where fairly frequent washing is required, and for wood, plywood, and hardboard paneling. Semi-gloss or gloss alkyd is always used on doors, windows, and woodwork because of its superior washability.

Natural-finish woodwork and paneling generally require a hard protective coating to keep them from soiling. This can be achieved with two coats of varnish or with a coat of white shellac followed by a coat of varnish (shellac serves as a knot-sealer and usually dries fast enough to permit application of the finish coat the same day).

Penetrating floor sealer is the most satisfactory finish for wooden floors because it has good resistance to wear and can be touched up when it becomes scratched without showing lap marks.

Clear finishes are best applied with a brush. Latex and alkyd paints are usually applied to walls and ceilings with a roller to save time. The resulting finish, however, has a slight pebbly texture. For a smoother finish, the paint should be applied with a brush or, better, a spray gun.

PAINTING

A colored picture executed in oil, water color, or acrylic paint. So much emphasis is currently being placed on the value of paintings as investments that doubt is raised as to whether they are appreciated for the contribution they make to the beauty of the home and the minds of the viewers.

Money aside, if a painting has merit, it should be hung where it can be enjoyed and where it complements or perhaps dominates the decorative scheme. In other words, it should be—

1 / In clear view—not hidden in shadows, obscured by too much light or by light striking it from the wrong direction, or blocked by furniture.

2 / Reasonably isolated from other paintings. The practice of grouping paintings for mass effect is laudable if the paintings are of little merit. A good painting can—and should—hang alone.

3 / Hung slightly below the eye level of the average viewer.

4 / In scale with the furniture under and around it.

5 / In general proportion to the wall space. Wide pictures generally look best on horizontal walls, tall pictures on vertical walls.

PAISLEY

A light wool fabric with woven figures or a silk fabric printed to imitate the woolen. It is used for hangings and coverings.

PALDAO

A Philippine hardwood with a gray to reddish-brown background color and darker streaks of varying colors. The wood is hard and very strong, and used in furniture.

PALLET

A square board platform used in shipping and warehousing manufactured goods. Pallets of redwood timbers are now made for flooring decks. The boards in adjoining pallets are laid at right angles, as in a parquet floor.

PANEL

That part of a surface which is sunk slightly below or raised slightly above the surrounding surface, or which is on the same plane as the surrounding surface but set off from it by some kind of frame. Sunken panels are usually identified as recessed or raised. A *recessed panel* is a flat surface. In a *raised panel*, a narrow border around the sides is beveled backward, and the large middle area (the *field*) is on the same plane as the surrounding framework or set slightly back from it.

Large sheets of plywood, hardboard, gypsum board, or the like are also called panels.

PANELING

Originally, paneling was a decorative wooden surface applied to walls, ceilings, or furniture. It consisted of an assortment of panels (*see above*) set off from the surrounding surface by a framework of stiles and rails. Panels which were recessed (the common type) were allowed to float—that is, they were not fixed with glue, nails, or screws, in order to allow for expansion and contraction of the wood. This kind of paneling is still used to some extent in custom-built homes.

Today, however, paneling is more likely to consist of boards (usually beveled or otherwise milled along the edges), plywood, hardboard, particleboard, or even plastics. This is considerably simpler in appearance as well as construction.

Wooden and plywood paneling is usually given a transparent finish to bring out the grain, texture, and natural color of the wood. It may be painted, however; and in some cases, it is covered with wallpaper, vinyl, fabric, etc.

PANTRY

A small room most often used for storage of dishes, foods, utensils, etc., and with a sink for washing dishes, serving drinks, etc. The usual location is between the kitchen and dining room; thus, the pantry helps to mute kitchen noises heard in the dining room and keep out kitchen odors. But it may be placed anywhere in the vicinity of the kitchen. Pantries were common in old houses but disappeared almost completely after World War II.

PARAPET

A low wall, or sometimes a railing, along the edge of a roof, balcony, or terrace.

PARGE

To apply a thin layer of cement plaster or other plaster to a wall or chimney flue. The principal function of parging is to waterproof foundation walls built of concrete blocks.

PARGET

Same as *parge*. This was the original word and had the same meaning. But it was also used to describe the practice of decorating walls with ornamental relief work.

PARQUET

A floor made of wooden blocks composed of narrow strips of wood glued together along the edges. The blocks are laid with the strips in one at right angles to the strips in the next.

PARTICLEBOARD

A strong, durable sheet material made of small scraps of wood bonded together under pressure. Pale brown in color, it has excellent dimensional stability—which makes it particularly suitable for cabinet doors and as a base for countertops. It is also used as an underlayment in resilient floors. Standard panels measure 4 x 8 ft. and are available in ½- and ¾- in. thicknesses.

PARTING STRIP

The protruding strip attached to a jamb which separates the sashes in double-hung and horizontal sliding windows.

PARTITION

An interior wall in a house or piece of furniture. In a house, some partitions are bearing partitions; most are nonbearing.

PARTY WALL

A wall dividing apartments in an apartment or a two-family house. Building codes often require party walls to be of fireproof construction. In all cases, they should be well sound-proofed.

PASS-THROUGH

An opening made in a wall—commonly the wall between the kitchen and dining room—so that things can be passed directly from one side to the other. A rather deep shelf should be provided on one or both sides of the opening, and a means of closing the opening is desirable.

A pass-through is a good illustration of the truth that few things in a house are quite as simple as they seem. Here apparently is a very uncomplicated functional device; yet if it is to be completely satisfactory on all counts, various small details must be considered in planning it. For example:

1 / The shelf must be deep enough to accommodate the things that are likely to be placed on it but not so deep that a person cannot reach across it.

2 / If the pass-through is located between a kitchen and dining room, the bottom should be high enough to prevent diners from seeing through into the kitchen, and the top should be high enough so that the servers don't have to stand on their heads to see through to the other side.

3 / The door must be designed so it can be easily operated and will not smash closed on the servers' hands.

4 / A means of locking the door should be provided in a pass-through which is used to facilitate delivery of groceries from garage into kitchen.

PASTEL
A painting done with colored chalk-like sticks. It must be kept under glass to prevent smearing and soiling.

PATCHING PLASTER
A white powder which is mixed with water and used to fill holes in plaster and gypsum board. It is the best common patching material for large holes since it dries more slowly than plaster of Paris and is therefore easier to place, and since it dries faster than spackle and is therefore less likely to sag.

PATINA
The mellow color acquired by wood or metal as it ages.

PATIO
A terrace (*see below*).

PATIO TILE
See Concrete Tile.

PAW FOOT
A furniture foot carved to resemble the paw of an animal, usually a lion. The leg immediately above it is usually carved with a leaf motif.

PEARWOOD
Often called *fruitwood,* pearwood is a lovely brownish rose. Very fine-grained and uniform, it is used largely in furniture. It is tough, hard, and moderately strong.

PECAN
Cut from a species of hickory, pecan wood is hard, strong, heavy, and reddish brown in color. It has rather large pores. It is made into furniture, cabinets, paneling, and flooring.

PEDIMENT
An ornamental triangular or arched section over a door or portico or at the top of a highboy or similar piece of furniture. An arched pediment has a gently curving top; a triangular pediment has a tentlike top with slight pitch to the sides. In a broken pediment, the slanted sides do not meet at the apex of the triangle. In a scroll pediment, the sides are shaped like cresting waves and are separated at the top.

PEELING
A common paint problem in which paint peels either from the base material or from the next coat below. If the base material is exposed by peeling, it indicates that the material was damp when painted or has absorbed moisture since. Peeling between coats usually occurs on exterior surfaces when there is a long delay between application of the first and second coats. *See* Intercoat Peeling.

PEG
A small piece of wood, usually cylindrical, used instead of nails or screws to fasten furniture, cabinets, etc., together. In some

cases—especially in pegged floors—pegs are only a fraction of an inch long and are used to conceal screws.

PEGBOARD

A popular type of hardboard that has small holes spaced 1 in. apart vertically and horizontally covering the entire surface. It is used for hanging everything from dishmops to lawnmowers.

Pegboard is usually sold in 4 x 8-ft. sheets that are 1/8 or ¼ in. thick. The 1/8-in. panels are used for light loads, the ¼-in. for garden tools and other heavy loads. The panels are normally nailed directly to studs, but can be installed over a finish wall if they are furred out approximately 1 in. An open space behind the board is necessary so the special hangers used with it can be inserted in the holes.

PELLON

A nonwoven fabric used as a lining material in curtains, etc.

PENALTY CLAUSE

A condition written into a building contract that the builder will pay a penalty if he fails to complete a house on schedule. But builders will accept such a clause only if they are desperate for work.

PENCIL

A painting or drawing done with pencils. It should be kept under glass to prevent smearing and soiling.

PENNSYLVANIA DUTCH

A rather simple style of furniture and furnishings produced by the people of German, Dutch, and Swiss extraction who settled in eastern Pennsylvania. The pieces were often decorated with painted tulips, birds, hearts, etc.

The preferred name is *Pennsylvania German.*

PENNY

A nail size. It is abbreviated by the letter "d". *See* Nail.

PENT EAVE

A small rooflike projection across the front of a house betweeen the first and second stories. Its original purpose—in medieval times—was to provide protection for people passing by on the sidewalk below.

PERCALE

A plain, closely woven cotton fabric used for curtains and bed linens. It is lightweight, strong, and durable.

PERCOLATION TEST

A test to determine the ability of soil to absorb the effluent from a septic system. The design of septic system fields is largely dictated by the results of percolation tests.

PERFORATED METAL

A metal sheet with numerous openings made by stamping. The material is used in radiator covers, cabinet and furniture doors, dividers, etc.

PERFORMANCE BOND

A bond posted by a building contractor in effect guaranteeing that he will complete construction of a building on schedule and, if not, will pay a penalty. However, few house builders today will pay the premium for a performance bond.

PERIMETER

All the outer edges of a building, room, material, etc.

PERIMIFLOR

A new installation system used with sheet vinyl flooring. The adhesive, an epoxy, is applied to the floor in a ribbon around the perimeter and to all cut edges of the sheet. The system reduces installation time and can be used to apply sheet vinyl not only over a conventional subfloor but also over an old resilient floor which is still in good condition.

PERIOD

A specific period of time; for example, the Federal Period.

PERLITE

A lightweight, glass-like mineral substance made from lava which is sometimes used instead of sand to improve the insulating properties and fire resistance of plaster.

Vermiculite is a similar material but is not recommended as an aggregate because of its low strength.

PERMANENT PRESS

Used interchangeably with *durable press*, permanent press is a loose name for fabrics which require little or no ironing after laundering. These are usually made by blending cotton or rayon with a thermoplastic fiber such as polyester, acrylic, or nylon. They are widely used for draperies, curtains, slipcovers, bedspreads, and other coverings.

Early permanent press fabrics were difficult to wash, but most today are treated with an anti-soiling and/or a soil release chemical which permits automatic washing and drying.

PERMIT

See Building Permit.

PETIT POINT

The basic type of needlepoint stitch, characterized by very small stitches. Because of this construction, petit point is more durable than gros point or bargello, and is therefore preferable to them in upholstery and rugs.

PEWTER

A semi-dull, gray alloy used in various kinds of ware, candlesticks, and lamps. The composition has varied considerably over the years. The first pewter had little lead and was quite hard. Later alloys contained a lot of lead and were soft. Modern alloys with little lead are very hard. Pewter is also plated on more common metals.

The low luster of pewter is maintained with a brass polish. Lacquer is rarely applied but can be used to stop tarnishing.

PHENOLIC RESIN PRIMER-SEALER

A primer-sealer made especially to equalize the density of the grain of Douglas fir and other softwood plywoods, and to prevent it from showing through a paint finish in irregular, wavy streaks.

PHOSPHORIC ACID

A chemical put up in liquid or jellied form for treating metal, such as aluminum and steel, before it is painted. The acid removes light rust and etches the surface.

PHYFE, DUNCAN

A furniture style developed by America'a most famous cabinetmaker. It is similar to the Sheraton style but features the lyre motif in chair backs, sofa arms, and table bases. Phyfe (1768-1854) was also especially known for his pedestal tables.

PIANO

No matter what its design, a piano requires space in a house because it is large itself and because people like to congregate around it when someone is playing. Average dimensions of upright pianos are 2 x 5 ft.; of baby grands, 5 ft. wide (keyboard length) by 6 ft. long; of grand pianos, slightly over 5 ft. wide by 9 ft. long.

Upright pianos are usually placed against a wall. If at right angles to a wall, something must be done to cover the back of the piano. A grand or baby grand piano can be placed with the straight side close to a wall; the curved side should face the room for best distribution of sound.

Since pianos are sensitive to weather changes, they should always be placed as far as possible from windows, heating outlets, and air conditioning outlets. The humidity of the room should be moderate, since too much causes rusting and sluggish action and too little opens joints and may crack the soundboard.

PIAZZA

A porch.

PICKLED-PINE FINISH

A variable blond finish for pine paneling and furniture. It is made by bleaching the wood, filling the pores with pale brown or gray paste filler, and applying two coats of white shellac.

PICTURE FRAME

The purposes of a picture frame are to define the limits of the picture and to focus attention on it. It should not, therefore, be of such size, color, or ornateness that it draws attention to itself, away from the picture.

Picture-framing can hardly be called an art. Anyone can do it. But to do the job well every time usually calls for a professional picture-framer with wide experience and a full supply of stock framing materials.

Picture-framing involves not only the selection and construction of frames but also the selection and making of mats and the selection and cutting of the glass.

A mat is a piece of cardboard, usually colored, which is cut out in the center and laid over a picture to separate it from the frame and give it a greater sense of depth. It may also be used to make a small picture occupy more space and thus have greater importance. Only pictures which are covered with glass are matted—and many of these are not. Whether a picture needs matting can be settled precisely only by testing.

The glass used to cover pictures is lightweight picture glass, nonreflecting glass (sometimes improperly called nonglare glass), and a clear acrylic or polished styrene. The plastics are used in large pictures because they are nonbreakable and weigh much less than picture glass. They also transmit light better. Nonreflecting glass, which has a frosted appearance when viewed from some angles, is occasionally used on pictures hung opposite windows or bright lights because the reflections of the light are not seen in its surface. However, the glass is not popular with artists because it may distort colors and completely obscure pictures seen from the side.

PICTURE MOLDING

A shaped wooden strip applied to the top of a wall about an inch below the ceiling. It is used for hanging pictures and mirrors from long wires that attach to S-shaped metal clips fitting over the molding.

PIER

A masonry column. It is used to support the end of an arch and also to stiffen a wall. A more common use in homes is to support one of the wooden or steel posts which in turn support decks and "stilt" houses. Such piers are sunk deep into the ground and project just far enough above it to protect the posts resting on them against decay or termites.

PIER GLASS

A tall, rather narrow mirror with a large, often ornate frame hung on a wall just above the floor so a person can see a full-length image.

PIGMENT

A substance added to paint or stain to give it color. The more pigment that is used, the greater the opacity of the paint or stain.

PIG-TAIL

A short, heavy cable with a plug used to connect a range, dryer, or water heater into an electrical system. It is also a little wire on the plug of some old-style small-appliance cords which is used for grounding the appliance.

PILASTER

A rectangular column attached to a wall or pier. It is usually ornamented and used either for decorative effect and/or to support a weight above. It may be made of masonry or wood.

PILE

A large, long, usually cylindrical timber driven deep into unstable soil to support a building. It is also occasionally made of steel or concrete.

Piles—or *piling*—are not much used for houses except for those near the seashore, where they serve to stabilize the houses in the sand, raise them above storm-driven water and anchor them against storms. They may also support small houses built on steep hillsides.

PILGRIM FURNITURE

Early American furniture in the Jacobean style. It is usually referred to as *Jacobean furniture.*

PILLAR

A rather slender, circular or square vertical support. The word is synonymous with *column*, although a pillar is often nothing more than a shaft without the capital and base characteristic of a column.

PILLOW

Pillows used primarily for decoration and secondarily for padding out a chair or sofa which is too deep to sit in comfortably should be reasonably firm and resilient, and covered with tightly woven, nonslippery, soil-resistant fabric with strong seams.

The most luxuriant—and expensive—pillow stuffing is goose or duck down. Down mixed with goose or duck feathers produces a firmer, more resilient pillow.

Duck or goose feathers without down are also desirable, even though they cost much less. But turkey and chicken feathers—sometimes called *crushed feathers*—should be avoided because they mat quickly.

Foam pillows made of molded foam and shreds are available in almost every possible degree of firmness, and in some cases, pillows are made firmer on one side than the other. The main advantage of foam, however, is that it is nonallergenic and resistant to mildew and moths.

Polyester pillows are also nonallergenic and mothproof, but unless a one-piece batting is used for filling, the pillows are likely to become lumpy; and even with batting, lumpiness occurs.

PILOT HOLE

The hole drilled for the threads of a screw or to prevent a nail from splitting wood. The pilot hole for a screw is often enlarged slightly near the top for the smooth shank (this is called the *shank hole*) and further enlarged at the surface for the screw head.

PILOT LIGHT

A small light connected with an electrical switch to indicate whether a remote light is on. It is also a small, constantly burning flame used to start a gas appliance automatically.

PIN

A peg or dowel.

PINE, WHITE

Until the great forests of the East and Middle West were cut to the ground, white pine was the most important wood in the United States. It was used for just about every building purpose as well as for furniture. Because it is now relatively scarce, its main uses are confined to doors, windows, woodwork, and solid board paneling. Knotty pine is particularly popular for paneling and is employed either in solid or plywood form.

White pine is almost white to pale yellow in color. Its softness and close, straight grain make it extremely easy to work. It also takes paint and stain exceptionally well, but if knots are present, they must be sealed with a stain-killer to prevent the resins from bleeding through a paint finish.

Eastern white pine is especially valuable but is now the hardest species to buy. Western white pine, sugar pine, and ponderosa pine (the last two also grow in the West) are more generally available and commonly used in windows and doors.

PINE, YELLOW

Although classified as a softwood, yellow pine is a very hard, heavy, strong wood; it is yellowish in color and contains a great deal of resin. It is widely used for structural timbers, rough lumber, and structural plywood. The principal sources of yellow pine are the fast-growing southern pines called longleaf, shortleaf, loblolly, and slash.

PIPE

The pipes used in plumbing systems and wet heating systems are made of a considerable variety of materials. Although the list has been expanded by the development of new plastics, many old materials are still going strong.

Vitrified clay • A very heavy, glazed clay pipe used for house sewers. The pipes are made in short lengths with an inside diameter of 4 in. or more.

Cast Iron • For many years cast-iron pipe was the standard for house drains and soil stacks. It is still used for the largest drains but has been pretty well replaced by copper and plastic in other parts of drainage systems.

Galvanized Steel • Galvanized pipe is still occasionally used for fixture drains and vents in drainage systems made with cast iron. But it is rarely used any longer for water supply and heating pipes.

Brass • Brass has almost completely disappeared (except in old houses) because of its cost. However, if water is exceptionally corrosive, brass pipe is the best metal pipe to use.

Copper • Because of its resistance to corrosion and clogging, copper is the standard piping material—used throughout the country—for carrying water. It is also used in hot-water heating systems;

and in the past 20 years has been the standard material for interior drains up to 3 in. in diameter. (Because of their smooth bore, copper pipes with an inside diameter of 3 in. can be substituted for cast-iron pipes with an inside diameter of 4 in. The copper pipes fit into a standard stud wall; the cast-iron pipes require a 6-in.-thick plumbing wall.)

So-called soft copper tubing is put up in 60-ft. coils and used for underground supply lines and for vertical supply lines indoors. Hard tube is rigid and made in 20-ft. lengths. It can be used indoors and out for horizontal runs as well as vertical risers.

Copper drains are always made with rigid tubes. The thickness of the walls required depends on local plumbing codes. Type M tubes should be used—where permitted—for economy.

All types and sizes of copper pipe are best installed with sweated (soldered) joints.

Plastic • Plastic pipe for plumbing systems has been in use for many years, but it has only recently been perfected for carrying water in the house. All types of plastic pipe enjoy a number of advantages: They are low in cost, lightweight and easy to install, remarkably durable, and resistant to corrosion and clogging by hard water.

Polyethylene pipe is a flexible tube available in long coils for carrying water underground from a well or city main to the house. Joints are made with hard plastic fittings which slip into the pipe and are held with stainless-steel clamps.

PVC pipe is a rigid pipe sold in 10-ft. lengths for carrying cold water indoors and out. Unlike polyethylene, it is damaged by freezing. Joints are made with female fittings which are cemented to the pipe.

CPVC pipe, a rigid pipe sold in 10-ft. lengths, is suitable for carrying both hot and cold water indoors and out. It is joined with fittings which are cemented to the pipe. Although closely related to PVC pipe, it should not be mixed with it in an installation.

ABS pipe is made in large diameters and 10-ft. lengths. It is rigid, highly resistant to ordinary household chemicals, and used for drainage systems in the house.

RS pipe is available in 4-in. and larger diameters for sewer and septic systems. It is also used for footing drains and to carry rainwater from gutters to dry wells or other disposal areas. Perforated pipes are used in footing drains.

PIPING
A tubular band of fabric used for trimming.

PIQUÉ
A lightly textured, neat-appearing fabric with raised cords running lengthwise, or lengthwise and crosswise to form a waffle pattern. It is used in draperies and bedspreads.

PITCH
The slope of a roof, stair, or other inclined surface. The pitch is measured in the number of inches that a roof, etc., rises in each horizontal foot. For example, a roof with a 3-in. pitch rises 3 in. in 1 ft. This may be written 3:12.

PITCH BLOCK
A triangular piece of board which a carpenter cuts to help him set a rail at an angle exactly parallel to a stair.

PITCH STREAK
A well-defined streak of resin in a piece of wood.

PITH
Spongy tissue in wood. Lumber with too much pith has little strength.

PLAID
A fabric or wallcovering with a pattern of colored stripes at right angles to one another.

PLAIN-SAWED
A term applied to hardwood lumber in which the growth rings form an angle of less than 45° to the wide faces. Softwood lumber sawed in the same way is said to be *edge-grained.*

PLANCIER
The hardboard, plywood, or lumber covering for the underside of a cornice. It is the same thing as a *cornice soffit.*

PLANK
A piece of lumber at least 6 in. wide and 2 to 4 in. thick.

PLANK-AND-BEAM
A type of construction employing 2-in.-thick planks laid over widely spaced beams. The beams should be

tongue-and-grooved or joined with splines, and should not be more than 8 in. wide.

Used to build roofs or floors, plank-and-beam reduces the number of framing members required in conventional construction and thus lowers cost. In a roof, the beams may be left exposed underneath so that they serve as the finished ceiling. The tops are covered with a vapor barrier, rigid insulating boards, and finally the roofing.

PLANTER

A raised planting bed surrounded by low walls. It generally forms a long, narrow rectangle, like a window box, and is built into the house; but it may be of any shape and dimensions, and free-standing.

Indoors, planters are commonly installed in living areas at the foot of interior walls or between areas (where they serve as low dividers). Outdoors, they are sometimes built across the facade of a house or used as low walls around porches.

Ideally, all planters should be designed so water can drain off through the bottom, and they should be deep enough that a thick layer of gravel can be placed in the bottom to keep plant roots from becoming waterlogged.

PLANT POCKET

An opening in a floor indoors or out which is filled with soil and plants.

PLANT TRAY

A large tray, usually made of copper, installed in a bay window just below the stool and used to hold potted plants. It is surrounded by a frame to make it look built in.

PLASTER

Long the standard material for surfacing interior walls and ceilings, plaster has lost out to gypsum board in the past 25 years because it requires more skilled labor to install, because it may develop unsightly cracks, and because the moisture in it often warps the framing of the house. On the other hand, it produces a smooth, strong, durable surface which is an excellent base for paint, wallpaper, and other finishing materials; it is a first-class sound and fire barrier, and it is thick and dense enough to support heavy objects hung with nails or screws.

Plaster is applied over gypsum or metal lath nailed to studs and joists. On gypsum lath, it is put on in at least two coats with a total thickness of at least ½ in. The first coat is called the *base coat*, the second the *finish coat*. On metal lath, three coats with a total thickness of at least 5/8 in. are required. They are called the *base*, or *scratch, coat, brown coat,* and *finish coat*. In all cases, the finish coat can be given a smooth or textured finish.

After plaster has dried for a week, it can be painted with latex paint. But if alkyd or oil-base paint is to be used, the plaster should be allowed to dry for six months. A similar waiting period is required before wallpaper or other flexible wallcovering is applied. The long wait is necessary to assure that the plaster is free of concentrations of chemicals which might damage the wall finish (these are called *hot spots*).

PLASTER BOARD
Gypsum board (*see above*).

PLASTER OF PARIS
A very fast-drying patching plaster for plaster and gypsum board walls.

PLASTIC ANCHOR
A plastic fastening device similar to a lead anchor or rawl plug for supporting light weights on masonry and ceramic tile walls.

PLASTIC, LAMINATED
The type of tough plastic sheet which is used to cover kitchen and bathroom countertops and—to some extent—bar tops, furniture tops, windowsills, doors, and walls. It is made by bonding together several phenol-impregnated paper sheets and a decorative surface layer of melamine-saturated paper or wood veneer. The resulting homogeneous material is very durable; resistant to heat, stains, and damage; and easily cleaned.

Standard dimensions of the sheets are 4 x 8 ft., but there are other widths from 30 to 60 in. and lengths from 5 to 12 ft. The general-purpose grade for horizontal surfaces is 1/16 in. thick; the vertical surfacing grade is 1/32 in. thick. Available patterns are legion, and increasing and improving every year. They are produced in gloss, satin, and textured finishes.

Laminated plastic sheets must be glued to a rigid backing to hold them flat and give them strength. The mounting is best done by a firm specializing in it, but any good workman can do a good job if he proceeds with care. On countertops—no matter how large—the plastic sheets are glued edge to edge to form what is, in effect, a single, unbroken surface. But if the laminates are mounted on plywood or particleboard for installation on walls, the joints between panels must be sealed with mastic and covered with battens or moldings.

When laminated plastic is used to cover an object with several surfaces at angles to one another—a countertop, for example—the corners between surfaces are usually sharp and square and show a thin seam between the abutting sheets. But the corners can be rounded in a prefabricating shop by postforming.

See Plastic Paneling.

PLASTIC PANELING

Interior wall paneling made of rigid plastics. It is colorful, tough, durable, damage resistant, waterproof (if the joints are properly sealed), fade resistant, and very easily cleaned. The commonest use is in bathtub recesses and shower stalls, and in dry areas where the walls are subjected to heavy wear or traffic.

Laminated plastic sheets (*see* Plastic, Laminated) are applied to walls only if they are bonded to a rigid backing of plywood, particleboard, hardboard, or moisture-resistant gypsum board. Installations fabricated on the job are rare, mainly because of difficulties in handling joints between panels. But prefabricated wall systems, as well as thick plastic materials which do not need special backing, are on the market; and although the choice of colors and patterns is limited, use is growing.

General-Purpose Wall Panels • These are made of a laminated plastic sheet glued to 3/8-in. particleboard. The panels are 16 or 24 in. wide and 8 to 10 ft. long. They are applied over horizontal furring strips and held together with splines.

Laminated Plastic Bathroom Panels • Used in tub recesses or shower stalls, these consist of a plastic laminate bonded to a layer of dense polystyrene foam which conforms to irregularities in the subwall. The panels can be glued to any sound subwall. They come in sizes up to 5 x 10 ft.

Fiberglass Panels • Panels made of plastic reinforced with fiberglass and shaped for installation over a standard-size recessed tub. They are fastened to a sound, smooth wall with pressure-sensitive tape.

Methacrylate Panels • Closely resembling marble, these are made of solid methacrylate with the color and veining running all the way through. Panels made specifically for wall covering are ¼ in. thick, 30 in. wide, and 98 in. long. They are glued to a smooth subwall or to furring.

The panels are also produced in ½ and ¾ in. thicknesses, primarily for making tops for counters and furniture.

PLASTIC-SHEATHED CABLE

An electrical cable incorporating two or more insulated wires and encased in tough, flexible plastic. It can be used indoors or out or underground, but it is not permitted for residential wiring in all communities. Types of plastic-sheathed cable with especially tough jackets for underground service are identified as *underground-feeder (UF)* or *direct-burial cables.*

PLASTIC TILE

Thin, 4¼ x 4¼-in. tiles made of durable plastic in several colors which extend all the way through. Glued to smooth, level walls, they are recommended by the makers for installation in tub and shower recesses; but the joints are not sufficiently watertight to support this idea. They are best applied to walls in dry locations. For appearance's sake, the joints should not be grouted.

Installation is easy and low-cost in comparison with installation of ceramic tile.

PLASTIC WOOD

A fast-drying mixture of wood fibers and chemicals used to fill holes and cracks in wood and other materials. It is dense, granular, and unattractive when dry, and will not take a stain; but it is durable and can be sanded and drilled. Most plastic wood is yellow, but other colors are available.

PLAT

A map of a subdivision or town on which the boundaries of individual properties are shown.

PLATE

A horizontal timber supporting part of a house. A *sole plate* is the timber at the base of a wall on which the studs stand. A *top plate* is the timber at the top of a wall to which the studs beneath are nailed and which supports the floor joists above. Both sole plates and top plates may be called *wall plates*.

A *rafter plate* supports the lower ends of rafters.

A *sill plate* is the timber on top of a foundation wall which supports the first-floor joists. This is more commonly known simply as a *sill*.

The covers for electric switch boxes and outlet boxes are also called plates.

PLATED

A metal object which is covered with a thick film of silver, gold, brass, chrome, etc. Plated ware is obviously not as durable or valuable as that made of solid metal; but some ware, such as Sheffield silver, is prized anyway.

PLATE RACK

A wall-hung rack for the display of plates, trays, etc. Cups are sometimes hung from the bottom of the shelf on which the plates stand.

PLATE RAIL

A rather large, L-shaped molding which is nailed to a wall to display plates.

PLEATED

A fabric which is folded and stitched at regular intervals in order to achieve an attractive fullness. The pleats take a variety of shapes as indicated by such names as *box pleats*, *knife pleats*, *accordion pleats*, and *cartridge pleats*.

PLENUM

An air space. The space between the actual ceiling of a room and a suspended ceiling is a plenum. The word, however, is most often applied to the large chamber in a warm-air heating system from which the heated air is distributed into ducts running throughout a house.

PLINTH
The square, slablike base on which a column rests. Also, a projecting course of bricks or stones at the base of a wall.

PLINTH BLOCK
A rectangular block sometimes placed for ornament at the bottom of a door casing and abutting the baseboard. It projects slightly beyond the face of the casing and baseboard.

PLISSÉ
A lightweight, puckered or crinkled fabric of cotton or rayon. It is used in bedspreads and curtains.

PLOT PLAN
A scale plan of a property showing the building and other pertinent features. In applying for a building permit, a plot plan is required for a new building or an addition to a side of an existing building.

PLUG-IN STRIP
A type of electrical outlet. It consists of a long, enclosed metal channel with receptacles for lamp and appliance cords spaced every 18 to 24 in. Plug-in strips are most often used in kitchens.

PLUMB
Straight up and down; absolutely vertical. A wall, column, etc., is checked for plumb with a plumb bob hung at the end of a plumb line, or with a spirit level.

PLUMBING SYSTEM
The entire system of pipes and fixtures which supplies water to a house and carries away the liquid and solid wastes. It consists of the hot and cold water supply lines, water heater, and water conditioning equipment (if any); the sinks, lavatories, bathtubs, shower stalls, toilets, bidets, and miscellaneous cold-water outlets; and the drain pipes, vents, and traps in the sanitary drainage system.

PLUMBING WALL
A wall containing the plumbing stack. If cast-iron pipes are used in the stack, the wall must be framed with 2

x 6-in. studs to accommodate the pipes. When copper or plastic drains are used, however, the studs are made of 2 x 4s because the pipes are so much smaller.

PLUMB LINE

A chalked line struck on a wall, door, etc., to serve as the vertical checkpoint for work to be done. The line is made with a long piece of cord tied to a weight or plumb bob—the whole thing being called a plumb line.

PLUSH

A velvet with a higher but less dense pile used for upholstery and draperies. Also, a thick carpet pile.

PLYWOOD, HARDWOOD

A decorative plywood made with a face veneer of hardwood (or sometimes a softwood such as knotty pine). It is used for interior paneling and also for construction of furniture, cabinets, etc.

The face veneer is usually made of straight slices of wood glued to the core side by side. Such a veneer is said to be plain-sliced or quarter-sliced. In some plywood, however, the veneer is rotary-cut, meaning that it is peeled from the circumference of a log in a continuous slice like a potato skin. Rotary-cut veneer is rarely as beautiful as sliced veneer.

The back veneer of hardwood plywood panels is made of either hardwood or softwood. Panels graded G2S (good two sides) are less common than those graded G1S.

The core of hardwood plywood may consist of three or five thin plies of softwood or hardwood, a thick slab of particleboard, or solid wooden boards glued edge to edge to form a lumber core. The last two constructions are used mainly in cabinetwork because the cores are easier to cut and finish, and because they hold nails and screws better than thin plies.

For purposes other than paneling, hardwood plywoods are made in sheets up to 4 x 8 ft. and in thicknesses from 1/8 to 1 in.

PLYWOOD PANELING

Plywood paneling has gained in popularity at the expense of solid wood paneling because it is somewhat less expensive and is made in a great variety of unusual and exotic woods.

It is a little easier to install on unbroken walls because it is made in large sheets and is generally pre-finished at the factory. On the other hand, because it is only a third of the thickness of solid wood (at best), it does not block transmission of sounds through the walls unless installed over a 3/8- or ½-in. gypsum backer board.

Most plywood panels have vertical V grooves to increase the resemblance to solid wood, to eliminate the necessity for covering the joints between panels with battens or moldings, and to conceal nails, which should be driven through the grooves. (The grooves are spaced so that when a panel is installed, they are centered over studs spaced 16 in. on center.)

Ungrooved panels are available on special order. In addition, there are numerous specially textured panels—made to resemble rough-sawn lumber, driftwood, etc. There are also panels covered with small stone chips of various colors, sizes, and shapes. Many of the panels which look like wood are actually made of inexpensive plywood surfaced with a plastic film and then given the color and grain of wood by printing.

The standard size of plywood panels is 4 x 8 ft., but 7-, 9-, and 10-ft. lengths are available. The standard thickness—the only one which should be used—is ¼ in. Thinner panels are made for low-cost installations, but are likely to bulge or ripple and are easily damaged.

The paneling is applied directly to studs or to furring strips, either with small finishing nails or with adhesive applied with a caulking gun. In an existing house, it can be nailed or glued directly to a wall, provided that it is level; otherwise, it should be put up over furring.

Unless the plywood is painted (which it rarely is), moldings should be purchased from the plywood manufacturer. They are made of wood, aluminum, or vinyl in very simple designs and in colors to match different types of paneling.

PLYWOOD SIDING

Plywood used for siding is an exterior grade made of softwood. It is installed either in large panels 4 ft. wide by 8, 9, or 10 ft. long or as a lapped siding (the panels measure 6 to 12 in. wide and 8 to 16 ft. long).

The siding is produced in a variety of textures and patterns—rough-sawn, V-jointed, board-and-batten, etc. Some are unfinished and must be painted or stained after installation; most come either with an overlay which serves as a long-lived base for paint or with a tough final paint finish which is guaranteed for many years.

An unusual type of plywood siding is surfaced with small stone chips permanently embedded in an epoxy matrix to resemble a rough-textured, colored stucco or concrete.

Because of its strength and rigidity, plywood siding can be applied to studs or over sheathing. If no sheathing is used, the maximum stud spacing for 3/8-in. plywood, 5/8-in. grooved plywood, and lap siding (which is a uniform 3/8 in. thick) is 16 in. on center. If the siding is nailed over 3/8-in. sheathing, maximum stud spacing can be increased to 24 in.

In all cases, large siding panels should be secured with nails spaced 6 in. apart around all edges and 12 in. apart through the center.

PLYWOOD, STRUCTURAL

A simple, often crude-looking form of plywood used for sheathing, subflooring, roof decks, painted cabinets, etc. It is widely used in preference to solid lumber because the large sheets cut the time and cost of installation. In addition, they are very strong and rigid, and eliminate the need for bracing the framing to which they are nailed. The quality is uniform.

Structural plywood was originally made of Douglas fir but is now made of roughly 30 wood species—mostly softwoods. It consists of three, five, or seven layers of wood glued together alternately at right angles. The front and back layers are known as *faces*, the layers directly under these are *cross-bands*, and all other inside layers are *cores*. A five-ply panel is made up of two faces, two cross-bands, and a core; a three-ply panel has two faces and a core.

The standard panel size is 4 x 8 ft., but other sizes are available in some types of panel. Available thicknesses are ¼, 5/16, 3/8, ½, 5/8, ¾, 7/8, 1, and 1-1/8 in.

All structural plywoods are made for either exterior or interior use, depending on whether the plies are bonded together with waterproof or nonwaterproof glue. Interior plywood should never be used outdoors or in a very damp location indoors.

The grading label printed on the back of each sheet designates whether it is an exterior or interior grade. The grading label also gives other information about the plywood panel on which it appears, but the coding is so complex that only a plywood manufacturer or dealer can keep it in mind.

So-called appearance grades of plywood carry a "group" number indicating the type of wood used to make the panel and its relative strength. On sheathing grades, a pair of numbers separated by a slant indicates the maximum permissible spacing of the framing members to which the plywood panel is nailed.

Appearance grades are also classified by hyphenated letters indicating the quality of the face and back veneers. *A*, for example, indicates that the veneer is smooth and paintable, and can even be given a natural finish in less demanding applications. *C* veneer, on the other hand, is marred with knotholes and splits.

Despite structural plywood's strength, it must be securely fastened to the framework of a building. Around all edges, nails should be spaced 6 in. apart and through the center 10 to 12 in.

POINT

To trowel mortar or adhesive into masonry joints. The primary purpose is to keep out moisture. For how to point masonry, *see* Mortar Joints.

POINTS

Fees charged by a mortgage lender for making a loan. They constitute an extra charge which the borrower pays in a lump sum at the closing. Lenders usually charge points when mortgage money is tight and interest rates have reached the ceiling permitted by state law. The points enable the lender to stay under the ceiling, yet make the extra money to which he thinks he is entitled.

A point equals $1 per $100 of loan value. In other words, if a mortgagee is charged three points on a $10,000 mortgage, he pays a lump sum of $300 to the lender at the closing.

POLYESTER

One of the commonest plastics in the home, polyester reinforced with fiberglass is made into tough, durable, colorful roof panels, garage doors, etc. *See* Fiberglass, Reinforced. Polyester fibers are used in draperies, home furnishings, and carpets. The fibers have exceptional wrinkle resistance and dimensional stability, and are blended with cotton, rayon, wool, and other fibers.

POLYETHYLENE

This strong, tough, flexible, chemical-resistant plastic serves many utilitarian purposes. As a flexible tubing, it carries water underground from the source to the house. As a tough film made in enormous sheets, it is used in vapor barriers to prevent condensation within the framework of a house and also to keep moisture from penetrating through concrete slabs and bare ground into a house.

POLYPROPYLENE

A strong plastic found in various household articles but most prominently in indoor-outdoor carpets and upholstery fabrics. The fibers are highly resistant to stains and dirt.

POLYSTYRENE

See Styrene.

POLYURETHANE

Proper name for urethane (*see below*).

PONGEE

Originally a plain-woven silk fabric made with uneven yarns which give it a broken crosswise texture. It is now imitated in cotton and synthetic fibers. It is used in draperies and curtains.

POPLIN

A durable, tightly woven fabric with fine crosswise ribs. Usually made of cotton or rayon, it is used in draperies.

PORCELAIN

A high-grade, expensive china used in table and ornamental ware.

PORCELAIN ENAMEL

A form of glass fused to metal to produce a dense, hard, durable heat- and stain-resistant material used in lavatories, sinks, bathtubs, and ranges. The best plumbing fixtures are made of porcelain enamel on cast iron. Those of porcelain enamel on steel are less durable and less expensive, and because of their lighter weight, they are easier to install. Ranges are made of porcelain enamel on steel.

PORCH

Few outdoor sitting areas are now known as porches, although many areas called by other names are in fact porches. A porch has no features which clearly label it. It is always connected to the house and raised above the ground (but terraces may be connected and raised also). It generally has a roof—but not always. The floor may be made of wood (as on a deck) or of masonry (as on a terrace).

PORTECOCHERE

A porch at the front entrance of a house with a roof extending out over the driveway so people can step out of their automobiles without getting wet.

PORTICO

A roofed front porch with columns.

PORTIERE

A drapery hung across a doorway.

PORTLAND CEMENT

The cement used in most masonry work. Patented in 1824 in England, it was named portland cement because when hard, it forms a yellowish-gray mass resembling the stone in quarries on the Isle of Portland, England. *See* Cement.

PORTLAND-CEMENT PAINT

A paint made by mixing dry portland cement and a pigment with water. It is used indoors and out on masonry walls because it resists moisture and alkalies; but it is not suitable for floors because it is worn by abrasion.

The paint is applied only to unfinished masonry or to masonry previously finished with portland-cement paint. Two coats are required. They are applied to a damp surface and kept damp for two days thereafter.

POST

A vertical timber supporting a load. It measures at least 4 x 4 in. Posts may also be made of steel or reinforced concrete.

POST-AND-BEAM

A construction system in which widely spaced posts are used to support beams which, in turn, support the joists or roof planks (*see* Plank-and-Beam). The system saves structural lumber by eliminating closely spaced studs. It also permits building a house on piers rather than continuous footings. (Decks are also built on posts and beams.)

The system lends itself particularly to modern architecture because it facilitates installation of large picture windows and sliding glass doors between the posts.

POTEAUX

An early form of construction using logs set upright, close together, to form the exterior walls of buildings.

POTTERY

Anything made of baked clay, including china, but usually thought of as thick, heavy earthenware. It may or may not be glazed. Unglazed types stain readily and are difficult to clean. Simple dinnerware as well as vases, bowls, ornaments, etc., are made of pottery.

POUF

A hassock resembling a big, thick, puffy cushion. Pouf is also used as an adjective to describe a very fluffy or billowy kind of drapery.

PRECUT

To cut lumber to size at a mill so it is ready for assembly at the site.

PRECUT HOUSE

A house for which all lumber is cut to the required sizes and delivered to the site in a package for assembly.

PREFAB

To build with assembled parts—prefabricate a prefabricated house.

PREFABRICATED HOUSE

A house with walls, floors, ceilings, and roof composed of panels or sections which have been put together in a factory prior to erection on the foundations. The house is ordered as a unit from a manufacturer and delivered to the building site by truck, where it is assembled by the builder, who is usually a dealer for the manufacturer.

The principal advantage of a prefabricated house is that it is speedily constructed. In addition, the quality is consistent and generally good, and the design is usually superior to that of a house designed by a local contractor. On the other hand, prefabricated houses are not adapted to all sites, and because the design is standardized, the house has no individuality (but neither do houses in a conventional development).

PRESS CUPBOARD

A companion piece to a court cupboard (*see above*), a press cupboard is a wide, rectangular storage unit with two large cupboards, one above the other.

PRESSURE-SENSITIVE

An adhesive or adhesive tape which sticks tight when slight pressure is applied. Pressure-sensitive adhesives are often used in making things because of their tenacious bond, but they must be handled carefully because once an object is glued, it is permanently fixed.

Pressure-sensitive tapes are made with adhesive on one or both sides. The latter are used to install such things as lightweight tiles and acrylic mirrors.

PRIMAVERA

A very valuable Central American wood used in furniture veneers. It is close-grained, moderately soft, and yellowish-brown.

PRIMER

A type of paint or finish used as the first coat under a final finish. It helps to bond the final finish to the surface and protects the final finish from chemicals in the surface. Metal primers also prevent formation of rust on the surface.

Primers are formulated for use indoors, outdoors, and on metal. The type used depends primarily on the surface to be finished and secondarily on the final finish. As a rule, it is advisable to use a primer made with a vehicle similar to that in the final finish—but this requirement is often overridden. For example, even though gypsum board is to be given a final finish of alkyd paint, it should be primed with a latex primer since this does not raise the fibers on the paper covering as an alkyd primer would.

Most primers are pigmented; but shellac, which is frequently used to prime wood, is not.

A few paints can be used without a primer.

PRIMER-SEALER

A finishing material which not only serves as a primer (*see above*) but also penetrates and seals the pores of the surface being finished.

PRIMITIVE

An adjective applied to art objects, furnishings, etc., of very simple, unsophisticated design. Such things were created by early man, by modern peoples cut off from the world, or by modern men and women (for example, Grandma Moses) who have had no training in the arts.

PRINT

A picture printed from an engraved plate or block. It is usually mounted, framed, and hung on a wall for decoration. The monetary value of a print depends on the fame of the artist and the number of printed copies he makes.

PROFILE

The contour of a wall, molding, piece of furniture, etc.

PROVINCIAL

Furniture and furnishings designed in the provinces in imitation of that designed in large cities. Used in a derogatory way, the word implies that such things are less refined than the pieces copied, although in actual fact they are often lovely and delightful.

PULL

A knob or handle without a latching or locking mechanism used on furniture and cabinets.

PULLEY STILE

See Stile.

PURLIN

A horizontal roof timber. On a very long roof slope, it is installed midway between the eaves and ridge to support the rafters. It is also installed between rafters to support planks or narrow insulating panels. And it may be laid on top of rafters to support metal roofing sheets.

PUSHPLATE

A metal or glass plate screwed to the latch-side face of a door to protect the finish against skin oils. It is used mainly on swinging doors.

PUTTY

A thick, plastic filler. *Oil-base putty* is the conventional type used for filling holes and covering nailheads—particularly on the exterior of a house—and is sometimes used for setting window panes. After aging, it becomes almost as hard as concrete.

Latex putty—also called *elastic putty*—is used primarily for setting window panes. It retains some elasticity after many years.

Water putty, or *wood putty*, is a white, plaster-like powder which is mixed with water and sets hard within 24 hours. It can be used for filling holes but is most valuable for molding into intricate shapes. It is particularly useful for replacing missing chunks in moldings and capitals.

PVC

Polyvinyl chloride. A plastic used to make rigid plastic pipe for carrying cold water outdoors and in. *See* Pipe.

QUARRY

A small, diamond-shaped or square pane of glass in a leaded window.

QUARTER-ROUND

A simple molding shaped like a broom handle which is cut lengthwise into quarters. It is used mainly as a shoe molding at the bottom of baseboards.

QUARTER-SAWED

Hardwood lumber cut from a log so that the growth rings are at an angle of 45° to 90° to the faces of the lumber.

QUARTZITE

A compact, granular rock composed of quartz crystals. It is as hard as many granites, but it is quarried in stratified layers with very smooth surfaces and is therefore an excellent material for building exterior walls.

QUEEN ANNE

A furniture style and, less importantly, architectural style during the reign of Queen Anne of England (early 1700s). It was designed for comfort and had fluent, refined lines (with an emphasis on curves). Cabriole legs were especially popular.

QUILTED

Any thick, soft fabric consisting of a front and back layer of cloth with a fluffy filling sandwiched between and held in place by stitching in a definite pattern. Quilted fabric is used for bedspreads.

QUOIN

One of a series of large rectangular blocks forming the corner of a building. In a masonry building, the blocks are made of stone, etc., and are set into the walls so they are a structural part of the corner. They are distinguished from the other masonry units by their size and, usually, their contrasting color.

In a wooden building, the quoins are thick wooden pieces applied to the sheathing and clearly separated from the siding by size, shape, and color.

All quoins are used for decorative purposes. They are associated mainly with handsome Georgian architecture.

RABBET

A rectangular groove cut in the corner of an edge or end of a board.

RABBET JOINT

A joint used to form a corner or to join the side of one board to that of another.

In a corner joint, the rabbet is cut in the end of one member, and the squared end of the other member is set into this.

In edge joining, a rabbet is cut in the face edge of one board, and a corresponding rabbet is cut in the back edge of the other board. The rabbets are then fitted together. In a less common method of edge joining, rabbets are cut in the back edges of both boards, the boards are fitted together to form a wide rectangular groove, and the groove is filled with a glued spline.

RACEWAY

A rectangular metal channel through which electric wires are run. It is attached to the face of a wall, baseboard, etc.

RADIANT HEATING

A heating system in which the floors, walls, and/or ceilings of a house serve as giant radiators. The result is very even warmth throughout the house and very comfortable floors. All heat outlets are completely hidden. Operating costs are often lower than those for a conventional hot-water system. On the other hand, the system is slow to respond to the thermostat; installation is costly; and if a leak develops, the entire house may have to be pretty well torn open.

Radiant heating is forced hot-water heating in which the heated water is circulated not through ordinary radiators but through coils of copper tubing embedded in floors, walls, or ceilings. The engineering layout should be made by an expert, but installation is well within the capabilities of a good heating contractor.

The system was briefly popular in the early 1950s but is rarely put in today.

RADIATOR

A cast-iron source of radiant and convected heat used with hot-water and steam heating systems. Radiators installed in houses today are much smaller and slimmer than old-fashioned types. Conventional units are designed to be either free-standing or recessed in a wall. Baseboard radiators are long, slender, horizontal units installed at the base of walls in place of wooden baseboards. They are generally preferred over conventional designs because they are more attractive, warm the floor, and produce more uniform temperature throughout the room.

RAFTER

One of the timbers which support a roof with a pitch of 3 in. or greater. It is made of 2-in.-thick lumber 4 to 10 in. wide. Normal spacing is 16 in. on center.

The precise nomenclature of rafters is as follows:

Common Rafter • A long rafter extending from the ridge to the rafter plate and at right angles to them.

Jack Rafter • A shortened common rafter. A *hip jack* runs from a hip rafter to the rafter plate. A *valley jack* runs from the ridge to a valley rafter. A *cripple jack* runs either from one valley rafter to another or from a valley rafter to a hip rafter.

Hip Rafter • A corner rafter in a hip roof extending from the end of the ridge to a corner of the exterior walls.

Valley Rafter • A rafter in a valley formed by intersecting roof slopes.

On roofs with less than 3-in. pitch, joists are used instead of rafters.

RAFTER PLATE
See Plate.

RAGGLE
A groove made in masonry to receive an edge of a piece of flashing.

RAIL
The horizontal or sometimes inclined member in an architectural or furniture assembly. On a chair, the rails connect the legs below and above the seat. On a window sash, the rails are the thick crossbars at top and bottom. On a door, they are the wide crosswise members. On the railing around a deck, they are the horizontal members connecting the uprights. On stairs, they are the hand rails.

RAISED PANEL
See Panel.

RAKE
The slanted edge of a sloping roof. Also, the trim applied to the slanted edge.

RANCH HOUSE
An early name, still used to some extent, for a contemporary house. It stemmed from the fact that early contemporary houses were derived from the original ranch houses of the Southwest—houses with gently pitched gable roofs and wide roof overhangs.

RANDOM WIDTH
Boards of different widths used in floors, and in wall and ceiling paneling. They are normally installed in no set sequence.

RANGE
No other kitchen appliance is produced in as many basic designs as the range. Gas and electric models currently on the market are the following:

Free-Standing Range • The original type of range which is finished on the front and sides so it can be placed anywhere—

between counters, at the end of a counter, or all by itself. The cooking surface, usually with four burners, is 36 in. high. The oven—or sometimes two ovens—is underneath.

Slide-In Range • Actually a free-standing range but designed to fit into a niche between counters so it looks built in.

Two-Oven, Eye-Level Range • Another free-standing range which looks built in. The base consists of a cooking surface and oven underneath. Above the cooking surface is a second oven, more or less at eye level.

Stack-On Range • This consists of a cooking surface with an oven mounted above it at eye-level. The cooking surface is level with the adjacent counters and set on a base cabinet approximately 30 in. high.

Drop-In Range • This is a complete range with surface burners and an oven underneath. It is built into a niche with counters on both sides and a raised platform (sometimes containing a drawer) beneath.

Built-In Range • This is really a two-piece range consisting of a cooktop with surface burners which is recessed in a countertop and a separate oven which is built into a cabinet or wall. It permits greater kitchen-planning flexibility than all other types of range but is usually more costly.

Stack-On Oven • A box-like oven with built-in controls which can be placed on a counter or deep shelf anywhere in the kitchen. Most electronic, or microwave, ovens are stack-ons.

Except for built-in models, the average range is 30 in. wide. But it is possible to buy free-standing ranges from 20 to 40 in. in width. Other ranges are produced in fewer widths.

The average built-in cooktop can be recessed in a 30-in.-wide base cabinet. A single built-in oven or a double oven (in which one oven is placed atop another) fits into a cabinet 24 or 27 in. wide by 24 in. deep.

A range should always be installed with counter space on one or, preferably, both sides. It should never be installed at the open end of a counter or peninsula where people walking by might knock off hot pots, under a curtained window, or deep in a corner where the heat of the burners might scorch a side wall.

Installation should also be made near an outside wall so that the moisture, smoke, odors, and grease given off in cooking can be efficiently dissipated to the outdoors through a ducted ventilating fan (*see* Fan, Exhaust).

An electric range requires a 240-volt wiring circuit fused to carry the maximum load of the range (usually 50 amps). A gas range is connected into a 15-amp, 120-volt lighting circuit.

RATTAN

Strong, slender, light-brown woody strips which are woven into furniture, chair seats and backs, baskets, etc. Also called *cane*, it is taken from an unusual climbing palm called the rattan and sold in 1000-ft. hanks. After soaking in a solution of glycerin and water to make it pliable, it is easily woven or otherwise shaped. Although it doesn't require a finish, a coat of clear wood sealer helps to prevent drying and cracking.

Plastic rattan is also made.

RAWL PLUG

A small cylinder of compressed jute fibers for fastening things to masonry and other walls which will not hold nails or screws. It is similar to a lead anchor but not as strong. The plug is tapped into a predrilled hole, and when a screw is driven in, the plug expands and grips the sides of the hole.

RAYON

The first man-made fiber, rayon is used to produce fabrics with a general resemblance to silk and to make inexpensive rugs and carpets.

REBATE

See Rabbet.

RECAMIER

A so-called Grecian couch with scrolled (S-curved) ends. Some examples are without a back; others have a gracefully curved back which extends only part way from the head of the couch.

RECEPTACLE

Another name for an electrical outlet into which lamp and appliance cords are plugged.

RECESSED PANEL

See Panel.

RECLINER
A reclining chair. *See* Chair.

RECORD PLAYER
If the number of people who have record player components strewn around their living rooms is any criterion, Americans enjoy music more than attractive homes. This is perhaps worth debate, but hardly anyone can be brash enough to claim that record changers, amplifiers, speakers, and miles of wires placed here, there, and everywhere add to the beauty of a house.

Building the system into furniture or walls improves matters immeasurably. It also adds in a strange way to the enjoyment of the music since the source is difficult to pinpoint.

The alternative to a built-in system—at least for people who do not pretend they can tell the difference between the music emanating from speakers placed close together and that from speakers set far apart—is to buy a console record player. These are low cabinets about 16 in. deep, 24 to 40 in. long, and 20 to 26 in. high.

RECREATION ROOM
A room for the family to play in. The walls and floors should be made of very durable materials which are easy to keep clean. Hardboard, plywood, and solid wood paneling and Class B vinyl wallcoverings are good for surfacing frame walls; a glaze coating is desirable on concrete block. Quarry and resilient tile, brick, and flagstone are good floor surfaces.

Soundproofing of the walls and ceiling (or floor) is desirable, especially if the room is used by children when the adults are elsewhere in the house.

RED LEAD
A paint pigment used in primers which are applied not only to clean iron and steel but also to iron and steel which are partially rusted. Since such primers cannot withstand much exposure to weather, they should be over-coated with a final finish as soon as they are dry. *Compare* Zinc Chromate. However, red lead has recently been legally banned from the market.

REDUCER
A threaded or soldered plumbing fitting used to connect a large pipe to a smaller pipe. *Compare* Bushing.

REDWOOD

Redwood is a widely advertised softwood having a straight grain and ranging from pinkish to deep red-brown. It is extremely resistant to decay and termites. Though used for structural timbers, it is not as strong as other lower priced softwoods; consequently, it is best reserved for siding and to a lesser extent for interior paneling and woodwork.

REEDING

A decorative motif for moldings, furniture legs, etc. consisting of a series of narrow, closely spaced convex beads carved in the surface. It is the opposite of fluting.

REFLECTANCE

The ratio of light reflected by a surface, such as a wall or ceiling, to the light reflecting on it. This depends on the color of the surface and is stated in percentages. For example, a new, clean white surface has a reflectance value of 90%, whereas medium gray has a value of 50% and leaf green a value of about 21%.

For the most efficient lighting, the walls, ceilings, floors, and large furnishings in a room should have a dull finish—not a gloss finish which produces disconcerting and uncomfortable mirror-like reflections. The reflectance value of the ceiling should be somewhere between 60% and 90%; of the walls, 35% to 60%; and of the floors, 15% to 35%.

REFRIGERATOR

The refrigerators in use in American homes are gradually growing larger and larger. Thirty years ago the average household refrigerator had a capacity of 8 cu. ft. Today, the smallest standard refrigerator holds 11 cu. ft.; the largest, 30 cu. ft. (So-called compact refrigerators as small as 1.5 cu. ft. are on the market but are used only as auxiliary units in bars, family rooms, outdoors, etc.)

Despite this increase in capacity, the space occupied by refrigerators has not gone up proportionally. Most refrigerators are 30 in. wide, 27 in. deep, and 66 in. tall. To permit pulling a refrigerator out for servicing, an additional 1 to 1½ in. of space should be provided on both sides and at the top.

Ideally, a refrigerator should be installed close to the kitchen door through which groceries are delivered. A counter space at least 18 in. wide is provided on the latch side. The refrigerator should be placed so its door swings open away from the center of the kitchen;

otherwise, it is necessary to walk around the door to get into the refrigerator.

Although small refrigerators which are defrosted manually can be plugged into a 120-volt, 15-amp lighting circuit, most refrigerators should be installed on individual 20-amp circuits to assure uninterrupted operation at full efficiency.

REGISTER

A grilled, louvered, or baffled opening through which heated or cooled air enters a room and stale air leaves. The air is carried to the supply registers (inlets) from the furnace or air conditioner by the supply ducts, and is drawn back to the furnace or air conditioner through return registers (outlets) and the return ducts.

The supply registers are placed in the exterior walls of a room, the return registers in the interior walls. The best supply registers are designed so that the incoming flow of air can be adjusted up or down. The return registers, however, have simple, fixed grilles.

REINFORCED CONCRETE

Poured concrete which is strengthened by embedded steel rods or heavy steel mesh.

RENAISSANCE

The period from about 1400 to 1600 in which there was a great rebirth of all the arts. Architecture and furniture during the period were dominated by classic details and proportions. Both private buildings, such as the Rucellai Palace in Florence, and churches, such as St. Peter's in Rome, displayed a form which was at once coherent, strong, formal, and reposed.

RENDERING

A sketch or simple painting of a house or an interior. It is prepared by or at the instigation of the architect, builder, or decorator to give the owner a better idea of what he is paying for.

REPRODUCTION

A copy of a piece of furniture, art, etc.

RESILIENT FLOORING

Flooring made of vinyl, linoleum, rubber, vinyl-asbestos, cork, or asphalt. Which of these materials is used depends on a number of things:

1 / The desired appearance of the floor.

2 / Whether tiles or large sheets are preferred. The former are easier to install. The latter have fewer, if any, joints and therefore produce a more uniform appearance and prevent moisture from penetrating to the subfloor.

3 / Whether the floor to be covered is below grade, on grade, or above grade (suspended).

4 / The characteristics of the resilient flooring. Some, for example, are easier to maintain than others. Some are quieter and more resilient underfoot than others. And so on.

Regardless of the flooring selected, all require the same careful preparation of the subfloor before installation. This must be reasonably level and smooth, firm and clean, and not subject to deterioration. Concrete subfloors should be tested to make sure they are completely dry.

In new construction, wooden subfloors are generally made of 5/8-in. plywood covered with ¼-in. hardboard, plywood or particleboard underlayment. They can also be made of ¾-in. plywood and ¼-in. underlayment, or of 2-4-1 plywood (1-1/8 in. thick) applied to joists spaced 48 in. on center.

In an existing house, old wooden floors are best covered with ¼-in. hardboard underlayment to prevent the joints between boards from showing through the resilient surface.

For the best appearance, tiles are laid from the center of the floor toward the walls. The border tiles on opposite walls should be equal in width, and, ideally, the border tiles at the end walls should be nearly equal to those at the side walls.

The way in which sheet goods are laid—the length of the room or across the room—depends on which will produce the better appearance and which will be more economical of material.

Installation of all resilient flooring is made with adhesive. Newer types of adhesive are applied to the subfloor with a paint brush, other types with a notched trowel. Self-stick resilient tiles are made for do-it-yourself application.

RESIN

The gooey substance exuded by coniferous trees. If not well seasoned, softwood lumber may continue to ooze resin long after it is purchased. This appears in hard yellow streaks on the surface of the wood and may penetrate a paint or varnish finish. It cannot be prevented unless every piece of lumber is sealed with shellac or stainkiller simply on the chance that the resin will appear. Once the oozing stops, however, the resin can be scraped off, and the surface neutralized with turpentine and refinished.

RETARDER

A chemical mixed with concrete to make it set more slowly. It is used mainly in hot weather to overcome the accelerating effect that high temperature has. Retarder solutions are also occasionally applied to the surface of concrete to facilitate its removal in order to produce a textured effect.

RETURN

A surface turned at an angle backward from the front surface. On a valance, the short side pieces that touch the wall are the returns.

REVEAL

When a door or window is set into a masonry wall, that part of the wall visible between the jamb and the corner of the wall is the reveal.

REVIVAL STYLE

Any out-of-date design style which is later revived. The revival style, however, is always a modification of the original style and rarely as popular.

Most decorating and many architectural styles have been revived at one time or another. For example, the Gothic style of the Middle Ages came to life again in the middle 19th century as the Gothic Revival style. Similarly, we have had an Egyptian Revival style, Greek Revival style, Louis XVI Revival style, Rococo Revival style, etc.

RIBBON STRIP

A ledger (*see above*).

RIDGE

The peak of a gable, gambrel, hip, or mansard roof. The horizontal timber at the peak is also called a ridge, *ridge pole*, or *ridge piece*. Its purpose is to tie the rafters together and align them.

RIDGE CAP

An inverted-V-shaped strip of boards or shingles laid over the roofing at the peak of a roof. When shingles form the cap, they are laid lengthwise of the ridge. Asphalt shingles are bent over the ridge; other shingles—as well as solid boards—are beveled along the top edges to make a tight joint between those on opposite sides of the ridge.

RIGHT OF WAY

An easement involving the grantee's right to move or pass something through the grantor's property.

For example, John Smith's title may contain a clause granting his neighbor to the south the legal right to drive his car into his property over a specified strip of Smith's property. Or if the local water company has a pipe running through a person's property to a neighboring property, it has a right of way; and the specified strip of land through which the pipe runs is also called a right of way.

Rights of way often cause problems, and for that reason, properties which are encumbered by them should be considered carefully before purchase. The rights cannot be abrogated at will by the grantor. And as long as they are extant, the grantor lacks full authority over his property.

RIGID CONDUIT

A steel pipe used in wiring. Standard conduit is rather heavy, threaded pipe rarely used in residential work except outdoors. Thin-wall conduit is much lighter, easily cut and bent, and installed with special connectors which obviate the necessity for threading the pipes.

Rigid-conduit wiring is approved in all communities in the United States and is the only system permitted in a few. It is generally used only in new construction because installation is difficult in closed-in buildings. After the conduit is installed and connected to the outlet and switch boxes, etc., insulated wires are snaked through it and connected as in other wiring systems.

RIPARIAN RIGHTS

If a stream or other watercourse runs through or along the edge of a property, the property owner has the right to draw water from it, even though the rest of the stream is owned by someone else.

RISE

The distance between the low point and high point of something which rises. For example, the rise of a roof—measured from the plates on which it rests to the top of the ridge—might be 6 ft. *Compare* Pitch.

RISER

The vertical board under the front edge of a stair tread. In a properly designed stairway or flight of steps, the height of the riser should be roughly proportional to the depth of the tread. *See* Stair.

The vertical runs of pipe in a plumbing or heating system are also called risers.

ROCKING BENCH

Also called a *cradle rocker* and *mammy bench*, a rocking bench is a settee with rockers designed in the fashion of a Windsor chair. A railing along the front of the bench, at one end, forms a cradle so a baby can be rocked without falling off the seat.

ROCKING CHAIR

Considered to be an American invention, rocking chairs, or rockers, started out in the early 1700s as straight chairs with rockers attached. From here they progressed to the Boston rocker, with its slightly S-curved seat and high spindled back, and the similar but smaller Salem rocker. Since then, other rocker designs have been introduced. The most distinctive was the platform rocker—an upholstered chair which was attached to a fixed platform.

ROCOCO

Furnishings and, to a lesser extent, architecture characterized by light-hearted but lovely design which was rather definitely feminine. Pieces were small in scale, curvilinear, and exuberant. The Rococo period ran through the early and middle 18th century and was confined mainly to France and Italy.

ROLL-ON FABRIC

A Japanese-developed material for covering interior walls. It is a mixture of fibers such as cotton, nylon, and rayon; metallic-like glitter; and a powdered glue. When mixed with water and applied to a wall with a short-napped paint roller, it resembles a thick, coarse-textured brocade, grasscloth, or marble.

The material can be used over any clean, sound surface, and because of its texture and thickness, it conceals almost all imperfections in the surface. But it is easily damaged and shows dirt and stains.

ROOF

The design of residential roofs is dictated primarily by the architectural style of the house. Types in use are the gable, gambrel, hip, louvered, and mansard (all of which are more or less tent-shaped), flat, and shed. Butterfly, barrel, and domed roofs are also built but are rarities.

Traditional pitched roofs are fairly expensive to build because they must be well braced to prevent them from exerting outward pressure against the exterior walls. They must also be strong enough to withstand wind pressure, and carefully flashed at all breaks in the roof line to stop leaks. The framing consists of a system of rafters which rest on the rafter plates at the top of the exterior walls and are tied together at the top by the ridge. Collar beams installed below the ridge are used further to link the rafters on opposite sides of the roof and strengthen the entire structure.

Flat and shed roofs are simpler to build and less expensive because the total area is reduced. In climates with heavy snows, however, they require larger-than-normal timbers to carry the weight of the snow. Roof joists rather than rafters support the roof deck.

In normal construction, the rafters or joists are spaced 16 in. on center and are sheathed with ½-in. exterior-grade plywood sheets laid with the outer plies at right angles to the framing members. The plywood is secured with nails spaced 6 in. apart around the edges and 10 to 12 in. apart through the center. The deck thus formed should be covered with asphalt building paper before the roofing is applied.

One-inch boards can be substituted for plywood sheathing but are seldom used today except on wood-shingle roofs. In this case, the boards are 3 or 4 in. wide and are laid with open spaces between them.

In plank-and-beam construction, the roof deck is made of 2-in.-thick tongue-and-groove planks laid on beams spaced up to 6 ft. apart. If the underside of the planks serves as a finished ceiling, fiberboard insulation is laid over the planks and a vapor barrier is sandwiched in between.

Plank roof decks are also made with 2 x 8-ft. rigid insulating panels nailed to framing members spaced 2 to 4 ft. apart. The panels are made in 1½-, 2-, and 3-in. thicknesses; have a built-in vapor barrier; and are finished on the underside to serve as ceiling panels.

The selection of roofing material for a house is influenced by the following considerations:

Effect Desired • The basic choice is between materials which produce definite shadow lines and those which form a more or less smooth expanse. Once this point is settled, the homeowner faces the difficult job of deciding which texture and color come closest to his aim.

Roof Pitch • Shingle-type materials which overlap can be laid only on roofs with a fairly steep pitch. Only sheet-type materials are suitable for flat or nearly flat roofs.

Roof Contour • This becomes a problem when a roof has curves which complicate waterproofing. Silicone-rubber roofing is the only material which can be made to conform exactly to any surface.

Life Expectancy • In the proper exposure, almost all materials can be counted on to last about 20 years, but a number will last indefinitely.

Fire Rating • Fire resistance of inflammable materials is rated by the Underwriters' Laboratories. Moderate fire resistance earns a Class C rating; better resistance, a Class B rating; excellent resistance, a Class A rating. Nonflammable materials such as slate and metal have no fire rating. All wooden shingles are considered combustible unless treated with an approved fire-retarding chemical.

Wind Resistance • A serious problem only with ordinary asphalt shingles. Top-grade asphalt shingles have seal-down tabs.

Weight • Conventional materials of all types are light enough to be laid on roofs framed in the conventional manner. Extra-thick clay and concrete tiles and slates require a reinforced framework, however.

Availability of Light Colors • White and other light-colored materials, as well as permanently reflective materials such as aluminum, are preferred on air conditioned houses because they reflect 15% to 20% of the sun's rays, and thus help to keep the space underneath cooler than dark roofing materials.

Whether the Roof Is Exposed to Shade • Shade encourages the growth of moss on some roofing materials but not on others. This is an unsightly but not usually a serious problem. Wooden shingles exposed to heavy shade, however, not only collect inordinate amounts of moss but also decay far more rapidly than they do in sunny locations.

Types of roofing material are discussed elsewhere. They include aluminum sheets and shingles, asbestos-cement shingles, asphalt roll roofing, asphalt shingles, built-up roofing, ceramic tiles, concrete tiles, copper sheets, galvanized steel sheets, silicone-rubber roofing, slate, terne, and wood shingles.

ROSE
A metal keyhole escutcheon.

ROSETTE
An ornamental detail, circular in shape and with a flower or foliage carving.

ROSEWOOD
A now rare, exotic wood of a rich, deep brown with black and almost yellow streaks. It is hard and smooth, and takes an excellent polish. Today it is used in the finest furniture and for veneer.

ROUGH GRADE
The land around a new house after it has been brought to approximately the desired contour with a back-hoe or bulldozer. In contract building, the land is usually rough graded by the contractor. Finish-grading is the responsibility of the owner.

ROUGH IN
To install plumbing and heating pipes, heating ducts, and electric wires and boxes in the framework of a house. After the work has been inspected and approved by the building inspector, the plumbing and electrical fixtures, etc., are installed. This work is not part of roughing in.

ROUGH OPENING
The opening made in the framework of a house for a door, window, etc.

ROUND
A strip of wood of circular contour; a dowel. As a verb, round means to cut or smooth off a sharp corner or edge.

ROWLOCK
Also spelled *rolok*, a brick laid horizontally on one of its thin (2-in. side) edges. It may be used as a stretcher or header.

RS
Rubber styrene. A plastic used to make drainage and sewer pipes for outdoor use. *See* Pipe.

RUBBLE
Broken stones, bricks, concrete, and other masonry materials.

RUBBLE MASONRY
Walls and floors built of irregular, uncut, or roughly cut stones.

RUFFLE
A gathered strip of fabric used for trimming.

RUG CUSHION
Padding under rugs and carpets not only protects them against wear but also increases their resiliency and makes them feel more luxurious. The cushions used are made of jute, rubber foam, or urethane foam roughly ½ in. thick or of solid sheets of rubber about 1/8 in. thick. The foam types are preferable because they are more resilient and do not fray or mat like jute. They are also nonallergenic and protect the floor against moisture sinking through a rug.

To allow for stretching, rug cushions should be cut 2 to 3 in. smaller than the rug; and to prevent skidding, they should be laid with the textured side down.

RUNG

A fairly slender, horizontal member tying together the legs of a chair. *Compare* Stretcher.

RUNNER

A long, narrow piece of fabric—for example, a rug used in a narrow hall or a piece of embroidery or scarf used on a table top.

RUNNING FOOT

See Lineal Foot.

RUSH

A tough marsh plant which is woven into chair seats, rugs, baskets, and mats. It has an attractive, informal appearance but needs frequent dusting. With age, it tends to break or ravel.

RUSTIC SIDING

Boards with beveled edges on the face. When applied horizontally to the exterior wall of a house, the boards are separated by wide, deep V joints. The edges of the boards are interlocked to keep out water.

R VALUE

Resistance value. The letter, followed by a number, denotes the resistance to heat transfer of an insulating material when installed in a house; that is, the R number indicates the amount of heat the insulation plus adjacent air spaces and surfaces will keep from escaping from a house in winter or from entering it in the summer. The higher the R number, the more effective the insulation. For example, the insulation recommended for use in roofs, with a value of R-19, is thicker than that for outside frame walls—R-13.

SABER LEG
     A chair or sofa leg which is shaped like a saber and curves outward at the bottom.

SADDLE
     A small gable roof inserted between a chimney and the high side of the main roof to direct water and debris around the chimney.

SADDLE SEAT
     A solid wooden seat with a center ridge running from the front edge of the seat part way toward the back.

SAILCLOTH
     A smooth, stiff cotton or cotton-and-rayon fabric used for draperies and slipcovers.

SAILOR
     A brick laid vertically in a wall. One of the wide faces is exposed.

SALT BOX
     A gable house with a back roof slope which runs down considerably lower than the front.

SAMPLER
A small piece of embroidery mounted in a frame and hung on a wall for decoration.

SAND
Sand used in mortar should be clean, sharp building sand free of all organic matter. Sand from dry deposits and rivers is suitable (if clean). Beach sand should not be used because the salt affects setting of the mortar. Sand sold for building purposes is known as *builder's sand.*

SANDED PAINT
A latex paint in which fine sand is suspended. Used to give interior walls and ceilings a sandpaper-like finish, its chief value is in covering imperfections in such surfaces. It is applied with a texturing brush.
Any ordinary paint can be mixed with clean builder's sand or a synthetic granular material called Perltex to produce a sanded finish.

SANDSTONE
A sandy sedimentary rock normally light brown but sometimes of other colors. It is relatively easy to cut and therefore makes a good building stone.

SAPELE
A West African wood much like mahogany but harder and heavier. The color is reddish brown. Depending on the way the log is cut, the wood shows light and dark alternating stripes. It is used in furniture.

SAPWOOD
The newly developed wood under the bark of a tree and surrounding the inner heartwood. As a rule, sapwood has a lighter color than heartwood, is less resistant to decay, and is not quite as hard or strong.

SARAN
A type of vinyl with excellent resistance to weathering, sunlight, and chemicals, and therefore used in indoor-outdoor

carpets, awnings, and webbing for garden furniture. It also goes into upholstery and drapery fabrics.

SARASA
A Japanese dying process similar to batik, it is best applied to unbleached cottons, linens, and silks. The resulting fabrics are used for curtains, hangings, and coverings.

SASH
The moving part of a window. It includes the glass and surrounding framework. The framework is also the sash.

SASH WEIGHT
Now obsolete but still very common, a sash weight is a heavy, cylindrical piece of cast iron which controls the movement of a sash in a double-hung window. Each sash is connected to two weights which are hidden in pockets behind the side jambs. They are attached to the sashes by ropes (*sash cords*) or sometimes chains.

SATEEN
A fabric like satin with a special finish to give it luster. It is usually made of cotton and is used for drapery linings or by itself in draperies and upholstery.

SATIN
A soft, smooth, lustrous fabric going into draperies, bedspreads, and upholstery. It is made of various fibers and in several forms and weights.

SATIN, ANTIQUE
A drapery, bedspread, and upholstery fabric. It is heavy and has a dull luster resulting from its slubbed texture. It is made from several different fibers.

SATINWOOD
An East Indian wood which has a satiny luster when finished for furniture. Unusually heavy and tough, it is yellowish brown with pretty stripes.

SCAB

A piece of wood used to join timbers which are butted together or to strengthen weak spots in timbers. A special use of a scab is to provide a level, unbroken surface between the ends of floor joists which project above a girder that separates them. In this case, the scab is laid across the top of the girder and nailed to the sides of the joists.

A scab may be called a *fishplate* when used to splice timbers. It is simply laid over the sides of the timbers and nailed or bolted to them.

SCAFFOLDING

A temporary structure on which workmen stand when they build, paint, etc., the upper part of a house. It can be built on the job out of lumber or assembled from prefabricated steel parts.

SCANTLING

A relatively small timber such as a 2 x 2, 2 x 3, or 2 x 4.

SCARF

To bevel the end of a timber for splicing to another timber. The resulting beveled end is also a scarf.

SCARFED SPLICE

A splice made by beveling the ends of the timbers or boards to be joined. The beveled surfaces are then coated with glue, fitted together, and held with screws or glue. The result is a much neater, less obvious joint than a butt joint, and should always be used when moldings, baseboards, etc., are joined end to end.

If a scarfed splice is subjected to stress, it can be strengthened by nailing fishplates over it on both sides.

SCENIC WALLPAPER

An expensive wallpaper composed of several strips which together depict a scene.

SCHEDULE

A hand-lettered list of the doors and windows for a house. It is included in the working drawings and gives the actual dimensions of the doors and windows. The purpose is to eliminate such details from the plans themselves.

Windows are indicated on the plans and in the schedule by numbers, doors by letters.

SCHRANK
A cupboard similar to a kas (*see above*). It was made by the Pennsylvania Dutch.

SCONCE
A decorative wall bracket used for lighting. It has one or more arms holding candles or incandescent bulbs.

SCORE
To scratch a surface so that glue, plaster, cement plaster, etc., will stick to it better.

SCOTIA
A deep, concave molding.

SCRATCH COAT
The first, or brown, coat of plaster applied to a wall. It is criss-crossed with lines—scored—so the second coat will adhere well.

SCREED
A dot or strip of plaster applied to a wall or ceiling to assist the plasterer in applying a level plaster surface of the proper thickness. A screed is also a tool for leveling poured concrete.

SCREENCLOTH
Also called *screenwire, screen mesh*, and *screening*, screencloth is the material used in window, door, and porch screens to keep out insects.

It is fabricated in long rolls from 2 to 4 ft. wide if made of metal, or 2 to 7 ft. wide if made of fiberglass. It comes in two meshes: 18 x 16 and 18 x 14—meaning that there are 18 squares per inch in one direction, 16 or 14 in the other direction.

Screencloth is made of four materials, but galvanized steel and bronze are no longer widely used (the former because it is short-lived, the latter because it is expensive). This leaves the field to aluminum and fiberglass. Both are durable and fire resistant, and have good resistance to impact (although fiberglass tends to belly, it can be pulled straight again, whereas aluminum is more resistant to bellying but cannot be pulled straight once it does). Both are also available in various colors.

SCREEN DOOR

Screen doors have hardly changed at all since they were invented. The conventional door has a wooden or aluminum frame with large inserts of screencloth. Combination storm-and-screen doors are similar, except for the fact that the screen panels are taken out in the fall and replaced with glass panels.

Since exterior doors almost always swing inward, screen doors swing outward. Both doors are hinged to the same jamb.

SCREEN, WINDOW

In northern climates, screen windows are generally the other half of combination storm-and-screen sash. The screened section is a single panel which covers the lower part of the window in summer. In winter, it is pushed to the top and one of the two glass panels is pulled down, thus closing the window against wind and cold. (The screened panel can also be removed entirely from the sash, but then a place must be found to store it.)

Conventional window screens are made, as they have been for years, with wooden frames which usually cover the entire window. Similar screens can be made with aluminum frames. These are a great deal more attractive because the frames are so slender that they are barely visible, and the screens not only are much lighter and therefore easier to put up and take down but also need less space in storage. On the other hand, the frames are not very rigid and can easily be damaged; and they require an inordinate amount of hardware to hang them.

Tension screens are unframed. An aluminum bar at the top is fastened to the head jamb; another bar at the bottom is clamped to the sill. If properly installed, the screencloth is stretched so tight against the side jambs that insects cannot get in. But no matter how desirable these screens may appear at first inspection, they are a poor choice because they are hard to store, are easily damaged, and come unclamped readily.

Roll screens are similar to window shades. They roll up to the top jamb in winter, and roll down and attach to the sill in summer. The side edges are enclosed in built-in metal channels. The cost is high.

SCREW

Screws are used when it is necessary to fasten two things together more securely than is possible with nails. They are also used when it may be necessary to take things apart without damaging them.

Wood Screws • The type most often used, they are made of steel, brass, bronze, and aluminum with flat heads, oval heads, or round heads. The heads usually have a straight slot for a standard screwdriver, but Phillips-head screws have cross slots for a Phillips screwdriver.

The screws are classified by length and gauge (diameter). Lengths range from 3/16 to 5½ in., gauges from 0 to 24 (approximately ¾ in. in diameter). Most lengths are made in several gauges.

Wood screws are used primarily to join wood to wood or metal or plastics to wood.

Lag Screws • Big screws with square heads which are turned with a wrench. They are used for joining large timbers and also for anchoring heavy objects, such as gates, in lead anchors set into masonry.

Set Screws • Small screws with blunt ends used to keep bolts, etc., from coming loose. The most familiar type is the tiny screw which secures door knobs to spindles. The heads are formed in several ways.

Sheet-Metal Screws • For fastening thin sheets of metal together as in kitchen and laundry appliances. They are also known as *self-tapping screws* because threads do not have to be cut in the metal in which they are used.

Machine Screws • Used for joining metals in which threaded holes have been cut. Like sheet-metal screws, they are threaded for their entire length but have blunt points.

SCRIBE

To fit a piece of lumber, cabinet, countertop, etc., to an irregular wall surface. The work is done by placing the board, etc., against the wall and drawing a pair of dividers from one end to the other. One leg of the dividers is held against the wall; the other scratches a line on the board parallel with the wall. The board is then cut along the scratched line.

SCRUTOIRE

See Escritoire.

SCULPTURE

A three-dimensional work of art executed in stone, wood, metal, glass, pottery, etc., and displayed on tables, shelves, mantels, etc., strictly for its ornamental value.

SCUTTLE

A hatch; an opening with a trapdoor into an attic, basement, etc.

SEALER

A finish applied with a brush to close the pores of the base material. Pigmented sealers are called *primer-sealers* because they prime the surface as well as sealing it. Sealers without pigment are called *clear*, or *transparent*, *sealers* and are used to help prevent soiling and staining of the surface. No final finish is required.

SEAMLESS FLOORING

A floor covering made by pouring plastic from a can and spreading it across the floor in a thin, unbroken layer. When carefully applied to a well-prepared plywood or concrete base on or above grade, the flooring is quite durable and cleanable and never needs waxing. But it must be reglazed periodically and resurfaced in heavy traffic areas.

The product has almost disappeared from the market, however, mainly because of poor workmanship by installation crews.

SECRETARY

A tall, handsome piece of furniture for writing and storage. The lower part is a chest of drawers. The upper part—about half the depth of the bottom—is a cabinet with shelves and hinged doors. The writing shelf sometimes pulls out, but usually it folds out and is supported on wooden arms. In the latter case, when the shelf is closed, it conceals the contents of the desk.

SECTION DRAWING

A drawing of part of a house in cross-section. *See* Working Drawing.

SEEPAGE PIT

A large hole in the ground which is used for disposal of the effluent from a septic system if there is not space for a tiled field. It is lined with masonry blocks or stones laid without mortar. *See* Septic System.

SEERSUCKER

A light fabric with lengthwise crinkled stripes used for bedspreads, curtains, and slipcovers. It is generally made of cotton or a cotton-polyester blend.

SELF-EDGED

See Edging.

SEMI-GLOSS FINISH

A hard, smooth, partially shiny paint or varnish finish which washes well. Midway in luster between flat and gloss finishes, it is the best finish for all woodwork and also for kitchen and bathroom walls and ceilings, which need to be washed frequently. Gloss finish is even more washable, but its shine is objectionable on large surfaces.

SEPTIC SYSTEM

The approved system for disposing of sewage if a house cannot be connected to a town sewer. The system consists of a large, watertight tank which is filled by the house drain. Bacterial action in the tank breaks the wastes down into sludge, liquid, scum, and gas. The sludge settles to the bottom of the tank where it slowly collects and from whence it must be pumped every few years by a septic tank service. The liquid, with the scum on top, forms a pool above the sludge, and when deep enough, it flows out of the tank into the disposal field. It is called the effluent. The gases flow back through the house drain and up through the stack into the open air.

Septic systems must be built by a qualified contractor in accordance with local building and health codes. The size of a system, dictated by the codes, is dependent on the number of bedrooms in the house. In the absence of local or state regulations, authorities usually call for a minimum tank capacity of 750 gal. This is adequate for one- and two-bedroom houses. If there are three bedrooms, tank size is increased to 900 gal.; four bedrooms, 1000 gal. Each additional bedroom above four requires an additional 250 gal. If there is a garbage disposer in the kitchen, tank size in all cases must be increased approximately 50%.

The size of the disposal field is also regulated, but the basis on which it is figured is more complicated.

A septic tank can be built on the job but is generally prefabricated of poured reinforced concrete. The best design is divided into two compartments. The tank should be buried deep enough (at least 6 in.) so grass will grow over it, but not so deep that it is hard to get at when cleaning is required.

The disposal field normally comprises a network of shallow trenches lined on the bottom with crushed rock. Perforated drain pipes are laid on the rock and covered with rock and soil. In situations where a tiled field requires too much space, the effluent may be disposed of through dry wells, seepage pits, or an enormous concrete-block-lined gallery.

A septic system must be carefully located. The ground should be reasonably porous—the more so, the better; not subject to flooding or a high water table; and well removed from willows, poplars, and other trees with aggressive roots which are likely to work into and clog the pipes. From a practical standpoint, the system should be placed in front of a house so the plumbing system can be connected into a city sewer if one is ever built.

The tank should be no less than 5 ft. from the house, 10 ft. from the property line, 10 ft. from all water lines, and 50 ft. from a well or other water source. The disposal field must be no less than 5 ft. from the house and all property lines, 100 ft. from a well, 25 ft. from a stream not used as a water source, and 20 ft. from a dry well which collects water from the roof. (The exact distances may be different in any given community.)

SERPENTINE FRONT
An undulating front on a chest of drawers, sideboard, or other case piece. It is convex at the center, concave on either side. *Compare* Oxbow Front.

SERVICE DROP
The wires running from the electric utility pole to the first point of attachment to the house. Three wires are required to provide 240-volt ser ˙

SERVICE ENTRANCE

That part of the electrical system between the service drop and the fuse box or circuit breaker panel. It consists of the cable running from the service drop to the meter, the meter, the cable running from the meter to the master switch, the cable from the master switch to the fuse box or circuit breaker panel, and finally the fuse box or circuit breaker panel. The service entrance should be rated at no less than 100 amp.

SETBACK

The distance between the boundary lines and the building lines. No part of a house, except possibly a flight of steps or bay window, is permitted to extend forward of a setback (which is the same thing as a *building line*).

Setbacks vary with the community, the zoning, the size of the lot, and the location of the setback. For example, in a quarter-acre residential zone, the front and rear yard setbacks may be 35 ft.; the side yard setbacks, 10 ft. In a one-acre zone, by contrast, the front and rear yard setbacks may be 50 ft.; the side yard setbacks, 25 ft.

Setbacks are sometimes referred to as *yard requirements*. That is, a 50-ft. front yard requirement is similar to a 50-ft. setback.

SETTEE

A bench or small sofa. Originally the framework was exposed and the seat caned, rushed, or of solid wood. The back was caned, or solid, or made of carved or shaped wood in the manner of chair backs. Later settees were often upholstered.

SETTLE

A long wooden bench with arms and a high solid back. A chest was often built in under the seat, which was hinged.

SETTLEMENT

Sinking or lowering of a house as a result of unstable soil, weak foundations, or skimpy use of materials in the structure.

SEWER

Two types of sewer system serve large communities: sanitary and storm. They are not connected.

A *storm sewer* is designed to remove storm water from streets and large paved areas as fast as possible. If a house is equipped with footing drains or drains carrying off water collected by gutters, these may usually be connected into the storm drains.

A *sanitary sewer* carrying household and factory wastes to the sewage disposal plant must be connected to every house and other building it passes. This means that if a person builds a house with a private septic system and later a public sewer is extended past his house, he is required by law to help defray the cost of the sewer by paying a sewer assessment, to hook into the sewer (for which he pays a modest connection fee), and to pay an annual sewer maintenance tax.

SEWING MACHINE CABINET

A piece of furniture in which a sewing machine is concealed in a small cabinet under the top. When the machine is to be used, the actual top of the cabinet folds out to one side to form a large work surface, and the machine, which is mounted in a secondary top, is pulled up to the level of the work surface. When closed, most sewing machine cabinets look like a small table with drawers or a knee-hole desk.

SEWING TABLE

A small table—usually an antique—with several drawers for sewing supplies.

SHADE

Roller Shades • The simplest and least expensive devices for screening windows against sun and sight. The conventional fabric shade is made of solid vinyl (least expensive), vinyl-coated cotton (medium price), or fiberglass laminated to vinyl (most expensive). Most of these materials are translucent, but some are treated to give complete darkness, and a few are treated on the back to reflect the sun's rays. All can be decorated with oil or latex paint or covered with iron-on fabric.

Roller shades are also made of slender wooden or bamboo strips which admit light through the joints between strips but are otherwise opaque.

Fabric shades are best installed within the window opening just below the top jamb because they are somewhat less noticeable when rolled up. But installation on the casings is sometimes necessary, in which case the shades should overlap each side casing about 1½ in. and should be installed above the bottom edge of the top casing about the same distance.

Because wooden and bamboo shades are much bulkier, installation within the window opening is always preferable; otherwise, they interfere with curtains or draperies.

Accordion Shades • These are decorative fabric shades which open and close in accordion fashion. Made of a firm fabric bonded to a stiff backing, the shades have crisp lines resembling those of a standard Venetian blind and are operated in the same way by three cords threaded through the folds.

Austrian Shades • These are an elegant type of shade made of a thin fabric, such as silk or nylon, with a deep fringe and tassels along the bottom. Usually used on very wide windows, they are separated into narrow shirred panels by cords running through eyelets on the back. When the cords are pulled to raise a shade, the fabric in the panels crumples together in multiple soft folds.

Roman Shades • Roman shades are quite similar to Austrian shades except that they are made of firmer fabrics and therefore fold into more stiffly precise pleats. They also are weighted by a rod which gives them a straight bottom line. The shades are made with special tapes sewn to the back. Cords inserted through rings in the tapes raise and lower the shades.

SHADOW LINE

Dark shadow lines are often valued in architecture because of the decorative, sometimes dramatic effect they give to exterior walls and roofs. One of the easiest ways to create shadow lines is to use bevel siding with thick butts or in double courses. But shadow lines can also be created in masonry by the manner in which the joints are made, in vertical-board walls by the use of thick battens or deep grooves, and so on.

SHAKE (1)

A wood defect characterized by a separation of the wood fibers as a result of natural causes.

A *heart shake* starts from decay at the heart of the tree and develops into radial splits running out toward the bark in one or more directions. As opposed to a check (*see above*), a heart shake is wider at the center of the log than at the circumference.

A *wind shake*, or *cup shake*, is a split between the growth rings and is shaped like a bow. It is caused either by high winds racking a tree or by expansion of the sapwood.

SHAKE (2)

A thick, handsplit wooden shingle with very rough texture. It is used on roofs and exterior walls.

Cedar shakes—the commonest type—are sold in bundles covering 20 sq. ft. and containing an assortment of random widths ranging from 4 to 14 in. Standard lengths are 18, 24, and 32 in. The best grade is labeled No. 1 Handsplit and Resawn; then comes No. 1 Handsplit, followed by No. 1 Straightsplit.

Shakes are installed much like wooden shingles. Maximum exposure on roofs is 8½ in. for 18-in. shakes, 10 in. for 24-in. shakes, and 13 in. for 32-in. shakes. When application is made to a wall, the exposures for 24- and 32-in. shakes are slightly greater.

Shakes are either stained or allowed to weather naturally. The life expectancy of a shake roof is approximately 20 years.

SHAKER

Furniture made by the Shakers, a religious sect in the Northeast. It is simple, functional, and charming but with a minimum of decoration.

SHAKE, SIDEWALL

A cedar shingle with deep grain-like grooves made on the face by machine. It is used to cover exterior walls and is always double-coursed to produce a deep shadow line.

The shakes are made in standard shingle sizes and are also available in pre-assembled 4- and 8-ft. panels. They come either with a factory-applied color or in their natural state.

SHEATHING

The subsurface in exterior walls and roofs to which the finish wall surface or roofing is applied. It stiffens and strengthens the structure, increases insulating value, and helps to reduce air and water infiltration. Roof sheathing is normally called the *roof deck.*

Sheathing was for many years made of wide boards nailed to studs and rafters, usually on the diagonal. Exterior-grade plywood and a heavy grade of insulating board are used today because the large panels are easier and faster to install, and impart so much strength to the framework that the special bracing sometimes required with board sheathing is no longer needed.

In some cases the siding or roofing is nailed directly to the sheathing, but in quality construction, building paper is inserted between.

Sheathing is sometimes eliminated if 3/8-in. plywood siding is applied to studs spaced 16 in. on center. But the insulation in the wall should be increased to compensate for the loss.

SHEATHING PAPER

Building paper applied between the sheathing and siding to keep out moisture, air, and dust. It is usually asphalt-saturated or laminated kraft paper.

SHED ROOF

A roof pitched in one direction.

SHEER

An adjective applied to a fabric which is transparently thin: for example, organdy and marquisette. Sheer fabrics are used for curtains and dressing table skirts.

SHEETROCK

Gypsum board (*see above*).

SHELF

Shelves in the home are built of wood, steel, glass, and even stone. Those of steel are factory-made and come with a baked enamel finish. Wooden shelves are generally finished by the home-owner with alkyd enamel, varnish, or shellac; but to reduce wear and facilitate cleaning, surfacing with laminated plastic is advisable.

The finish of a shelf, however, is less critical than its thickness and the way it is supported, because if these matters are not attended to properly, the shelf will sag, break, or topple.

Minimum thickness of boards used for shelving which is to bear books, records, china, and other heavy articles is 1 in. (nominal dimension). The boards should be supported at or near the ends and at 3-ft. intervals along the back edges. If 1¼-in. boards are used, the spacing of supports can be increased to 5 ft.

Glass shelves will bear comparable loads if made of ½-in. plate and supported at 3-ft. intervals. Spacing of supports under steel shelves should be specified by the manufacturer.

Methods of supporting shelves are numerous.

If they are permanently built in, as in a closet, the simplest kind of support is a wooden cleat or rabbeted wood shelf molding nailed to walls under the ends and backs of the shelves. For adjustable shelves, the alternatives are L-shaped shelf hangers which are plugged into drilled holes and V-shaped hangers which clip into slotted metal strips that are screwed to the walls.

If a tier of shelves is cantilevered from a wall and the ends are left open, another type of slotted metal strip is screwed to the wall at the back of the shelves, and the shelves are laid across metal brackets which fit into the slots. If the strips are screwed into studs spaced 16 in. on center, shelves made of 1-in. boards will carry any load put on them.

Individual shelves are cantilevered on large angle irons or ornamental shelf brackets.

Tiers of shelves which are used as dividers between rooms are built with slotted standards similar to but much larger than those made for cantilevering shelves. Wedged upright between the floor and ceiling, they support shelves on one or both sides.

SHELF STRIP

A wooden molding which is rabbeted along the top edge to receive a shelf.

SHELLAC

An alcohol-base transparent finish applied to wood which is not exposed to weather. It is used for finishing furniture and paneling, as a base for varnish and paint, and for sealing knots and stains. Shellac producers also recommend it for finishing floors, but it is readily worn, scratched, and damaged by water.

Natural shellac is orange colored and used only if it is to be covered with another finish. White shellac is colorless. Stainkiller is a shellac containing white pigment.

A major advantage of shellac is that it dries within a few hours, even in subfreezing weather. If it has been in the can more than six months, however, drying is erratic.

SHELLAC STICK

A more of less pencil-shaped piece of hard shellac which is melted and used to fill holes in wood. It comes in various colors.

SHELL HOUSE

A partially completed house which the buyer finishes himself. The extent of the work the buyer must do depends on how much is completed by the builder.

SHERATON

A furniture style named for its originator, Thomas Sheraton (1751-1806), an English cabinetmaker. No furniture actually made by Sheraton has been found, but his manuals, *The Cabinet-Maker and Upholsterer's Drawing Book* and *The Cabinet Dictionary* were widely influential. Sheraton furniture is small in scale and characterized by classic lines, delicate grace, painted medallions, inlay work, and Wedgwood plaques.

SHIELD BACK

The back of a chair or settee which is shaped like a shield. It was a design much favored by Hepplewhite.

SHIELDING

Any device for protecting or completely covering something else. The word, however, is most often applied to a device used to prevent direct view of a light bulb in a fixture. In many built-in fluorescent fixtures, the shielding is nothing more than a board placed between the tube and the room. In other fixtures, it is a sheet of translucent glass or plastic, a louver, a grille, etc.

SHIKI SILK

A silk wallcovering with a delicate texture and horizontal weave resembling grasscloth. It is put up in 3-ft. widths laminated to a paper backing. Installation is made over lining paper.

SHIM

A thin, flat or wedge-shaped strip for making slight adjustments in the position of something. For example, shims are used under base cabinets in a kitchen to raise them to the proper height or to level them. They are also inserted behind the leaves of hinges in a door jamb to make the door close more easily. They are also used to steady stones in a dry wall.

A shim can be made of any material which is appropriate to the purpose—wood, metal, cardboard, or stone chips.

SHINGLE

A thin, oblong piece of material which may or may not be thicker at one end than the other. Used for roofing or siding, it is installed with the bottom edge—butt—overlapping the top of the shingle in the next course below.

SHIPLAP

A horizontal siding board with rabbeted edges which interlock with the rabbets in the adjacent boards. The siding produces a smooth wall.

SHIRRED

Fabric which is drawn up or gathered by pulling three or more parallel threads or cords through it. The informal effect is particularly suited to window curtains. *Compare* Gathered.

SHOE MOLDING

A small molding—normally a quarter-round—applied along the bottom edge of a baseboard to conceal and seal the joint between the baseboard and floor. The molding should be applied with finishing nails driven at an oblique angle so that open joints do not appear between the molding and baseboard or the molding and floor. Sometimes simply called a *shoe.*

SHOJI

Floor-to-ceiling sliding panels used in Japanese houses to admit light without sacrificing privacy. They are divided into small rectangles by slender wooden strips and covered with translucent paper.

SHORING

Timbers set at an angle to brace a building during construction or reconstruction or to prevent earth from sliding during excavation. A single timber used in this fashion is a *shore.*

SHORT CIRCUIT

A malfunction in an electrical system which results when bare wires cross or touch metal outside the system. It blows the fuse or trips the circuit breaker and will continue to do so until the condition is corrected.

SHOWCASE LIGHT

A long, slender light fixture similar to those in store showcases. It may contain a fluorescent tube or several tubular incandescent showcase bulbs. It is used in houses to illuminate large paintings, collections of art objects on shelves or in cabinets, etc.

SHOWER CURTAIN

A shower curtain is an inexpensive but only semi-effective way to keep water from escaping from a shower stall or tub with shower. The curtain is usually a single thickness of waterproof material which hangs down inside the front of the stall receptor or tub. There are usually gaps at the ends through which water leaks, and mildew inevitably forms on the inner surface, marring the appearance of the curtain inside and out. The better solution, therefore, is to hang two shower curtains. The inner one is made of vinyl; the outer one—which hangs outside the stall or tub—is made of any decorative fabric which resists spotting by the water that gets past the liner. This arrangement minimizes leakage and maintains the beauty of the outer curtain.

Further to prevent escape of water, the inner curtain can be weighted at the bottom—preferably by small magnets which cling to the side of the tub.

SHOWER DOOR

Shower doors are better than curtains in preventing escape of water from stalls and tub enclosures, but they must be installed carefully to be fully effective. They are made with chrome-plated steel or anodized aluminum frames surrounding plastic or glass panels. The glass should be shatterproof, and both the glass and plastic should be translucent, textured, or rather fully decorated so that water spots on the inside do not show through.

Doors for shower stalls are usually made in one piece hinged at the side and opening outward. But some designs are bi-folds which open inward like the doors on telephone booths.

The conventional door for tub enclosures consists of two sliding panels in parallel tracks, but these allow access to only part of the tub and therefore make cleaning difficult. This problem is obviated by two other kinds of door. One is a bi-fold which opens back against the wall at the rounded end of the tub. The other consists of narrow panels which open and close in accordion-fashion.

SHOWER HEAD

The spray head used in a shower bath. It is normally installed at a height of 5½ to 6 ft. above the base of the tub or shower stall.

SHOWER RECEPTOR

The panlike base of a shower stall. It is often an integral part of prefabricated metal or fiberglass stalls, but is separate otherwise. If a separate receptor is surfaced with ceramic tile, it should incorporate a lead liner to ensure against leaks. Separate receptors are also made of artificial stone.

SHOWER STALL

Despite some differences in size and shape, the only basic difference between shower stalls is that some are prefabricated and others are built on the job. The prefab units are made of enameled steel or of fiberglass or plate glass in a metal frame. Custom-built shower stalls, on the other hand, are usually built of ceramic tile or sometimes of laminated plastic panels or glass. A primary concern in the case of all stalls is that the floor is watertight.

Although shower stalls are often installed simply because they take up less space than tubs, they actually save space only if the opening is closed with a shower curtain, folding door, or bypass sliding doors. If they have hinged doors which swing outward, almost as much space must be allowed for the door to swing open as for the stall itself.

A more serious problem with small shower stalls is that they are too cramped for the bather to use easily. A 3 x 3-ft. unit is about the smallest size for comfortable bathing if the door is solid. If a curtain is installed instead of a door, the front-to-back dimension can be reduced to about 30 in.

SHRINKAGE CRACK

A hairline crack in a plaster wall.

SHUTTER, EXTERIOR

Although exterior shutters, or *blinds*, rarely serve a useful purpose today, they are frequently used for decoration. But the effect in many instances is unfortunate because they are too obviously undersized and inoperable.

A pair of shutters should equal the width of the window they adorn. The normal height equals the distance from the sill to the top casing, but if an ornamental wood panel is installed below a window to emphasize its vertical lines, the shutters are lengthened to cover the panel as well as the sash.

The tendency to screw shutters permanently to walls has grown with the increasing use of aluminum and plastic shutters which do not need painting. This simplifies installation but results in a flat, appliqued effect rather than the three-dimensional appearance of wooden shutters hung on hinges.

Prefabricated shutters are available with louvers and solid recessed panels. Like all louvered articles, the former collect dirt, need frequent cleaning, and are tedious to paint. They are less expensive, however.

SHUTTER, INTERIOR

Shutters are used inside windows instead of shades or Venetian blinds to give privacy and keep out the sun. They are generally made in narrow panels (approximately 6 to 9 in. wide) which are hinged together in pairs so they will collapse into small bundles on either side of the window when opened.

The shutters are built of wood. Most stock designs have adjustable louvers. Some are made with open centers over which the homeowner stretches decorative fabric.

Interior shutters often cover only the bottom half of a window. If used to cover an entire window, they may be made in full-length panels extending from the sill to the top casing, or in half-lengths.

SIDEBOARD

A handsome, long dining room piece used for storage, serving, and display of silverware, etc. It contains drawers and cabinets under a slightly overhanging top. The beautiful sideboards by Hepplewhite and Sheraton had four slender legs under the front edge and two at the back corners.

SIDE LAP

The point at which the side edge of one piece of material overlaps the side edge of another piece in the same course or in the next course below. For example, when installing metal termite shields over foundation walls, the edges of adjacent strips are side-lapped and soldered to keep out the termites. On the other hand, on a wooden shingle roof, the shingles in the top course are installed so that the joints do not fall directly over the joints in the next course below; and in this case, the top shingle is side-lapped over the shingle below.

SIDELIGHT

A fixed window beside an exterior door—usually the front door. Whether composed of several small panes or one large pane, it is a narrow, vertical strip.

SIDING

Any material used to surface the exterior walls of a house. For example, shingles, clapboards, board-and-batten, bricks.

SILICONE

A man-made chemical product used to make a water repellent for application to a masonry, a lubricant, an adhesive, and a caulking compound.

SILICONE-RUBBER ROOFING

A flexible roof coating of particular value on barrel, domed, curving, and other oddly shaped roofs. It is applied directly to a plywood or concrete deck with a paint brush or roller. Since the material dries rapidly and a total of only three coats is required, one man can complete an 800-sq.-ft. area in a standard workday.

Although silicone-rubber roof coating is thin, it is watertight and durable, remains flexible in extremely cold weather, and is resistant to damage by extremely high temperatures. It has a Class A fire rating when applied to a concrete base and a Class C rating on plywood.

The material is made in several colors.

SILK

Silk is one of the most highly prized fabrics because of its beauty, luster, softness, and strength; it is therefore woven into many fabrics used for draperies, bedspreads, etc. But it must be kept clean and out of direct sunlight to prevent fairly rapid deterioration.

Silk is sometimes identified, according to its source, as cultivated, raw, wild or tussah, Duppioni, or spun. The characteristics of the fibers vary somewhat. Wild silk, for instance, is of uneven texture, tan in color, and nonbleachable.

Silk must be labeled "weighted" if it contains more than a small percentage of metallic salts. It is cheaper and more easily draped than pure silk but less serviceable.

SILK SCREENING

A process for printing decorative designs on fabric, paper, wood, plastic, glass, etc. The basic process consists of cutting a stencil and adhering it to a piece of silk. This is stretched on a frame, placed over the material to be decorated, and coated with heavy ink. The ink is rubbed through the silk with a squeegee on to the material.

SILL

A timber bolted to the top of a foundation wall and on which the first-floor joists rest. It is made of 2 x 4s, 2 x 6s, or 2 x 8s installed flat side down. Sometimes the timbers are doubled.

The sills completely encircle a house. They must, of course, be installed several inches above grade to prevent decay and termite attack. They are also called *sill plates.*

The lowest horizontal exterior member of a window frame or exterior door frame is also a sill. It is a thick board angled slightly toward the ground to shed water.

SILVER

Most valuable and beautiful metal in common use in the home. But because of its rising cost and the rapidity with which it tarnishes, many young homeowners have passed it by in favor of pewter.

SILVER LEAF

Very thin sheets of silver sometimes used to decorate furniture, trays, boxes, etc. It is applied like gold leaf.

SILVER-OAK FINISH

A blond finish for oak furniture consisting of a very thin basecoat of diluted light-gray lacquer, white paste filler worked into the wood pores, and two final coats of water-white lacquer.

SINGLE-COURSE

To install wooden shingles and other siding in a single course on walls. This is the conventional installation method. *Compare* Double-Course.

SINK

Sinks for the kitchen and other locations are made of porcelain enamel on steel, porcelain enamel on cast iron, stainless steel, or rigid plastic reinforced with fiberglass. Porcelain on steel has long been the most popular because of its low cost, but it is not very durable. Porcelain on cast iron is very durable but expensive, and its weight makes installation difficult. Because of these problems, stainless steel is now near or at the top in usage. Though the best stainless-steel sinks are expensive, they are exceptionally durable, easily formed into many shapes and sizes, and simple to install. However, they are noisy, show scratches, and are hard to keep looking clean (although they may be perfectly clean). (*See* Stainless Steel.) Fiberglass sinks are too new to have been proved. The quality is uneven.

Almost all modern sinks are designed to be recessed in a countertop. They are secured in place and the joint around them made water-tight by several methods. The faucets are mounted either on the rim of the sink or behind it on the counter.

Sinks have one, two, or three bowls. If a single-bowl sink is installed, it should have inside dimensions of no less than 16 x 21 in. to give ample working space. At least one of the bowls in a multi-bowl sink should be equally big; in the newest sinks, the other bowl (or bowls) is usually smaller.

Because kitchen sinks are ordinarily installed under a window (although there is no rule that they must be), the bowls in multi-bowl models are arranged in a straight line. But corner sinks are made which, in effect, wrap around an inside corner in a counter— with the bowls at right angles to each other. One three-bowl sink designed for installation in a peninsula or island is arranged with two medium-size bowls side by side behind the third oversize bowl.

The faucet for a kitchen sink should be long enough to reach the center of the sink and high enough to place a big kettle underneath. Hot and cold water are regulated by separate control handles or by a single handle which can be adjusted from cold through any degree of warm to hot. In many cases, a separate spray outlet on a flexible, retractable hose is provided for the sink.

Other sinks for household use include:

Bar sinks—small sinks with high gooseneck faucets. One and two-bowl models are available.

Laundry sinks—also called *tubs* or *trays*. These are very large, deep sinks with one or two bowls.

Floor sinks—resemble small, low-sided bathtubs. Placed on the floor, they are used for cleaning mops, filling buckets, draining rain-soaked clothing, etc.

SISAL
A strong, durable plant fiber which takes dye well. It is woven into informal rugs.

SIZE
A thin glue applied to walls and ceilings which are to be wallpapered. It should be used on all surfaces except those covered with lining paper or old wallpaper. It aids in the adhesion of the paper and facilitates hanging.

One kind of size is made for brushing on walls prior to paperhanging. A second kind is mixed right in with the wallpaper paste and applied to the back of the paper with the paste.

SKINTLED BRICKWORK
Skintled brickwork is used to give walls a rough or rustic effect. In one form, the bricks are set in and out—at random or in a planned design—from the normal plane of the wall. In another form, the mortar squeezed out of the joints is allowed to remain as it is rather than being struck off.

SKIRT
Another name for the apron under the top of a table or at the base of a chest of drawers or other case piece.

A skirt is also a fabric covering fitted over the box spring of a bed and hanging down around the edges to the floor. Like a dust ruffle, it is used for decoration and to conceal the space under the bed, but it differs from a dust ruffle in that it is usually tailored and formal. The skirt is stitched to a sheet of muslin which covers the top of the box spring.

SKOTCH FASTENER
A patented metal fastener hammered across a joint to reinforce it. The fastener is a small, flat strip of steel with sharp prongs projecting from the underside.

SKYLIGHT
Skylights, or roof windows, if improperly selected and installed, cause problems because they admit too much glare, raise the house temperature sharply during the day, and allow heat to

escape in cold weather. But they are useful for five reasons which more than counterbalance their shortcomings:

1 / They permit greater flexibility in the planning of a house because they make it possible to have brightly lighted rooms without windows. Consequently, it is unnecessary to arrange a house so every room has at least one window, and this, in turn, permits construction of a more compact house at lower cost.

2 / Because skylights admit more light than windows and distribute it more evenly, rooms with only a few windows or very small windows can be as bright as those with large picture windows.

3 / They admit natural light to interior halls, stairways, and bathrooms.

4 / They increase privacy.

5 / They make it easier to arrange furniture in small bedrooms where windows might be partially blocked by chests and the headboards of beds.

Skylights can be built to special design and size of wired glass or glass blocks, but prefabricated units are used most often because of their economy. They are available in a wide range of shapes and sizes, usually with domes of clear or translucent plastic. The translucent domes are preferable because they diffuse the incoming light and thus reduce glare, and because they give privacy from higher surrounding buildings. The clear domes are used when a view of the sky is important to the spirits or for aesthetic reasons.

All domes should be double-glazed to reduce heat loss and prevent condensation.

Hinged domes are made to provide ventilation. And some units are made with built-in exhaust fans.

SLAB CONSTRUCTION

A system in which a house is built on a concrete slab laid directly on the ground. In addition to supporting the structure, the slab serves as the base on which flooring is laid.

Houses built on slabs are generally less expensive than those built on conventional foundations over a basement or crawl space, and they need not be any colder (contrary to popular opinion); but they are more subject to attack by termites.

On well-drained soils, monolithic floating slabs are used. In these, the foundations, which are about 1 ft. deep, are poured in one piece with the slab. The slab itself is poured on a 6- to 8-in. base of crushed rock covered with a polyethylene moisture barrier. The slab is 4 in. thick and reinforced with steel mesh. To keep the slab warm, rigid waterproof insulating boards 1 to 3 in. thick are secured to the edges and extend down to the bottom of the foundations. An alternative is to make the slab of concrete containing expanded mica or a similar insulating material.

On poorly drained soils, slabs should be of the suspended type. These are laid across the tops of foundation walls which extend below the frost line. The slab is constructed like a floating slab and insulated with rigid boards secured to the perimeter and extending from the top of the slab to a depth of at least 2 ft. below grade.

Both floating and suspended slabs are relatively termiteproof, provided the top of the slab is 8 in. above grade and provided at least 6 in. of the outside edges are clearly visible.

Other types of slab are poured within the foundation walls on a moisture barrier laid over crushed rock. These are insulated by wrapping rigid insulation around the vertical edges of the slab and down around the bottom for a distance of 2 ft. However, such slabs are very vulnerable to termites, which enter the house through the insulated joints between the slab and the foundations.

SLANT FRONT
A desk or secretary with a backward-slanted front which opens outward on hinges to form a writing surface.

SLAT BACK
See Ladder Back.

SLATE
A fine-grained, striated stone which splits into flat slabs with smooth surfaces. Generally black, dark gray, or red, it is used in houses on roofs, floors, walls and hearths, and to cover the jambs around fireplaces. It is available—usually on order—in precut rectangles and squares and in miscellaneous, untrimmed shapes. Natural cleft slate has a vigorous irregular surface texture and is suitable for all applications. Sawed slate has a less pronounced texture and is generally restricted to floors.

Roofing slates are laid on a solid deck covered with building paper. Additional framing may be required to support the weight, which runs to about 8 lb. per square foot for thin slates. The roof must have a pitch of at least 4 in. per foot.

Slate roofs are very handsome, fire resistant, and windproof, and have an indefinite life expectancy. But they are fairly difficult to repair when a slate is broken. And snow and ice cascade off them with such a rush that plantings under the eaves may be beaten to the ground—which is why slate roofs are often equipped with one or two rows of steel snow guards.

SLEEPER

A 2 x 2 or 2 x 4 timber laid on a concrete subfloor to serve as the base for a wooden floor or subfloor. It is embedded in asphalt to immobilize it. If there is any chance of moisture in the concrete, sleepers should be treated with a wood preservative and covered with polyethylene sheets to keep moisture out of the finish floor.

SLIPCOVER

Removable covers are sometimes used on upholstered furniture to protect the upholstery when the furniture is not on display. But their primary purpose is to change the appearance of furniture in different seasons or to improve the appearance of old furniture at low cost. In all cases, the covers should be fitted snugly so that they look almost as much a part of the furniture as the upholstery and so they do not slip or wrinkle. At the same time, they must be securely stitched to prevent ripping of the seams and be equipped with zippers to permit easy removal.

Fabrics used for slipcovers should be durable and, ideally, stain resistant. Materials which are especially suitable include tightly woven cottons, linens, sailcloth, barkcloth, and chintz.

SLIPPER FOOT

A furniture foot shaped like a slim, pointed woman's shoe.

SLIPPER STOOL

A stool with a compartment for slippers under the hinged lid.

SLIP SEAT

A removable upholstered seat like that on many dining room chairs.

SLUBBED

A term describing fabric with thick, uneven places in the yarns.

SLUSHED JOINT

In masonry work, a slushed joint is a vertical joint which is filled after the masonry units are laid by troweling mortar down into it. Such a joint is undesirable because it may have voids and is therefore weak—so it should be made only when it is impossible to form a buttered joint.

SNAKE

A long, stiff but flexible flat steel ribbon with an attached arrow-like head which is used by plumbers to clean out drains. As a verb, snake means to pull electric cables, etc., through the framework of a house.

SNAKE FOOT

A furniture foot curving sharply outward and shaped like a snake's head. It was used on Queen Anne and Chippendale pieces.

SNOW GUARD

An L-shaped metal device inserted under the butts of roof shingles to prevent avalanche-like snow slides.

SOFA

A sofa is a handsome piece with upholstered seat, back, and arms, usually sized for three persons. It has been an important, almost essential, feature of living rooms since the early 1800s, although it was used before then. Popular styles which have survived from earlier periods are Queen Anne, Chippendale, Hepplewhite, Sheraton, Duncan Phyfe, Louis XVI, Victorian, and American Empire. Current styles include the Lawson sofa (a rectangular piece with arms lower than the back and removable cushions at the back and on the seat), the tuxedo sofa (basically like the Lawson sofa but with arms the same height as the back), and the contemporary sofa which has no definite earmarks except its simple lines.

A sectional sofa is a distinct modern type consisting of two or more separate units which can be placed end to end to make what appears to be an enormous straight or curved one-piece unit. The sections have no arms or a single arm at either the right or left end.

Another modern sofa is the sofa bed, which can be converted at night into a single bed or twin beds.

Conventional sofas and sofa beds are commonly made in two more or less standard sizes—72 x 33 in. and 84 x 33 in. Other pieces which seat two or more persons but which differ from sofas in size or construction are the love seat, conversational, settee, settle, Chesterfield, Davenport, and divan. These are described elsewhere.

SOFFIT

The underside of a beam, cornice, arch, lintel, etc. It is also the vertical board enclosing the space between a ceiling and the top front edge of a kitchen wall cabinet.

SOFTWOOD

A tree, or the wood of a tree, with needle-like leaves. Pines, spruces, and redwoods are softwoods. But the wood of some softwoods is harder than that of some hardwoods. Yellow pine, for example, is much harder than poplar, which is a hardwood.

SOIL BRANCH

The pipe through which a toilet is emptied into the soil pipe which leads to a community sewer or septic tank. Soil branches are usually 4 in. in diameter.

SOIL PIPE

The large central drain pipe into which all plumbing wastes from toilets, lavatories, tubs, sinks, etc., are discharged. The pipe extends through the roof, where it serves as the vent for the plumbing system. A soil pipe is also called a *soil pipe stack* or simply a *stack*.

SOLAR CONTROL

An effort to reduce sun heat and glare in houses with large expanses of glass without resorting to awnings or blinds. Eyebrows extending out over the windows and tinted glass are most often used. In existing houses, glass can be sprayed with a tinted alkyd resin or covered with tinted polyester film.

SOLAR HEATING

A much discussed, long studied idea for capturing and using the heat of the sun to heat a house. The systems developed to date are experimental and vary in some respects; but in all of them a large flat box is installed on top of a roof facing south. The box is painted black on the bottom and has a glass top. Water circulating through a long, continuous coil or pipe inside the box is heated by the sun and then piped to a tank or chamber in which the heat is given off and stored. Air passing through the tank is used to circulate the heat through the house.

Solar heating has been slow to catch on because the system is fully effective only in regions with a great deal of sunshine; but it has been used with considerable success in cold climates because some heat is picked up by the pipes, even on cloudy days, and because of the storage tank. Nevertheless, an auxiliary heat source is needed to warm a house during long inclement spells.

In some systems, the domestic water used for bathing, etc., is also heated by the sun. Systems using solar cells on the roof are used to generate electricity as well.

SOLDER

A metal alloy with a low melting point used for permanently joining most common metals. In the house, it is used primarily to install copper plumbing and heating pipes, and to seal joints in flashing, especially around chimneys.

Metals to be soldered must be completely cleaned to remove oxides, fluxed, and heated with a propane torch, soldering iron, or soldering gun. The solder is melted by touching it, not with the soldering tool but to the hot surfaces being joined.

Solder is put up in wire form and bars, and also as a paste which is applied with a brush. Some wire solders contain a core of flux, but in most cases, the flux is applied separately to the metal just before it is heated.

SOLDIER

A brick laid upright on one of its ends and with a narrow face exposed. Soldiers are used in courses, rarely individually.

SOLE PLATE

      See Plate. A sole plate is also called a *sole.*

SOUND CONTROL

      Muffling sounds within a room is easily done by lining the room with materials that soak up noise. The material most often used is acoustical tile (*see above*) which is glued or stapled to the ceiling and, if necessary, to the walls. Heavy draperies, thick upholstery, and deep carpets achieve the same end.

      Transmission of noise from room to room is more difficult to control and has become a much more common problem in the past 25 years. Somewhat surprisingly, success in stopping sound or at least lowering it to an unobjectionable point is achieved not by trapping it in fibrous insulation but by increasing the density of walls and ceilings.

      In a new house, the easiest way to minimize sound transmission between adjoining rooms is to install 5/8-in. gypsum board on both sides of the walls. A better solution is to nail a ½-in. gypsum backer board to the studs and cover it with ½-in. standard gypsum board.

      In extreme situations, sound control is further improved by staggering the studs so that the odd-numbered studs touch one side of the wall and the even-numbered studs touch the other side of the wall.

      To stop noise from rising from the first floor to the second (usually not a bad problem), 5/8-in. gypsum board or two layers of ½-in. board are applied to the first-floor ceiling. But stopping the sounds of steps from penetrating to the first floor from the second is more difficult. Most people settle for a thick rug cushion and deep-pile carpet on the second floor. A better solution is to nail 1½-in. insulating board of the type used for roof decks to the floor joists in the second floor, and to cover this with rug cushion and carpet.

      Another source of trouble most people overlook is interior doors. These can be quieted slightly by fitting them more tightly into the frame or installing weatherstripping. But a more important step is to substitute solid-core flush doors for hollow-core doors or to use traditional raised-panel doors.

SOURCE

      A nylon-and-polyester carpet fiber with resistance to abrasion and crushing. The fibrils in the fiber refract light like a gem, thus giving carpets a soft glow.

SPACE HEATING

Heating individual rooms rather than the entire house with a central furnace. Until the advent of electric heating, space heaters were used to supplement the central system—to heat areas which for one reason or another did not have a heating outlet or were inadequately heated. Today, however, electric heating done with individual room units controlled by individual room thermostats is actually space heating, although it is not known as such (*see* Heating).

Space heating in the accepted sense is done with several types of built-in heater as well as with portable units. The built-ins include:

Room Heat Pumps • These are similar in operation to large heat pumps (*see above*) but resemble room air conditioners and are installed in windows or through openings in exterior walls in the same way. They heat the room in which they are located in winter and cool it in summer.

Oil and Gas Space Heaters • Large box-like units installed in a room, about a foot out from all walls, and vented to the outdoors through metal flues. Though efficient, they are unattractive and are usually used only in vacation homes.

Floor Furnaces • Gas- or oil-fired heaters which are installed in a basement or crawl space under the floor of the room requiring heat. Heat rises through a grate in the floor.

Wall Heaters • Using gas or electricity, these are rather small units which are recessed in a wall. They heat primarily by radiation, but some units have a built-in fan to circulate the heated air. Heaters of this type have been used in bathrooms for many years.

Ceiling Heaters • Small electric heaters which are recessed in or surface-mounted on a ceiling. They incorporate a fan for circulating the heated air.

SPACKLE

A material used for filling holes in wood, plaster, gypsum board, etc. Conventional spackle is made for interior use only, but interior-exterior grades are sold.

Spackle is sold either as a dry plaster-like powder which is mixed with water just prior to application or as a thick paste ready for immediate use. The latter, though a bit more expensive, is better since it is smoother, dries more slowly, and requires no mixing. Both types can be applied to most untreated materials, but wood should first be primed with paint or shellac.

SPADE FOOT

A slender furniture foot shaped like a flower pot with four flat (rather than circular) sides.

SPALL

To break off in small chips. Bricks, stones, and other masonry units spall when struck a sharp blow with a hammer. They may also spall in winter when moisture gets into them and freezes. This is an especially aggravating problem with old bricks.

SPAN

The distance between the supports under joists, beams, etc. The permissible span depends on the material of which the spanning member is made (usually wood or steel), its size, the load on it, and how many members are used.

For example, if floor joists are spaced 16 in. on center, a joist cut from 2 x 8-in. Douglas fir timber of No. 1 Dimension grade has a maximum allowable span of 14 ft. under a 30-lb. live load; 13 ft. under a 40-lb. load. By contrast, a comparable 2 x 12 can be used for 19 ft. 8 in. and 18 ft. 8 in. spans, respectively.

SPANDREL

In current architecture, a spandrel is the wall area between the head of one window and the sill of the window directly above.

SPANISH FOOT

An outcurved furniture foot with flutes.

SPATTER FINISH

A paint finish applied to floors and large furniture surfaces. The effect ranges from that of fine rain on a dry pavement to a violently polka-dotted dress.

The paint is spattered on a basecoat of paint, varnish, shellac, etc. Application is made with a sprayer or a paint brush slapped against a stick. The spatters may be one or many colors.

SPECIFICATIONS

A written document detailing the way a house should be put together. Primarily it stipulates the kind and quality, and perhaps the brand and quantity, of materials and equipment to be used. But it may also describe the way in which certain parts of a house are to be assembled or erected.

The specifications amplify the plans for a house. If a contractor were not given written specifications, he would either waste the homeowner's time asking hundreds of questions about what was wanted here and there, or he would make his own decisions with perhaps disastrous results to the owner's pocketbook or to the quality of the house.

Like the plans for a house, the specifications are made a part of the contract when that is drawn up and signed.

SPICE CHEST

A compact cabinet with drawers in which spices were kept in earlier periods. It can be made to stand on a table or shelf, hang on a wall, or stand on the floor (like a miniature chest of drawers).

SPIKE

A common nail from 6 to 12 in. long. It is specified by its length, not by the penny.

SPLASH BLOCK

A troughlike rectangular slab of masonry placed at the outlet of a gutter to direct water away from the foundations.

SPLAT

A rather wide, flat piece centered vertically or horizontally in the back of a chair, such as a fiddle-back chair. It is sometimes pierced.

SPLAY

A surface that angles outward from an opening. If an opening cut for a window does not form a true rectangle, it has a splay, or is splayed.

SPLICE (1)

To connect boards, timbers, or moldings end to end in a straight line. The result is a splice. By contrast, if pieces of lumber are connected at an angle, the connection is called a *joint* (*see above*).

In the construction of a house, splicers are most often made when it is necessary to join two lengths of baseboard or molding. Since the baseboard or molding is nailed to the wall, the only purpose of the splice is to produce a neater, less obvious joint than if the boards were simply butted end to end. The splice used is a *scarfed splice.*

When it is necessary to join timbers for the framework of a house, however, the splice must be made with care to ensure that it will hold up under the stress to which it is subjected. Among the several splices used for this purpose, the simplest are the *fished, halved, square,* and *scarfed splices.*

SPLICE (2)

A joining of electrical wires. It may be made by wrapping one wire around the other, soldering or with a wire nut. In a permanent wiring system, splices are always made in a box. Extension cords are often spliced and wrapped with insulating tape.

SPLINE

A strip of wood or metal used as a fastener. Boards can be joined edge to edge by cutting grooves in the edges and inserting a spline. Splines are also used to hold screen wire in grooves in screen frames.

SPLINT

A thin wooden strip which is woven into a chair seat or basket.

SPLIT

A lengthwise crack in lumber usually caused by man, as when a large nail is driven into a yellow pine board near one end. Splitting caused by nailing or screwing can generally be prevented by drilling a pilot hole for the nail or screw.

SPLIT LEVEL

A house with one or more of the floors less than a full story (usually 8 ft.) above another. The flights of stairs between floors are only about half as long as those in a conventional two-story house; but, of course, there are more flights. The houses are best suited to gently sloping lots, but are often built on flat lots by speculative builders because they take up less space than one-story houses of comparable square footage. This is their main advantage. Their other advantage is that they require less stair-climbing than two-story houses because there is relatively little traffic between the main level and the lowest level, which usually contains the family room and garage.

On the other side of the coin, splits (as they are also called) are sometimes ugly. They are difficult and expensive to build. Water often seeps into the lowest levels, especially when the floor is below grade. The houses are hard to heat. The short flights of stairs are often dangerous because they are not expected (this is especially true in splits on more than three levels). The family room on the lowest level frequently resembles a railroad car, and the garage may be too wide for one car but not wide enough for two.

SPOON RACK
A small, wall-hung rack with notches in the front edge for displaying pretty spoons. The rack can usually be used also for display of cups and/or plates.

SPRINGWOOD
The wood formed by a tree in the spring. *See* Summerwood.

SPRUCE
Spruce is a straight-grained, fine-textured softwood with unusual strength in relation to weight. It is used for many building purposes because it works easily, takes a finish well, and shrinks very little. Eastern spruce is pink to reddish; Englemann spruce from the West is off-white.

SQUARE
One hundred square feet. Some building materials, such as roofing, are specified or sold by the square.

SQUARE FOOT
The unit of measure for lumber materials such as plywood, hardboard, and clapboards under ½ in. thick. The term *surface foot* is also used.

Many other building materials such as gypsum board and asbestos-cement board are sold by the square foot.

SQUARE SPLICE
A relatively simple splice made to connect timbers which are under tension in a straight line. The opposing ends are shaped so they overlap and interlock (in much the same way bent index fingers on both hands are overlapped and interlocked). Fishplates are then nailed, screwed, or bolted over the splice.

STABILE
A piece of sculpture composed of several parts which are secured to a permanent base but which are designed to move when struck by a breeze or activated by mechanical means. *Compare* Mobile.

STACK
The vertical run of drain pipe into which all plumbing wastes in a house are discharged. Known also as the *soil pipe*, it is connected into the house drain at the bottom and extends through the roof at the top end, where it serves as a vent. Careful placement of a stack is important so it does not interfere with the floor plan of a house and so the vented end is not visible from the street.

A chimney is also called a stack.

STAGING
Scaffolding.

STAIN
A pigmented liquid for changing the color of wood. Interior stains for use on furniture, paneling, woodwork, floors, etc., have an oil, water, or alcohol base; exterior stains have an oil base.

Water and alcohol stains give an excellent effect but are difficult to handle and should be applied by professionals. Interior oil stain is applied to a small section of wood and allowed to stand for about five minutes. Then the excess is removed with clean, dry rags, and the surface is rubbed hard to a uniform color. If a deeper color is desired, the process is repeated as often as necessary. The stain should then dry for 48 hours before a final protective finish of varnish, shellac, etc., is applied.

Regardless of the interior stain used, it is very difficult to achieve exactly the same color on two dissimilar woods, such as pine and mahogany or maple and oak.

A true *exterior oil stain* is a lightly pigmented, clear finish which colors wood but does not conceal its texture or grain. It can be applied to any unfinished, previously stained, or water-repellent-treated wood, but it is most effective on rough-sawn wood because it will last for eight to ten years, whereas it has a life of only two to four years on smooth wood. Two coats should be brushed on, the second within 30 minutes of the first. Thereafter, the color can be renewed with a single coat.

A second type of exterior stain is called an *opaque* or *solid-color stain* by the paint industry, but it is actually more like a thin paint made with penetrating oil because it leaves a film of pigment on the surface and conceals fine grain and texture. It does not, however, conceal very rough grain, saw marks, or other imperfections. Two coats are applied with a brush; the second after the first is fully dry.

An opaque stain can be applied to new wood. It can also be used over a previously stained surface to change from a light to a darker color. It can even be used on a painted house, provided the paint has worn very thin. In all cases, it has about the same life—four years—as paint.

STAINED GLASS

Glass colored by a chemical process for use in windows and lampshades and simply as ornaments. It is commonly set in slender lead frames.

Much stained glass today is more accurately called *fused glass* because the glass is set in layers, heated in a kiln to the point of softening, and then framed in epoxy or other plastic material.

STAINKILLER

A white-pigmented finish with an alcohol base which is used for sealing knots in softwood lumber so they won't bleed through the final finish.

STAINLESS STEEL

A very tough, durable, rust-resistant steel alloyed with chromium. Its principal uses are in sinks and utensils.

Because stainless steel sinks are very noisy, the best type for installation is made of 18-gauge metal with an automobile-like undercoating on the bottom. But even these scratch readily, show fingermarks, and are hard to keep looking clean.

STAIN WAX

A wood finish which stains and waxes simultaneously. It is used on paneling, floors, furniture, and other surfaces, but it is less durable than some other finishes.

STAIR

The design of a stairway is dictated by the plan of the house; but if the result is dangerous, tiring, or unattractive, the house plan should be changed.

The simplest, least expansive stair is the *straight-run* type which leads from one floor to the next without any turns or landings. But it is dangerous, tiring to climb, and rather unattractive.

An *L stair,* also called a *dog-leg* or *platform stair,* is safer, less tiring, and more attractive—but also more expensive—because it incorporates a landing part way up. If the landing is near the top or bottom, the stair is called a *long-L* or *quarter-space stair;* if it is halfway between floors, the stair is a *wide-L stair.*

A *double-L stair* makes two turns and has two landings, one near the bottom and the other near the top.

A *wide-U stair* is similar to a double-L except that both landings are closer to the middle of the stair. By contrast, a *narrow-U stair* doubles straight back on itself; there is only one landing, but it is twice the width of each run of stairs. Both types of U stair as well as a double-L rank first in safety because no one can fall very far. They are also least tiring.

Winder, or *winding, stairs* can be L-shaped or U-shaped. Both are dangerous because, instead of having landings, there are steps which wind around the corners. As a result, the treads are wedge-shaped and provide very little surface to step on close to the corner.

Curving stairs which curve more or less continuously from top to bottom are dangerous for the same reason. On the other hand, a well-designed curving stair is more graceful than any other design.

If a stair has walls on both sides, it is known as a *closed-string stair*. An *open-string stair* has a wall on only one side. Some stairs are open-string at the bottom and closed-string at the top. Others are open on both sides. Whatever the arrangement, all closed areas should have a railing on at least one side, and all open areas should have a balustrade on the open side. On stairs which are open on both sides and on all stairs more than 44 in. wide, there should be railings or balustrades on both sides. The top rails are normally 30 in. above the treads and 34 in. above landings. Additional rails or balusters should be installed under the top rail on the open side of a stair so there is no chance of a person falling through to the floor below.

The safety of a stair and the ease with which it is climbed also depend on the dimensions of the stair.

The height of the risers and depth of the treads are figured first. The risers are the vertical surfaces or spaces between the top of one tread and the top of the next. The treads are the horizontal boards on which a person steps. They are measured from the face of one riser to the face of the next (the nosings which overhang the risers are not included in the measurement). Two rules are used to establish the dimensions of risers and treads:

1 / On the main staircase, the risers should be no less than 7 in. and no more than 7-5/8 in. high. (On a service staircase, riser height up to 8 in. is permissible.)

2 / The height of one riser plus the depth of one tread should total between 17 and 18 in. In other words, if a riser is 7 in. high, the tread can be 10 to 11 in. deep. If a riser is 7-5/8 in. high, however, the tread should measure between 9-3/8 and 10-3/8 in. deep.

On any single staircase, the dimensions of every step (riser and tread) should be the same.

The width of a main staircase should not be less than 3 ft.; otherwise, two people cannot pass. Somewhat greater width is preferable. Minimum width of a service staircase is 30 in.

The minimum headroom required by the FHA between stair treads and the lowest part of the ceiling above is 6 ft. 8 in., but it should actually be at least 7 ft. 4 in. for safe passage of the average person and movement of furniture.

STAIR, DISAPPEARING

A prefabricated stair used to provide access to an attic. Installed in the attic floor above a hatch, it automatically folds or slides down into the space below when the hatch is opened.

STAIR, SPIRAL

Steel or wooden stairs winding in a tight spiral around a central steel column. They take up less floor space than any other type of stair but are very tiring, hazardous, and, for some people, frightening. As used in modern or rustic houses, the stair is almost always fully exposed to view. In very old houses, on the other hand, spiral stairs were built for the servants' use and were fully enclosed.

STAIR WELL
The enclosed space surrounding a stair.

STAKE OUT
To outline with stakes and strings the plan of a house or other structure on the ground on which it is to be built. For a person who has difficulty understanding blueprints, staking out the house he is about to build helps him to visualize it better.

STAPLE
With the development of automatic staplers, the use of staples instead of nails or tacks has grown in building, decorating, and furniture manufacture. The staples are similar to office staples but made of heavier wire and in lengths ranging from ¼ to 9/16 in.

Much heavier, hammer-driven staples are used for fastening down wires, cables, etc.

STARTER
A small metal can needed to turn on fluorescent tubes of the preheat type. Such tubes require a few seconds to heat up before the light goes on. By contrast, rapid-start, trigger start, circline, and moduline fluorescent tubes light instantly without a starter.

STARTING STEP
The bottom tread in a flight of stairs. When the stair is not built between walls, the starting step commonly projects beyond the other treads and supports the newel post.

STATIC ELECTRICITY
Static electricity is an annoying cold-weather problem which results when a person walks across a wool or nylon carpet and touches a piece of metal, a person, or an animal. It can be minimized by raising the humidity in the house and prevented by using carpets made of other fibers or by treating wool and nylon carpets with an anti-static spray.

STEMWARE

Goblets, wine glasses, and other types of drinking glass with relatively slender stems between the bowls and the bases.

STENCILING

A technique for applying a painted design, letters, numerals, etc., to furniture, paneling, walls, floors, etc. The stencil used is a thin sheet of stiff, oil-treated cardboard with the design cut out. Paint is applied through the cut-outs with a short-bristled stencil brush.

Stenciling is also done by pressing paint through a patterned silk screen.

STICK BACK

A chair or settee back made with slender spindles. Windsor chairs, for example, are sometimes called stick-back chairs.

STILE

One of the vertical members of a door or window sash. The horizontal rails are fastened between them.

In a double-hung window, a stile is one of the grooves in which a sash slides up and down. In old-style windows, it was called a *pulley stile* because it incorporated a pulley at the top.

On cabinets, the stiles are the vertical facing boards to which doors are hinged or into which drawers slide. In kitchen cabinets, the stiles are often made much wider than necessary—so they extend beyond the side panels of the cabinets. These are called *extended stiles* and serve the same purpose as filler strips when cabinets are fitted to walls or when a row of cabinets needs to be filled out to fit a wall space.

STIPPLED FINISH

A furniture or wall finish with a random dotted effect. It is generally made with a short-bristled stippling brush which is jabbed into a sticky coat of alkyd enamel or glaze. Stippling can also be done with a stippling roller or ordinary sponge.

STIRRUP

A hanger (*see above*).

STOCK

Standard. Virtually all building materials and equipment are made and sold in stock sizes and/or designs. This means that they are—or can be—produced in large quantities and marketed in anticipation of demand; and as a result, they sell for less than materials and equipment which must be made to order.

Just because something classifies as a stock item does not mean, however, that it is available in a lumberyard, etc., for immediate delivery. In fact, it may not be available at all unless the customer is willing to place a minimum order which may be far larger than he needs.

STONE

Used in building from time immemorial, stone is laid up in walls for houses and used in fireplaces and chimneys and for floors:

Walls • Sandstone, limestone, granite, and quartzite are the most popular stones for building exterior walls. Artificial stones made by combining stone aggregates with cement are also used. In earlier days, the walls were solid—12 to 18 in. thick—and uninsulated. Today, the stones are laid up as a fairly thin veneer over a frame wall which is stuffed with fiber insulation. An air space between the stone and sheathing keeps moisture from entering the house and also helps to insulate it.

To simplify construction, stones are usually cut into exact or irregular rectangles which are laid up in uniform or random horizontal courses. This is called *ashlar facing. Rubble facing*, made of irregular stones left more or less as they are quarried or found in a field, is more difficult to construct; but if skillfully handled, it has a tapestry-like effect of exceptional beauty.

Floors • These are commonly built of flagstone, slate, or marble. The stones are embedded in a concrete base and separated by mortar joints approximately ½ in. wide.

STONEWARE

Also called *stone china*, a very hard, opaque kind of pottery which does not absorb water and is more durable than earthenware. It is used for tableware as well as for decorative pieces.

STOOL (1)

The flat board on the inside and at the base of a window frame. It is popularly called a *windowsill*, although the sill is actually the corresponding thick, slanted board on the outside of the frame. Stools are normally made of wood finished with paint or varnish, but for ease of maintenance they may be covered with sheet plastic or ceramic tile. In some parts of the country, they are made of marble.

STOOL (2)

Stools for sitting are made tall or short; with fixed or swivel seats; with or without chair backs; with a single central pedestal or three or four legs. They are identified according to their principal uses as bar stools, bathroom stools, children's stools, kitchen stools, and dressing table stools.

Other kinds of stool are called foot stools, or crickets, and step stools. The latter are generally made of steel and have one, two, or three steps so a person can reach into high cupboards and shelves.

STOOP

A very small porch—really nothing more than a landing at the top of steps leading up to the front or back door.

STOP

A simple molding or wooden strip which restricts the motion of a door or window. In a doorway for a hinged door, the stops are nailed to the jambs and prevent the door from swinging shut past the latch. They also help to prevent drafts around the door edges. The same type of stop is used in a casement or hopper window.

In a double-hung or horizontal sliding window, one set of stops is installed along the inside edges of the jambs; the other set is installed along the outside edges. The latter are called *blind stops*. All window stops are designed to hold the windows in the frame and to prevent drafts.

In wooden doors and windows, the stops are fastened with finishing nails or screws so they can be readily removed. The blind stops, however, are a permanent part of the jambs.

A stop is also a rubber-tipped metal bumper which keeps a door from banging against a wall.

STORAGE WALL

A thick wall built of lumber and plywood which is divided into closets, cabinets, shelves, and drawers for the storage of large numbers of articles. It has no bearing strength and can be simply shoved up against a framed wall or used in the center of a room as a divider. Divider walls are frequently only 6 or 7 ft. high rather than full ceiling height.

A storage wall can be built to any dimensions and compartmentalized in any way to suit the homeowner. Those used as divider walls may be accessible from one or both sides.

STORM DOOR

A door installed outside a regular exterior door to keep out cold. It usually has glass panes.

Stock doors are made with wooden or aluminum frames. In a combination storm-and-screen door, the glass inserts can be removed in warm weather and replaced with screens. Stock storm doors are generally available in three designs:

High Light • With two large glass inserts, the top being longer than the bottom. There is a wide kickplate below the lower light.

Even Light • With two glass inserts of equal size and a kickplate.

Cross-Buck • With a single large glass insert in the upper half of the door. The bottom half is solid and has a large X design.

STORM WINDOW

The best storm windows are those which can't be seen and never have to be bothered with. They are made of large panes of insulating glass which take the place of ordinary glass in window sash or of single-thickness plate glass in picture windows.

Insulating glass has many advantages in addition to the fact that it is indistinguishable from ordinary glass except under closest examination, and that once installed, it can be forgotten. For one thing, it reduces heat loss roughly 50%. Because it is made of plate glass, it gives a distortion-free view indoors and out. And it can be made with tinted glass, patterned glass, etc. On the negative side, it is much more expensive than ordinary glass. If one of the sheets is cracked or broken, the whole piece must be replaced. And it is not made in small enough panes for multi-paned windows. This last fault has been corrected—theoretically—by fitting a window sash with a large piece of insulating glass. Then thin, flexible, snap-in-and-out mullions are set into the frame against the glass, converting the single pane into several small panes. When the homeowner wants to wash the window, he takes out the mullions. This is a perfect solution to a problem except for one thing: From outside the house, the windows look like the obvious fakes they are.

All other kinds of storm window are installed separately from the house windows. Most popular are combination storm-and-screen windows with aluminum frames which are screwed to the jambs outside double-hung and horizontal sliding windows (but not outside swinging windows such as casements). The so-called three-track combination is the most common. This consists of two glass panels, each sliding in its own track, and a screen panel in a third track. In winter, one glass panel covers the top half of the window, and the other glass panel covers the bottom half. The screen is pushed up to the top of the window where it is stored. In summer, the lower glass panel is pushed to the top of the window, and the screen panel is pulled down to take its place.

The worst fault of combination sash is that they detract from the appearance of the window, even when the sash and its frame are painted white (sometimes they are unpainted). It is also impossible to get more than 50% ventilation through the window in summer.

On the other hand, once combinations are installed, they can be forgotten. Nothing has to be taken down and stored. When the windows need washing, the storm sash panels lift out easily.

Other storm windows are large put-up-and-take-down units with wide wooden or narrow aluminum frames. The latter are preferable simply because they are much lighter and easier to handle, and because they do not spoil the lines of the windows so badly. But they are tricky to anchor and tend to sail away in a high wind if they are not well secured. (As in the case of combination storm-and-screen sash, installation of conventional storm windows should be made outside the house windows so that condensation forms on them rather than on the house windows.)

STORY

A story is that part of a house between any floor and the ceiling or roof above. A basement is not considered a story unless the larger portion of the space is above ground.

A half-story is an occupiable space under a sloping roof. A story-and-a-half house is generally thought of as one with a full first story and a steep gable, hip, or gambrel roof which rises from the top plates of the first floor walls to a height of 8 ft. or more at the ridge.

The definition of a story, however, is not uniform among local building departments and zoning boards.

STORY POLE

A long strip of wood used by carpenters, masons, etc., to mark and determine the height of door and window openings, shingle and brick courses, etc. Also called a *story rod.*

STRAIGHT FRONT

A plain front on a case piece such as a chest of drawers.

STRAW

Straw is woven into rugs, table mats, baskets, basket-like stools, and other small articles. It is not durable and collects dirt, but it has an interesting texture and charming simplicity.

STRESS

A load or force or system of forces producing strain. All structures, such as houses or pieces of furniture, are subjected to stress and must be designed and built to withstand it.

STRETCHER

A brick or other masonry unit laid lengthwise of a wall.

Also, a horizontal member tying together and bracing the legs of a piece of furniture. It is larger in cross-section than a rung (*see above*).

STRIKE

Also called a *strikeplate,* a strike is a metal plate mortised into or sometimes mounted on the face of a door jamb to receive the latch and lock tongues.

STRING

The slanting timber supporting a stair—more commonly called a *stringer.* A mason uses the word to describe the act of spreading mortar into a long, narrow ribbon to receive a new course of bricks.

STRING COURSE
A narrow, horizontal band on an outside wall. It is ornamented with carving and may be flush with the wall or slightly projecting. *Compare* Frieze.

STRINGER
A long, heavy, horizontal timber between posts and used to support floor joists. It is 5 in. or more thick and at least 2 in. wider than its thickness.

A stringer is also the inclined timber supporting one side of a stair. The simplest stair stringer—usually used only in basement or temporary stairs—is a straight-sided timber with cleats nailed to the side to support the treads. Another type of stringer is cut in a sawtooth pattern on one edge. This is also used primarily for basement and outside stairs.

The main stair in a house is usually built with housed stringers, in which grooves are cut to receive the treads and risers. The half of the stringer exposed above the stair is, in effect, a baseboard.

STRIP
A narrow piece of lumber. Boards less than 2 in. wide are strips.

As a verb, strip means to damage threads of a bolt, screw, or other threaded object. It also means to remove paint or other finish from a surface.

STRIPE
A striped fabric or wallcovering.

STRUCTURAL CRACK
A large, jagged, often gaping crack in plaster or masonry caused by settlement of the building.

STRUT
A structural member installed between two other pieces to keep them apart. Its purpose is to resist pressure or a load. The short diagonal pieces between the main members of a truss are struts.

STUCCO

A cement plaster used on exterior walls. It is applied in three coats to metal lath over wooden sheathing or to masonry. The first two coats are made of 1 part portland cement, 3 parts sand, and hydrated lime to 10% of the weight of the cement. The finish coat—the actual stucco coat—is mixed to the same proportions but contains white portland cement. If the stucco is to be colored, mineral pigment is added to the mix.

Stucco may be given a smooth, stippled, sand-floated, sand-sprayed, or rough-cast (also called spatter-dash) finish.

STUD (1)

One of the upright timbers in a frame wall. It is usually a 2 x 4. But 2 x 3s may be used in nonbearing partitions to save a little floor space, and 2 x 6s are used in plumbing walls containing cast-iron drains. Normal spacing of studs is 16 in. on center, but this may be increased to 24 in. or decreased to 12 in.

STUD (2)

A nail-like, hardened-steel device used to fasten things to masonry walls. Unlike other masonry anchors, it does not require a pre-drilled hole into which it is set. Instead, it is driven directly into masonry, either with a pistol-like stud driver using gunpowder or with a stud driver which is actuated by hitting with a hammer.

Because of the speed of installation, studs are used primarily when a large number of fasteners are required—as in attaching furring strips to a basement wall.

STUDIO COUCH

A couch which serves during the day as a sofa and converts at night into a bed or sometimes twin beds.

Studio couches generally consist of a frame with a built-in innerspring, mattress, and removable innerspring pillows which form the back of the sofa during the day. The couches are approximately 75 in. long and 30, 33, or 39 in. wide.

STUDY

A room, usually small, for reading, writing, and any other similar pursuits. It is usually characterized by bookshelves, although these may be omitted by nonreading families. A study is also called a *den*.

STYLIZED

A design that strays from reality but clearly depicts the subject of the design. For example, roosters, whales, and horses on weathervanes are stylized. Similarly, the designs printed on toile de Jouy fabrics and matching wallpaper are stylized.

STYRENE

Properly called *polystyrene,* this is a variable and versatile solid plastic for which new uses keep cropping up. In homes, it most often appears in the disguise of carefully carved and finished wooden parts of furniture. It is also used to make rigid slabs of moisture-proof, chemical-resistant insulation which are installed under and around the edges of concrete slabs.

SUBCONTRACTOR

A subcontractor is a skilled tradesman who is responsible for the construction of a specific part of a house. Subcontractors include carpenters, plumbers, electricians, masons, painters, etc.

In conversation, a subcontractor is often called a *sub*; to build with subcontractors is to *sub out* the job.

Building with subcontractors saves money because the owner does not pay for a *general contractor's* supervision, overhead, etc. On the other hand, the owner or someone designated by him should act as the general contractor; otherwise, the subcontractors are without supervision, and there is no one to coordinate when they report for work.

SUBFLOOR

A floor forming the base for a finish floor. In times past, when flooring boards may have been more than 1 in. thick, subfloors were often omitted, but today they are a standard part of every floor.

Subfloors are usually made of plywood laid perpendicular to the joists. Half-inch thickness is adequate if the joists are spaced no more than 16 in. on center; 3/4-in. is used otherwise. If boards are used instead of plywood (no longer a common practice), they are ¾ in. thick and laid at a 45° angle to the joists.

If a room is to be carpeted wall to wall, a finish floor may be omitted. Ideally, the subfloor should be ¾ in. thick, but frequently it is only a ½ in.

When a floor is covered with resilient flooring, the subfloor is made of 5/8-in. plywood covered with ¼-in. hardboard, plywood, or particleboard underlayment. To make the tile floor level with a wooden floor in an adjoining room, ¾-in. plywood is used instead of 5/8-in.

An alternative is to use 2-4-1 subfloor underlayment, which can be laid over beams spaced as much as 4 ft. apart.

A concrete slab also serves as a subfloor in rooms below grade and in some built on grade. The finish flooring should be put down on it only after it is ascertained that the concrete is completely dry.

Also see Floor.

SUBSTRUCTURE
The bottom part of a building—the foundations.

SUBWALL
Comparable to a subfloor, a subwall is a wall surface which serves as the base or backer for a finished wall surface made of rigid materials. Sheathing is an exterior subwall. The gypsum board, plywood, etc., to which ceramic tile, plastic panels, etc., are glued forms an interior subwall.

The wall surface to which wallpaper or other flexible coverings are applied is not called a subwall.

SUEDE
A soft, velvety, undressed leather sometimes used for upholstery, although it soils badly and is hard to clean.

SUITE
A set of furniture. Also, a group of related rooms.

SUMMER
A large, horizontal timber or stone used as a principal beam in a house or as a lintel.

SUMMERWOOD
The wood formed by a tree during the summer. Examination of the growth rings will show that each ring has two parts. The inner part is light colored and called the springwood; the outerpart is darker and is the summerwood.

Summerwood—occasionally called *autumnwood*—is stronger than springwood because it has smaller cells with thicker walls. For structural purposes, therefore, it is desirable to select lumber with a high proportion of dense summerwood.

SUMP
A hole in a basement floor made to collect water which seeps into the basement. To be effective, obviously, the floor should be slightly sloped from all sides toward the sump.

SUMP PUMP
An automatic pump installed in a sump to get rid of water which leaks into the basement. The pump turns on when the level of water in the sump reaches a pre-set height.

Since a sump pump does not prevent leakage, it should be a last resort if a house is frequently flooded.

SUPPLY PIPE
One of the plumbing pipes which distribute water throughout a house.

SURFACE FOOT
See Square Foot.

SURVEY
To measure and map out property. The result is called a survey.

SWAG
A piece of fabric hung horizontally over a window and allowed to droop. Reproductions of swags are often seen carved in furniture, etched in metal, etc.

SWEAT
To solder copper or brass pipes and fittings together. A fitting designed for installation with solder is called a sweat fitting, and has smooth inner walls.

Windows, walls, and other surfaces on which water vapor consenses are also said to sweat.

SWITCH

An electrical device which controls the flow of current to a light. Portable lamps contain their own switches, as do some appliances such as ranges, washers, and toasters. Built-in light fixtures and other appliances are controlled by wall switches as a rule. Outlets into which portable lamps are plugged may also be controlled from wall switches.

The standard wall switch makes a sharp click when the toggle is flipped on or off. The most desirable switches are silent. There are two types. The better, because it lasts longer, is a mercury switch which must be installed with the end marked "top" up. The less expensive type can be installed with either end up.

Switches are normally mounted 4 ft. above the floor on the latch side of doors and the traffic side of arches. They should be placed in the room in which the light or outlets they control are located; however, outdoor lights are switched from indoors, and lights on closed-off stairways and in storage rooms are switched from outside these areas. No switch should be placed within arm's reach of a plumbing fixture or clothes washer. In a few communities, the code requires that bathroom switches be installed outside the room.

A single-pole switch is used when the light or outlet is controlled from that switch alone. Three-way or four-way switches are used when a light or outlet is controlled from two or more switches. For convenience and safety, three- or four-way switches should be installed in any room, hall, stairway, or other enclosed area which can be entered from two or more directions; thus, it is possible to turn on, say, a stairway light when you start up the stair and turn it off when you get to the top.

SYCAMORE

A hard, tough American wood of light reddish brown. When quarter-sawed for veneer, it has a distinctive, lovely, but variable mottled effect sometimes characterized as lacy.

SYMBOL

The plans for a house must obviously incorporate a great deal of information—so to simplify them without adding too many words or details, architects use a variety of symbols. For example, a concrete wall is indicated by hundreds of dots and spots, a brick wall by closely spaced diagonal lines. A double-hung window is four parallel lines, a water heater a circle, a ceiling light a small circle with four short lines radiating from it, and a three-way switch an S with a tiny 3 just to the right and slightly below (S_3).

$\left[T \right]$

TABLE

Next to chairs, no furniture piece is designed in as many ways or has acquired as many names as the table. The following is a list of tables which have been or are being made. Some are distinct types; others differ in minor features. A number can be used interchangeably; for example, many end tables are used as bedside tables. Similarly, there is little reason why an antique pier table cannot take the place of a modern sofa table.

Bedside • Also called a *night table* or *night stand*, a small table placed at one side of the head of a bed.

Butler's • A low table with a top rim in which holes are cut for handles.

Butterfly • Comparable to a gateleg table except that the drop leaves are supported on wing-shaped brackets that swing out from the stretchers.

Card • The modern version has folding legs. Antique tables were permanent (never put away) pieces of several designs, almost all handsome.

Chairside • A small, low table of many designs.

Children's • A very low, utilitarian play and/or eating table.

Coffee • Also called a *cocktail table,* a low, usually long table for use in front of a sofa.

Console • A narrow, rectangular table placed against a wall as in a front hall. *See* Console.

Dinette • An inexpensive, usually plastic-topped, metal-legged table for dinettes and kitchen eating areas.

Dining • *See* Dining Table.

Dressing • *See* Dressing Table.

Drop-leaf • Any table with end leaves that drop.

Drum • A smallish table with a round top with drawers beneath. In some tables, the entire top rotates on a pedestal.

End • Also known as a *lamp table,* a small table placed at the end of a sofa to hold a lamp.

Folding • A metal utility table used for picnics, meetings, etc. Open, it forms a long rectangle. Closed, it folds into a bundle roughly a third of the size of a bedroom door.

Gaming • A special type of antique card table.

Gateleg • A table with out-swinging gate-shaped legs which support the end leaves of the table top when they are raised.

Harvest • A very long, narrow, rather rustic dining table.

Library • A medium to large table used in libraries and living rooms.

Nested • Several small tables that nest one inside another. Also called *bunching tables.*

Pembroke • Named for the Earl of Pembroke, a rectangular or oval table with a wide fixed leaf flanked by drop leaves of half width.

Pier • A long, rectangular table designed to stand against a wall; consequently, the back is unfinished. The top is usually marble but may be wooden.

Reading • A rectangular table with a top hinged along one edge so it can be tilted up to support a book.

Sawbuck • A simple dining table with a long, narrow board top and X-shaped legs.

Serving • A rectangular table on casters usually with drawers and a shelf below the top.

Sewing • *See* Sewing Table.

Sideboard • Also called a *serving table,* an antique rectangular table with a marble top. Food heated by alcohol lamps was served from it.

Sofa • A rectangular table placed across the back of a sofa set out from the walls.

Tea • A small table from which tea was served.

Tilt-top • A table which is more ornamental than useful because the top tends to wobble under weight. The top, hinged to a shaft supported on a tripod pedestal, tilts from vertical to horizontal. It is circular or square.

Tray-Top • A smallish rectangular table with a top shaped like a shallow tray.

Trestle • A very long, narrow table from the early days. It is supported on T-shaped trestles.

Tripod • Any table, such as a tilt-top, that is supported on a pedestal with three out-curved legs.

TABLE LINEN

The tablecloths and mats used to protect and ornament dining tables, and the napkins for the diners.

Because of the difficulty of laundering large, formal linen tablecloths and napkins, these have been almost completely replaced by smaller, colorful cloths and napkins of easy-to-launder permanent press fabrics. Vinyl cloths—but not napkins—are also used. For durability and beauty, however, the old-fashioned linens are difficult to equal.

Mats are made of linen, rayon, vinyl, vegetable fibers—almost anything.

TABOURET

A low, drum-shaped stool or table.

TACK

Familiar, sharp-pointed fastener for holding flexible materials in place. Although there are slight differences in design, most tacks can be used interchangeably. They come in lengths up to almost 1 in. and are made of steel, copper, or aluminum.

TAFFETA

A fine, crisp, lustrous fabric which rustles when it moves. Made of silk, rayon, nylon, or wool, it is used in curtains, draperies, bedspreads, and dressing table skirts.

TAIL

A shortened joist or beam which is perpendicular to a header. It is comparable to a *cripple (see above).*

TAMBOUR

A flexible door or shutter made of thin wooden strips glued to a canvas backing. It slides in grooves. Roll-top desks are of tambour design. And some cabinets have vertical tambours which slide sideways.

TAPESTRY

A heavy, rough fabric of silk, rayon, cotton, or wool with a strong pattern or design woven in. It is used for draperies and upholstery, and the finest hand-woven tapestry is used for wall hangings. In fact, so many hangings are made of tapestry that tapestry has become a synonym for hanging.

TAR AND GRAVEL

Roofing made of alternate layers of felt and asphalt, and covered with gravel, slag, or stone. *See* Built-Up Roofing.

TATAMI

A thick, woven straw mat used by the Japanese for floor covering. It normally measures 3 x 6 ft. A plastic finish is sometimes applied to increase durability.

TEA CART

A table-like cart with two wheels at one end, a horizontal handle at the other, and a large bottom shelf.

TEAK

Teak is an even, rich, medium-brown wood with a pro-nounced straight grain. It is heavy, hard, and very strong, and has such good resistance to decay and termites that it is widely used in boat building. In the home, it is found primarily in modern furniture and occasionally in handsome floors.

TELEVISION SET

The importance that a television set gains in a house is directly proportional to the importance the homeowner attaches to television as an entertainment and news medium. Regardless of the size of the set or whether it shows black and white or color pictures, several basic rules influence its placement.

It must not be exposed to direct heat. The vents in the back and bottom should not be obstructed by draperies, furniture, etc. If a set is built into a cabinet or wall, the space around it must be commodious and well ventilated.

The set must be placed where sunlight or bright lamp light will not obscure the picture on the screen.

The screen should be at the eye level of the viewers when they are seated in chairs.

Depending on the size of the family, ample space must be provided for chairs to be drawn up for all to watch a show.

In a new or remodeled house, the location of the set should be established early so that a grounded electrical outlet and an antenna lead can be built in behind it. Ideally, the antenna wire should be carried through the house to the antenna in a raceway.

TEMPER

To mix water into mortar or plaster until of working consistency. Unused mortar and plaster can be retempered as they grow stiffer but only for a few hours after they are originally mixed.

TEMPLATE

A pattern made of wood or metal which is used in carpentry and other forming work. Also spelled *templet.*

TENON

A tongue-like projection formed in the end of a piece of wood to fit into a mortise of similar size. *See* Mortise-and-Tenon Joint.

TENSION

The state of being stretched or pulled. In construction, steps must be taken to counteract the effects of tension. For example, since the rafters in a roof are under tension, they are held together with collar beams.

TERMITE CONTROL

Termites are likely to be more of a problem in new houses than old. But they can be held at bay by the following measures.

Install poured, reinforced concrete foundations rather than concrete block foundations. If block foundations are used, cap the tops with continuous slabs of 4-in.-thick, poured, reinforced concrete.

Sills must be at least 8 in. above grade; joists and beams under the house at least 18 in. above the soil in a crawl space.

If a house is built on a slab, the slab should be of the monolithic type or suspended type. In all cases, the top of the slab should be at least 8 in. above grade, and 6 in. of the outside edges must be exposed to view. *See* Slab Construction.

All wood and other cellulose material must be removed from the ground around the house.

The soil around and under the house should be treated with a recommended chemical such as chlordane. This is advisable for all houses, essential for those on slabs.

The house should be framed with lumber which is pressure-treated with wood preservative. The sills are the elements most needing treatment, but all framing pieces benefit by it.

TERMITE SHIELD

A solid metal sheet which is installed between the top of a foundation wall and the sill to keep out termites.

Since installation of termite shields is rarely made properly, shields are no longer recommended, though they can be effective. They must form a continuous strip all the way around a house, and the joints between strips must be soldered. In addition, the metal should extend beyond the sides of the foundations a couple of inches and be bent down at an angle to the ground.

TERNE

Steel coated with a lead-tin alloy which is used as a roofing material. Made in long rolls up to 28 in. wide, it is laid vertically over a solid roof deck covered with resin-sized paper. The strips are interlocked along the edges. If standing seams are made, terne can be used on a roof with a minimum pitch of 2½ in. per foot. If the seams are flat-locked, the roof can be almost flat.

Terne is fire and wind resistant, but must be painted regularly with acylic emulsion paint. Thus protected, it lasts almost indefinitely.

TERRACE

Since World War II, terraces (also called *patios* or *lanais*) have achieved the same importance in the home as family rooms. They are the hub not only of most family activities in warm weather but also of parties and of efforts by individual family members to relax alone.

Terraces are generally located more or less as a matter of course behind a house as close as possible to the living room (or family room) and kitchen. This gives privacy from the street and allows for easy access to the indoor areas which are the source and destination of most traffic to and from the terrace. But if a terrace is to be of maximum enjoyment, other points should also be considered about its location:

1 / All the ways in which it will be used.

2 / The plan of the house and its placement on the lot.

3 / The shape and contour of the lot.

4 / The orientation of the terrace to the sun.

5 / The exposure to strong winds.

6 / Whether there is a view or unusually pleasant outlook.

The location of a terrace may automatically determine its size, shape, and elevation. But this is usually not the case.

In size, a terrace should be at least equal to the living room. Even more space is preferable since terrace furniture is large, and the people occupying it are less sedentary than those indoors.

A simple rectangular terrace generally conforms best to the lines of the house and is easiest to fit into the average lot, but no restrictions should be placed on a competent architect or landscape architect.

The height of the terrace in relation to the first floor of the house becomes a problem only if the ground around the house is sloping. The ideal is a terrace which is on the same level as the room off which it opens—or just a few inches below—because it is easy to walk out on; and if it is separated from the room by sliding glass doors, it becomes a visual part of the room and makes both areas feel that much larger. On the other hand, if a house is raised off the ground, raising the terrace increases its cost; and building a deck instead of a terrace does not alter the situation. So a terrace built at ground level may be preferable, provided a long, tiring flight of steps is not required to reach it.

Once the area for a terrace is leveled, building is essentially a paving job. Favorite paving materials are brick, concrete patio tiles, cut stone blocks, flagstones, slate, wooden blocks, exposed-aggregate concrete, and ceramic tiles. The first five can be laid in mortar or without mortar on a bed of sand and gravel. Wooden blocks are always laid without mortar.

Terraces are left open to the sky or are wholly or partially roofed. In most climates, roofs are designed to keep off rain as well as to provide shade. They are built like the house roof or with corrugated, translucent fiberglass panels.

In dry climates, open roofs which let in some sunlight and facilitate air circulation on the terrace are preferred. One of the simplest types—the so-called *lath roof*—is made with 1 x 2-in. boards laid parallel and spaced 1 in. apart for deep shade, 2 in. for half shade. Other popular permanent roofs are the *louvered* and *eggcrate types*.

Large canvas awnings are often used instead of roofs in all climates. They protect against rain, yet let in a little light.

TERRA COTTA

An orange-brown earthenware used for vases, cooking utensils, and decorations. It is easily broken, and if not covered with a glaze, it soils and stains badly.

TERRAZZO

A beautiful, colorful, smooth flooring material made of marble aggregates and white portland cement laid in relatively small sections between brass strips. It is very strong, durable, and, when properly finished, impervious to stains and cleanable.

Terrazzo is laid directly over a concrete base or over a concrete base covered with a thin layer of sand. The terrazzo should be mixed so that 70% or more of the finished surface is marble and less than 30% concrete. After curing, the terrazzo is ground and polished by machine, and should then be given a coat of penetrating sealer.

TESTER

A canopy covering a bed. It is usually supported on the bedposts but is sometimes hung from the ceiling or cantilevered from the wall out over the head of the bed.

A tester consists of a wooden frame (which is sometimes partially exposed) covered with fabric. It may be flat or arched (resembling an inch-worm humping along); severely simple in design or very frilly. In some cases, draperies hang from the corners of the tester to the floor.

TETE A TETE
See Conversational.

TEXTURED PAINT
A thick latex or oil-base interior wall and ceiling paint which is used to produce a variety of textured effects and to conceal imperfections in the surface. It is applied with a brush and immediately textured with special rollers, crumpled newspapers, a broom, etc. Usually available only in white, it is most easily colored by overcoating with a conventional paint. Once dry, it is very difficult to smooth or remove.

T FITTING
A T-shaped pipe fitting into which three pipes are connected.

THERMOSTAT
The electrical control which turns on the furnace when the house gets cold and turns it off when the temperature rises to the pre-set point.

One type of thermostat—the least expensive—has open contacts made with metal strips which react to changes in temperature. Some work on 120 volts, others on 24. The latter are generally more reliable; and all incorporate an anticipator which shuts off the burner before the desired house temperature is reached. The furnace blower or circulating pump continues to operate, however; thus, it uses heat left in the furnace to bring the house temperature up to the exact point. (A 120-volt thermostat without an anticipator shuts the furnace off precisely at the pre-set temperature, but the house temperature keeps on rising as the blower or pump continues to run.)

Sealed-contact thermostats with anticipators are similar to the open-contact type but better because dust cannot settle on the contacts. They usually last forever.

The third type of thermostat is a mercury unit with anticipator. In this, a spring attached to a glass envelope containing mercury reacts to changes in house temperature. As it does so, it tilts the envelope until the mercury flows to the other end and opens or closes the circuit. This is the most expensive standard thermostat, but also the most sensitive and reliable.

Clock thermostats are usually mercury units. They are designed so that once the clock is set, the thermostat not only controls the heating system throughout the day but also automatically turns it down at night to conserve fuel and turns it up again at a pre-set time in the morning.

Still another type of thermostat for gas-fired heating plants is actually not a thermostat but an entire system. It is ideal for new furnaces in new homes because it gives high performance and does not have moving parts which can cause trouble. But its extremely fine temperature control—to within a fraction of a degree—is not perceivable to the human body.

Whatever its design, a thermostat must be located carefully. The following rules apply to most houses but not necessarily all:

1 / Install the thermostat 4 ft. off the floor in a central location which the family frequently occupies—the dining room or central hall, but never a bedroom, bathroom, or kitchen. Living and family rooms are also good locations, provided they don't have a fireplace which is used often (a fireplace makes for trouble because the fire raises room temperature and also pulls in air from surrounding rooms, causing the thermostat to feel warm when other rooms are too cool).

2 / Avoid a central hall, outside walls, and locations near the furnace or on a wall containing heating pipes or ducts or a chimney.

3 / Place the thermostat far from sunny windows, radiators, registers, the TV set, a heating appliance. Also, keep it away from exterior doors, picture windows, and glass walls.

4 / Install the thermostat in an open location—not behind a door or draperies, for example—so it is exposed to circulating air.

THINNER

A liquid which gives paints and other finishes more fluid consistency. The type of thinner used depends on the composition of the paint. Water is the thinner for latex and other water-based paints, mineral spirits for alkyd and oil-base paints and varnishes, denatured alcohol for shellac, and lacquer thinner for lacquer.

Modern paints generally are put up in cans ready for application and should not be thinned arbitrarily. If a paint is difficult to apply, however, it may be thinned to the degree specified on the label.

THIN-WALL CONDUIT
See Rigid Conduit.

THREE-WAY SWITCH
See Switch.

THRESHOLD
The slightly raised strip, usually of wood or aluminum, attached to the floor under a door. In the past, all exterior doors and doors between rooms had thresholds, but today they are generally used only under exterior doors and doors from the house to the garage, basement, or other cool areas.

Thresholds may be simple strips of material. Many are made of aluminum and incorporate vinyl gaskets which press against the bottom edge of the door to stop drafts.

THROW
A fabric with finished edges which is thrown seemingly casually over a piece of furniture for added interest or protection. There is little difference between a throw and a throw cover, except that the latter is often cut to rather precise size to fit the furniture it covers.

THROW COVER
A flat, unfitted fabric cover which is draped over furniture to protect it. It is sometimes made of laminated fabric with a foam-rubber backing which gives it extra weight and keeps it from sliding. *Compare* Slipcover.

TICKING
A strong, durable cotton or linen fabric. Usually off-white with color stripes, it is used for upholstery and coverings.

TIE
Anything which holds together parts of a building. It may be a beam used to tie together the rafters in a roof or a metal strap tying a brick veneer wall to the sheathing.

TIEBACK

A device for pulling a drapery back to the sides of a window. It serves the purpose of letting light through the window while softening the window's lines.

Many tiebacks are decorative J-shaped metal pieces. Many others are simple strips of fabric or thick yarn which are looped around a drapery and tacked to the window casings.

TIE BEAM

A timber which links structural timbers of a house so that they cannot pull apart. A collar beam is a tie beam.

TIER

In a football stadium, each horizontal row of seats is called a tier. In building, similarly, a tier is one of a series of horizontal rows—or thicknesses—arranged from front to back (as compared with a course, which is a series of horizontal rows moving from bottom to top).

Brick walls, for example, are generally built in two tiers— meaning they are made of two 4-in.-wide bricks laid side by side to give a total depth of 8 in. Such tiers are also called *withes.*

TIGERWOOD

A West African furniture and paneling wood, tiger-wood ranges from gray-brown to gold and has longitudinal black streaks. Often called *Australian walnut* because of its similarity to true walnut; also, *benin* and *orientalwood.*

TILE

A tile was originally a small, flat ceramic piece; but the word has been extended to other materials made in small, flat pieces. The latter are almost always square and used in building construction. But while most ceramic tiles are square and used in construction, they are also made in other shapes and used for surfacing furniture tops and for various decorative and sometimes practical purposes.

See Acoustical Tile, Ceramic Tile, Cork, Marble Tile, Metal Tile, Plastic Tile, and Resilient Tile.

TIMBER CONNECTOR

A metal device attached to the surface of timbers to secure joints and transfer loads from one timber to another. Connectors of several kinds and known by various names such as *shear plates, claw plates,* and *spike grids* are made. However, they are not often used in houses except in truss and post-and-beam construction.

TINWARE

Articles made of thin iron or steel coated with tin. The most highly prized tinware is decorated with paint.

The design and production of painted tinware flourished in America in the 18th and 19th centuries. Objects turned out included coffeepots, teapots, dishes, trays, mailboxes, banks, small storage boxes, etc.

TITLE

Evidence of ownership. Title to a house passes from seller to buyer at the closing.

TITLE SEARCH

A study made of public records—usually by a lawyer—to ascertain ownership of a property and bring to light any cloud upon it.

TOENAIL

To drive a nail diagonally through the end or edge of one piece of wood into another. Studs are toenailed to plates; strip flooring boards are toenailed to the subfloor.

TOGGLE BOLT

A device for fastening things to hollow walls. It consists of a long, slender bolt and a special nut. In most cases, the nut has two large wire wings which are actuated by a tiny spring (hence, the bolt is called a *spring-wing toggle bolt*). When the nut attached to the end of the bolt is pushed through a hole drilled in a wall, the wings spring open and grip the back of the wall as the bolt is tightened.

TOILE DE JOUY

A light-colored cotton or linen fabric printed in a monochrome with pictures of people, landscapes, fruits, etc. The fabrics are frequently made to match wallpapers or vice versa.

TOILET

Four types of toilet, or washcloset, are used in homes:

Wash-Down • This is the simplest, noisiest, and least expensive. Water enters through the rim and washes down the walls of the bowl until there is enough head to expel the contents down the drain in the front of the bowl.

Reverse-Trap • Somewhat more expensive, quieter, and with better cleaning action. The contents drain out through the back of the bowl.

Siphon-Jet • This is the best type of toilet and also the costliest. It has excellent cleaning action, despite the fact that it is very quiet.

Ventilated Siphon-Jet • This toilet operates like the ordinary siphon-jet, except that it has a vacuum action which removes odors from the bowl more effectively.

Most toilets have pedestal bases and are bolted to the floor, but a number of models are hung from the wall to permit easy floor cleaning.

Other differences between toilets: In some, the bowl and water tank are molded in one piece; in others, the tank is separated from the bowl and bolted to it. In some, the bowl is more or less round; in others, it is elongated.

Average dimensions for toilets are 21 in. wide by 28 to 30 in. long (measured from the wall to the front rim of the toilet).

TOILET, SELF-CONTAINED

A toilet which does not require a water supply or sewage disposal system. One type, like that used on airplanes, operates by electricity. The chemically treated water in the toilet is reusable many times before it must be finally disposed of.

A somewhat similar but larger unit consists of a toilet and separate treatment tank which is large enough to serve a family of eight for roughly two years.

TOLE

Painted tinware. The word is particularly applied to lamps and lampshades.

TON

A word sometimes used to rate the capacity of an air conditioner. One ton of refrigeration is the equivalent of the cooling produced by melting a ton of ice in 24 hours.

However, the capacity of air conditioners today is generally stated in British thermal units. Twelve thousand Btu's equal one ton.

TONGUE-AND-GROOVE

A joint used to fasten boards edge to edge or, in some cases, end to end. It consists of a short tongue cut in the edge (or end) of one board and a corresponding groove cut in the edge (or end) of the next board. Tongue-and-groove lumber may be labeled T & G.

TOOTHING

A wall end in which every other brick or concrete block projects so that a new wall can be added and tied into position.

TORCHERE

An oversized candlestick very often made of black iron. The earliest torcheres stood on the floor and were roughly 6 ft. high. Today, some torcheres are much smaller and hung on walls. They may also be wired for incandescent light.

T PLATE

A flat, T-shaped piece of steel or brass for reinforcing a butt joint in which one piece of wood is attached at right angles to the middle of another piece. It is secured with screws or sometimes nuts and bolts.

TRACK LIGHT

An incandescent lighting unit consisting of a long, slender track which is screwed to a wall or ceiling and to which one or more light fixtures can be attached at any point. The fixtures are adjusted to direct light in any direction.

Straight tracks are made in up to 8-ft. lengths. Additional tracks can be attached to form an L, T, etc.

TRADITIONAL

Taken from the past. All architecture and decoration can be broadly categorized as traditional, contemporary, or—rarely—futuristic; but the lines between them are often hard to draw.

TRANSFORMER

An electrical device for reducing voltage. A large, canister-like transformer is mounted on utility poles to step down the high voltage of the power lines to the requirements of a house. Small transformers are installed in residential wiring systems to convert 120-volt power to the lower voltages required for doorbells, thermostats, and low-voltage wiring systems.

TRANSITIONAL

An in-between stage in which some of the recent past is combined with something new. Actually, almost all architectural and decorative styles are transitional; the totally new rarely bursts suddenly on the scene. But in the history of the arts, certain styles were so dominant in certain periods that they have become, in effect, benchmarks to which everything else is related.

TRANSOM

A small operating or fixed window above a door. Also, the horizontal dividing piece between such a window and door.

TRAP

A device which is supposed to be filled at all times with water in order to prevent sewer gases from entering a house. The trap for a toilet is built into the base of the fixture. All other traps are U-shaped sections of pipe.

Every plumbing fixture in a house has its own trap, and there is, in addition, a large house trap installed at the end of the house drain. Each trap is vented by a pipe installed on the sewer side of the trap.

TRAPDOOR

The door in a floor, ceiling, or roof.

TRAPROCK

A kind of crushed rock which is used as a base for masonry floors.

TRAVERSE ROD
See Drapery Hardware.

TREAD
The horizontal part of a step. *See* Stair.

TREILLAGE
Decorative latticework often used indoors on walls and ceilings and around windows.

TRIACETATE
A man-made fiber very much like acetate but with greater resistance to damage by heat. It is used in laminated fabrics and is excellent for permanently pleated curtains.

TRIFID FOOT
See Drake Foot.

TRIM
Material applied to articles and surfaces for decoration.

In interior decorating, trim is the braid, banding, piping, etc. applied to curtains, draperies, upholstery, lampshades, etc.

In building, the trim is the exposed wood used on the interior and exterior of a house to conceal joints and generally embellish the appearance of a room—for example, the casings around doors and windows, baseboards, moldings, corner boards, etc.

TRIMMER
A joist or beam which forms the long side of an opening through a floor. For strength, a double trimmer is usually on both sides of the opening, and double headers are then nailed perpendicular to the double trimmer to complete the framing of the opening.

TRUMPET LEG
A turned furniture leg like a muted trumpet pointing skyward.

TUBE

The same thing as a pipe, except that it is manufactured by drawing whereas pipes are made by piercing a rod or by rolling and welding. Professional craftsmen call copper, aluminum, and plastic pipes tubes.

TUCK

A fold made by doubling a fabric back on itself and stitching it parallel to the edge. The purpose is to take up fullness and thus improve the fit. Tucks made in a well-spaced series are also used for decoration.

TUCK-POINT

To fill an old worn-out or cut-out joint with fresh mortar. Tuck-pointing is also a process, rarely used, to finish joints to a selected color.

TUDOR

An English style of architecture and furniture in the 16th century. Houses were built of dark wood and light-colored masonry. Windows were large—often with leaded panes. Wainscots were high and divided into panels. There was still a good deal of ornate carving reminiscent of the Gothic period.

Furniture was massive and covered with much carving.

TUFTED

A fabric with small clumps of fibers on the front. Also, a pillow or upholstery with a somewhat waffled or puffy surface made by drawing the facing down tight to the stuffing with buttons. Also, a type of carpet in which tufts are inserted in the backing.

TURNBUCKLE

A coupling inserted between two threaded rods to adjust the total length of the rods. The device is often encountered on screen doors where it is used to correct a sag at one corner.

TURNING

A piece of wood which is symmetrically cut on a lathe. Stair balusters and chair spindles are turnings.

TURNIP FOOT
A furniture foot shaped like an upturned turnip after the leaf stems have been chopped off just above the flesh.

TURPENTINE
A strong-smelling liquid for thinning oil-base paints and varnishes. Because of its odor and relatively high cost, however, mineral spirits are generally used instead.

TWEED
A heavy, coarse, rough-textured fabric usually made of wool which is sometimes used in draperies.

2-4-1 UNDERLAYMENT
A 1-1/8-in. tongue-and-groove plywood panel which serves as a subfloor under resilient flooring. It takes the place of a layer of 5/8-in. plywood covered by ¼-in. underlayment. Because of its thickness, it can be laid over beams spaced as much as 4 ft. on center. Thus, it reduces framing.

UNDERCOATER

The primer used under enamel. It is particularly important to the attainment of a very smooth finish in gloss and semi-gloss enamels. Normally white, it can be tinted like the final finish.

UNDERLAYMENT

A hardboard, plywood, or particleboard panel used as a base for resilient flooring. It is ¼-in. thick.

In certain circumstances, resilient flooring can be laid without an underlayment (*See* Floor, Resilient). But it is generally desirable, especially in remodeling work.

UNDERWRITERS' LABORATORIES

Abbreviated *UL*, this is an organization which tests electrical equipment and many other materials and equipment used in building for safety and quality.

UNION

A fitting installed in a length of plumbing or heating pipe so the pipe can be easily taken apart and, if necessary, removed. It has three parts: two sleevelike pieces which are fastened to the ends of the opposing lengths of pipe and a large central nut which ties the pieces together.

Unions are necessary primarily in piping systems made with threaded pipes. The reason: When a pipe is threaded at both ends, it cannot be removed with a wrench, because as one end is loosened, the other end is tightened.

UPHOLSTERY

While the upholstery on a furniture piece is generally thought of as the fabric covering, it properly includes the cushioning, springs—everything down to the frame of the piece.

In high-quality chairs and sofas, seats are made with coiled steel springs individually sewn to a webbing of jute. In pieces of lower quality, coiled springs are prefabricated in a metal frame, or the springs are flat, serpentine strips or straight bands. In all cases, coiled springs are covered with burlap or other tough material, and this, in turn, is covered with padding, the composition of which must by law be described on the label. It is usually made of cotton or thick rolls of rubber or urethane foam. Finally, the padding should be covered with muslin before the upholstery fabric is applied.

Upholstered backs and arms are made in the same way but without springs.

Cushions are filled with synthetic fibers, a mixture of feathers and down, or rubber or urethane foam (*See* Pillow).

While color, pattern, and texture generally outweigh other considerations in the selection of upholstery fabric, practicality cannot be ignored. For maximum durability, the fabric should be a close, firm weave which does not absorb dust rapidly. Long floating threads, big loops, and fluffs which are easily snagged should be avoided. Fabrics containing nylon or polypropylene give superior abrasion resistance.

Pure nylon, polypropylene, and vinyl are the best fabrics from the standpoint of cleaning, since spills can usually be wiped off with a damp cloth. The alternative is to use a fabric which has been factory-treated with a soil-and-oil repellent finish.

Fading of upholstery fabric is not preventable, although some materials fade more slowly than others. Fading can be minimized, however, by selection of more nearly neutral colors rather than intense bright colors.

UPRIGHT

A vertical timber or board.

URETHANE

Properly called *polyurethane*, this is an extraordinarily versatile material. As a flexible foam, it is used to cushion seats, backs, and arms of conventional upholstered furniture, and it is also formed into one-piece modern chairs and sofas without any framework. As a strong, rigid foam, it is molded into doors, window trim, false ceiling beams, chair legs, backs, etc., which so closely resemble wood that they are difficult to distinguish.

Foamed urethane is blown directly into the walls and onto the roofs of houses to insulate them against heat. The roofing is watertight and sun resistant if covered with a thin film of silicone or epoxy.

Applied to a cloth backing, urethane is made into an upholstery material and wallcovering resembling vinyl, but it is thinner, softer, and porous enough to breathe (even though it is waterproof).

Urethane is also a principal ingredient of a tough varnish applied outdoors and in.

The major drawback of the material is its apparent flammability.

U VALUE

The rate of heat transfer between the air inside a house and the air outside. The recommended maximum heat flow for ceilings and roofs has a U value of .05; for frame walls, .07; and for floors over crawl spaces, .07.

U values can be coverted into resistance units (*see* R Value) by dividing the U into the number 1. This gives total resistances of 20 for ceilings and roofs, 14.3 for walls, and 14.3 for floors over crawl spaces.

VACUUM CLEANER, BUILT-IN

A built-in, or central, vacuum cleaning system comprises an electric motor and a large dirt receptacle installed in a central location such as a basement, utility room, or garage; a network of plastic ducts installed in the walls, floors, and ceilings; and a long flexible hose and attachments used for cleaning. The system is operated by plugging the hose into a wall outlet and turning on the motor. Dirt picked up by the cleaning nozzle is carried through the hose and ducts into the dirt receptacle. Because of its size, the receptacle usually needs to be emptied only four or five times a year. In some systems, it is cleaned automatically by a stream of water which flushes the dirt down the drain.

The principal advantages of a built-in vacuum cleaner over the conventional type are that it is quiet, does not have to be emptied so often, and does not leak fine dust back into the rooms which are being cleaned. On the other hand, it is a great deal more expensive.

Installation can be made in new or old houses. Outlets into which the flexible hose are plugged should be located, if possible so that each serves several rooms. The system can be connected into a 15-amp lighting circuit or 20-amp appliance circuit.

VALANCE

A short drapery hung from a rod over the top of a window or under the edge of a bed (usually called a *dust ruffle*). Also, a frame of wood covered with fabric and hung over a window or on a blank wall to conceal the tops of draperies or a fluorescent light. The wooden type of valance is also known as a *cornice* (*see above*).

VALANCE HEATING AND COOLING

A new method of heating and air conditioning buildings with long, trough-like metal valances which are suspended just below the ceilings close to outside walls. It is used primarily in commercial buildings, but it is adaptable to houses.

Heating and cooling are done with water circulated through pipes hidden above the valances. The water is heated in a boiler fired with gas, oil, or electricity, and it is cooled in an electric chiller.

The thermostatically controlled system is efficient and silent but expensive to install. The valances virtually eliminate drafts, and during cooling operations, they dehumidify the air and remove dust and lint from it.

VALLEY

The V-shaped space at the juncture of two intersecting roof slopes. The actual point at which the roof decks are joined is particularly vulnerable to leaks; consequently, it must be flashed with care. The roofing is then laid over the valley flashing. If there is a fairly wide space between the edge of the roofing on one slope and that on the other slope, the valley is called an *open valley*. If the roofing meets at the joints, it is a *closed valley*.

VALLEY RAFTER

See Rafter.

VALVE, PLUMBING .

A device for controlling or shutting off the flow of water in a plumbing system. The following types are installed:

Gate Valve • A large valve with a flat disk which slides across the opening when the handle is turned. It is best suited to main supply lines.

Globe Valve • The commonest type of valve in houses. It operates like a compression faucet—that is, a disk paralleling the pipe is screwed down on a hole called the *seat*.

Globe valves installed on the branch lines in a water service are usually equipped with little bleeder valves which permit the pipes to be drained when the globe valves are closed.

Flush Valve • The large rubber ball in the bottom of a toilet tank which keeps water from flowing into the toilet bowl.

Float Valve • The valve in a toilet tank which controls the flow of fresh water into the tank. It opens and closes as the copper or plastic float in the tank drops or rises, respectively.

VANITY
Either a dressing table or a built-in lavatory cabinet.

VARIANCE
A deviation from the requirements of a zoning code. For example, if a local zoning code requires a front setback of 50 ft., a homeowner must apply for and be granted a variance in order to build an addition to his house 20 ft. or 5 ft. or even only 1 in. forward of the setback.

The zoning board or zoning board of appeals has authority to hear appeals for variances and to grant or deny them.

VARNISH
A hard, transparent wood coating usually with a slow-drying oil base but sometimes with a quick-drying spirit base. It produces a high-gloss, semi-gloss, or flat finish which protects the wood and is itself reasonably durable. But it gives wood a slight yellowish cast, deteriorates quickly in sunlight, and cannot be touched up invisibly if it is scratched.

For exterior work, spar and urethane varnishes are used because of their superior weather resistance. The latter can also be used indoors when a very tough finish is required. Generally, however, furniture varnish is used on furniture, paneling, and trim; floor varnish on floors; and bar varnish on surfaces exposed to alcohol.

Varnish is applied with a brush. For the best finish, it is flowed on with the grain, brushed across the grain, and then brushed with the grain. Two coats are needed on all new work. On furniture and paneling, the first coat may be varnish or white shellac.

VARNISH STAIN

An inferior product which should be used only on cheap furniture to give a fast finish, varnish stain is a varnish containing a pigment to give a colored finish.

VASE

A vase is used not only to hold flowers but also to contribute to their beauty. An ugly vase fails because it detracts from the flowers. On the other hand, a beautiful vase may also fail if it is not shaped to give proper support to the flowers.

Too much faith should not be placed in the ability of flower holders to compensate for the deficiencies of poorly designed vases. The holders are useful only if they can be seated properly in vases, and this also depends on vase design. It follows that the selection of a vase should be made only by a person who understands the intricacies of flower arranging.

Generally, the only vases which fulfill their purpose without aid of flower holders are rather deep and narrow. Shallow vases are equally effective if holders are used, but only if the vases have a flat bottom area which is large enough to support a holder firmly.

VEHICLE

The liquid part of a paint. Water is the vehicle in latex paint, for example.

VELLUX

A fabric made of thin urethane foam covered on both sides with nylon flock, or on one side with flock and on the other side with tricot or another fabric. It is used in bedspreads.

VELOUR

A soft, heavy, velvet-like fabric. Cotton velour is used in draperies.

VELVET

A variable fabric but always luxurious in appearance and feeling. It is soft and lustrous and has a low pile and plain back. It is used in draperies, upholstery, and bedspreads.

Velvet is also a type of carpet.

VELVET BOARD

A wall paneling made of plywood covered with colored velvet plush. It is ¼-in. thick and produced in 4 x 8-ft. panels and 1 x 8-ft. strips.

VELVETEEN

A drapery fabric resembling velvet but made in a different way. It is strong and durable.

VENEER

A thin layer of attractive material applied over a base of sturdy utilitarian material. Houses are built with brick and stone veneer. A tough vinyl sheet made in imitation of wood or leather is sold as vinyl veneer for bonding to furniture, cabinets, etc. Laminated plastics on countertops are veneers, although they are not known as such. But the material instantly associated with the word veneer is the wood used to surface plywood wall paneling and furniture.

Veneers have been applied for many years to tables, bureaus, and other case pieces; but despite the fact that the resulting furniture was often beautiful, many people avoided it because the veneer sometimes cracked or came loose. This rarely happens today because of improvements which have been made in adhesives.

VENETIAN BLIND

Venetian blinds with horizontal wooden, metal, or plastic louvers permit nearly total control of light and air coming through a window because they can be slanted toward the floor or ceiling to any degree, pointed straight in, or closed tight. They are more durable than roller shades but require more frequent cleaning.

Standard blinds have 2-in. slats held in wide cloth tapes. Mini-blinds have very thin, 1-in. slats and are controlled by slender cords. These are made in fewer sizes than standard blinds but are more attractive because they are less visible when the slats are slanted straight in.

If Venetian blinds are to be hung inside a window opening, there must be sufficient flat space on the jambs to mount the brackets. Otherwise, the blinds must be hung over the opening, in which case they should overlap the casings on both sides at least 1½ in.

VENT

One of the several pipes used to exhaust sewer gases from a sanitary drainage system and to maintain atmospheric pressure in the system. Atmospheric pressure is necessary to prevent loss of water in traps, retardation of flow through the drains, and deterioration of the pipes by the chemical elements in plumbing wastes.

The principal vent in a house is the upper part of the soil pipe, which extends through the roof. In addition, individual vent pipes are installed on the sewer side of all traps and connected into the main vent.

VENTILATING FAN

See Fan, Exhaust.

VENTILATOR

Any device or opening allowing air to escape from a house, such as an exhaust fan in a kitchen or an attic louver.

VERANDA

A porch, usually roofed.

VERGEBOARD

See Bargeboard.

VERTICAL BLIND

A Venetian blind with vertical louvers. It is used mainly to emphasize the height of a window and is therefore most effective on floor-to-ceiling windows. Metal and plastic louvers are 2 in. wide or wider; cloth louvers are 4 to 6 in. wide.

VESTIBULE

A front hall; also, an entry outside the main entrance door. *See* Entry and Front Hall.

VICTORIAN

The architecture and decoration prevailing during the reign of Queen Victoria from 1857 to 1901. They were an elaborate and intricate combination of many older styles and were often mixed with designs from the Orient and Near East.

VINYL

A strong, abrasion-resistant, colorful plastic, vinyl goes into the best types of resilient flooring, and also into wallcoverings, siding, gutters, upholstery, shower curtains, and other familiar items. In addition, polyvinyl chloride, a special form of vinyl, is used in plumbing pipes; polyvinyl acetate is a widely used adhesive.

VINYL-ASBESTOS TILE

A medium-price resilient floor tile which can be laid below grade or on grade as well as above grade. It is made in 9- and 12-in. squares in a reasonably wide selection of colors and textures. In most important characteristics it ranks about midway between the best and worst resilient flooring materials. But its durability and ease of maintenance are suspect, if not actually poor.

VINYL FLOORING

The best of the resilient flooring materials, vinyl is produced in large sheets (rarely in tiles) which come in an almost bewildering array of patterns, colors, and textures. It can be installed below, on, or above grade; is very durable; has good resistance to grease, staining, alkalies, and sunlight; is easily maintained; and is reasonably soft and quiet underfoot.

The differences in types and grades of vinyl flooring are confusing, however.

Sheet vinyl with a thin backing is generally the best; that with a cushioned backing is exceptionally soft underfoot but less durable. Homogeneous vinyl is of uniform composition throughout and has no backing. It is slightly less durable than backed vinyl. Least desirable is rotovinyl, in which the design is printed rather than inlaid.

Another difference in vinyls is that some are made with a very glossy, never-needs-waxing finish while others have a semi-gloss finish which must be waxed periodically if the homemaker likes a fairly high luster. However, the gloss on the shiny vinyls deteriorates rather rapidly in traffic areas and must be restored with a special finish.

VINYL SIDING

Vinyl siding is made of solid vinyl in the form of clapboards, vertical boards, and strips resembling cedar shingles or shakes. Since the color is an integral part of the material, no painting is required. In addition, the siding is very resistant to impact because of its resiliency, it it is relatively quiet when hail or rain pounds against it, and there is no danger of electrical shock as there sometimes is with aluminum siding, its chief competitor. On the other hand, it is more expensive than aluminum siding.

The boards are designed so they interlock to form watertight joints. All should be installed over a mineral-fiber backer board that helps to insulate against cold and noise.

VINYL WALLCOVERING

A material which is frequently substituted for wallpaper when an exceptionally durable, washable surface is desired. It is made with a paper or cloth backing on which the pattern is printed, and is then coated with a film of vinyl.

Vinyl wallcoverings are printed on presses or by hand. Many are pre-trimmed. Some are flocked. They are put up in rolls of the same widths and lengths as wallpaper.

Three weights are produced. Type A, lightweight, is the kind most often used in homes. It is stain-resistant, scrubbable, and durable enough to withstand most wear. Types B and C are heavier and are used primarily in schools, hotels, hospitals, and other public buildings where they are subjected to very hard wear and abrasion. They are also available in many fewer colors and patterns than Type A vinyl.

Vinyl wallcoverings are hung like wallpaper but with special adhesives. Since they are not porous and therefore do not breathe, blisters must be eliminated at the time they are hung; otherwise, they will remain and show up in the finished surface.

VINYON

A synthetic fiber with little strength but high resistance to almost everything except heat. It is used with other fibers to make embossed carpets, pressed felts, and other nonwoven fabrics.

VITRINE

A tall, free-standing, glass-enclosed cabinet with shelves for the display of art objects. If lighted from within—as it often is—the shelves are made of plate glass. Vitrines are often mistakenly called etageres.

VOILE

A sheer, soft cotton fabric made of various fibers as well as the traditional cotton. It is used in curtains.

VOLT

The unit of electrical pressure. The rate of pressure exerted on current flowing through a wire is similar to the pounds of pressure on water flowing through a plumbing pipe.

Most electrical equipment in an American home has a standard voltage of 115-120 volts. Large equipment operates at 230-240 volts. The modern residential electrical system is designed for operation at both levels, and there are three wires leading from the utility pole to the house. If there are only two wires between a pole and house, it indicates that the system is limited to 115-120-volt operation.

VOLTAGE DROP

The voltage loss which occurs when electrical wires are overloaded. The drop may occur in an individual circuit within a residential wiring system, or it may occur in the utility company's lines. The homeowner has no control over the latter type of drop, but he can prevent drops in individual wiring circuits by making sure that the circuits are of limited length and made with properly sized wires.

VOLUTE

An object carved in a spiral. At the bottom of many stair rails a horizontal volute—a continuous part of the rail—is supported on the newel post. Vertical volutes are used for ornament on Ionic and Corinthian capitals.

WAINSCOT

When an interior wall is divided into two horizontal sections by moldings or a change in materials, the wainscot (also called *dado*) is the lower section. It is normally 30 to 40 in. high, but in bathrooms the tiled wall area behind lavatories and toilets is usually 48 in. high.

In early architecture, wainscots were paneled in wood—usually oak—and served the practical purpose of protecting the walls against damage from traffic, furniture, etc. Today, wainscots are used primarily for decorative effect, although they still have protective value if constructed for that purpose. They may be surfaced in wood, plaster—almost anything contrasting with the upper part of the wall.

WALL

The walls of a house include exterior walls, interior walls or partitions, foundation walls (*see* Foundation), and dividers (*see* Divider). All exterior walls support the structure overhead. Interior walls are classified as either bearing or nonbearing (*see above*).

In American homes, the standard method of framing both exterior and interior walls is with 2 x 4-in. timbers. The horizontal timber at the base of a wall is the *sole plate*. The studs are nailed to this to form the principal wall surface, and they are held together at the top by the *top plate*. The top plate, in turn, supports floor or roof joists.

Studs are usually spaced 16 in. on center, but the spacing may be decreased to 12 in. or increased to any measurement up to and including 24 in. The use of nonstandard spacing is dictated partly by the load or stresses to which a wall is exposed, by the size of the framing members, and by the type of wallcovering.

Exterior frame walls are covered on the outside with sheathing (*see above*). Building paper is generally tacked over this to keep out dirt, air, and moisture. And the siding is applied over the paper.

Interior walls—as well as the interior surfaces of exterior walls—are most often surfaced with gypsum board. Numerous other materials are also used.

For other types of wall construction, *see* Concrete Block, Masonry, and Post-and-Beam.

WALLBOARD

Any rigid material made of cellulose fibers which is applied to walls and ceilings.

WALLCOVERING

Any flexible material used to cover interior walls. Included are the following, which are described elsewhere; wallpaper, vinyl wallcovering, metal foil wallcovering, cork wallcovering, shiki silk, felt, burlap, grasscloth, leather, carpet, cork, laminated wood veneer, bamboo, fabric wallcovering, and gypsum-coated wall fabric.

WALL HEATER

See Space Heating.

WALL-HUNG

A term usually applied to something hung on a wall which is normally used in another position. Some toilets are wall-hung.

WALL PANEL MOLDING

A molding applied to a flat wall to divide it into panel-like areas. Any simple molding such as a half-round may be used for the purpose. But special designs are also made.

WALLPAPER

Next to paint, wallpaper is the most widely used interior wall and ceiling finish. Its popularity is attributable primarily to the fact that it is available in a vast array of colors, patterns, and textures. But it is also relatively inexpensive, increasingly durable, and easy to install once the technique is mastered.

Wallpapers are categorized in the following way. Most patterns fall into several types; for example, many machine-printed papers are also washable and pre-trimmed.

Machine-Printed Wallpaper • The great majority of wallpapers are machine prints—meaning they are printed on high-speed presses. They fall into the low to medium price brackets, and are easy to hang and durable. One roll is an exact or close match for another.

Hand-Printed Wallpaper • Wallpaper produced one roll at a time by the silk screen process. It is unusually beautiful but expensive, hard to hang, and easily soiled and worn.

Hand-prints are widely available in stock patterns and colors, but special colors or stock patterns can be ordered.

Pre-Trimmed Wallpaper • A paper from which the selvages have been removed at the factory. Most machine-printed papers are pre-trimmed, but hand-prints are usually untrimmed.

Pre-trimming of wallpaper reduces installation time, especially for do-it-yourselfers. But extra pains must be taken to cover the edges with paste.

Pre-Pasted Wallpaper • This is a machine-printed wallpaper coated with adhesive at the factory. It is supposed to simplify installation since all the paperhanger has to do is to roll each strip through water and smooth it on the wall. However, some people find the procedure messy and unreliable.

The best base for pre-pasted wallpaper is a porous surface or a layer of old wallpaper.

Washable Wallpaper • A paper which can be washed with water without running or showing obvious wear. The actual degree of washability varies between brands and patterns, and depends on the thoroughness with which it has been treated with a clear plastic. A way to test washability is to place a drop of water on the patterned surface. A paper that absorbs the water is less washable than one that does not.

Washable papers are for the most part machine-prints, but some hand-prints are washable, too.

Strippable Wallpaper • A washable, machine-printed wallpaper which can be ripped off a wall in one big piece. It is useful primarily to people who redecorate frequently. But it has the added advantage of being more resistant to damage than a conventional paper. On the other hand, because it tends to be stiff, it has less stretch than a conventional paper and is harder to hang on uneven walls.

Flocked Wallpaper • A hand-printed wallpaper with flock applied to the surface. Although used mainly for its decorative value, it is useful for concealing imperfections in walls.

Sand-Finished Wallpaper • A hand-printed wallpaper with a sandpaper-like texture. It also hides imperfections in walls.

Scenic Wallpaper • A hand-printed wallpaper which forms a large picture on the wall when strips are hung in the order specified by the manufacturer.

All wallpaper is priced by the single roll. The average single roll contains 36 sq. ft., but because of waste in hanging, it is generally assumed to cover only 30 sq. ft. of wall. The width of rolls ranges from 18 to 28 in. after removal of the selvages.

Despite the way they are priced, most machine-printed papers are put up in double or sometimes triple rolls.

The actual amount of wall which a single roll of wallpaper will cover depends on the pattern and how often it is repeated up and down a strip. The two basic patterns in use are the *straight pattern* and *drop-match pattern*. In the former, the pattern at one edge of a strip exactly matches the pattern directly across the strip. In a drop-match pattern, the pattern at one edge of a strip is halfway between the matching pattern on the opposite edge.

The frequency with which a pattern appears on a strip of wallpaper is called the *repeat*. This may be every 2 in., every 6 in., every 24 in., or whatever the case may be. Some straight-pattern papers have no repeat at all; this is true of solids and vertical stripes, for example.

Before hanging wallpaper, the run number printed on the back of each roll should be checked to make sure that it is the same as the run number on all other rolls. If they are the same, it means that all the rolls were printed during the same press run and are therefore exactly alike. But if the run numbers are different, the rolls were printed during different press runs, and the colors may not match perfectly. This can be checked by unrolling all the rolls side by side and comparing colors. This is called *shading*. If there are differences in colors, it is advisable to return all the rolls to the dealer and ask for a new set from the same run.

Wallpaper can be hung on any sound, smooth, clean surface that is free of flaking paint, scraps of wallpaper, etc. The surface should be washed thoroughly, holes and cracks should be patched, and rough spots should be sanded down. A new gypsum board wall should be primed with latex paint. All walls except those covered with old wallpaper should be sized. The size can be applied before the paper is hung and allowed to dry, or a paste containing size can be used.

Old wallpaper should be removed from a wall before new paper is hung. If not removed, the applicator must make sure it is securely attached to the wall at all spots, and he must sand down the joints so they will not show through the new paper.

Lining paper is required only under hand-printed and scenic wallpapers. It can also be used under machine-printed paper if the wall has a rough texture.

WALL PLATE
See Plate.

WALL SYSTEM
A wall of cabinets and shelves; a storage wall.

WALNUT
Black walnut is the United States' foremost furniture and cabinet wood. It is also used in paneling. The heavy, hard, tough, strong wood is the color of rich chocolate. The texture is rather coarse, but the grain is normally straight.

Two other excellent woods are the Circassian walnut and Australian walnut (the last is actually tigerwood). They are approximately the same color as black walnut and have a finer texture.

WANE
A missing piece of wood along the edge or at a corner of a board or timber. Since a wane is not large enough to effect the strength of wood, it is categorized as a blemish.

WARDROBE
A tall, free-standing cabinet for clothes.

WARP
A bend or twist in a piece of wood caused by uneven shrinkage of the cells as the wood dried out. Warps can be sub-classified as *bows, cups, crooks,* and *twists.* Whether a warped

board can be used in construction depends on the kind of warp and its severity.

WASH

To bathe a large surface—usually a wall—with relatively uniform, not-too-bright light.

WASHER (1)

Although wringer and spinner washers are still made, they have been supplanted in most households by automatic machines which can be set to soak, wash, rinse and damp-dry loads weighing up to 20 lb. (dry weight).

The standard automatic washer is 36 in. high, 28 in. deep, and 25 to 31 in. wide. It should be installed on its own 120-volt, 20-amp wiring circuit, and should be drained into either a laundry tub or a 30-in.-high standpipe connected into the house drain.

Combination washer-dryers are similar in size and are installed in the same way, but they require a 240-volt circuit.

WASHER (2)

A washer is a metal ring used under nuts and bolts. A *flat*, or *punched-hole*, *washer* is a smooth, unbroken ring used to keep the head of a bolt or nut from being pulled through the hole drilled for the bolt or from being pulled into the wood.

A *lock washer* is designed to keep a nut or bolt from loosening. The commonest lock washer is a split ring of spring steel with offset ends. Other lock washers are slightly concave and have serrated edges.

WASTE PIPE

One of the pipes through which all plumbing fixtures, except toilets, discharge wastes into the house drainage system. Waste pipes are usually made of 2-in.-diameter pipes and are connected into the soil branches or sometimes the house drain.

WATER CLOSET

A toilet (*see above*).

WATER COLOR

A painting done with paints which are soluble in water. Since it cannot be readily cleaned, it should be kept covered with glass to protect against damage and soiling.

WATER CONDITIONER

A water softener or other device for removing or counteracting unpleasant elements in water. Some units can handle only a single element; others are used to get rid of several.

A good many types of water conditioner are on the market. And it is generally possible to find one which can correct any common problem. If not, there are water experts (but not the companies that sell residential water conditioners) who can devise an answer.

Also see Water Softener.

WATER HEATER

Water heaters are of either the storage or the indirect type. The former is more widely used.

In a *storage heater*, water is warmed and stored in a round, insulated tank. Heaters operating on oil, gas, or LP gas must be vented into a flue and are therefore usually placed in a basement or utility room near the furnace. Electric heaters require no venting and can be installed anywhere.

Storage heaters are classified as *fast-recovery* or *slow-recovery* units. The word "recovery" refers to the speed with which a heater will heat a tank of fresh water to the pre-set temperature. A slow-recovery heater is the more efficient and economical. But a fast-recovery unit costs less originally and is better able to satisfy peak-period demands for hot water.

The size of heater a family requires depends on the size of the family and its bathing habits, and whether it has a dishwasher and an automatic clothes washer; but it also depends on the recovery rate of the heater. In other words, the average family of four needs either an 82-gal. slow-recovery heater or a 50-gal. fast-recovery heater.

Indirect water heaters—which can be installed only in automatically fired boilers used to heat houses with forced hot water or steam—do not heat by direct flame. Instead, the water is circulated through a copper coil which is surrounded by hot water from the boiler; consequently, in winter, domestic hot water is largely a by-product of normal house-heating operations. In summer, however, all the fuel burned by the boiler is used for water heating. Actual cost of heating water is difficult to figure, but the system is generally thought to be quite economical.

Indirect heaters are also sized according to their recovery rate. The fastest heaters are known as tankless units because they consist of nothing more than a very long copper coil inside a steel jacket that is mounted outside the boiler. Indirect storage heaters, which are less popular, have a shorter coil and a small storage tank.

Because hot water is more corrosive than cold, the life expectancy of any water heater depends in good part on the materials of which it is built. The tanks in storage heaters are especially vulnerable. In the past these were usually made of galvanized steel; but because the steel rusted out in only a few years in areas with very aggressive water, it is rarely used today. The majority of tanks are now "glass-lined"—meaning that they are made of steel coated with porcelain. The best are guaranteed for ten years. Even tougher—and more expensive—tanks are made of solid copper or copper on steel. Plastic tanks are on the market but should be considered in the experimental stage.

Since indirect heaters are equipped with solid copper coils, corrosion is rarely a problem. But in areas with hard water, the coils may become so clogged with chemicals that they must be flushed out periodically with acid.

WATER PRESSURE

The pressure in a water system determines the speed at which water flows from the outlets in the house. The minimum desirable pressure is 20 lb.; the maximum is 75 lb.

Municipal water utilities generally provide water to all homes within the proper pressure limits, and if they fail to do so, they should correct the situation promptly. If they don't, the property owner must take action himself.

If the water pressure is too high or fluctuates violently, special valves can be installed in the house. If the pressure is too low, the homeowner can either install a larger main supply line to the house or put in an electric pump which carries water from a tank connected into the supply line to a small pressure tank, from which it is distributed throughout the house.

If a house draws its water from a well, the water pressure is controlled by a pressure tank into which the well water is pumped and from which household water is drawn. The pressure gauge on the tank is generally set to operate between a low point of 25 to 30 lb. and a high point of 50 to 60 lb.

WATERPROOFING

Despite the fact that the entire shell of a house is designed to keep out water, several steps in the construction process have the specific purpose of waterproofing the house:

1 / Foundation walls are protected by laying drain tiles around the footings and parging the walls with cement plaster. *See* Foundation.

2 / In very wet locations, a membrane, usually of polyethylene film, is installed in the basement floor.

3 / Flashing is used in the roof to protect vulnerable spots.

4 / Joints between dissimilar siding materials are caulked.

5 / Metal drip edges are installed along the eaves and rakes of roofs to force water running off the roof to drop straight to the ground.

WATER REPELLENT

A liquid applied to a material to repel water. There are three types.

One is applied to fabrics to minimize waterspotting and staining. *See* Fabric Finish.

The second is a colorless, transparent liquid containing silicone which is applied to masonry walls to prevent seepage of water. It makes the wall resistant to dampness but does not stop active leaks. It must be renewed after about five years.

The third is also a colorless liquid applied to wood—usually that outside a house—to make it retain its natural color and to minimize splintering and cracking. It may also prevent mildew if formulated with a mildewcide. Two coats are applied originally; an additional coat is applied when the wood begins to darken.

WATER RIGHTS

Having legal authority to enjoy or make some use of a lake, ocean, stream, or other water course, even though the property does not front on the water.

A property owner also has water rights if he draws water from a public main running through another person's property. In the event the main develops leaks, the holder of the water rights and the utility can dig it up and replace it.

WATER SERVICE

The system of pipes supplying water throughout the house and grounds. One set of pipes carries cold water; the other hot water. Both must be completely separated from the house drains.

Most water services are made with copper tubing and soldered copper or brass fittings. Although the size of the tubing varies with the size of the house and household requirements, ¾-in. pipe (inside diameter) is generally used for the mains; ½-in. for the branch lines, called *branches*; and 3/8-in. for the supply risers which serve individual outlets.

The horizontal pipes are called *runs*, the vertical pipes *risers*. In a new house, all the piping is usually done with rigid pipes. In remodeling, the risers are often made with soft copper tubes because they can be easily snaked up through the framing. Soft tubes should never be used in runs, however, because the runs have low spots from which water cannot be drained.

The entire water service should be equipped with an adequate number of valves to control the water flow and facilitate repairs. One valve is installed near the water meter so the entire system can be drained, and each supply riser has its own valve. Additional valves on the branches are advisable.

The practice of insulating pipes is usually ignored by plumbing contractors, but homeowners can make up for this oversight themselves. Insulation of hot water lines is desirable to prevent rapid heat loss, but the actual fuel saving is negligible, except in the case of pipes serving outlets that are turned on frequently. Cold water lines in warm basements are insulated to keep moisture from condensing on the pipes and dripping on to the floor.

WATER SOFTENER

Also known as a *water conditioner*, a water softener is a large tank containing a mineral called *zeolite* which removes the hardness from the water flowing through.

Hardness in water is proportional to the content of calcium and magnesium salts. It is expressed in grains per gallon. Soft water has less than 3.5 grains per gallon; all other water is considered hard. If the water has between 3.5 and 7 grains, it is moderately hard; between 7 and 10.5 grains, hard; and above 10.5 grains, very hard.

Most water in the United States is hard to some degree. This not only interferes with effective washing of laundry, dishes, and glasses, but also causes dirty deposits to form in tubs, toilets, pitchers, etc. It also forms a scale in hot-water pipes and water heaters which reduces heating efficiency, wastes fuel, and leads to premature failure of the heating system.

A water softener installed to prevent such problems is connected into the main water supply line so that all water passing through it is treated. However, since the size and cost of the installation depend on the water usage by the family as well as on the hardness of the water, and since the cost of operation depends on how often the zeolite becomes clogged and must be regenerated, water used outside the house should be bypassed around the tank. Some people also bypass the water used in toilets.

WATER SUPPLY

The source of water—and related equipment—from which a household draws for drinking, bathing, cooking, etc. The great majority of houses are served by a municipal water system, but approximately 10% are served by wells, and a very small number are served by cisterns, springs, streams, or ponds.

A water supply is considered adequate if it has a sustained flow of 5 gal. per minute. However, a smaller yield can be made adquate by the installation of a storage tank holding 1000 gal. or more.

An adequate water supply must also deliver water to the faucets and other outlets at sufficient pressure to maintain a good flow.

Finally, and most importantly, an adequate water supply is one which delivers water that is pure enough to drink.

WATER SYSTEM

The mechanical system used to supply water from a well—or, in rare cases, a cistern or other private water source—to a house. It consists of a pump and a pressure tank.

The type of pump used depends on whether the well is shallow—less than 25 ft. deep—or deep. The most commonly used deep-well pump is a submersible unit which is installed inside the well fairly close to the bottom. Jet pumps are also used for deep wells but are used mainly for shallow wells. (Some pumps can be converted from shallow- to deep-well use.) They are installed above ground, usually next to the pressure tank. The choice of pump for a water system is best made by the well driller. In all cases, the pump should be served by an individual 120- or 240-volt wiring circuit.

Operation of a water pump is automatically controlled by the air pressure in the pressure tank. This is a closed steel or fiberglass tank containing water and a cushion of air. When a faucet in the house is opened, water flows from the tank, and as the water level in the tank drop's, the air cushion expands and loses pressure. When the air pressure drops to a pre-determined point—usually about 25 to 30 lb.—a pressure gauge turns on the pump, which introduces fresh well water into the tank. This compresses the air cushion, and when the pressure reaches a pre-set point—usually 50 to 60 lb.—the pump turns off. In the newest type of pressure tank, the water is contained in a vinyl bag separate from the air cushion. This prevents the slow loss of air from the tank as the water is drawn out; thus, it is unnecessary to recharge the air supply (as in older water systems) or to equip the tank with an automatic air control.

The pressure tank for the average residential water system has a capacity of 82 gal. Smaller tanks can be used for small homes. Larger tanks are sometimes installed to reduce pump operation. The tanks can be installed in a well house or pit at the well or in the main house. In the latter case, the tank should be insulated so it does not sweat and drip water on the floor.

WATER TABLE (1)

A slight horizontal, ledge-like projection designed to divert water from the foundation wall below. It may be built into the foundation near the top or installed just at the base of the siding.

WATER TABLE (2)

The depth at which the ground is normally saturated with water. If this rises to within a few feet of the soil surface, it exerts tremendous pressure on building foundations and basement floors and causes leaks.

WATER TANK

See Water System. Pressure tanks for home water systems are made for the most part of galvanized steel which is frequently lined with porcelain or epoxy to resist corrosive waters. Fiberglass-reinforced plastic tanks are made but have not gained wide acceptance.

WATER-THINNED PAINT

Any paint which is thinned with water, including latex paint, portland-cement paint, and linseed-oil emulsion paint.

WATT

The unit of electrical power, determined by multiplying volts by amperes. For example, 1 ampere times a pressure of 1 volt equals 1 watt. A small light bulb uses 50 watts; a typical electric range, over 10,000 watts. The wattage of an appliance multiplied by the hours the appliance is in use determines the rate charged by an electric utility.

WATT-HOUR

One watt of electricity used for one hour. One thousand watt-hours equals one kilowatt-hour, which is the unit by which electricity is metered and sold.

WEATHERHEAD

A hood-like device to keep out the weather. One type is used at the top of the service entrance in an electrical system. Another type is used to seal a ventilating fan duct where it projects through the exterior wall of a house.

WEATHERSTRIPPING

Weatherstripping of doors and windows to keep out moisture and air is accepted as a matter of course in new construction. Virtually all new windows are weatherstripped at the factory. Exterior doors, however, are weatherstripped at the time of installation with interlocking metal strips.

Many kinds of weatherstripping are used in old houses. The most effective and durable is a flexible spring-metal strip which is nailed to the jambs of both doors and windows.

WEEPHOLE

Any hole made in a wall or other surface to allow moisture to escape.

WELL

Wells are the principal source of water for houses which are not served by municipal water systems. They should be installed by professional well drillers under contract with the homeowners.

The kind of well put in is determined by the availability of safe drinking water on the property. There are four:

Drilled Wells • These are also called *deep wells* because they are usually more than 25 ft. deep. They are constructed by making a hole of fairly small diameter in the ground with either a rotary drill, which operates like a hand drill, or a cable-tool drill, which punches out a hole. The upper part of the well is lined with a *casing*—a pipe over 4 in. in diameter which prevents the well walls from caving in and which also helps to keep out pollution.

Dug Wells • These are dug by hand and lined with rocks. They range in depth from about 6 to 30 ft., in diameter from 2 to 8 ft.

Bored Wells • These are fairly deep wells made with an auger up to 3 ft. in diameter. They are put in only in the rare instances when a drilled or dug well would be unsatisfactory. A large pipe, perforated at the bottom, is placed in the center of the well and surrounded by crushed rock.

Driven Wells • These are usually shallow wells made by hammering a pipe into porous, rock-free soil.

No matter how it is constructed, a well should be no less than 50 ft. from all septic tanks, 100 ft. from all disposal fields, and 10 ft. from the property lines. (The exact distance depends on local health codes.) It should never be within the foundation walls of a house, except in arctic and subarctic regions. Before a well is put into service, the water should be tested for purity and, ideally, for chemical content.

WELTING
Thick cord covered with fabric and inserted in seams of upholstery, slipcovers, bedspreads, etc., for decorative effect.

WET LOOK
A flexible plastic which is so glossy that it looks wet. It is used for upholstery and sometimes wallcoverings. It is also a type of paint finish sold in aerosol cans.

WHATNOT
A tier of open shelves, either standing on the floor or hung on a wall, for display of decorative objects. It was popular during the Victorian era. Also called an *etagere*.

WHITE POCKET
Also called *white speck*, white pocket is a small white pit in wood caused by a fungus disease. It does not affect the strength or utility of the wood.

WHITE PRINT
A blueprint in reverse—that is, with blue lines on a white background.

WHITEWASH
An inexpensive paint made with lime, salt, alum, molasses, and water which is used indoors and out. Because it is not durable, latex paint is normally used instead.

WHORL FOOT
A Chippendale furniture foot carved like a scroll. Also called a *knurl foot*.

WICKER
Furniture, baskets, and other articles woven of slender willow twigs. Pieces made of entire twigs are more durable and attractive than those made of split twigs.

The natural color of wicker is yellowish-white, but if it is not finished—either with a clear finish or paint—it soils rapidly. All wicker catches and holds dust and dirt.

WIDOW'S WALK
A captain's walk (*see above*). It was called a widow's walk because women used to watch from there for ships returning with their seafaring husbands. Often the men never came home.

WILLIAM AND MARY

An English furniture and architectural style in the late 1600s. Furniture was of small scale, highly polished, and elaborately inlayed.

Buildings were higher than wide. Walls were two-dimensional with windows set in at regular intervals. The Governor's Palace at Williamsburg is an outstanding example of the style.

WILTON

A type of carpet produced in narrow widths.

WINDER

A wedge-shaped stair tread used on a winding or spiral stair.

WINDOW

The manner in which windows are used in a house can be one of the most difficult problems for architects and homeowners to figure out. Windows not only serve a variety of purposes but also create problems which must be anticipated if a house is to be completely successful.

The role windows play in illuminating houses is imperfect unless they are installed in two or three walls of each room. Used in only one wall, they give very uneven distribution of light.

Windows should also be used in at least two walls to serve as efficient ventilators. The ideal arrangement is to install some of the windows just above the floor in the wall facing the prevailing breeze, and to place the others at ceiling level on the opposite side of the room.

When one of the purposes of a window is to admit a view, the usual practice is simply to put in the largest picture window possible. Actually, the size, shape, and placement of a window should be tailored to enhance the view. For example, when the view is a close-up of a garden, a floor-to-ceiling window tends to bring the garden right into the house. On the other hand, if a view across a beautiful valley is spoiled by a clutter of unkempt buildings in the immediate foreground, a large window placed well above the floor may be called for. Similarly, if the view is of a lone pine or tiny backyard waterfall, a small window which concentrates and frames this one special spot is likely to be preferable to a large window.

The final purpose of windows—to enhance the exterior of the house—is probably the most difficult to achieve because there are no rules to go by unless the house is of traditional style requiring careful balancing of the windows in the facade. In less formal architectural styles, effective window treatment depends on the ability of the architect to attain balance without symmetry.

Other factors which must be weighed in planning the fenestration of a house are:

Orientation to the Sun • This raises such questions as: To which point of the compass should the house be oriented? How can the sun be kept out while admitting a view? Should a house which must face west be air conditioned, and how can it be done economically?

Climate • This affects the selection of window types and sizes, the placement of the windows in relation to prevailing winds, the need for storm windows, the need for screens, and so forth.

Immediate Surroundings • Proximity to neighboring houses, the street, sources of objectionable noise, etc., influences the placement of windows and the way in which they are shielded or curtained. Clerestory windows, for instance, are often used in bedrooms to assure privacy and facilitate furniture placement.

Possible Hazards Created by Windows • For example, floor-to-ceiling windows are dangerous because people sometimes walk into them. Very low windowsills are a hazard in children's rooms.

Curtaining • This is very difficult with certain kinds of windows such as two-story windows, wall-to-wall windows, triangular gable-end windows, and others.

Effect on Placement of Furniture and Built-Ins • A particular problem in bedrooms, where furniture is likely to be large and tall, and kitchens, where cabinet space is more important than window area.

Washing • Despite removable mullions and lift-out sash, window washing remains a thorn in the side of all homeowners, whether they have multi-paned windows (which take longer to wash) or single-paned windows (which must be washed more carefully since dirt shows up on them worse). Efforts should therefore be made not to aggravate the problem further by installing windows which are hard to reach or are exposed to excessive soiling (mainly because they are not protected by wide overhangs).

Lighting • Seen from inside a lighted room at night, all windows are black, impenetrable mirrors. This is especially true of picture windows—which means not that these should be avoided but that steps to alleviate the problem by curtaining and/or installation of outdoor lighting should be taken.

A final problem in planning fenestration—although it is usually less difficult than some of those cited—is the selection of the windows themselves. The following types are used:

Fixed • Inoperable windows are usually large plate-glass units but may be small and multi-paned. Floor-to-ceiling windows should be glazed with shatterproof glass. Natural ventilation may be tricky to provide with all big windows.

Double-hung • The most familiar window type because it is economical, weathertight, and easily covered with screens or storm sash; it develops few problems; and it is fairly easy to operate (except when installed high in a wall or behind a ccunter). But the ventilation area is only half of the total opening. And most windows have to be washed from the outside and inside.

Single-hung • Almost obsolete. Resembles a double-hung window with an inoperable top sash.

Horizontal Sliding • Basically a double-hung window laid on its side. It has similar advantages. Washing is simpler, however, since the sashes are usually removable. On the other hand, the breeze always blows straight in and cannot be split as with a double-hung window.

Casement • These are hinged at the side and operate like doors. They are installed singly or in pairs; they usually swing outward but can be purchased to swing inward. Screens are installed inside, but storm sash should not be used. They are fairly easy to open and close with a crank or lever; but they are not easily washed, they admit rain when wide open, and they tend to sag or warp.

Awning • Consist of one or more framed horizontal panes which swing upward and outward at the turn of a crank. They give 100% ventilation without admitting rain. Some, but not all, can be washed on both sides from indoors. But they collect dirt and cannot be protected with storm sash.

Hopper • Similar to an in-swinging casement which is laid on its side and hinged at the bottom jamb, hopper windows are used mainly in basements and clerestories. They are easy to wash from inside and can be screened and storm-windowed on the outside, and they give excellent ventilation and admit little rain; but they are hard to shade or curtain.

Jalousie • Like awning windows but made with innumerable, slender unframed panes which overlap in louver fashion when closed. They permit extremely flexible ventilation but are not completely airtight. Washing is easy. Screens and storm windows are installed on the inside. The overlapping panes, however, spoil the view.

Except for fixed windows, all types are sold in stock sizes and can be made up in other sizes (at fairly high cost). They come pre-assembled in frames ready for fast installation. Large frames containing two or three types of window are available.

Sashes are made of wood, wood sheathed with vinyl, aluminum, or steel. All have advantages and disadvantages. For example, wood is the best insulator, but it must be painted regularly and is subject to sticking and decay. Steel is very strong and stable, but it also needs regular painting to prevent rusting and it transmits cold. Aluminum transmits more cold than the other materials, but it needs no finishing. It may, however, deteriorate in seacoast and industrial areas. Wood covered with vinyl combines the best features of wood and metal sashes, but it is expensive, not used in all types of window, and available in white only.

WINDOW SEAT
A built-in bench below the inside face of a window. It is usually built into a bay window recess. The top is cushioned and the space beneath it used for storage.

An upholstered piece of furniture built in the 18th century for placement in window alcoves was also called a window seat. It resembled a love seat with arms but no back.

WINDOW WELL
A basement areaway. *See* Areaway.

WIND SCREEN
A high fence or wall used to protect an area—usually a terrace or porch—against wind. If the area is not roofed, the most effective screen is perforated or slatted. The wind strikes it head on, and in passing through the holes, loses its force. By contrast, wind striking a solid screen vaults over the top and comes down, with force unbroken, on the lee side. However, if the protected area has a roof, a solid screen is more effective than a perforated one.

Wind screens can be made of almost any material. In the past they were sometimes of extremely intricate design—like an elaborate carving in a church.

WIND SHAKE

A split in wood paralleling the growth rings and therefore bow-shaped. It is also called a *cup shake*. The cause is debatable.

WINDSOR

A famous style of chair with a solid wooden seat; slender, spraddled legs; and a back with stick-like spindles. It has been popular in America since its introduction in the early 18th century. It is thought to have originated in the town of Windsor, England.

WING

A section of a house extending out from the central body and subordinate to it in importance and usually in size.

On an upholstered chair, a wing is one of the side pieces, attached to the back and projecting forward from it.

WIRING

The importance of good wiring in the home is indicated by the fact that average annual consumption of electricity has risen from roughly 700 kilowatt-hours in 1944 to 7000 in 1974. Such heavy usage is made possible only by giving each home an electrical capacity of at least 24,000 watts, and by installing enough circuits of large enough size and enough outlets to permit operation of lights and increasing numbers of appliances. If electric heating is added, requirements more or less double.

Although an electrical system is relatively easy to install in a new house, the work should be done—for safety's sake—by a licensed electrical contractor in compliance with the local electrical code or, lacking this, the National Electrical Code. For what constitutes good wiring, *See* Circuit, Conductor, Fuse, Outlet, Service Entrance, and Switch.

WITHE

Also spelled *wythe*. A tier of masonry. Also the thickness (usually 4 in. or better) of masonry separating one flue from another in a chimney.

WOODENWARE

Bowls, trenchers, spoons, and other utilitarian pieces made out of a hardwood such as maple or birch. Antique pieces are usually displayed for their decorative value. They are sometimes known as *treen*.

WOOD FLOORING

The favorite woods for flooring are red oak and white oak. Maple is a distant third. Other woods which are used to a limited extent include birch, yellow pine, fir, teak, and pecan.

The most commonly installed type of flooring is called *strip flooring* because the boards are cut in narrow strips. The nearest thing to a standard width is 2¼ in. Standard thickness is 25/32 in. The boards are sold in bundles of assorted lengths, all of which are tongue-and-grooved at the ends as well as along the sides.

Plank flooring consists of long boards ranging from 6 in. upward in width. These are generally laid in random widths. They are tongue-and-grooved along the edges but not at the ends.

Parquet and *block flooring* are made with square blocks in several sizes. In parquet blocks, strips of wood are glued together side by side. Ordinary blocks are made of solid wood or of laminations glued one atop the other, as in plywood.

Strip Flooring • In new construction, strip flooring is usually laid over a ½-in. plywood base. The direction in which the boards run is immaterial from a structural standpoint, but for the sake of appearance, they should parallel the flooring in adjacent rooms. If the subfloor is made of boards rather than plywood, the flooring is put down at right angles to the boards.

If very short, even-length flooring strips are laid in herringbone design, the long rows usually run the length of the room.

To lay strip flooring over a concrete slab, the slab is coated with asphalt cement, 2 x 4-in. sleepers spaced 16 in. on center are laid in the asphalt while it is wet, a subfloor of plywood is nailed on top, and then the finish floor is installed. If there is any likelihood of moisture penetrating a concrete slab, this installation is further improved by substituting 1 x 3-in. boards for sleepers. One layer of boards is embedded in the asphalt cement and covered completely with a continuous layer of polyethylene film. Then a second layer of boards is nailed over the first, and the floor is completed with a plywood base and finish strips.

In the actual laying of a floor, the strips are arranged for the best possible combination of colors and grains. End joints in adjacent rows are staggered at least 6 in. Care is taken not to bunch up short pieces or long pieces. A ¼-in. expansion joint is provided between the flooring and the wall. This is later hidden by the baseboards and shoe moldings. The flooring strips are nailed to the subfloor with 2¼-in. screw nails or 2½-in. cut nails driven at a 45° angle through the tongues. Only the last boards next to a wall are face-nailed.

Strip flooring can be purchased pre-finished or unfinished. The former type is more expensive but saves work, provided it is installed with care. If unfinished boards are used, the entire floor is sanded when completed, stained (if desired), and finished with two coats of floor seal or varnish.

Plank Flooring • Because plank flooring comes in longer lengths than strips, it is laid with fewer joints. The boards are fastened down with 1¼-in. flat-head screws which are countersunk and covered with wooden plugs ¾ in. in diameter and ¼ in. deep. Holes for screws and plugs can be drilled simultaneously with a special drill bit called a *countersink-counterbore*. The screws, like the boards, are generally installed at random.

Since plank flooring does not come prefinished, it must be sanded after it is laid. Plugs which project from the surface are sanded down to the proper height at the same time.

Parquet and Wood Blocks • Both types of flooring can be laid over a subfloor of plywood or smooth boards, but they are used today mainly over concrete slabs on or above grade. The slabs must be free of moisture and primed with a coat of unfibered asphalt roofing cement. The blocks are then set in mastic applied with a notched trowel.

Blocks are set from the middle of the room toward the four walls so that the border blocks on opposite walls are of equal width. An espansion joint is allowed between the perimeter of the floor and the wall.

Since the blocks are pre-finished, no final on-the-job finishing is called for.

WOOD PANELING

The highly decorative wood paneling with raised and recessed panels set into a framework which characterized many early homes is still found in expensive new homes or in period reproductions, but it lives up to the original only if designed by an expert and constructed by a true craftsman. It is therefore very expensive. But paneling made of straight solid boards is widely used because it is relatively cheap and easily installed by anyone handy with tools. This does not mean, however, that it is lacking in historic antecedents because it was frequently used in many lovely but simple Colonial homes.

The boards now most often used for paneling and generally available in lumberyards are cut from pine—usually knotty pine—tongue-and-grooved and chamfered on the edges. It is possible, however, to buy paneling of other woods on special order and to have them milled to special designs. Old barn boards are also to be had from collectors of antique materials and by razing buildings which are on the verge of collapse.

Solid boards are generally installed vertically, edge to edge, either in uniform or random widths. On a frame wall, they are best nailed through the edges to horizontal 2 x 4-in. blocking installed between studs. But they can be applied to furring strips nailed to studs or over an existing wall. They are also applied over furring strips on masonry walls. In all cases, if the boards are to be painted, they should be given a prime coat on the face and edges before installation; if they are to be stained, the edges should be given a preliminary coat of stain. This assures that, if the boards shrink, the edges will not show up as white lines.

Other vertical paneling patterns include board-and-batten, batten-and-board, and board-and-board. Paneling is also installed horizontally, on the diagonal, or in herringbone pattern. A fairly popular installation incorporates a wainscot of horizontal boards and an upper wall of vertical boards. This has the practical advantage of minimizing the appearance of scratches on the lower part of the wall—especially in halls and other traffic areas—since most scratches and gouges are made on the lower wall in a horizontal direction.

WOOD PRESERVATIVE

A liquid chemical applied to wood to improve its resistance to decay, fungus attack, insect attack (especially termites), and growth of moss. It also tends to reduce warping, expansion, and contraction by stabilizing the moisture content in wood.

The best preservatives for wood which is not to be painted or finished are creosote, pentachlorophenol, and copper naphthanate in a heavy oil vehicle. For exterior wood which is to be painted, pentachlorophenol or copper naphthanate in a light oil vehicle is used. For painted wood indoors, water-borne preservatives are recommended because they are somewhat easier to paint over, but they are fully effective only in the absence of moisture. The chemicals used in these preservatives include zinc chloride, tanalith, chromated zinc arsenate, and chromated copper arsenate.

The value of a preservative depends largely on how well it penetrates the wood. Lumber which is treated under pressure in a mill has a longer life than that which is dipped in an open vessel; and dipped wood, in turn, lasts longer than that treated with a brush.

Effective treatment also requires that all cut and drilled surfaces be treated separately before the lumber is assembled. This is necessary even for pressure-treated lumber.

In the home, the wood most requiring treatment includes that installed near the ground (sills, first-floor joists and beams, etc.), horizontal surfaces exposed to rain, and window and door frames.

WOOD SEALER

A transparent liquid which penetrates and seals the pores of wood without changing its appearance materially. It helps to prevent discoloration and staining, and simplifies cleaning. The sealer requires no final finish but can be waxed. It can also be used as a prime coat under a clear finish such as varnish.

WOOD SHINGLE

This popular roofing and siding material is almost always made of red cedar, but it is also made in small quantities from eastern white cedar and redwood. All shingles are put up in bundles covering 25 sq. ft. The lengths in each bundle are a uniform 16, 18, or 24 in.; but the widths range up to a maximum of 14 in. The best grade of red cedar shingle is No. 1 Blue Label. Other grades are, in descending order, No. 2 Red Label, No. 3 Black Label, No. 1 or No. 2 Rebutted-Rejointed, and No. 4 Undercoursing.

The life expectancy of a wood-shingle roof averages 30 years if it is exposed to the sun. In shade, and especially in damp locations, decay becomes a problem. A wall should last years longer than a roof.

Wood shingles should be used on a roof only if it has a pitch of 3 in. or more. If the pitch is from 3 to 5 in., 16-in. shingles are laid with a maximum exposure of 3¾ in., 18-in. shingles with an exposure of 4½ in., and 24-in. shingles with an exposure of 5¾ in. On a roof with a pitch of 5 in. or more, the exposures can be increased to 5, 5½, and 7½ in., respectively. One roof is as watertight as another. Choice of shingle length is dictated by the effect the homeowner wants to achieve.

Shingles are applied to a roof deck of solid or spaced boards. A solid deck is generally recommended in snowy climates, although there is some evidence that it shortens the life of the roof. Spaced sheathing is best in warm climates, although it can be used in cold. It is made of 4- or 6-in. boards nailed horizontally to the rafters. The spacing of the boards from center to center should not exceed the exposure of the shingles.

On walls, the recommended exposures for wood shingles are 5½ to 7½ in. for 16-in. shingles, 6 to 8 in. for 18-in. shingles, and 8 to 12 in. for 24-in. shingles.

The shingles are either single-coursed or double-coursed. In single-coursing, the shingles are laid much as in roof construction, but the solid sheathing is covered by only two layers of shingles at any point. In double-coursing, each course is made up of two shingles laid one over the other. The bottom shingle is an undercoursing grade; the top is any of the four superior grades. Double-coursing produces deep shadow lines at the butts and permits greater exposures than are possible in single-coursing.

On walls, shingles may be left unfinished, treated with a water repellent, stained, or painted. Roof shingles are generally allowed to weather naturally.

Wood shingles can be treated with a fire retardant approved by Underwriters' Laboratories, but the cost is very high. Shingles with specially shaped butts similar to those often used in the Victorian era are available at about double the price of standard shingles.

WOOD SIDING

Even with the advent of materials which are easier to maintain, wood remains the No. 1 siding for American homes. This is partly because we are used to it and builders are used to working with it; but it is also because solid wood has a texture, warmth, and solidity which cannot be equalled by man-made materials. It can be shaped in numerous ways and applied in many more ways. It lends itself particularly to treatment with the transparent oil stains which have soared in popularity in recent years. And it has good thermal insulating characteristics.

Wood is generally applied in horizontal courses. The materials used in this way include shingles, clapboards, Colonial siding, rustic siding, shiplap, and flush board siding, all of which are described elsewhere.

The most commonly used vertical siding is board-and-batten. Less well known are batten-and-board and board-and-board. Simple vertical board siding is made with ordinary flat, tongue-and-groove boards or tongue-and-groove boards with chamfered edges (to produce a V-jointed effect).

Simple board siding is also occasionally installed at an angle of about 45°.

All wood sidings are applied to plywood or insulating board sheathing covered with building paper. Common nails of galvanized steel should always be used to prevent formation of rust spots on the siding. If the nails are not concealed under overlapping siding, the heads are usually countersunk and covered with putty.

WOODWORK

The exposed finished wood inside a house. Floors are not included, and doors and window sash are sometimes not included.

WOOL

Obtained from the fleece of lambs and sheep, wool is used in carpets and blankets of outstanding quality. It is beautiful, durable, resilient, warm, and resistant to fire. On the other hand, it shrinks, soils easily, loses strength when wet, and is attacked by moths.

Fabrics labeled "wool", "new wool", or "virgin wool" are made of fibers which have never been used or reclaimed. "Reprocessed wool" has been reclaimed from unused wool products. "Reused wool" has been reclaimed from used textiles. New wool is best.

WORKING DRAWING

A fully completed plan from which a person works when building a house, a piece of furniture, etc. Actually, working drawings are the original pencil drawings from which blueprints are made, and it is the blueprints which the builder follows.

Working drawings are almost always drawn to a scale, but sometimes drawings of details are actual size. A quarter-inch scale is most often used for house plans. That is, ¼ in. on the plan equal 1 ft. of building.

Several types of line are used on working drawings:

Full, or Visible, Lines • Used to show the border lines and visible parts of the structure, such as walls and doors.

Dash, or Invisible Lines • Lines composed of dashes of equal length. They are used to show the invisible parts of a house, such as the joists under a floor.

Center Lines • Fine lines composed of alternating very long and very short dashes. They indicate the center lines of studs, a stairway, etc.

Dimension Lines • Fine lines with arrows at the end used to indicate the distance from one point to another.

Ceiling, or Floor Lines • Heavy lines of alternating long and short dashes which mark the location of ceilings and floors.

Working drawing for a house incorporate several types of plan:

Floor Plans • These show the house as it might be viewed by a bird.

Elevations • Plans for the walls and other vertical surfaces.

Section Drawings • Plans showing a cut-away view of part of a house, such as an exterior wall or stairwell. The existence of a section drawing is indicated on floor plans and elevations by a line with arrowheads and duplicate letters at both ends. The section drawing itself is identified by the same letter—that is, Section A-A or Section F-F.

Detail Drawings • Plans for specific details, such as a mantel, stair rail, or corner cupboard. They are usually drawn to a larger scale than floor plans and elevations.

The working drawings of a house are the legal property of the architect who creates the plan. The person hiring the architect purchases only the right to use the plan one time. If he wants to use it again, he should pay the architect a second fee. On the other hand, if the architect wants to sell rights to the plan to a second person, there is nothing to keep him from doing so except professional ethics.

WRINKLING

A paint problem characterized by rough wrinkling of the paint when it dries. Application of paint in an overly thick coat is the usual cause.

WROUGHT IRON

An almost pure form of iron, it is malleable, strong, gray in color, and highly resistant to rust. Its main use in the home is in pipes and ornamental ironwork. In the latter use, it is preferable to cast iron because of its greater strength and rust resistance. However, if painted—as it usually is—it should be primed with red lead or zinc chromate before an alkyd or oil finish is applied.

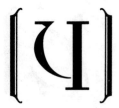

YARDPOLE

A central power pole from which feeder wires run to separate buildings on a property. It is found mainly on farms. The electric meter is mounted on the pole.

Y FITTING

A plumbing fitting shaped like a Y.

ZEBRAWOOD

A straw-colored West African cabinet wood with parallel brown stripes which may be thin and wavy or wide and straight.

ZINC CHROMATE

A pigment used in primers for metal. Such primers are recommended above all others for application to aluminum. They are also often used on iron and steel, but they are effective only if all traces of rust have been removed. *Compare* Red Lead.

ZINC DUST

A pigment used in a primer made specifically for galvanized steel and iron. The only paint that sticks to new galvanized metal, zinc-dust primer not only prevents rust but also can serve as a durable finish coat. It is light gray but can be tinted almost any color.

ZONING

An effort made by a town to control the development of the land in the town in order to protect the lives and health of the citizens and to prevent downgrading of property values, disruption of traffic, and so on.

The execution of this program is entrusted to a zoning commission which promulgates a zoning code spelling out the purposes of the regulations, defining them in precise language, and outlining both the manner in which they are administered and enforced and the methods by which the homeowner or home builder can appeal for relief.

Under a zoning code, a town is divided into areas to be used for residences, commercial businesses, manufacturing businesses, etc., as well as into areas which may not be built up at all. The residential zones are then subdivided by the size of the lots and also by the type of dwellings. For example, one New York City suburb has eight different kinds of residential zone. The two lowest zones are for multi-family dwellings; all others are limited to single-family dwellings. In the single-family zones, the minimum permissible lot size in Zone R-7 is 7500 sq. ft.; in Zone R-12, 12,000 sq. ft.; in Zone R-20, 20,000 sq. ft.; in Zone RA-1, 1 acre; in Zone RA-2, 2 acres; and in Zone RA-4, 4 acres.

In addition to specifying lot sizes and the types of building allowable, zoning codes spell out what the minimum road frontages must be, how far houses must be set back from the lot lines, the maximum height and area of the houses, and so forth.

Enforcement of a zoning code starts, as a rule, with the town building inspector. When he receives an application for a building permit, one of his first acts is to check whether the building is of a type permitted in that particular zone and whether it complies with all zoning restrictions. If the building fails to pass this test, the permit application is denied forthwith—and renewed applications are also denied until all zoning requirements are met.

If for one reason or another the home builder wishes to appeal the building inspector's ruling, he can demand a hearing before the zoning commission or whatever authority is set up to consider such appeals. And if he convinces the commission that the zoning regulations subject him to an unjustifiable hardship, he is granted a variance which allows him to proceed with construction as planned. On the other hand, if his appeal for a variance is denied, he must either change his plans to comply with the zoning code or appeal to the state courts.

Among some people, zoning is a controversial subject, and they are making constant attempts to do away with it or water it down. Whether such thinking is justified is a matter of personal opinion. But at the moment, zoning codes are in force in almost all parts of the country; and as a result, anyone building or remodeling a house should become familiar with the code for his community and with the rulings made by the zoning commission in cases it has heard.

Useful Lists

BUILDING LISTS, 447-453

DECORATING AND FURNITURE LISTS, 453-456

LISTS USEFUL IN BUILDING AND DECORATING, 456-458

BUILDING LISTS

ARCHITECTURAL STYLES

Adam 3
Baroque, 27
Carpenter Gothic, 63
Colonial, 90
Contemporary, 98
Federal, 147

Georgian, 178
Greek Revival, 184
International, 214
Modern, 259
Neoclassic, 267
Queen Anne, 311

Renaissance, 320
Revival, 322
Rococo, 324
Tudor, 401
Victorian, 411
William and Mary, 430

HOUSES—TYPES
(*also see* Architectural Styles)

Log cabin, 244
Precut house, 307
Prefabricated house, 307

Ranch house, 315
Salt box, 330

Shell house, 345
Slab construction, 355
Split level, 365

REAL ESTATE

Abstract of title, 1
Agreement of sale, 6
Apportionment, 15
Appraisal, 15
Assumption of mortgage,
  20
Bid, 40
Bill of sale, 40
Binder, 40
Boundary line, 48
Building site, 56
Closing, 87
Closing costs, 87

Cloud on title, 88
Contract, 98
Conveyance, 100
Covenant, 106
Deed, 112
Deed restriction, 113
Earnest money, 134
Easement, 135
Encroach, 137
Encumbrance, 137
Equity, 139
Escrow, 139
Frontage, 168

Land contract, 229
Lien, 235
Lot line, 244
Mortgage, 261
Option, 272
Plat, 298
Points, 304
Right of way, 323
Riparian rights, 324
Survey, 382
Title, 396
Title search, 396
Water rights, 423

ZONING

Building area, 55
Building height, 55

Building line, 55
Cluster zoning, 88

Setback, 340
Variance, 408

CONSIDERATIONS WHEN BUILDING OR REMODELING

Architect, 16
Architectural review
  board, 16
Bid, 40
Builder's allowance, 54
Building inspector, 55
Certificate of
  occupancy, 75

Code, building, 88
Code, Life Safety, 89
Code, National
  Electrical, 89
Code, National
  Plumbing, 89
Completion bond, 92
Completion date, 92

Contract, 98
Contract builder, 99
Contractor, general, 99
Insurance, 211
Penalty clause, 285
Performance bond, 286
Subcontractor, 380
Zoning, 444

HOUSE PLANS AND SPECIFICATIONS

Blueprint, 43
Detail drawing, 114
Elevation, 136
Floor plan, 161

Plot plan, 300
Rendering, 320
Schedule, 333
Section drawing, 338

Specifications, 363
Symbol, 383
White print, 429
Working drawing, 440

ROOMS AND AREAS IN AND CONNECTED WITH THE HOUSE

STRUCTURAL MEMBERS OF THE HOUSE

NONSTRUCTURAL PARTS OF THE HOUSE
(in addition to those listed elsewhere)

ROOFS—TYPES

WALLS—TYPES

FASTENERS
(devices and materials for holding things together)

A anchor, 1
Adhesive, 4
Adhesive anchor, 5
Angle iron, 13
Bolt, 45
Brad, 50
Connector plate, 98
Dowel, 125
Drift pin, 130
Drive anchor, 130
Fishplate, 157
Gusset, 186

Hollow-wall screw anchor, 203
Lag screw, 225
Lead anchor, 234
Machine-screw anchor, 250
Mending plate, 254
Nail, 265
Nylon anchor, 269
Peg, 284
Pin, 291
Plastic anchor, 296

Rawl plug, 317
Screw, 336
Skotch fastener, 354
Solder, 360
Spike, 364
Spline, 365
Staple, 371
Stud, 379
Tack, 386
Timber connector, 395
Toggle bolt, 396
T plate, 398

FLOORING MATERIALS

Asphalt tile, 20
Brick, 51
Canvas, 62
Carpet, 63
Carpet tile, 66
Ceramic tile, 73

Concrete tile, 95
Cork, 101
Flagstone, 157
Linoleum, 241
Marble, 252
Parquet, 282
Resilient flooring, 321

Seamless flooring, 337
Slate, 356
Terrazzo, 391
Vinyl, 412
Vinyl-asbestos tile, 412
Wood, 435

HARDWARE
(*also see* Fasteners)

Bolt, locking, 45
Bracket, 49
Catch, 68
Door chain, 122
Door closer, 123
Door holder, 123

Drapery hardware, 128
Drawer slide, 129
Hanger, 192
Hasp, 194
Hinge, 201
Hook and eye, 204

Kickplate, 218
Latch, 230
Lock, 243
Pushplate, 310
Strike, 377
Turnbuckle, 401

MASONRY MATERIALS

Adobe, 5
Aggregate, 6
Brick, 51
Brick, concrete, 52
Brick, surface-applied, 52
Cast stone, 68
Cement, 72
Cement plaster, 73

Cinder block, 82
Concrete, 92
Concrete block, 94
Concrete, exposed-aggre-
gate, 94
Concrete, prestressed, 94
Concrete tile, 95
Facebrick, 144

Fire clay, 153
Grout, 186
Hollow tile, 203
Lime, 240
Portland cement, 306
Reinforced concrete, 320
Sand, 331
Stone, 373

MOLDINGS

Astragal, 20
Back-band, 23
Base-cap molding, 28
Bead, 35
Bed molding, 45
Bolection molding, 45
Ceiling panel, 71
Chair rail, 76

Cock beading, 88
Corner bead, 102
Cornice molding, 103
Cove molding, 106
Crown molding, 108
Drip cap, 130
Half-round, 191

Ogee, 271
Picture molding, 289
Plate rail, 299
Quarter-round, 311
Scotia, 334
Shelf strip, 315
Shoe molding, 347
Wall panel molding, 414

PAINTS AND RELATED FINISHING MATERIALS

Alkyd, 10
Aluminum paint, 12
Barn paint, 27
Bleaching oil, 41
Block filler, 42
Calcimine, 61
Casein paint, 67
Catalytic coating, 68
Cementitious coating, 72
Chlorinated rubber paint, 82
Dripless paint, 130
Emulsion paint, 137
Enamel, 137
Fire-retardant paint, 155
Fluorescent paint, 162

Glaze, 181
Glaze coating, 181
Gym seal, 188
Lacquer, 225
Latex paint, 231
Linseed oil, 241
Masonry sealer, 253
Metallic paint, 255
Multi-colored paint, 263
Oil paint, 271
One-coat house paint, 272
Phenolic-resin primer-sealer, 287
Portland-cement paint, 306
Primer, 308
Primer-sealer, 309

Red lead, 318
Sanded paint, 331
Sealer, 337
Shellac, 345
Stain, 367
Stainkiller, 368
Stain wax, 369
Textured paint, 392
Undercoater, 403
Varnish, 408
Varnish stain, 409
Water repellent, 423
Whitewash, 429
Wood sealer, 438
Zinc chromate, 444
Zinc dust, 444

ROOFING MATERIALS

Aluminum, 12
Asbestos-cement shingle, 18
Asphalt roll, 19
Asphalt shingle, 20
Built-up, 57

Ceramic tile, 73
Concrete tile, 95
Copper, 100
Fiberglass, rigid, 149
Galvanized steel, 174
Shake, 343

Silicone-rubber, 351
Slate, 356
Tar-and-gravel, 387
Terne, 389
Urethane, 405
Wood shingle, 438

SIDING MATERIALS

Aluminum, 12
Asbestos-cement, 18
Asphalt shingle, 20
Barn, 27
Batten-and-board, 34
Beaded bevel, 35
Bevel, 39
Board-and-batten, 44
Board-and-board, 44
Brick, 51

Brick, concrete, 52
Brick, surface-applied, 52
Clapboard, 84
Colonial, 90
Concrete block, 94
Dolly Varden, 119
Drop, 131
Hardboard, 193
Plank-and-beam, 294

Plywood, 302
Rustic, 329
Shake, 343
Shake, sidewall, 343
Shiplap, 347
Stone, 373
Stucco, 379
Vinyl, 412
Wood shingle, 438
Wood, 439

WALLCOVERINGS
(must be applied to a subwall)

Acoustical tile, 2
Burlap, 57
Ceramic tile, 73
Cork, 101, 102
Fabric, 143
Felt, 148
Grasscloth, 184
Gypsum-coated wall fabric, 189

Laminated wood veneer, 226
Marble tile, 252
Masonry, plastic, 253
Metal foil, 255
Metal tile, 255
Mirror, 257

Mirror tile, 258
Plastic, laminated, 296
Plastic tile, 298
Roll-on fabric, 325
Shiki silk, 346
Vinyl, 413
Wallpaper, 416

WALL PANELS
(usually applied directly to studs)

Acoustical board, 2
Asbestos-cement board, 18
Fiberboard, 149
Fiberglass, rigid, 149

Gypsum board, 188
Hardboard paneling, 192
Pegboard, 285
Plastic paneling, 297

Plywood paneling, 301
Velvet board, 410
Wallboard, 416
Wood paneling, 436

DECORATING AND FURNITURE LISTS

FURNITURE—TYPES

FURNITURE—SEATING PIECES

FURNITURE—STORAGE PIECES

FURNITURE—TABLES

FURNITURE—DESKS

FURNITURE—STOOLS

FURNITURE—MIRRORS

FURNITURE–OTHER PIECES

Bed, 36
Crib, 108

Dry sink, 131
Folding screen, 163
Piano, 288

Record player, 318
Television set, 388

ACCESSORIES
(Small furnishings used for decoration and/or utility)

Acrylic (2), 3
Bedspread, 38
Bell pull, 38
Bolster, 45
Bric-a-brac, 51
Britanniaware, 53
Candelabrum, 61
Candlestick, 61
Carpet, 63
Chalkware, 77
Clock, 85
Collage, 89
Coverlet, 106
Curtain, 109
Decorative beads, 112
Drapery, 126
Dust ruffle, 132
Earthenware, 134
Enamel, 137
Faience, 144
Fireplace tools, 155
Fire screen, 156
Flatware, 160
Floorcloth, 161

Girandole, 178
Glassware, 180
Hanging, 192
Hassock, 194
Hollowware, 204
Jabot, 215
Kakemono, 217
Lambrequin, 226
Lusterware, 249
Majolica, 251
Mobile, 259
Montage, 260
Mosaic, 263
Moucharabi, 263
Mural, 264
Objet d'art, 270
Oil, 271
Painting, 280
Pastel, 283
Pencil, 285
Picture frame, 288
Pillow, 291
Plate rack, 299
Portiere, 306
Pouf, 307

Print, 309
Runner, 329
Sampler, 331
Sconce, 334
Sculpture, 337
Shade, 341
Slipcover, 357
Spoon rack, 366
Stabile, 367
Stemware, 372
Stoneware, 373
Swag, 382
Table linen, 386
Tapestry, 387
Throw, 394
Throw cover, 394
Tole, 397
Torchere, 398
Valance, 406
Vase, 409
Venetian blind, 410
Vertical blind, 411
Water color, 421
Woodenware, 435

FURNITURE PARTS–BACKS OF CHAIRS AND OTHER SEATING PIECES

Arch back, 15
Arrow back, 18
Balloon back, 25
Banister back, 25
Bow back, 48

Camel back, 61
Drawing book chair back,
 129
Fan back, 145
Fiddle back, 150

Ladder back, 225
Loop back, 244
Medallion back, 254
Shield back, 356
Stick back, 372

FURNITURE PARTS–FRONTS OF BUREAUS AND OTHER CASE PIECES

Block front, 42
Bow front, 48
Cylinder front, 110

Fall front, 144
Oxbow front, 276

Serpentine front, 339
Slant front, 356
Straight front, 377

FURNITURE PARTS–LEGS AND FEET

Ball foot, 24
Block foot, 42
Blunt arrow leg, 44
Bracket foot, 48
Bun foot, 57
Cabriole, 60
Claw and ball foot, 85

Drake foot, 126
Eagle-head foot, 134
French foot, 167
Gate leg, 177
Pad foot, 277
Paw foot, 284
Saber leg, 330

Slipper foot, 357
Snake foot, 358
Spade foot, 363
Spanish foot, 363
Trumpet leg, 400
Turnip foot, 402
Whorl foot, 429

FURNITURE PARTS—MISCELLANEOUS

Apron, 15
Arm stump, 17
Bonnet top, 47
Carcase, 63
Caster, 67
Crest rail, 107
Drop leaf, 131
Footboard (see Headboard, 194)

Glide, 181
Headboard, 194
Pediment, 284
Pull, 309
Rail, 315
Rung, 329
Saddle seat, 330
Skirt, 354

Slip seat, 358
Splat, 364
Splint, 365
Stretcher, 377
Tambour, 387
Tester, 391
Upholstery, 404
Wing, 434

FABRICS AND YARNS

Acetate, 1
Acrylic, 3
Alpaca, 11
Anidex, 14
Batiste, 34
Beta fabric, 39
Bouclé, 48
Brocade, 53
Brocatelle, 53
Burlap, 57
Calico, 61
Candlewick, 61
Canvas, 62
Casement cloth, 67
Challis, 77
Chenille, 78
Chintz, 81
Corduroy, 101
Cotton, 104
Crash, 106
Crepe de chine, 107
Cretonne, 107
Damask, 111
Denim, 113
Drill, 130
Duck, 132
Faille, 144
Felt, 148

Fiberglass, 149
Frieze, 168
Gauze, 177
Georgette, 177
Gingham, 178
Haircloth, 191
Homespun, 204
Hopsacking, 205
Indian Head, 209
Jaspé cloth, 216
Kettle cloth, 217
Lace, 225
Lamé, 226
Laminated fabric, 226
Lawn, 233
Linen, 240
Marquisette, 253
Matelasse, 254
Metallic fiber, 255
Modacrylic, 259
Mohair, 259
Moiré, 260
Monk's cloth, 260
Mull, 263
Muslin, 264
Ninon, 267
Nylon, 269
Organdy, 273
Osnaburg, 274

Paisley, 280
Pellon, 285
Percale, 286
Permanent press, 287
Piqué, 294
Plissé, 300
Plush, 301
Pongee, 305
Poplin, 305
Rayon, 317
Sailcloth, 330
Sateen, 332
Satin, 332
Satin, antique, 332
Seersucker, 338
Silk, 351
Taffeta, 386
Tapestry, 387
Ticking, 394
Triacetate, 400
Tweed, 402
Vellux, 409
Velour, 409
Velvet, 409
Velveteen, 410
Vinyon, 413
Voile, 413
Wool, 440

LISTS USEFUL IN
BUILDING AND DECORATING

METALS

Aluminum, 11
Brass, 50
Bronze, 53
Cast iron, 68

Chrome, 82
Copper, 100
Galvanized steel, 174
Lead, 234

Pewter, 287
Silver, 352
Stainless steel, 358
Wrought iron, 441

FINISHES

PAINTING PROBLEMS

WOOD JOINTS AND SPLICES